Ian A. Fraser
June 1998.

ENGLISH PLACE–NAME SOCIETY. VOLUME LXXIV
FOR 1996–1997

GENERAL EDITOR

VICTOR WATTS

THE PLACE–NAMES OF
CHESHIRE

PART V (2)

THE SURVEY OF ENGLISH PLACE–NAMES
UNDERTAKEN WITH THE APPROVAL AND SUPPORT OF
THE BRITISH ACADEMY

THE PLACE–NAMES OF

CHESHIRE

BY

†JOHN McN. DODGSON

completed and edited by

ALEXANDER R. RUMBLE

PART FIVE
Section 2

INTRODUCTION, LINGUISTIC NOTES AND INDEXES
WITH
APPENDIXES

NOTTINGHAM
ENGLISH PLACE–NAME SOCIETY
1997

Published by the English Place–Name Society

Registered Charity No. 257891

© English Place–Name Society 1997

ISBN 0 904889 54 8

Typeset by Paul Cavill & Printed in Great Britain
by Woolnough Bookbinding, Irthlingborough, Northants.

ACKNOWLEDGEMENTS

The Society gratefully acknowledges donations received towards the preparation of this volume from Cheshire County Council, the Historic Society of Lancashire and Cheshire, and the Department of English, University of Manchester.

CONTENTS

EDITOR'S FOREWORD

THE PRESENT VOLUME completes the set covering the county of Cheshire, surveyed for the Society by the late Professor John McN. Dodgson, comprising EPNS volumes 44–8, 54 and 74. Almost all of the final volume has been edited from manuscript notebooks and slips upon which John Dodgson was working at the time of his death in 1990. The index covers all the place–names treated in the Cheshire survey. Also included is an analysis of the distribution of field–name elements and various sections relevant to the context against which the place–names of the county were coined, used and recorded. The place–name forms collected in the survey are subjected to linguistic analysis in the 'Linguistic Notes', which should prove of particular importance for the study of medieval orthography in a county whose Middle English dialect is the product of a Mercian–Scandinavian background tinged in places by Celtic survivals and influences. The three sections of the 'Introduction' represent all that had been finished by John Dodgson in 1990. They are supplemented to a substantial degree by the reprinting, as Appendix I, of five detailed studies on Cheshire place–names which John Dodgson published between 1957 and 1985, and by Appendix II, a summary by Dr Denise Kenyon of the county's environmental characteristics which was both commissioned and read with approval by John Dodgson before his death. The section of Addenda and Corrigenda to the Cheshire survey presented here includes only those which are essential to discussion contained elsewhere in the present volume; further material will appear in JEPNS in due course.

As the completing editor of the present volume, I have received help and encouragement over the last seven years from a number of individuals, here gratefully acknowledged. I am particularly touched to have been trusted by Mrs Joyce Dodgson to use and edit the materials left by her husband. She herself spent a large amount of time in completing and checking the index slips and joined Mr David Mills and myself in a marathon four–day exercise to put them in a preliminary alphabetical ordering. Dr Gillian Fellows–Jensen has given essential guidance on the Scandinavian material and, with Mr Mills and Mr Victor Watts, has made useful comments on the 'Introduction' and 'Linguistic Notes'. Invaluable practical help and advice with the word processing and setting up of the present volume at the Universities of Sussex, Manchester and Nottingham has been given by Professor Richard Coates, Ms Jane 'Espinasse, Ms Celia McInnes, Ms Maggie Bailey and Mrs Janet Rudkin. Dr Paul Cavill has produced the camera–ready copy with great patience and care.

Map 1, with its explanatory notes, was originally published by Cheshire Record Office and Chester Diocesan Record Office and is reissued here by the kind permission of its compiler, Mr Ian Dunn, the County Librarian. Map 2 is reproduced from the *Victoria History of Cheshire*, volume ii, p. 30, by permission of the General Editor.

Thanks for permission to reprint the copyright articles in Appendix I are due to the following: The Viking Society for Northern Research; The Historic Society of Lancashire and Cheshire; The Chester Archaeological Society; The Royal Library, Stockholm; Carl Winter Universitätsverlag; Dr Folke Sandgren; and Professor Rudolf Schützeichel.

A continuing personal debt, here in small part repaid in kind, is acknowledged to my mentor and friend John Dodgson for giving me a thorough training in, amongst other subjects, the essential skills of onomastic editing. It is therefore fitting to end by recording that one of the first tasks of my apprenticeship to him as Research Assistant to the Society was to help in 1969 with reading the proofs of Part I of *The Place–Names of Cheshire*.

ALEXANDER R. RUMBLE

University of Manchester
St Swithun's Day, 1997

AUTHOR'S PREFACE

THE FINAL PART of *The Place-Names of Cheshire* has been too long delayed, to the inconvenience of the author as much as that of Members of the Society and of the public. I regret the delay, because the publication comes too late for some whose approbation, congratulation, and criticism I would have valued, Hugh Smith, Olof von Feilitzen, Melville Richards, Bruce Dickins, Frederick Wainwright, Benno Timmer, Bernard Lucas, Betty Garbutt, W. Fergusson Irvine, Archdeacon Burne and, above all, Harry and Margaret Dodgson late of Boothfield, Pilling Lane, Lancs. I wish they had seen the finish.

I have been much beholden to these. And some new names now come into the list of acknowledgements — those colleagues and Members and correspondents who have read, consulted, criticised, augmented and corrected the previous volumes and the draft of this one.

Especially, in the volume which contains Chester, I thank Miss Annette Kennett, [former] City Archivist of Chester, and her predecessors Mrs Elizabeth Berry, Dr Mary Finch and Miss Helen Boulton (Mrs J. Parkinson). I continue indebted to Mr Brian Redwood, [former] County Archivist of Cheshire, and to [his successor] Mr Dunn, as, indeed, to the former members of that department. This Society's work is very dependent upon the skill, erudition and service of the staff of the local record offices up and down the country, and we can never thank them too much. We owe our local archivists more than selfishness allows us to remember or their modesty allows them to claim. I sincerely commend Dr Alexander Rumble, Joy Hubble (Mrs H. Jenkyns), Celia Parker, Helen Thomas, Dr Catherine Coutts (now Cubitt), and Dr Mark Bateson, former Research Assistants to the Society, for all their industry, erudition, help and advice in the compilation of this volume. Last, but never the least, here, I would mention [the late] Mrs Doris Lord, who was ever at hand with her patient, graceful and imperturbable assistance, as secretary, typist and indexer and in all sorts of ways.

My colleagues at University College London, to whom I am much indebted in many departments, but principally in English, in Geography (here especially to Miss Anne Oxenham and Mr Kenneth Wass of the Cartographic Section), in Geology (here Dr Eric Robinson), in Medieval Archaeology and in History, will share (I hope) my relief that it is over, as would (I suppose) Mr J. Crabtree and Captain W. MacConochie who have in many ways kept up my spirits. Especially, however, I mention the late Mr J.W. Scott, Librarian of University College London, and his staff, for his unfailing service and encouragement.

I am grateful to the Members of the English Place-Name Society for their faith and patience. At the end, of course, and before all, I am, have been and shall be ever grateful and beholden to Joyce Dodgson, who married it, and my children John Robert Dodgson and Sarah Jane Dodgson who were born to it, weaned and reared on it, and grew up with it, for courageously enduring the thankless lot of the family of one of the English Place-Name Society's editors.

JOHN McNEAL DODGSON

University College London
[c.1989]

ADDENDA AND CORRIGENDA

VOLS. XLIV–XLVIII, LIV

THE PLACE–NAMES OF CHESHIRE, PARTS I–V

The following reference is used for a contributor.

K.G.G. Kathleen G. Goodchild of Knutsford

VOL. XLIV
THE PLACE–NAMES OF CHESHIRE, PART I

p. xxx. Add '*Gros* Grosvenor of Eaton, Ancient Charters in the possession of His Grace the Duke of Westminster.'.

p. xxxiv. Add 'NPM   *Neuphilologische Mitteilungen.*'.

p. xxxviii, s.v. Reaney. Add 'Reaney[2] 2nd ed. 1976, revised R.M. Wilson'.

p. xxxviii, line 7 from foot. For 'C. Ritter' read 'O. Ritter'.

p. 27, s.n. R. GOYT. Add '*Gwit, aqua de Gwid* 1285 *DuLaMinAcct*, see BBCS 22 (1967), 112, note 6'.

p. 29, s.n. HOLYWELL BROOK. Add 'Hollywell Ridding **4** 49 (**5:2** Add.)'.

p. 71, FIELD–NAMES, (*b*), s.n. *le Rotindebroke*. Add 'Cf. *Ricand(e)brigge*, **1** 141'.

p. 90, s.n. BODKIN. Add 'This is a name–type Bodkin Hall, Lane, etc., also seen in La, meaning a small cramped place in which one lies *bodkin*, see EDD and NED, s.v.'.

p. 106–7, s.n. HURDSFIELD. For 'Open land . . . hurdle–fence' read 'Open land at a shelter, *v.* **hūder**, occasionally confused with **hyrdel**, –es[2], **feld**, cf. Hurleston **3** 146–7' and add 'Addenda at **5:1** xv s.n. Hurdsfield and xxxv s.n. Hurleston report contributions by Arngart and Löfvenberg. But see now discussion of Hurdsfield, Huddersfield WRY **2** 295, Hothersall La 145, Hudswell NRY 245, in LSE NS 18 (1987), 136–7. The first el. in these appears to be OE ***hūder** 'shelter', an *–r* extension of the PrGer stem **hūd(h)* which lies behind OE *hȳd* 'skin, hide', *hydan* 'to hide, to cover up', *hȳð* 'a harbour', OHG *hutta* 'a hut'. Hurdsfield, Huddersfield and related p.ns. discussed LSE loc.cit. which contain the putative OE els. ***hūding**, ***hȳdel(s)**, ***hūd**, ***hūde**, ***hūda**, ***hydde**, or the OE pers.n. **Hūda*, would signify the use of huts, shelters and sheltering–places in herding, foraging, woodcutting, or hunting, at an epoch of the settlement in their districts'.

p. 109, FIELD–NAMES, (*b*), s.n. *the longshutt*. Add '1611'.

p. 133, s.n. THE ARK HILL FIELD. After '**hnutu**' add 'or ON **hnot** 'a nut'.'

p. 137, FIELD–NAMES, (*b*), s.n. *Culuercrofte, Calvercrofte*. Add 'Arngart, *Stud Neophil* 43 (1971), 575 considers *calfra* 'calves'field' to be as likely as *culfra* 'doves' field'.

    s.n. *Luysotesrudyng*. For '*Lisote*, 'probably' read '*Lisote*, probably'.

p. 140, s.n. SPULEY. Add 'cf. *le Rotindebroke* **1** 71'.

p. 154, s.n. LINGERDS. After '79 *supra*' add '226 *infra*'.

p. 162–3, s.n. TONGUE SHARP WOOD (p. 163, l. 8). After '335 *infra*' add 'also *tunkezarppelond* 1230–70 **5:1** xxxvi (**3** 158–9: Church Minshull).'

p. 170 (and **5:1** xvii), s.n. TOLLS. Add 'Cf. *toll* 'clump of trees, row of trees' EDD K, Sr, Sx, Ha, but Kristensson, *Studier i modern språkvetenskap* NS 8, 53–4 proposes OE ***tolle** fem. wk. (as also Middendorff, *Altenglisches Flurnamenbuch* 135 for OE *tollan dene*) 'tree trunk'.'

p. 172, s.n. TAXAL. Add 'Compare *Taxley* **2** 271'.

p. 173, s.n. NORMANWOOD. For '134 113' read '134, 113'.

p. 173, s.n. DERBYSHIRE BRIDGE. Add 'BBCS 22 (1967), 112, note 6 cites *DuLaMinAcct* for 1285: the bounds of the forest of the Peak begin on the south side *ad novum locum de Gwit* and then follow the water of *Gwid* to the water of *Ederou*. I think this point would have been Derbyshire Bridge.'.

p. 175, FIELD–NAMES, (*a*), s.n. Oldham Fd. After '**hulm**' read 'but the basis may be **hamm** or the surname derived from Oldham La 50.'.

p. 192, FIELD–NAMES, (*b*), s.n. *the black Earth*. Read '('black ploughland or soil', *v.* **blæc, eorðe**, or **erð**)'.

p. 240, line 17. For NORTHERN ETCHELLS read NORTHEN ETCHELLS.

p. 268, s.n. BRINNINGTON. This may contain OE ***bryning** 'a burnt place, scene of a fire'.

p. 271, s.n. ORMESTY. The final el. could be either OE **stiga** 'sty, pigstye' or ON **stía** 'a sty'.

p. 276, FIELD–NAMES, (*b*), s.n. *Wharnedg(e)*. Add 'Cf. *Qwerneegge* (Lyme Handley) **5:1** xix, Add. to **1** 201–2'.

p. 286, s.n. WHITECROFT. This is now in Db, SJ 974867.

p. 287, FIELD–NAMES, (*a*), s.n. Walve Hill. Add 'perhaps containing a dialect word for a culvert or drain from OE **hwalf**'.

p. 307, s.n. HATTERSLEY. The first el. could be an OE *–es, –os* stem noun with alternative uninflected and *–es* gen. sg. *Hatter–, Hattres–*. The noun would be OE **hæter* deduced from OE *hæteru* 'garments, clothing'. The supposed noun would mean 'garments, dress, clothing'. Such a place–name would probably mean 'woodland estate held at the rent of a suit of clothes' (cf. OE *scrūdland*), or perhaps 'glade where clothing is made or aired or laundered'.

p. 320–1 (and Add. **3** xiv), s.n. TINTWISTLE. Eventually, one must settle for an OScand el. in Tintwistle, the ON pers.n. *Þengill* (Rygh, *Gamle Personnavne* 246; Lind, *Islandska Dopnamn* 1122).

VOL. XLV
THE PLACE–NAMES OF CHESHIRE, PART II

p. vii, line 1. For '1419' read '1490'.

p. viii (addendum to 2 181). See further addendum *infra*.

p. 31, s.n. TIMPERLEY. The etymology given here (and in DEPN) will not do. The phonetic conditions for so absolutely consistent an unvoicing of the bilabial plosive in [mb] are not apparent, so the first el. can hardly be OE **timber**. Compare with Timberley Sx 1 125.

No success has attended attempts to find analogy with Timperley in such p.ns. as Timble WRY 5 128, 130, Timperley Bank Db 1 90. Templing Lane WRY 1 296, Tempernacre WRY 1 50, Tymparon Cu 1 188, Temperness Pembrokeshire NCPNW 81. Templand La 197 would be a promising comparison, if the first el. in that name and Timperley were taken to be OE *timple, –an*, sb., fem., 'a weaver's temple' (see NED s.v. *temple* sb.[3] 'spar for stretching the woven cloth in a loom', cf. OE *atimplian* 'to stretch as on a loom or rack') the basic sense of which is 'a spur, a rafter' (which also lies behind Latin *templum* 'a purlin', *templum* 'a sanctuary'). It would be feasible to interpret Templand La and Timperley Ch as, respectively, 'a grove (**lundr**)' and 'a woodland glade (**lēah**) where temples were got' (cf. Staveley Db 2 301, from **stæf**). But this interpretation of Timperley runs into a phonological problem just as grave as that of the [mb] > [mp] substitution. For there are no spellings representing **Timple–leah*, i.e. the name appears always as *timper–l* never *timp(e)l–l*: and whilst it would be easy to explain the *–r–* spellings as the result of Anglo–Norman interchange of [i] and [i̭] and the dissimilation of [l–l], the complete uniformity of the *timper–* form in a fairly often reported place–name gives rise to misgivings.

Now, the discovery of *Timpresdale* 113 *Gros* 81, a place–name in Poulton, 4 155 (**5:2** Add.), affords independent evidence of a first element which we may provisionally identify as either OE **timper*, **timpor* (*–es/os* stem sb.), gen. sg. *timper(es)*, or OE **timpre* (*–ra* suffix sb.), gen. sg. **timpres* (OE **timpre* adj. is ruled out by the *–es* gen. inflexion of *Timpres–*). These postulated words, related to OE *timple, supra*, would be from the root *temp–* in IE *tempos* 'a span, a spread, a stretch, an extent', Pokorny IEW I 1064. OE **timpor*, **timpre* probably meant 'spar, stretcher' but it could have meant 'an extent; a precinct'. The words could be the basis of the obscure Cumb dialect *timperon* (EDD), e.g. in OE dat. pl. *timperum* or compounded with OE **ærn** 'house' or ON **runnr** 'thicket'; cf. Tymparon Cu 1 188–9 whose middle syllable rules out analogy with the Ch **timper* names.

p. 41–2, FIELD–NAMES, (*b*). Add from 1463–4 *CRO Deed* (DXX 78/2) *Cruehurst* (*v.* **crew, hyrst**), *the Broadhey, Brod(e)hey* (*v.* **brād, (ge)hæg**), *The Cuehurst dich* (*v.* **cū, hyrst, dīc**), *the Overthwert way* (*v.* **oferþwart, weg**), *videcall way* (*v.* **weg**; first el. obscure). Mr Hughes reports (1444 *CRO Deed*) *le Brome* (*v.* **brōm**), *Ollerker* (*v.* **alor, kjarr**), *le Rede Meddow* (*v.* **hrēod, mæd**).

p. 58, s.n. YARWOODHEATH. The first el. could just as well be OE ***gear** 'yair, fishweir', cf. *Iarewell* 2 247, Yarwood 3 5.

p. 64, the site of NORSHAW (lost) has been located through fieldwork by K.G.G. at SJ 757828.

p. 65, s.n. GOLDEN BROOK PITS. Add '*The Golden Brow* 1733 J. Hussey's *Map of Tatton Park*'.

p. 65, s.v. FIELD–NAMES. Add 'The undated forms in (*a*) are reported by K.G.G. from 1733 J. Hussey's *Map of Tatton Park*'. Also add the following paragraph:

(*a*) The (Eight, Five, etc.) Acre; The Alice Croft; The Allors (*v*. **alor**); Antrobus Park; The Backside; (The) Bank(s); Baxter's Moss; The Beams (*v*. **bēam**); The Birken (Fd, Heath, Heys) (beside Birkin Brook **1** 15; cf. Birkin Lodge **2** 64, and Birkin **2** 58); The Black Acre; The Blackmoor Croft (*v*. **blæc**, **mōr**[1]); The Blake Fd (*v*. **blæc**); The Bostock Fd; The Three Bottoms (*v*. **botm**); The Bower Hey; The Brickhills (*v*. **bryke–kyl**); Bride Mdw (perhaps dower land); The Brow Fd; The Calf Croft; The Carr (*v*. **kjarr**); Cartwright's New Hey; The Castage (cf. Castedge **1** 173; the final el. may be **stede**); The Chamber End; The Church Fd; The Clay Croft; The Coe (Mdw); The Coney Greave (Fd); The (Little, Mare, Pump, Walley, Wheat, Will's) Coppy; The Crow Bank; The Dam Fd (*v*. **damme**); The Dams Head Mdw; Lt Day Math; Dean Mdw; Fidler's Hill; The French Wheat Croft & Fd; Furnivall Park; The Furry Fd (2x); The Gig Hole Fd (*v*. **gigge**); Glebe Land; The Gorsty Fd & Nook; Harrison's Croft; The Harrop Moor (*v*. **hara**, **hop**); Hemp Croft & Yard; The Hib Croft; The Higher Pleck; The Hill; The Hob Fd; Hobson Croft; The Hodge Hey (*v*. **hocg**); The Horsley (*v*. **hors**, **lēah**); Hulm's Acre; Hunt's Fd & Flatt (*Hunt* was the surname of a family at the Walk Mill 16, K.G.G.); The Intack (several); Kirfoot's Croft; The L (a shape); The Lime Croft; The Linley (*v*. **lind**, **lēah**); The Long Earths (2x) (*v*. **eorðe**); Lowe's Fd; The Mare Fd (several, named from Tatton Mere or Turn Mere, *v*. **mere**[1]); The Marl'd Fd; The Marliff Mdw; The Marsh; The Mdw before the door; (The) Meadow Spot(t); Miller's Croft; The Milly Croft (Nook); Hobson's, Hurlbott's, Leigh's & Pownell's Moss; The Nett Moor Ditch & The Nett Yards (perhaps named from wildfowl nets); Newhall's Croft; Newton's Hey; Newton's L (a shape); The Oaks Hey; The Oller Croft (*v*. **alor**); The Ound Fd; The Out Fd (*v*. **ūt(e)**); The Out Lett (*v*. **outlet**); The Paddock (several); The Page Hey; Patch; Phillip Clark's Land (a yeoman here e18, K.G.G.); The Piper's Heys (2x); The Pitt Loond; Prior's Mdw; The Pump Coppy; The Quarter Acre; The Rood Loons; The Rough Close; The Round Greaves; The Sheper Long (2x) (cf. *Chepfaldefurluc*' and *Sepefurlong* both **2** 65 (*b*)); The Shrogs (several) (*v*. **skrogge**); Sir Charles; The Slack (2x); Steel's Mdw (Steele was a surname in Norshaw, 16 K.G.G.); Streets; The Tentry Croft (*v*. **tentour**); The Three Corner'd Fd; Town Fd Croft; Turn Mare (Knowls) (a lake near Tatton Hall, *v*. **trun**, **mere**[1], **cnoll**); The Under Mill (a field downstream from the mill); The Wain Loons (2x) (*v*. **wægn**, **lane**); The Walley Croft; The Ware Mdw (2x) (*v*. **wær**); The Water Lees (*v*. **lǣs**); Whitely Top; The Yard Moor.

p. 71, FIELD–NAMES, (*a*), s.n. Twyford Mdw. For '**twī–**, **ford**' read '**twī–fyrde**, cf. Twyford, 87 *infra*'.

p. 87, s.n. TWYFORD. For '**twī–**, **ford**' read '**twī–fyrde**, cf. Twyford Mdw, 71 *supra*'.

p. 121. For ROLLYMOORS read ROOLYMOORS.

p. 142, FIELD–NAMES, (b). Add 'le Conyngr 1466 LeghW 290 (v. **coningre**; cf. Clapper, supra, and le Claper **5:1** xxviii'.

p. 161, s.n. MIDDLETON GRANGE. For 'Eston 958 (13) (17)' read 'Eston 958 (14) (17)'.

p. 166, FIELD–NAMES, (b), s.n. le Homormor. Add 'The tenement is named Clifton and **hamor** here may be the same as **hamor–wyrt**, a botanical el.'.

s.n. Ringestede. For '**hring, stede**' read '**hring–stede**, Sandred 103'.

p. 173, s.n. EANLEY. For 'Lambs' clearing . . . Handley 326 infra, **1** 98' read 'Nearby, convenient clearing or wood', v. **(ge)hende, lēah**. The modern pron. is not attested by spellings before 18th c., and then it can be explained as [ɪ:n(d)] < [in(d)] from original [en(d)]. The supposed analogy with Yeanley, Eanley **3** 292 will not stand in view of the quite different spelling tradition. The record of ME spellings for Eanley **2** 173 is largely second–hand, but it is consistent with an original form *(h)ende–. The DB spelling could be the result of overlay of the bow of d on the second minim of n, whence End– > Enl–. The first el. is occasionally replaced by OE **ende**[1] 'end of a district or township'.

p. 179, FIELD–NAMES, (a). For 'Po(p)y Butts' read 'Pop(p)y Butts'.

p. 181 (and p. viii), s.n. MURDISHAW. Although the surname Mottershaw may be connected with this p.n., note that the forms Modershale, Modreshale 1333, 1339 are from Moddershall St, see Reaney[2], s.v. Mothersale.

p. 181, s.n. ROSAM GRAVE. After '**ros**' insert ', **rosinn**'. The spelling Rosinene– indicates that Rosin was treated as if an –en adj. and strengthens derivation from **rosinn**.

p. 182, FIELD–NAMES, (b), s.n. the tend Bearne of Bold. For '**teōnde**' read '**tēonde**'.

p. 240, FIELD–NAMES, (b), s.n. Kelrridding, Kellridding. The first el. may be Kel (p) < ON Ketill. Cf. also Kelsall **3** 276.

p. 247, FIELD–NAMES, (b), s.n. Kelmeadow. As preceding addendum.

s.n. (le) Rosemeadow. The first el. is probably **ros**.

p. 256, FIELD–NAMES, (a), s.n. Edgrew Fd. For **hecg–ræw** read **ed–grew**.

p. 259, FIELD–NAMES, (a), s.n. Little Daylight. Add 'v. **lihte**'.

p. 268, FIELD–NAMES, (a), s.n. Colliers Croft. For **colere** read **colier**.

p. 271, s.n. TAXMERE. After 'Taxal **1** 172' add 'or the el. OE **þæc** 'thatch' proposed for Taxal at **5:1** xvii.'.

p. 289–90, FIELD–NAMES, (b), s.n. Cortusfeld. Another possibility is OE *cort(e) 'a short plot of ground, a piece of land cut off'.

p. 316, FIELD–NAMES, (b), s.n. Solinhac. Delete the cross ref. to Sulinesfeld **2** 186.

p. 325, before 'Bradford (Whitegate)' add 'Botterley Hill (Faddiley), 12, 60, 270: **3**'.

p. 327, for 'Stanlow, 160: **3**' read 'Stanlow, 160: **4**'.

VOL. XLVI
THE PLACE–NAMES OF CHESHIRE, PART III

p. 5, s.n. BARTHOMLEY. A preferable explanation is 'glade at (a place called) *Brighthamm', from OE lēah with a compound p.n. *beorht–hamm/homm in which hamm/homm occasionally alternates with hemm, cf. Mortomley YW, Marchamley Sa and Brightholmlee YW 1 222.

p. 267 (and 5:1 xxxviii). Delete reference to toll, tollr. The first el. is OE *tolle, fem., *toll, masc., as in The Taskar 4 317, 5:2 Add.

VOL. XLVII
THE PLACE–NAMES OF CHESHIRE, PART IV

p. 30, FIELD–NAMES, (b). Add 'Croft Iyagow 1308 Gros 147 ('Iago's croft', Welsh pers.n. Iago, croft)'.

p. 38, FIELD–NAMES, (b). Add 'Alwaldishalc 113/e14 Gros 145 (OE Ælfwald, halc); le Hechavedland 113/e14 Gros 145 (v. hēah, hēafod–land)'.

p. 49, FIELD–NAMES, (a), s.n. Flax Boughs. Add 'Flaxpolismos 113 Gros 141, v. mos. Adjoined Bickley land.'

s.n. Hollywell Ridding. Add 'Chaddewalle 1301 Gros 113, 'Chad's (= Cedd's) spring or well', v. wælla'.

p. 49–50, FIELD–NAMES, (b). Add:

s.n. Atenalgh. le Atenhaluh 1295 Gros 105

s.n. Castelward. However, Gros 165, dated 1314, records an assart in le Castelwode and a haya between the hall of Tushingham and le Castelwode, v. wudu.

s.n. Hauedlond. le hauidlond 1301 Gros 113.

s.n. Henlowe. campus de Hennelove 1295 Gros 99, Hennelowe 113, e14 Gros 143, 160, 164.

s.n. le Heye. 1305 Gros 126.

s.n. Hobbemede. Cf. Hobbecroft 1295 Gros 105.

s.n. Thurwardeslegh. Thorewardislegh, Thurwardesleg' 113 Gros 139, 141. Gros 141 locates it between Flax Boughs (TA Tushingham) and Willey Moor.

s.n. Quitemor. le quitemor 1305 Gros 126.

s.n. Wletghereslond. Wladriscroft e14 Gros 161.

p. 49–50, FIELD–NAMES, (b). Insert these additional f.ns.:

le blakebut 1295 Gros 99 (v. blæc, butte); le blakecroft 1295 Gros 104; le Bradelond 113 Gros 143 (v. brād, land); Candelannescroft 1316 Gros 167 ('Candelan's croft', from the ME pers.n. discussed 4 19); le Dichelond in Hennelowe 1316 Gros 143 (v. dīc, land, cf. Henlowe infra); le Feldyard e13 Gros 22 (v. feld, geard, cf. feltiard 2 232; perhaps there is a cpd. el. *feld–geard); Hakeryard e13 Gros 22 (v. æcer, geard); Ithelliscroft 1295 Gros 105 (from croft and Welsh pers.n. Ithell; probably Ithell le Clerk of Tushingham 1305 Orm² II 654, but cf. Richard son of Ithel son of Matthew 1347 ib 655); *?le lithemos* or *?le sichemos* 1316 *Gros* 169 ('bog at a hillside' or '– near a watercourse', *v.* **hlið, sīc, mos**); *le longland* 1295 *Gros* 99 (*v.* **lang, land**); *Magottisword* 1301 *Gros* 113 ('Magot's private enclosure', from the ME derivative of *Mag, Margaret* with **worð**, here shown in a ME cpd. Cf. *Magotestilth* **4** 196); *Meduwebroc* e13 *Gros* 22 (*v.* **mǣd, brōc**); *le Middilfeld* 1295 *Gros* 99 (*v.* **middel, feld**); *le mosfeild* 1317 *Gros* 179 (*v.* **mos, feld**); *le reddelond* 1295 *Gros* 99 ('the cleared land', *v.* **(ge)ryd(d), land**); *le redelewis* 1316 *Gros* 169, *Redeleus* (lit. *–lens*) 1415 Orm² II 655 ('reedy clearings', *v.* **hrēod, lēah**); *le Russicroft* 1295 *Gros* 105 (*v.* **riscig, croft**); *?Seggimor* e13 *Gros* 22 (perhaps **mōr**[1] with an adj. from **secg**[1]); *?sichemos* (see *?lithemos*); *Stevene parkes* 1295 *Gros* 105 ('paddocks with paling fences', *v.* **stæfen, pearroc**); *le Taylurishauetlond* 1301 *Gros* 113 ('the tailors's head–land', *v.* **hēafod–land**); *le Wolfislond* 113 *Gros* 143 ('selion called after a wolf or one *Wulf*', *v.* **wulf, land**); *le Wytelond* 1295 *Gros* 99 (*v.* **hwīt, land**).

p. 57, l. 22. *Sandonio* is probably an error in this part of RavGeog, see A.L.F Rivet, C. Smith, *The Place–Names of Roman Britain*, London 1979, 415.

p. 107, FIELD–NAMES, (*b*). Add the following names: *Aldemethwe, Blakemonnis heystow, Herewordiscroft* all m13/e14 *Gros*; *Thurberneswra* 112 *Gros* 8. The latter three contain respectively the pers.ns. OE *Blǣcmann, Hereweard*, and OScand *Þorbjorn.* Also add *tunkescarriphalliflond* 1257 *Gros* 43, *v.* **tonge–s(c)harp**.

p. 147, FIELD–NAMES, (*b*), s.n. *Caryngfeld.* See **5:1** xxiii, addendum to **2** 17, Carrington.

p. 155, FIELD–NAMES, (*b*). Add '*Edthelmesmedue* 113 *Gros* 81 ('Æthelhelm's meadow', from the OE pers.n. *Æthelhelm* and **mǣd**); *le Heyrekwyhenegreues* 113 *Gros* 81 ('the higher mountain–ash woods', *v.* **hearra, cwicen, grǣfe**); *le Stodefald* 113 *Gros* 81 (*v.* **stod–fald**); *Timpresdale* 113 *Gros* 81, *v.* addendum **5:2** to Timperley **2** 31.'.

p. 209, FIELD–NAMES, (*b*), s.n. *le Storgreues.* Add '*le Stortegreues* 1283–7 *Gros* 91 (this spelling represents ON **storð** 'a young plantation'. The same interchange of **storð** and **storr**[1] is noted at Storeton **4** 253.'.

p. 240, s.n. *Dingesmere*, line 16. For 'However . . . maintained' substitute the following: 'However, this was challenged by professorial opinion that the resultant OE **Dē–ing* would contract to **Deng* rather than **Ding*, and the poem–text is too early for the late OE, eME change *–eng* > *–ing*. The objection can now be countered by citing the analogy of Margaretting Ess 258 and its base OE **Gīgingas, *Gēgingas* (> ME *Ginge(s), Genge(s)*) from **gē** 'district' and **ingas**. Here, the resultant OE **Gē–ing–* formation has contracted to **Gēng–* and **Gīng–*.'

p. 287, s.n. FRANKBY. After '**Franki*' add 'Cf. the fact that in Ch **4** we find the el. ODan **klint** where we would have expected ON **klettr**.'.

p. 317, s.n. THE TASKAR. Delete reference to **toll, tollr**. Here and in *The Tolske* (**3** 267), the first el. is OE ***tolle** fem., ***toll**, masc., 'tree trunk, tree–stock'. See G. Kristensson, *Studier i modern språkvetenskap*, NS 8, 53–5, cf. Middendorff, *Altenglisches Flurnamenbuch*, 135 on OE *tollandene* 932 BCS 689 [Sawyer 417], Tolleshunt, Tollsbury Ess 304, 306, Tollington Mx 126.

VOLS. XLVIII and LIV
THE PLACE–NAMES OF CHESHIRE, PART V, SECTION 1

p. xvii. See addendum to **1** 170.

p. xxxviii. See addendum to **3** 267.

p. 161, s.v. **docga**. The reference to '*Hodg Croft* **1** 165' should read '**1** 158'.

p. 277. For **mān–drēam** read **man–drēam**.

p. 232, s.v. **holmr**. The reference to discussion, *infra*, in 'Linguistic Notes on Cheshire Place–Names' should be to §12.4.4.

p. 237, s.v. **hulm**. As preceding addendum.

p. 309, s.v. ***plocc**. The headword should rather be **plock** ME and ModE dial., *v.* Gl **4** 162.

p. 368. The names listed under **toll, toln** OE, **tollr** ON, **toll** ME 'a tax, a toll' should now be referred to †***tolle** OE, sb. wk. fem., or †***toll** OE , sb. str. m. or n., 'a tree trunk, a split tree stock', ModE dial. *toll, tolt* (< *tollet?) 'a clump of trees' (originally, perhaps, a clump of pollards). See G. Kristensson, *Studier i modern språkvetenskap*, NS 8, 53–5, cf. Middendorff, *Altenglisches Flurnamenbuch*, 135.

p. 406, line 2. For 'linguistics' read 'linguistic'.

p. 406, before *Brangwain*. Add '*Bleddyn* (f.ns. Blethums Croft **4** 29, Blethens Croft **4** 43).'.

p. 406, s.n. *Goff (e)*. For 'II *infra*' read 'E *infra*'.

s.n. *G(o)ronwy*. Add 'f.n. *Granowes* **4** 214, **4** xv Add.'.

s.n. *Iago*. Add 'f.n. *Croft Iyagow* **5:2** Add. (**4** 30)'.

p. 406, before *Llewelyn*. Add '*Ithell* (*Ithelliscroft* **4** 49–50, **5:2** Add.)'.

p. 407, s.n. *Ælfwald*. Add 'f.n. *Alwaldishalc* **5:2** Add. (**4** 38)'.

p. 407, before *Æthelhild*. Add '*Æthelhelm* (f.n. *Edthelmesmedue* **5:2** Add. (**4** 155))'.

before *Blunt. Add '*Blæcmann* (f.n. *Blakemonnis heystow* **5:2** Add. (**4** 107))'.

p. 408, s.n. *Ceadda*. Add 'f.n. *Chaddewalle*, s.n. Hollywell Ridding **5:2** Add. (**4** 49)'.

p. 410, before *Hildeburg*. Add '*Hereweard* (f.n. *Herewordiscroft* **5:2** Add. (**4** 107)'.

p. 410. For 'Hræfn' read '*Hræfn*'.

p. 412, s.n. *Wulf*. Add 'f.n. *Wolfislond* **5:2** Add. (**4** 49–50)'.

s.n. *Wulfhild*. Add 'or ON *Ulfhildr* fem.'.

p. 413, delete the entry for *Kári*, cf. addendum (**5:1** xxiii) to **2** 17.

p. 413, s.n. *Ketill*. Add 'For a surname *Kel* < *Ketill*, see addendum (**5:2**) to **2** 240, 247'.

p. 414, s.n. *Steinkell*. Add 'cf. ME by–name *Stenkel*, *infra* 423 and f.n. *Stenkelescroft* **3** 41'.

p. 414, before *Þóraldr*. Add '*Þengill* ON (?Tintwistle **5:2** Add. (**1** 320))'.

before *Þórir*. Add '*Þorbjorn* OScand (f.n. *Thurberneswra* **5:2** Add. (**4** 107))'.

before *Úlfr*. Add '*Ulfhildr* fem., cf. *Wulfhild* OE *supra* 412'.

p. 414, s.v. D. Old Irish. Add '*Béollan* (f.n. *Bolanescroft* **5:1** xxvi (**2** 44))'.

p. 415, s.n. *Candelayn*. Add 'f.n. *Candelannescroft* **5:2** Add. (**4** 49–50)'.

p. 417, last line, after '**3** 277'. Add 'but cf. **5:2** Add. (**2** 240, 247)'.

p. 418, line 1, after 'f.n.'. Add '*Kellrudding* **2** 240'.

p. 418, s.n. *Magot*, after 'f.n.'. Add '*Magottisword* **5:2** Add. (**4** 49–50)'.

p. 425, before *John*. Add '?Ithell the clerk of Tushingham 1305 (*Ithelliscroft* **5:2** Add. (**4** 49–50)'.

INDEX OF THE PLACE–NAMES OF CHESHIRE

This index includes all the major and minor names treated in volumes **1–4** or in the addenda and corrigenda sections (add.) in **5:1** and **5:2**. Unidentified or lost names are italicized. The overall alphabetization is letter–by–letter, but the definite article is ignored (e.g. The Mound appears under 'M').

The following abbreviations occur:

Fm	Farm	par.	parish
f.n.	field–name	P.H.	Public House
Gt.	Great	Pk	Park
Ho	House	R.	River
Hd	Hundred	Rd	Road
Lt.	Little	St	Street (also Saint)
Mdw	Meadow	Wd	Wood
nr.	near		

Aaron's Cottage **2** 125
Aaron's Well **2** 125
Abattoir Cottages **3** 192
Abbey, The **5:1** 40
Abbey Arms Wd **3** 211
Abbey Cottages **2** 46, 49
Abbeydale Ho **4** 106
Abbey Fm **1** 76
Abbeyfield **2** 269
Abbey Gate, The **5:1** 29
Abbey Gateway, Lt. **5:1** 8
Abbey Green **5:1** 8
Abbey Grove **2** 316
Abbey Square **5:1** 8
Abbey St (Birkenhead) **4** 314
    (Chester) **5:1** 8
Abbot's Barn, The **5:1** 29
Abbot's Clough **3** 16, 220, 246

Abbot's Grange
    (Lower Bebington) **4** 249
    (Chester) **5:1** 72
Abbot's Hall, The **5:1** 29
Abbots Moss **3** 182
Abbotsmoss Cottage **3** 217
Abbots Moss Hall and Moss Wd
    3 182
Abbot's Walk **3** 180
Abbot's Well **4** 109
Abney Hall **1** 248
Abraham's Chair **1** 322
Accommodation **1** 208
Ack Lane (Bramhall) **1** 259
    (Cheadle) **1** 249
Ackers Fm **2** 18
Ackers Lane (Carrington) **2** 18
    (Latchford) **2** 143 (add. **5:1** xxix)

Barnston (township) **4** 263 (add.
  5:1 xii)
Barnston Common **4** 263
Barnston Hall **4** 263
Barnton (township) **2** 105 (add.
  5:1 xxvii)
Barn Well **4** 29
Barn Wd Field **3** 94
Baronet Fm **2** 157
Baron's Quay **2** 196
Baron's Quay Mine **2** 196
Barony, The **3** 36
Barony Rd **3** 36
Barr, Big **2** 307
Barrack Hill **1** 264
Barrack Hill Fm and Lane **1** 264
Barracks, The (Burwardsley) **4** 94
  (Marlston cum Lache) **4** 164
Barracks Fm **2** 3
Barracks Lane **1** 121
Barrastitch Lane **3** 199
Barrelwell Hill **5:1** 78
Barrets Green (Alpraham) **3** 301
  (Calveley) **3** 308
Barrets–Poole **3** 149
Barrington Rd **2** 9
Barrow (par.) **3** 261
Barrow, Gt. and Lt.
  (townships) **3** 261
Barrow Brook (R. Gowy) **3** 264
  (R. Mersey) **1** 14
Barrow Fork Plantation **4** 98
Barrow Hall **3** 264
Barrow Hall, Lt. **3** 264
Barrow Hill **3** 264 (add. **5:1** xxxvii)
Barrow Lane (Hale) **2** 24
  (Ringway) **2** 29
  (Seven Oaks) **2** 134
Barrow Lane Fm **3** 254
Barrow Lodge **3** 264
Barrow Mill **3** 262

Barrowmore Fm, Gorse and Hall
  3 264
Barrows Green **3** 29
Barrsgate St **5:1** 75
Barry's Covert **2** 141 (add.
  5:1 xxvii)
Barry's Wd **3** 217
Bars, The **5:1** 79
Barsbank Fm and Lane **2** 38
Bartholomewse Inne **5:1** 29
Barthomley (par.) **3** 2
Barthomley (township) **3** 5 (add.
  5:1 xxxiii, **5:2**)
Barthomley Mill **3** 7
Barthomley Rd Fm **3** 10
Bartington (township) **2** 106 (add.
  5:1 xxvii)
Bartington Fm **2** 107
Bartomley **1** 168
Bartomley Bottoms **1** 168
Barton (township) **4** 68
Barton Lodge and Plantation **4** 68
Barton's Clough **1** 182
Basford (township) **3** 48
Basford Brook **3** 49
Basford Coppice **3** 7
Basford Hall **3** 48
Basford Ho **3** 59
Bate Heath **2** 103
Bate Mill **2** 87
Bate Mill Fm **2** 87
Bate Moss **2** 87
Bates **1** 312
Bate's Bridge **2** 177
Bates Lay **1** 259
Bates Ley **1** 249
Bate's Mill Bridge **3** 321
Batherton (township) **3** 50 (add.
  5:1 xxxiv)
Batherton Dairy Ho **3** 51
Batherton Hall and Mill **3** 50

Black Moss Covert and Fm **2** 21
Black Rock **4** 326 (add. **5:1** xlv)
Blackrock Fm **1** 142
Blackshaw Gap **1** 142 (add. **5:1** xvi)
Blackshaw Heys **2** 10
Black Spring **1** 121
Black Swan P.H. **1** 90
Blackthorn Wd **3** 62
Black Tor **1** 322
Blackwater Moss **3** 85
Black Wd
   (Ashton iuxta Tarvin) **3** 269
   (Dodleston) **4** 157
   (Kingswood) **3** 215
   (Marton) **1** 81
Blackyard Fm **2** 231
Blacon **4** 168
Blacon Cottages **4** 169
Blacon cum Crabwall
   (township) **4** 168
Blacon Hall **4** 169
Blacon House Fm **4** 169
Blacon Point **4** 170
Blacon Point Fm **4** 169
Bladehurst **1** 52
Blakeden **3** 171
Blakeden Gorse and Lane **3** 171
Blakefield **1** 55
Blakehey Wd **1** 133
Blakehouse Fm **1** 86
Blakelees **3** 242
Blake Lees Ho **3** 242
Blakeley Brow **4** 227
Blakeley Fm and Lane **2** 66
Blakelow (Sutton Downes) **1** 153
   (Willaston) **3** 79
Blakelow Bank, Fm and Gate **1** 153
Blakelow, Lower
   (Macclesfield) **1** 121
   (Sutton Downes) **1** 153
Blakelow Rd **1** 121
Blakemere (Norley) **3** 249

   (Oakmere) **3** 217
   (Weaverham cum Milton) **3** 208
Blakemere Moss **3** 213
Blakemoor Cottages **2** 310
Blakenhall (township) **3** 51
Blakenhall Moss **3** 52
Blakeswell Mdw **2** 18
Blakhall **5:1** 30
Blaze **1** 160
Blaze Hill **1** 142
Blazehill Fm **1** 194
Bleak Ho (Bollington) **1** 189
   (Newhall) **3** 103
Bleakhouse Fm **2** 211
Bleakley Lane 3 208
Bleaze Fm **2** 80
Blobb Hill **4** 77
Bloomsbury Lane **2** 31
Blossoms Fm **1** 254
Blossoms Mdws **1** 160
Blue Bache Fm **3** 103
Blueball **1** 104
Bluebell Fm (Tabley Superior) **2** 61
Blue Bell Fm (Tytherington) **1** 215
Blue Bell Fm, Old **1** 215
Blue Boar Fm **1** 142
Blue–Coat School, The **5:1** 70
Bluemire Fm **3** 7
Blueslate Fm **2** 231
Blueslates Fm **2** 236
Bluestone **3** 145
Blundering Hall Fm **2** 10
Blundering Lane **1** 312
Boarded–barn **2** 310
Boarded Barn Fm **2** 38
Boarding School Yd **5:1** 10
Boar Flat **1** 310
Boargreave, Higher **1** 153
Boathouse Lane **4** 219
Boat Lane (Buerton, lost) **4** 80
   (Northenden) **1** 235
Bobberhill **4** 35

Brookfold **1** 306
Brookfold Fm **1** 264
Brook Furlong Lane **3** 223 (add.
  3 xvi)
Brookhead **1** 249
Brookheys Fm **2** 21
Brookheys Rd (Carrington) **2** 18
  (Dunham Massey) **2** 21
Brook Hole (Golborne Bellow) **4** 96
  (Huxley) **4** 102 (add. **5:1** xl)
Brook Hole Cottage **4** 96
Brook Ho (Acton) **3** 127
  (Adlington **1** 183
  (Agden) **4** 3
  (Audlem) **3** 85
  (Bostock) **2** 202
  (Gt. Boughton) **4** 125
  (Buglawton) **2** 291
  (Burland) **3** 135
  (Chorley, nr. Wilmslow) **1** 225
  (Chorley, nr. Wrenbury) **3** 116
  (Cogshall) **2** 110
  (Cuddington) **3** 199
  (Eaton) **3** 290
  (Gawsworth) **1** 68
  (Godley) **1** 306
  (Gt. Warford) **1** 105
  (Handforth cum Bosden, 2x)
  1 257
  (Haslington) **3** 14
  (Huxley) **4** 102
  (Kelsall) **3** 278
  (Kinderton cum Hulme) **2** 238
  (Kingsley) **3** 242
  (Latchford) **2** 143
  (Mottram St. Andrew) **1** 204
  (Newbold Astbury) **2** 287
  (Old Withington) **1** 93
  (Over) **3** 171
  (Partington) **2** 27
  (Shavington cum Gresty) **3** 70

  (Stockton Heath) **2** 145
  (Tattenhall) **4** 98
  (Walgherton) **3** 74
  (Warburton) **2** 35
  (Whatcroft) **2** 215
  (Yeardsley cum Whaley) **1** 178
Brookhouse
  (Macclesfield Forest) **1** 127
  (Rainow) **1** 142
Brookhouse Bridge and Clough
  (Rainow) **1** 142
Brook House Fm
  (Kinderton cum Hulme) **2** 238
  (Newton by Daresbury) **2** 154
Brookhouse Fm (Allostock) **2** 218
  (Alsager) **3** 3
  (Bruen Stapleford) **3** 270
  (Lt. Budworth) **3** 186
  (Clotton Hoofield) **3** 272
  (High Legh) **2** 46
  (Ollerton) **2** 80
  (Plumley) **2** 92
  (Rainow) **1** 142
  (Smallwood) **2** 316
  (Lower Whitley) **2** 135
Brookhouse Fm, Upper
  (Foulk Stapleford) **4** 106
Brookhouse Green **2** 316
Brookhouse Lane
  (Bruen Stapleford) **3** 270
Brookhouse Moss **2** 316
Brookhouse Rd **3** 3
Brook Houses **1** 323
Brook Lane (Gt. Boughton) **4** 125
  (Chorley) **1** 225
  (Timperley) **2** 31
Brooklands
  (Church Coppenhall) **3** 24
  (Cuddington) **3** 199
  (Hough) **3** 64
  (Church Hulme) **2** 279

Brownhayes Fm **2** 199
Brown Heath (Christleton) **4** 109
Brownheath
    (Weaverham cum Milton) **3** 208
Brown Hill (Wincle) **1** 169
Brownhill (Rushton) **3** 292
Brown Hills (Spurstow) **3** 315
Brownhills (Gawsworth) **1** 68
Brown Ho (Offerton) **1** 290
    (Rainow) **1** 142
    (Stockport) **1** 297
Brown House Fold Brook **1** 297
Brown Knowl **4** 15
Brown Lane **1** 244
Brownley Green **1** 240
Brownlow (Newbold Astbury) **2** 287
    (Sutton Downes) **1** 153
Brownlow Fm and Heath
    (Morton cum Alcumlow) **2** 305
    (Newbold Astbury) **2** 287
Brownmoss **3** 66
Brownmoss Fm **3** 249
Brownough **1** 178
Brownroad **1** 314
Brown's Bank (Davenport) **2** 301
    (Newhall) **3** 103
Brown's Fm **1** 222
Brown's Lane **5:1** 49
Brownslow **2** 108
Brownswolds **2** 297
Brow's Fm **2** 98
Browside Clough and Fm **1** 199
    (add. **5:1** xviii)
Browtop **1** 111
Broxton (township) **4** 12 (add.
    5:1 xxxix)
Broxton Bridge (Broxton) **4** 15
    (Clutton) **4** 72
Broxton Fm, Small **4** 16
Broxton Hd **4** 1
Broxton Lower Hall **4** 15
Broxton Old Hall **4** 15

Broxton Wd **4** 15
Bruchis, le **1** 42
Bruera Chapelry **4** 115
Bruera **4** 122
Brugge, del, atte **1** 52
Bruggeende, le **1** 52
Brun **1** 323
Brundhurst **1** 153
Brundred Fm **1** 212
Brundrit, The **2** 13
Brund's Fm **3** 3
Bruneshurst **3** 53
Bruntwood Hall **1** 249
Brushes **1** 318
Brushes Reservoir and Quarry **1** 310
Brydges Fm **1** 284
Bryn **3** 198
Bryncaewannedd **4** 31
Bryn Common **3** 218
Bryndeyatefolde, le **1** 52
Bryn Fm **3** 198
Brynlow **1** 97
Brynn Bank (Cuddington) **3** 198
    (Weaverham cum Milton) **3** 203
Buckbean Pit **2** 227
Buckbean Pit Fm **2** 227
Buckhall **2** 29
Buckley Mill Cottage **3** 45
Bucklow Fm **2** 92
Bucklow Hill (Mere) **2** 51
    (Millington) **2** 55
    (Rostherne) **2** 58
Bucklow Hd **2** 1
Buckoak **3** 245
Buck's Hill **1** 86
Buckton Castle **1** 323
Buckton Grange and Vale **1** 318
Buddeley **2** 60
Budworth, Gt. (par.) **2** 95
Budworth, Gt. (township) **2** 107
Budworth, Lt. (chapelry, township)
    3 184 (add. **5:1** xi)

Burley Lane **2** 98
Burned Hey Wd **1** 231
Burnhousefold **1** 318
Burnt Acre **1** 93
Burntcliff Top **1** 160
Burnthouse **1** 169
Burnthouse Fm **2** 61
Burnthouses (Mere) **2** 52
   (Tabley Superior) **2** 61
Burnt Wd **3** 217
Burrow Coppice **3** 49
Burrows Hill
   (Castle Northwich) **3** 190
   (Weaverham) **3** 205
Burton (par.) **4** 211
Burton in Wirrall (township) **4** 211
   (add. **5:1** xii)
Burton, nr. Tarvin (township) **3** 270
Burton (Rainow) **1** 142
Burton Barn **4** 212
Burton Fm and Hall **3** 270
Burton–Head **4** 212
Burton Ho **3** 270
Burton Manor **4** 211
Burton Point **4** 212
Burwardestone **4** 1
Burwardsley (township) **4** 93 (add.
   5:1 xii, xl)
Burwardsley Hall **4** 93
Burwardsley, Higher **4** 94
Burwardsley Hill **4** 94
Burwardsley Hill Fm **4** 94
Burybrokes **1** 52
Burying Fd f.n. **1** 87, 156 (add.
   3 xiv)
Burymewick **1** 293
Burymewick Wd **1** 271 (add.
   5:1 xxi)
Bush Fm **4** 109
Butcher's Bank **3** 21
Butchersfield Bight **2** 38

Butley (township) **1** 193 (add.
   5:1 xvii)
Butley Ash **1** 195
Butley Bridge (Adlington) **1** 183
   (Butley) **1** 195
Butley Hall and Town **1** 195
Butter Bache **4** 117
Butter Bache Bridge
   (Gt. Boughton) **4** 125
   (Huntington) **4** 117
Butter Hill **4** 141
Butterhouse Green **1** 263
Butterlands **1** 165
Butterley Heys **3** 95
Butterley Moss **1** 323
Butter Market, The **5:1** 30
Buttermilk Bank **3** 107
Butter Shops, The **5:1** 22–3
Butterton Lane **3** 14
Butterton Lane Fm **3** 14
Butteryhouse Fm **2** 29
Butt Fm **3** 186
Butt Green **3** 72
Butt Lane **2** 321
Butt Lane Fm **2** 321
Button Brook **1** 17
Button Lane **1** 237
Butts, The **1** 97
Buttsclough **2** 29
Buttyfold Fm **2** 141
Buttymoss **1** 68
Buttymoss Wd **1** 68
Buxton Croft f.n. **1** 185
Buxton Rd (Macclesfield) **1** 122
   (Norbury) **1** 288
Buxtors Hill **1** 127
Buxtorstoops Fm **1** 142
Byatt's House Fm **4** 128
Byeflat Works **3** 192
Bye Pitt **1** 183
Bye Wash **2** 138

Coal Pit Lane (Beeston) **3** 304 (add.
  5:1 xxxviii)
  (Backford) **4** 173
  (Lea) **4** 176
  (Gt. Mollington) **4** 178
  (Gt. Saughall) **4** 204
Cobblers Cross **3** 297
Cobblers Gorse **2** 129
Cobbs, The **2** 98
Cobb's Lane and Moss **3** 64
Cobbs Quarry **2** 98
Cock A Burland **3** 135
Cock Brow **1** 307
Cocked Hat Covert **3** 165
Cocked Hat Plantation **3** 98
Cockerhill **1** 323
Cockers **1** 318
Cocker's Heyes **2** 129
Cockhall **1** 153
Cockhead **1** 272
Cock and Hen Lane **2** 178
Cock Knarr **1** 310
Cock–Knoll **1** 272
Cock Lane **2** 108
Cockmoss Cottage, Fm, Rd and Wd
  1 81
Cockshades **3** 64
Cockshead **1** 212
Cocksheadhey Fm **1** 189
Cockshead Wd **1** 212
Cock Wd
  (Henbury cum Pexall) **1** 79
  (Stayley) **1** 318
Cocle **3** 160
Cocuslane **5:1** 11
Coddesburie **1** 52
Coddington (par.) **4** 82
  (township) **4** 85
Coddington Bridge **4** 85
Coddington Brook **4** 86
Coddington Hall Fm and Mill **4** 85
Codlough **1** 52

Codyngeheye f.n. **4** 87
Cogshall (township) **2** 109
Cogshall Brook and Hall **2** 110
Cogshall Lane (Anderton) **2** 96
  (Cogshall) **2** 110
Cogshall Mill **2** 110
Cokesrowe **5:1** 23
Cold Arbour **1** 215
Coldelawe **1** 52
Coldharbour **4** 89
Cold Moss Heath **2** 270
Coldstream Cottages **2** 67
Collar Ho **1** 212
College, The **3** 306
College Fields **3** 87
College Lane **3** 306
Collesdale **3** 162
Colley Lane (Betchton) **3** 19
  (Sandbach) **2** 270
Colleymill **1** 59
Colleymill Bridge
  (Buglawton) **2** 291
  (N. Rode) **1** 59
Colleys Bridge **3** 28
Colleys Lane **3** 43
Colliers Lane **2** 103 (add. **5:1** xxvii)
Collinge Fm and Wd **4** 173
Collins Wd **1** 195
Colonel's Hatch **3** 211
Colshaw **1** 221
Colshaw Hall **2** 87
Colshaw Wd **1** 86
Colt Hovel Wd **1** 93
Colthurst Mill **2** 83
Colvesdale **3** 162
Comberbach (township) **2** 111
Comberbach Green **2** 111
Comberbach Ho **2** 134
Comber Mere **3** 93 (add. **5:1** xxxiv)
Combermere Abbey and Pk **3** 93
Combermere Wd **3** 98
Comberwheyn f.n. **1** 211

Cowbury Dale **1** 323
Cow Fields **3** 33
Cow Hey Covert **4** 255
Cowhouse Fm **2** 103
Cow Lane (Ashley) **2** 10
    (Bollington) **1** 189
    (Chester) **5:1** 65
    (Handforth cum Bosden) **1** 257
    (Macclesfield) **1** 115
    (Norley) **3** 249
    (Rainow) **1** 143
    (Foulk Stapleford) **4** 106
    (Stockport) **1** 297
Cowlane Bridge **5:1** 72
Cowlane Gate **5:1** 72
Cowley **1** 67
Cowlishaw Cottages **1** 303
Cow–Pasture Wd **4** 242 (add.
    5:1 xliii)
Coxbank **3** 85
Coxbank Brook **3** 85
Coxton Hall **1** 242
Crabmill Fm (Baddiley) **3** 124
    (Elton) **2** 258
    (Somerford Booths) **1** 64
Crabmill Ho **2** 270
Crab Moss **1** 68
Crabtree Cottage **4** 71 (add. **5:1** xl)
Crabtree Fm (Alvanley) **3** 220
    (Cuddington) **4** 29 (add.
    5:1 xxxix)
    (High Legh) **2** 47
    (Prestbury) **1** 212
    (Rainow) **1** 143
Crabtreegreen Fm **3** 217 (add.
    5:1 xxxvii)
Crabtree Lane **2** 47
Crabtreemoss (Gawsworth) **1** 68
    (add. **5:1** lxv)
    (Siddington) **1** 86
Crabwall **4** 169

Crabwall, Blacon cum
    (township) **4** 168
Crabwall Fm and Hall **4** 169
Cracow Moss **3** 58
Crag Cottage and Hall **1** 161
Craghouse Fm **2** 84
Crag Works **1** 161
Crampton Lane **2** 18
Cranage (township) **2** 223
Cranage Bridge and Hall **2** 224
Cranage Mill (Cranage) **2** 224
    (Wincham) **2** 136
Cranberry Moss (Alsager) **3** 3
    (Barthomley) **3** 7
    (Eaton in Astbury) **1** 61
Crane Bank **5:1** 62
Crane St **5:1** 62
Cranford Avenue **2** 74
Cranshawes **1** 74
Crappilous f.n. **2** 322
Craxton, The **4** 215
Creek Ho and Side **4** 330
Crescent **1** 208
Cresswellshaw Brook **3** 3
Cresswellshawe **3** 3
Cresswellshawe Fm **3** 3
Crewe (nr. Barthomley) (township)
    3 9 (add. **5:1** xxxiii)
    (nr. Farndon) (township) **4** 73
    (Monks Coppenhall) **3** 26
Crewe Bridge and Gate **3** 10
Crewe Gorse **4** 73
Crewe Green **3** 10
Crewe Hall
    (Crewe nr. Barthomley) **3** 10
    (Crewe nr. Farndon) **4** 73
Crewehall Fm **3** 10
Crewe Hill **4** 73
Crewe Mill and Pk **3** 10
Crewe Rd
    (Brereton cum Smethwick) **2** 274

Delavor Ho and Rd **4** 278
Dell, The (Higher Bebington) **4** 246
   (Hankelow) **3** 90
   (Wirswall) **3** 113
Dell Wd **2** 162
Demesne Fm **3** 61
Demesne St **1** 318
Demmage Fm **4** 176
Demmings **1** 249
Denamere **4** 75
Denbigh St **5:1** 65
Den Coppice and Fm **3** 52
Dene Brook **3** 174
Dene Cottage **2** 116
Dene Cottages, Ho and Pump **2** 108
Denfield Hall **2** 57
Denhall **4** 220
Denhall Gutter (Gayton) **4** 275
   (Gt. Neston) **4** 223
Denhall Ho and Quay **4** 220
Den, Higher **3** 52
Den Lane (Blakenhall) **3** 52
   (Checkley cum Wrinehill) **3** 58
Denman Wood **2** 267
Denna Lane **4** 220
Dennow Fm and Wd **2** 98
Dension's Bridge **4** 182
Denton **4** 71
Depleach Hall **1** 249
Depmore Fm **3** 242
Derby Arms P.H. **1** 127
Derby Ho **4** 246
Derbyshire Bridge **1** 173 (add. **5:2**)
Derby St **1** 115
Derwalshawe **2** 141 (add. **5:1** xxvii)
Deslayheath **2** 116
Devil's Bank **4** 242
Devil's Bridge (Hollingworth) **1** 310
   (Tintwistle) **1** 323
Devils Lane **1** 101
Devil's Nest **3** 114
Devisdale Rd **2** 20

Dewhill Naze **1** 323
Dewsbury Ho **3** 278
Dewsnap Fm and Lane **1** 277
Dewsnip Fm **1** 310
Dial Ho (Hollingworth) **1** 310
   (Stockport) **1** 297
Dialstone Lane **1** 297
Dialstone Lane Fm **1** 297
Dibbinsdale **4** 251
Dibbinsdale Brook
   (Bromborough) **4** 242
   (Poulton cum Spital) **4** 251
Dibbinsdale Lodge and Rd **4** 242
Dicken Bridge **2** 67
Dickens Fm **1** 101
Dickens Lane **1** 208
Dickens Wd **1** 101
Dickinson's Rough **3** 285
Dicklow Cob and Fm **1** 90
Dicks Mount **3** 211 (add.
   5:1 xxxvii)
Didsbury Intake **1** 323
Dighills, The **1** 68
Dighills Brook and Wd **1** 68
Diglake (Buglawton) **2** 291
   (Wybunbury) **3** 82
Dig Lane **3** 127
Dig Lane Fm **3** 127
Diglee **1** 178
Dilles Towre **5:1** 25
Dimples **1** 126
Dingers Hollow **1** 161
Dingle, The (Appleton) **2** 98
   (Chester) **5:1** 59
   (Cuddington) **4** 29
   (Lymm) **2** 39
   (Willington) **3** 285
   (Wimboldsley) **2** 257
Dingle Bank **5:1** 59
Dingle Bridge **2** 98
Dingle Brook (Appleton) **2** 98
   (Old Withington) **1** 93

Dogkennel Covert and Fm **4** 67
Dogkennel Wd (Capesthorne) **1** 74
   (Tabley Inferior) **2** 123
Dog Lane (Brereton cum
   Smethwick) **2** 276
   (Chowley) **4** 84
   (Middlewich) **2** 241
   (Nantwich) **3** 33
   (Newton by Malpas) **4** 44
   (Oldcastle) **4** 44
Dog Lane Fm (Brereton cum
   Smethwick) **2** 276
   (Oldcastle) **4** 44
Dog Lodge and Wd **2** 75
Dogmoor Well (Delamere) **3** 211
   (Kelsall) **3** 278
Dokunesforde, le **1** 52
Dolefield **1** 284
Dole Ho **2** 235
Doles Fm, Higher and Lower **1** 183
Dollards **1** 153
Dollards, Old **1** 153
Doncasterhill **1** 108
Done **3** 161
Donefields **2** 214
Dones Green **2** 113
Donkey Lane **3** 183
Donkinson's Oak
   (Church Coppenhall) **3** 24
   (Warmingham) **2** 262
Donnington **3** 61
Dood's Bridge **2** 98 (add. **5:1** xxvii)
Dood's Brook **1** 22, **2** 98
Dood's Lane **2** 98
Dooleylane **1** 284
Dooley's Fm and Grig **1** 90
Dorfold Cottage and Dairy Ho
   3 127
Dorfold Hall **3** 126
Double Wd (Clive) **2** 235
   (Ringway) **2** 30
Doudfield **1** 284

Doulak' **1** 52
Dove Ho (Godley) **1** 306
   (Hough) **3** 64
   (Marple) **1** 284
Dovehouse Croft **3** 39
Dove Light and Point **4** 298
Downes **1** 148
Downs, The **2** 8
Downs Bridge **1** 249
Downs, Higher **2** 20
Downs Rd, E. and S. **2** 15
Dowry **1** 173
Dowse Green **4** 23
Dragon Fm **4** 84
Dragons Hole **1** 143
Dragon's Lane **2** 259
Drakecar **1** 272
Drake Lane **3** 127
Drakelond **3** 1
Drakelow Fm (Allostock) **2** 218
   (Rudheath Lordship) **2** 198
Drakelow Gorse Fm **2** 199
Drakelow Hall **2** 198 (add.
   5:1 xxxi)
Drakelow Lane **2** 199
Drameleg' **1** 52
Dromedary Lodge **2** 227
Droppingstone Ho **4** 94
Droppingstone Well **4** 4
Drove Hey Fm, Lower **1** 153
Drumber Fm **3** 19
Drumber Lane **2** 310
Drumble Lake **2** 254
Drumbo, The **4** 15
Drury Lane **2** 262
Dry Clough **1** 319
Dryheath Wd **1** 68
Dryhurst **1** 272
Dryhurst Wd **1** 272
Dryknowl **1** 161
Dry Pool Plantation **3** 91
Drysike Clough **1** 323

Dunsdale Hollow **3** 230–1
Dun's Lane **2** 13
Dunstan Fm and Lane **4** 212
Dutton (township) **2** 112 (add.
    5:1 xxvii)
Dutton **3** 155 (add. **5:1** xxxv)
Dutton Bottoms, Dean, Dingles,
    Hall and Hollow Fm **2** 113
Dutton Lane **3** 197
Dutton Locks **3** 194
Dutton Lodge and Pk **2** 113
Dutton's Lane **3** 278
Dye Lane **1** 293
Dyer's Fm **4** 31

Each Man's **4** 5
Eagle Brow **2** 39
Eagle Hall Cottages **3** 103
Eanley **3** 292
Eanley Wood Fm **2** 173 (add. **5:2**)
Eanley Wood Fm, Lower **2** 173
Eardswick Bridge **2** 249
Eardswick Hall **2** 247 (add.
    5:1 xxxii)
Eardswick Wd **2** 249
Earle's Lane (Kelsall) **3** 278
Earles Lane (Wincham) **2** 137
Earlscroft **3** 278
Earl's Eye **5:1** 46
Earl's Wd **2** 204
Early Bank **1** 319
Early Bank Wd **1** 277
Earnshaw Hall **2** 188 (add. **2** viii,
    5:1 xxx)
Earnshaw Ho **2** 229
Earnslow Grange **3** 207
Easterlane Fm **2** 28
Eastford Rd **2** 157
Eastgate (Chester) **5:1** 25
East Gate (Macclesfield) **1** 115
Eastgate St **5:1** 13
Eastgate St Row, N. and S. **5:1** 22

Eastham (par. and township) **4** 187
    (add. **5:1** xlii)
Eastham Ferry and Rake **4** 188
Eastham Sands
    (Bromborough) **4** 242
    (Eastham) **4** 188
    (Hooton) **4** 190
Eastham Windmill and Woods
    4 188
East Lodge **1** 199
Easthoe Lane **1** 24
Eastwood **1** 277
Eastwood Fm **4** 199
Eaton (in Astbury) (township) **1** 61
Eaton (nr. Davenham)
    (township) **2** 204
    (nr. Eccleston) (township) **4** 148
    (add. **5:1** xli)
    (nr. Tarporley) (township) **3** 289
    (add. **5:1** xii)
Eaton Bank (Eaton in Astbury) **1** 62
    (Eaton nr. Tarporley) **2** 291
Eaton Bank Wd **2** 207
Eaton Boat **4** 150 (add. **5:1** xli)
Eaton Cottage **1** 62
Eaton Green **4** 148
Eaton Hall (Eaton in Astbury) **1** 62
    (Eaton nr. Davenham) **2** 205
    (Eaton nr. Eccleston) **4** 148
Eatonhill Fm **3** 290
Eaton Mill **1** 62
Eaton Pk **4** 148
Eaton Rd (Chester) **5:1** 52
    (Claverton) **4** 161
    (Eccleston) **4** 151
    (Tarporley) **3** 297
Eaton Stud **4** 151
Eaves Fm **1** 143
Ebnal Fm and Grange **4** 40
Eccles Bridge **1** 284
Ecclesfield Wd **2** 11
Eccleston (par.) **4** 148

Folly Cottage **2** 291
Folly Fm (Kingswood) **3** 217
Folly Fm, The (Swettenham) **2** 284
Folly Gut **4** 333
Folly Ho (Newton by Chester)
    4 146 (add. **4** xiv)
Folly Houses (Gt. Warford) **1** 105
Folly Lane **4** 333
Folly Mill **1** 169
Folly Wd **3** 252
Fools Nook (Gawsworth, lost) **1** 68
    (Sutton Downes) **1** 153
Ford **4** 309
Ford, Bidston cum (township) **4** 308
Fordbank **1** 24
Ford Bridge
    (Bidston cum Ford) **4** 309
    (Bruen Stapleford) **3** 270
    (Foulk Stapleford) **4** 106
    (Upton) **4** 306, 309
Ford Cottage (Norbury) **1** 288
    (Northenden) **1** 237
Ford Fm **4** 106
Ford House Fm **2** 157
Ford Lane (Aldford) **4** 78
    (Churton by Aldford) **4** 81
    (Monks Coppenhall) **3** 27
    (Newton by Tattenhall) **4** 96
    (Northenden) **1** 237
    (Tattenhall) **4** 98
Ford Lane Fm (Aldford) **4** 78
    (Churton by Aldford) **4** 81
Ford Rd (Upton) **4** 306
Ford's Rough **2** 98
Ford St **1** 248
Foregate St **5:1** 13, 65, 75
Foreign Hey **1** 195
Forest Barn **1** 127
Forest Fm (Eddisbury) **3** 214
    (Utkinton) **3** 299
Forestgate **3** 216
Forestgate Fm **3** 242

Foresthey **3** 208
Forest Hill and Hill Fm **3** 208
Forest Ho (Lt. Budworth) **3** 186
    (Delamere) **3** 211
    (Oakmere) **3** 217
Foresthouse Fm **3** 242
Forest Lane (Kingsley) **3** 242
    (Norley) **3** 249
Forest Rd (Macclesfield) **1** 122
    (Macclesfield Forest) **1** 127
    (Tarporley) **3** 297
Forest Smithy **1** 127
Forest St **3** 205
Forestview Inn **3** 199
Forge Brook **3** 67
Forge Brook Cottage and Pool
    2 118
Forge Fields **2** 270
Forge Lane **2** 298
Forge Mill (Congleton) **2** 298
    (Odd Rode) **2** 310
    (Warmingham) **2** 262
Forge Mill Ho **2** 262
Forgemill Cottages **2** 261
Forge Wd **2** 298
Fornall Bridge (Gt. Meols) **4** 298
    (Newton cum Larton) **4** 301
    (Saughall Massie) **4** 322
Fornalls Green (Gt. Meols) **4** 298
    (Newton cum Larton) **4** 301
Fornalls Green Lane **4** 301
Forster's Lane **5:1** 13
Forton Hey **4** 288
Forty Acre Lane **2** 282
Foulk Stapleford,
    v. Stapleford, Foulk
Foundry Lane **5:1** 65
Fountain Cottages **3** 312
Four Lane Ends (Alvanley) **3** 220
    (Timperley, lost) **2** 32
    (Tiverton) **3** 321
Four–Lane–Ends (Adlington) **1** 183

Hanging–Gate Fm **1** 154
Hangingstone Hill **3** 214
Hanging Wd (Darnhall) **3** 169
 (Moreton cum Alcumlow) **2** 305
Hangman's Lane (Birches) **2** 185
 (Hulse) **2** 186
 (Lostock Gralam) **2** 190
 (Smallwood) **2** 317
Hankelow (township) **3** 89
Hankelow Court, Green and Hall
 3 90
Hankelow Ho **3** 85
Hankelow Mill **3** 90
Hankins Heys **3** 87
Hannah's Walk **2** 245
Hanns Hall **4** 226
Hanns Hall Cottages **4** 226
Hanson Ho **2** 67
Hapsford (township) **3** 257
Hapsford Hall **3** 257
Hapsford Moor **3** 257
Harborough, Old **1** 100
Harbour **1** 317
Harbutt's Field **2** 238 (add. **4** x)
Hardgreue **1** 53
Hardinge f.n. **2** 23
Hardingland **1** 126
Hardings **1** 154
Hardings Bank **2** 292 (add. **2** ix)
Hardings Wd **2** 321 (add. **2** ix)
Hardtimes **1** 311
Hardy Fm **1** 260
Hardy Green **1** 112
Hardy's Covert **2** 11
Harebachesty **1** 41, **3** 208
Harebarrow Fm **1** 100
Harebarrow, Lower and New **1** 101
Harebarrowlake **1** 101
Harefield **1** 228
Harefield Fm **1** 228
Hareheys Fm **3** 242

Hare Hill (Tintwistle) **1** 324
Harehill (Over Alderley) **1** 102
Hare Hill Clough **1** 324
Harehill Rough **3** 52
Hare Lane (Gt. Boughton) **4** 125
 (Guilden Sutton) **4** 128
Hare Lane Fm **4** 131
Harelane Rough
 (Brereton cum Smethwick) **2** 276
 (Davenport) **2** 302
Haresclough **3** 183
Hare's Lane (Frodsham) **3** 223
 (Frodsham Lordship) **3** 231
Harewood **1** 272
Harewood–Hill **3** 211
Harewood Lodge **1** 314
Hargrave (Foulk Stapleford) **4** 105
 (add. **4** xiii)
Hargrave, Lt. Neston cum
 (township) **4** 225
Hargrave **4** 228 (add. **4** xv)
Hargrave Cottages **4** 229
Hargrave Fm (Huxley) **4** 102
 (Foulk Stapleford) **4** 105
Hargrave Hall (Lt. Neston) **4** 228
 (Tarvin) **4** 105
Hargrave Old Hall (Tarvin) **4** 105
Hargravehouse Fm **4** 229
Hargrave Lane **4** 228
Hargrave's Bridge **2** 67
Hargrave Stubbs **4** 105
Hargreave **4** 227
Haropgreen **1** 90
Harp and Crown, The **5:1** 32
Harp and Crown Row **5:1** 21–2
Harpers Bank Wd **2** 59
Harpley, Higher and Lower **1** 319
Harre Tower, The **5:1** 25, 27
Harridge **1** 311
Harridge Hall and Pike **1** 319
Harrington Arms Inn **1** 69

Heath, Lt. **4** 4
Heath Lodge **2** 75
Heath Rd (Higher Bebington) **4** 246
 (Lower Bebington) **4** 249
 (Weston) **2** 183
Heathside (Cheadle) **1** 250
 (Eaton in Astbury) **1** 62
Heath St **1** 248
Heath Wd (Backford) **4** 173
Heath Wd, Lower (Storeton) **4** 255
Heatley (Broomhall) **3** 115 (add.
 5:1 xxxv)
 (Lymm) **2** 37 (add. **5:1** xxiv)
Heatley, Lt. **2** 37
Heaviley **1** 296
Heawood Hall **1** 96
Hebden Green **3** 169
Hedge Row **1** 143
Heesomgreen Fm **2** 81 (add. **2** viii)
Hefferston Grange **3** 203
Heildend **1** 161
Heild Rocks and Wd **1** 161
Heir's Wd, The (Duckington) **4** 30
 (Edge) **4** 32
Helde, del **4** 168
Helle **5:1** 32
Helleswode **1** 53
Hell Hole **3** 124
Hell Hollow **2** 91
Hell Kitchen Bridge **2** 236
Helsby (township) **3** 235
Helsby Hill, Ho, Lodge, Marsh and
 Quarry **3** 236
Helsdale Brook and Wd **2** 39 (add.
 5:1 xxiv)
Helmesley **1** 161
Helmesley Rocks and Wd **1** 161
Hemp Gill **3** 231
Hempshaw Brook **1** 297
Hempshawgate Fm **1** 297
Hempshaw Lane **1** 297
Hempstones, The **2** 168

Hempstones Point **2** 168
Henbury **1** 78
Henbury cum Pexall
 (township) **1** 78
Henbury Hall **1** 79
Henbury Lee **3** 76
Henbury Lodges, Moss and Smithy
 1 79
Hengilhulm **1** 53
Henhull (township) **3** 145
Henhull Bridge **3** 145
Henhullbridge Fm **3** 147
Henhull Cottage **4** 98
Henhull Fm **3** 145
Henlake Brook **1** 28
Hen Lane (Audlem) **3** 85
 (Shavington cum Gresty) **3** 70
Hennegrave **1** 53
Henshall Fm **2** 21
Henshall Hall **2** 298
Henshall Lane **2** 21
Henshall St **5:1** 66
Henshaw Green **2** 92
Henshaw Hall **1** 84
Henson House Fm **2** 84
Henwalds Lowe **5:1** 68
Hepelegh **3** 162
Heppales **1** 299
Heppewod **1** 53
Heppley **1** 208
Hermitage (Cranage) **2** 224
 (Romiley) **1** 293
 (Tarporley, lost) **3** 296 (add.
 3 xvi)
Hermitage, The
 (Frodsham Lordship) **3** 231
 (Gt. Neston) **4** 223
Hermitage Bridge **2** 279
Hermitage Thorns **2** 224
Heronbridge (Chester) **5:1** 54
 (Claverton) **4** 161
Heron Copse **1** 169

Highash (Brindley) **3** 133
Highbank Fm **3** 308
Highbank Ho **2** 190
High Bank Mills **1** 306
Highbirch **1** 67
Highbirch Cottage and Wd **1** 67
High Cliff **1** 143
Higherbarn **1** 209
Higherbarn Fm **3** 285
Higher Fm
   (Mottram St Andrew) **1** 204
   (Norbury) **1** 288
Higher Fence **1** 107
Higher Fence Fm **1** 107
Higher Fold **1** 108
Higher Green **2** 233
Higher Hall (Edge) **4** 31
Higher Ho (Over Alderley) **1** 102
   (Dunham Massey) **2** 21
   (Mottram St Andrew) **1** 204
   (Sutton) **2** 181
Higherhouse (Ashley) **2** 11
Higherhouse Fm (Lymm) **2** 39
Higher Lane (Bollington) **1** 190
   (Dutton) **2** 113
   (Lymm) **2** 39
Higherlane (Rainow) **1** 143
Higherlane Fm **1** 143
Higher Moor **1** 199
Higher Pk **2** 321
High Fm **2** 249
Highfield (Bosley) **1** 56
   (Bredbury) **1** 264
   (Disley–Stanley) **1** 272.
   (Offerton) **1** 291
   (Pownall Fee) **1** 231
   (Poynton with Worth) **1** 209
Highfield Cottage (Cheadle) **1** 250
   (Hough) **3** 64
Highfield Fm
   (Aston iuxta Mondrum) **3** 128
   (Baddiley) **3** 125

   (Cuddington) **4** 86
   (Snelson) **1** 94
Highfield Hall **1** 264
Highfield Ho (Allostock) **2** 218
   (Cheadle) **1** 250
   (Gt. Neston) **4** 223
   (Castle Northwich) **3** 190
   (Pensby) **4** 272
   (Runcorn) **2** 178
   (Snelson) **1** 94
   (Stockport Etchells) **1** 245
   (Upton) **1** 216
Highfield Lane **1** 264
Highfields **3** 88
Highfields Fm **3** 88
Highfield Tannery **2** 178
Highfield St **1** 277
Highgate Rd **2** 20
High Grove **1** 244
High Ho **2** 199
High Lane (Bredbury) **1** 264
   (Marple) **1** 284
   (Romiley) **1** 293
Highlane (Gawsworth) **1** 69
High Lane Fm **1** 264
High Lee **1** 149 (add. **5**:1 xvi)
Highlees **1** 101
Highlees Wd (Over Alderley) **1** 101
   (Birtles) **1** 72
High Legh (township) **2** 45
Highlegh Hall and Pk **2** 47
Highlow **1** 154
High Moor **1** 154
Highmoor Brook **1** 154
High Park Corner **1** 69
Highstone Rocks **1** 324
Highstones **1** 324
High St (Congleton) **2** 295
   (Godley) **1** 306
   (Haslington) **3** 13
   (Malpas) **4** 40
   (Nantwich) **3** 33

Hollinlane (Pownall Fee) **1** 231
Hollin Lane Fm **3** 103
Hollins (Tintwistle) **1** 324
   (add. **5:1** xxiii)
Hollins, The (Bosley) **1** 56
   (Sutton Downes) **1** 154
Hollins Clough **1** 324
Hollinset **1** 150
Hollins Fm (Antrobus) **2** 128
   (Cranage) **2** 224
   (Tintwistle) **1** 324
   (Utkinton, 2x) **3** 298–9
Hollins Ferry **2** 35
Hollins Fold **1** 285
Hollins Green (Marple) **1** 285
Hollinsgreen (Barrow) **3** 264
   (Bradwall) **2** 266
Hollinsgreen Fm **2** 266
Hollins Hill **3** 298
Hollins Ho **1** 285
Hollin's Lane (Dukinfield) **1** 277
Hollins Lane
   (Marbury cum Quoisley) **3** 107
Hollins Mill **1** 285
Hollins St **1** 277
Hollins Wd **2** 266
Hollins Wood Fm **2** 266
Hollintongue, Higher and Lower
   1 128
Hollinwood Cottages **1** 272
Hollinwood Place **1** 285
Hollow **1** 268
Hollowacre Wd (Chelford) **1** 76
   (Old Withington) **1** 93
Holloway **2** 178
Hollow Bridge **3** 10
Hollowcowhey **1** 112
Hollow Fm **4** 109
Hollow Lane **2** 74
Hollowmoor Heath **3** 263
Hollows Bridge **3** 153

Hollow Wd **4** 41
Hollow–Wood Fm **2** 61
Holly Bank (Bredbury, lost) **1** 264
   (Buglawton) **2** 292
   (Cheadle) **1** 250
   (Leese) **2** 229
   (Marton) **1** 81
   (Oldcastle) **4** 44
   (Rowton) **4** 114
   (Utkinton) **3** 299
   (Weaverham cum Milton) **3** 208
Hollybank (Audlem) **3** 85
   (Delamere) **3** 212
   (Eddisbury) **3** 214
   (Moston) **2** 260
Hollybank Fm (Barnton) **2** 105
   (Macclesfield) **1** 122
   (Marton) **3** 183
   (Prestbury) **1** 212
Holly Banks
   (Somerford Booths) **1** 64
Holly Heath **1** 64, 65
Holly Fm (Buerton) **3** 88
   (Somerford Booths) **1** 64
Holly Grove **1** 311
Hollyhead Fm **3** 174
Holly Heath **1** 64
Hollyhedge
   (Northen Etchells) **1** 242
Hollyhedge Fm
   (Acton Grange) **2** 147
   (Weston) **3** 76
Hollyhey **2** 5
Holly Ho **4** 131
Hollyhurst **3** 107
Holly Mount **3** 70
Holly Rough **3** 107
Hollywell Cottages **1** 303
Hollywell Ho **3** 144
Holly Wd (Frodsham, lost) **3** 228
   (Newbold Astbury) **2** 287

Jack Lane (Bostock) **2** 203
   (Davenham) **2** 204
   (Moulton) **2** 207
   (Weston) **3** 76
Jack Lane Fm **2** 203
Jacksonbrow **1** 134
Jacksonedge **1** 272
Jackson Lane **1** 190
Jackson's Bank **2** 11
Jackson's Bridge **2** 5
Jackson's Lane **1** 288
Jack's Wd **4** 233
Jacob's Cabin **1** 174
Jacob's Well **5:1** 83
Janney's Fm **1** 108
Jarmin **1** 154
Jenkin Chapel **1** 140
Jenkins Hay Wd **1** 102
Jep Clough **1** 174
Jepson Clough **1** 183
Jericho **3** 67
Jerusalem **3** 64
Jessiefield **1** 291
Jillion Covert **2** 276
Jobs **1** 308
Job's Ferry **4** 188
Jodrell Bank **2** 223 (add. **2** viii)
Jodrell Bank Fm **2** 223
Jodrell Hall **2** 231 (add. **2** viii,
   5:1 xxxi)
Joel Lane **1** 303
John O'Jerusalem's Patch **2** 16
Johnson Brook **1** 277
Johnsonbrook Rd **1** 277
Johnson's Rough **4** 152
Jollycock Fm **1** 144
Jollye's Hall **5:1** 69
Joneslane Bridge
   (Kinderton cum Hulme) **2** 239
   (Mooresbarrow cum Parme)
   2 252

Jones's Lane (Bradwall) **2** 267
   (Kinderton cum Hulme) **2** 239
Jones's Wd (Willington) **3** 285
   (Lower Withington) **1** 91
Jordangate **1** 115
Joule Bridge **1** 178
Judkynesrudyng **1** 53
Jumber Clough **1** 134
Justing Croft **5:1** 73

Kale Yards **5:1** 66, 69 (add. **5:1**
   xlv)
Kaleyards Gate **5:1** 25
Kaleyard Wall **5:1** 25
Kay Lane (High Legh) **2** 47
   (Lymm) **2** 39
Kaylane Brook (High Legh) **2** 47
Kay Lane Brook (Lymm) **2** 39
Kay Lane Fm **2** 47
Kays Fm
   (Aston by Budworth) **2** 102
Kay's Fm (Marton) **3** 183
Keckwick (township) **2** 151
Keckwick Bridge and Brook **2** 152
Keckwickford Fm **2** 174
Keckwick Hill **2** 152
Keepers Cottage **2** 137
Keeper's Fm **2** 249
Keepers Wd **2** 137
Keer, le **1** 53
Keg **1** 303
Kell Green Fm and Hall **2** 84
Kellhouse **2** 67
Kelsall (township) **3** 276 (add. **4** xi)
Kelsall Common Fm **3** 278
Kelsall Hall **3** 276
Kelsall Hill **3** 278
Kelsborrow Castle and Ho **3** 212
Kemnay Cottage **4** 223
Kenmure **3** 212
Kennel Bank **1** 94

Lea Forge Mill **3** 67
Lea Hall
   (Lea nr. Backford) **4** 175
   (Lea nr. Wybunbury) **3** 68
   (Wimboldsley) **2** 257
Leahall Fm **4** 119
Leahead **2** 253
Leahead Fm **2** 267
Lea Mill **4** 78
Lea Newbold (township) **4** 119
Lea Newbold Fm **4** 120
Lea Pk **3** 68
Leasowe **4** 332
Leasowebank **4** 320
Leasowe Castle **4** 333
Leasowe Lighthouse **4** 298
Leasowe Rd
   (Bidston–cum–Ford) **4** 311
   (Moreton–cum–Lingham) **4** 320
   (Wallasey) **4** 332
Leasowe Side **4** 311
Lea's Wd **3** 54
Leathers **1** 273
Leathers Smithy **1** 154 (add.
   5:1 xvi)
Lea Woods **3** 68
Ledsham (township) **4** 217 (add.
   5:1 xii)
Ledsham Hall and Rd **4** 195
Lee **1** 154
Leebangs Rocks **1** 314
Leech Wd **1** 161
Leecot **1** 285
Lee Cottages **4** 119
Lee Green **3** 156
Lee Green Hall **3** 156
Lee Hall **1** 204
Lee, High and Low **1** 154
Leek Rd **2** 298
Leen Lane **5:1** 14, 22
Leese (township) **2** 229
Leese Fm **2** 263

Lees Fm **4** 41
Lees Hill **1** 311
Lees Lane (Bollin Fee) **1** 223
   (Newton) **1** 206
Lees Wd **3** 76
Leftwich (township) **2** 205
Leftwich Grange **2** 206
Leftwich Green **2** 205
Leftwich Hayes and Mount **2** 206
Leftwich Old Hall **2** 206
Legh, High (township) **2** 45
Legh's Folly **2** 47
Leigh Cottage **3** 250
Leigh Hall Fm **2** 116
Leigh iuxta Bartinton **2** 115
Leigh Lane **2** 116
Leigh, Lt. (township) **2** 115
Leigh Oaks Fm **2** 47
Leigh Pond, Lt. **2** 116
Leigh's Brow **2** 105
Leighton (nr. Nantwich) (township)
   3 28 (add. **5:1** xxxiii)
   (nr. Neston) (township) **4** 218
   (add. **5:1** xii)
Leighton **4** 219
Leighton Banastre **4** 219
Leighton Brook **3** 29
Leighton Cottages **4** 219
Leighton Court **4** 223
Leighton Hall
   (Leighton near Nantwich) **3** 28
   (Leighton nr. Neston) **4** 218
Leighton Ho **4** 219
Leighton, Low and Old **1** 282
Lemon Pool **3** 66
Leonard's Bridge, Fm, Lane and
   Wd **2** 119
Lester Ho **2** 134
Lethenhardesheye **3** 158
Lewinshill Wd **1** 56
Lewin St **2** 242
Ley, The **3** 192

Leycester's Firs **2** 68
Ley Fm **4** 255
Ley Ground Fm **3** 54
Leyhall **4** 311
Ley Hey Pk and Wd **1** 285
Leylands **1** 308
Ley Plantation **1** 74
Lightalders **1** 273
Lightfoot Green Fm **2** 276
Lightfoot's Lane **4** 275
Lighthassells **1** 177
Lighthey **2** 292
Light Ho **2** 35
Lighthouse Rd **4** 300
Lightly Hill **2** 271
Lightwood Fm (Dutton) **2** 114
    (Somerford Radnor) **2** 319
Lightwood Green **3** 97
Lilac Fm **2** 47
Lilliecroft **1** 273
Lily Fm and Lane **2** 234
Lily Wd **3** 269
Lima Fm and Clough **1** 144
Limbo Lane (Arrowe) **4** 262
    (Irby) **4** 265
Limefield **1** 122
Limefield Ho **1** 190
Limefield Mill **1** 314
Limekiln **4** 281
Limekiln Fm
    (Lostock Gralam) **2** 190
Lime–Kiln Fm
    (Newbold Astbury) **2** 287
Limekiln Lane
    (Poulton cum Seacombe) **4** 330
    (Witton cum Twambrook) **2** 196
Limekiln Wd **2** 305
Limepits **3** 107
Limes, The **3** 283
Limes Fm **3** 8
Limes Lane **2** 126
Limetree Fm **2** 6

Limetree Ho
    (Dunham Massey) **2** 21
    (Utkinton) **3** 299
Lime Wharf **4** 304 (add. **5:1** xiii)
Lindow **1** 226
Lindow Common and Cottage **1** 230
Lindow End (Chorley) **1** 226
    (Gt. Warford) **1** 105
Lindow Fm **2** 68
Lindow Grove and Ho **1** 230
Lindow Moss (Mobberley) **2** 68
    (Pownall Fee) **1** 230
Linen Hall, The **5:1** 32
Linenhall St **5:1** 15
Line Pits **1** 77
Lingard **1** 265
Lingard Lane **1** 265
Lingards (Chorley) **1** 226
    (Henbury cum Pexall) **1** 79
Lingdale **4** 270
Lingdale Hill **4** 318
Lingdale Ho and Quarry **4** 270
Lingerds **1** 154 (add. **5:2**)
Lingham **4** 319
Lingham, Moreton cum
    (township) **4** 319
Linley Lane (Alsager) **3** 3
    (Church Lawton) **2** 321
Linley Wd **2** 321
Linmer Cottage **3** 214
Linmere Moss **3** 214
Linnet Mill **1** 303
Linney's Bridge **1** 231 (add. **1** xxi)
Linney's Tenement **1** 260
Linstrete, le **1** 44
Lion Cottage **2** 310
Lisburne Ho **1** 297
Lisburne Lane (Offerton) **1** 291
    (Stockport) **1** 297
Liscard (township) **4** 324
Liscard Hall and Ho **4** 324
Liscard Lodge **4** 324

Manor Fm, New
  (Preston on the Hill) **2** 156
Manor Ho (Barnston) **4** 263
  (Barnton) **2** 105
  (Barrow) **3** 264 (add.
  5:1 xxxvii)
  (Bechton) **3** 19
  (Bollin Fee) **1** 223
  (Gt. Boughton) **4** 125
  (Bredbury) **1** 265
  (Brinnington) **1** 268
  (Lt. Budworth) **3** 186
  (Caldy) **4** 284
  (Chelford) **1** 77
  (Comberbach) **2** 111
  (Edge) **4** 32
  (Fallibroome) **1** 198
  (Frankby) **4** 288
  (Goostrey cum Barnshaw) **2** 227
  (Hampton) **4** 35
  (Haslington) **3** 15
  (Hatherton) **3** 63
  (Hunsterson) **3** 66
  (Leese) **2** 229
  (Leighton) **3** 29
  (Middlewich) **2** 245
  (Mobberley) **2** 68
  (Mottram in Longdendale) **1** 314
  (Gt. Neston) **4** 224
  (Newhall) **3** 104
  (Over) **3** 174
  (Peckforton) **3** 312
  (N. Rode) **1** 60
  (Saighton) **4** 122
  (Church Shocklach) **4** 65
  (Siddington) **1** 86
  (Smallwood) **2** 317
  (Stapeley) **3** 72
  (Tarporley) **3** 297
  (Thingwall, lost) **4** 273
  (Thornton Hough) **4** 231

  (Tytherington) **1** 215
  (Walgherton) **3** 74
  (Gt. Warford) **1** 105
  (Wistaston) **3** 46
Manor Ho, Old
  (Newton by Frodsham) **3** 248
Manor House Fm (Betchton) **3** 19
Manorhouse Fm (Bulkeley) **4** 18
  (Burwardsley) **4** 94
  (Hulme Walfield) **2** 303
Manor Lane (Church Hulme) **2** 279
  (Liscard) **4** 327
Manor Lock **2** 143
Manor Pk **2** 75
Manor Rd **4** 327
Manor Side **4** 306
Manor Tannery **2** 143
Manor Wd **4** 231
Manx Lane **5:1** 15
Maple Fm **2** 13
Maple Hayes **3** 3
Maple Rd **2** 13
Mar, The **1** 30
Marbury (township)
  (Bucklow Hd) **2** 117
Marbury cum Quoisley
  (township) **3** 106 (add. **5:1** xi)
Marbury Brook (Marbury) **2** 117
  (Marbury cum Quoisley) **3** 107
Marbury Chapelry **3** 105
Marbury Hall (Marbury) **2** 117
  (Marbury cum Quoisley) **3** 106
Marbury Heys **3** 107
Marbury Ho **2** 126
Marbury Lodge and Mill **2** 117
Marbury Mill **3** 107
Marbury Pk **2** 117
Marchington Fm **1** 174
Mare Clough **2** 161
Mareknowles **1** 169
Marfords, The **4** 242 (add. **5:1** xliii)

(Macclesfield) **1** 122
(Mere) **2** 53
(Minshull Vernon) **2** 249
(Mobberley) **2** 68
(Moore) **2** 153
(Moston) **2** 260
(Norley) **3** 250
(Pownall Fee) **1** 232
(Tabley Superior) **2** 61
(Timperley) **2** 32
(Tranmere) **4** 259
(Wybunbury) **3** 81
Moss Lane Fm
(Lostock Gralam) **2** 190
(Manley) **3** 246
Mosslee **1** 155
Mossley (Congleton) **2** 296
(Marple, lost) **1** 283 (add.
5:1 xxii)
Mossley Fm, Hall, Ho and Moss
2 296
Mossleyvale Fm **2** 292
Moss, Lt. **2** 310
Moss Lodge **2** 53
Moss, Lower **2** 80
Moss Mere **4** 23
Moss Nook **1** 242
Mossnook Wd **2** 81
Moss Oaks **2** 48
Moss Oaks Fm **2** 48
Moss Plantation
(Over Alderley) **1** 102
(Tatton) **2** 65
Moss Rd (Carrington) **2** 18
(Congleton) **2** 298
(Newbold Astbury) **2** 288
(Winnington) **3** 192
Moss–Side **1** 242
Moss–Side Brook **1** 144
Moss Side Fm **2** 174
Moss Side Fm, Upper **2** 174
Moss Side Ho and Lane **2** 129

Moss's Strip **2** 48
Moss Terrace (Bollin Fee) **1** 223
(Gawsworth) **1** 67
Moss View **2** 27
Mossway Cottage **2** 68
Moss Well **1** 122
Moss Wd (Acton Grange) **2** 147
(Bickley) **4** 10
(Cholmondeley) **4** 23
(Church Lawton) **2** 321
(N. Rode) **1** 60
(Odd Rode) **2** 310
(Siddington) **1** 86
(Toft) **2** 81
(Walton Inferior) **2** 157
(Woodford) **1** 218
Mosswood Hall **2** 121
Moston (township)
(Broxton Hd) **4** 141
(Northwich Hd) **2** 259
Moston Green **2** 260
Moston Hall **4** 141
Moston Ho **2** 260
Moston Manor and Mills **2** 260
Mostyn Ho **4** 224
Mostyn Place **4** 219
Mothall Lane **5:1** 15
Motleybank **2** 16
Motley Hall **2** 25
Mottershead **1** 203
Motterstall **2** 310
Mottram Bridge (Butley) **1** 195
(Mottram St Andrew) **1** 204
Mottram Cross **1** 204
Mottram Hall **1** 204
Mottram Hill **1** 314
Mottram Ho **1** 97
Mottram in Longdendale
(par.) **1** 305
Mottram in Longdendale (township)
1 313 (add **5:1** xix, xxii)
Mottram Moor **1** 314

Oldham's Wd **1** 102 (add. **5:1** xv)
Oldhouse Fm (Baguley) **2** 13
  (Kermincham) **2** 282
  (Sandbach) **2** 271
Old House Fold **1** 293
Old House Green **2** 311
Oldknow Rd **1** 285
Old Lane **2** 209
Old Lanes (Oulton Lowe) **3** 165
  (Rushton) **3** 293
Old Man of Mow **2** 311
Old Manor, The (Liscard) **4** 327
Old Margery's **4** 249
Old Mat's Fm **1** 112
Old Mill (Bosley) **1** 56
  (Dukinfield, lost) **1** 278
Oldmill Bridge (Dodcott cum
  Wilkesley) **3** 95, 98
  (Newhall) **3** 104
Oldmill Cottages **2** 59
Old Mill Fm (Allostock) **2** 219
  (Mottram in Longdendale) **1** 315
  (Higher Whitley) **2** 126
Old Moss (Tarvin) **3** 283
Old Moss Fm and Lane
  (Bruen Stapleford) **3** 270
Old Pale, The **3** 214
Old Park **1** 69
Old Parks **1** 69
Oldpool Wd **1** 93
Old Quay, The **4** 225 (add. **5:1** xii,
  xlii)
Old Rd (Hollingworth) **1** 311
  (Mottram in Longdendale) **1** 315
Old Warps, The **2** 139
Old Wd (Allostock) **2** 219
  (Odd Rode) **2** 311
Oldwood (Baguley) **2** 13
Oldwood Fm and Lane **2** 13
Oliver St **4** 314
Oliverswell **1** 308
Ollerbarrow **2** 24 (add. **4** ix)

Ollerbarrow Rd **2** 24
Ollerpool , –e **2** 244
Ollershaw Lane **2** 118
Ollerton (township) **2** 79
Ollerton Fm **2** 80
Ollerton Green **2** 78
Ollerton Lane (Ollerton) **2** 80
  (Toft) **2** 81
Ollerton Lodge **2** 80
Olren(e)legh **1** 53
One Ho **1** 140
One Mile Ho **4** 164
Onston (township) **3** 200
Onston Hall and Lane **3** 200
Onston Mill (Onston) **3** 200
  (Weaverham cum Milton) **3** 204
Opetone **3** 161
Orangetree Fm and Ho **1** 293
Orangetree Inn **1** 195
Orchard, The (Pensby) **4** 272
Orchard Croft **3** 237
Orchard Ho (Chester) **5:1** 78
  (Dunham Massey) **2** 21
Orchardhouse Fm **2** 35
Orford Ho **2** 27
Organ Lane **4** 195
Organ Lot (Frodsham) **3** 224
  (Frodsham Lordship) **3** 231
Organsdale Fm **3** 212
Organsdale Ho **3** 214
Ormelegh **1** 53
Ormes Moor **1** 325
Ormes Smithy **1** 145
Ormesty **1** 271 (add. **5:2**)
Orrel Cottage **4** 330
Orrelhouse Fm **2** 68
Orrells Well **1** 226
Orrishmere Fm **1** 250
Orton Fm **2** 27
Oscroft **3** 281
Oscroft Bridge **3** 281
Oscroft Hall Fm **3** 281

Priestland **3** 306
Priest Lane **1** 204
Priestsway **4** 213
Priesty Fields **2** 299
Primrose Bank (Delamere) **3** 212
Primrosebank (Bosley) **1** 56
Primrose Hall **2** 280
Primrose Hill (Delamere) **3** 212
Primrosehill (Darnhall) **3** 170
Primrose Hill Cottage and Wd
   3 212
Primrose Vale **2** 299
Primrose Wd **3** 170
Prim's Parlour **1** 315
Prince Hill **3** 54
Prince's Fm **4** 96
Prince's Incline **1** 210
Princes Spinney **2** 14
Princess St **5:1** 18
Prince's Wd **1** 210
Pringles, The **4** 263
Prior's Heys (extra-parochial) **3** 284
Priory, The **2** 16
Priory Bank and Gate **2** 6
Priory, Old **4** 314
Priory St **4** 314
Prisonball Bank **2** 271
Pritch Fm **3** 115
Privet Wd **1** 93
Prize Plantation **2** 311
Promised-Land Fm **4** 114
Promontory Wd **1** 77
Prophet's Ho **3** 243
Prospect Fm (Dutton) **2** 114
   (Gayton) **4** 276
   (Kingsley) **3** 243
Prospect Ho **2** 30
Puddinglake **2** 229
Puddinglake Brook **1** 34
Pudding Lane (Godley) **1** 306
   (Marley) **1** 312

Puddington (township) **4** 214
Puddington Hall **4** 216
Puddle Bank **2** 299
Puddle Hall **4** 322
Puddy Dale **4** 278
Pugh's Cottages **3** 216
Pulford (par.) **4** 153
Pulford (township) **4** 155
Pulford Bridge, Brook and Hall
   4 155
Pullehous, le **3** 162
Pump Fm (Odd Rode) **2** 311
   (Woodford) **1** 218
Pump Ho (Antrobus) **2** 130
   (Cheadle, lost) **1** 251
   (Church Coppenhall) **3** 25
   (Fulshaw, lost) **1** 228
   (Leese) **2** 229
   (Nether Peover) **2** 220
Pump Lane Wd **4** 83
Pump Tree **1** 123
Puppet Show Entry **5:1** 18
Purchase Lands **2** 220
Pursefield **1** 200
Pursefield Wd **1** 200
Purser, The **4** 67
Puseydale **3** 68
Pyeash **1** 56
Pyecroft St **5:1** 49
Pyegreave **1** 155
Pyethorne Wd (Gawsworth) **1** 69
   (Siddington) **1** 86
Pykford **1** 208
Pym Chair **1** 174
Pymchair Fm **1** 112
Pym Gate **1** 245
Pym's Lane
   (Monks Coppenhall) **3** 27
   (Woolstanwood) **3** 45
Pynche Wares Heys, The **2** 2

Slack i' th' Moor **1** 145
Slack Mills **1** 280
Slack Rd (Barnston) **4** 263
   (Gayton) **4** 276
   (Heswall cum Oldfield) **4** 278
Slacks, The **2** 104
Slack Wd (Bosley) **1** 56
   (Bromborough) **4** 243
Slade Cottage (Hunsterson) **3** 66
   (Mobberley) **2** 69
Sladegreen **1** 102
Slain **1** 251
Slatehurst **2** 60
Slatersbank **1** 179
Slatersbank Wd **1** 179
Slater's Fm **1** 112
Slatepit Moor **1** 311
Slatey Rd **4** 317
Slaughter Hill **3** 10
Slaughter Hill Bridge **3** 10
Slaughter's Rough **2** 155
Sliddens **1** 325
Sliddens Moss **1** 325
Slitten Brook **1** 35
Slobbercrofts Covert **4** 83
Slope Plantation **1** 69
Slopes **4** 333
Sloyne, The **4** 260
Slum Wd **2** 321
Small Brook (2x) **1** 35
Smallbrook **2** 271
Small Dale f.n. **1** 130
Smallegh **3** 2
Smallhurst **1** 155
Small Lane **2** 69
Smallwood (township) **2** 316 (add.
   5:1 xxxiii)
Smallwood, Higher **2** 311
Smallwood Ho **1** 232
Smallwood Mill **2** 317
Smeaton Hall **3** 97
Smeatonwood Fm **3** 97

Smellmoor Wd **4** 83
Smethwick, Brereton cum
   (township) **2** 274
Smethwick Green, Hall and Lane
   2 275
Smithfield (Bulkeley, lost), **4** 16
   (Poynton with Worth) **1** 210
Smithfield Lane **2** 269
Smithfield, Old **4** 197
Smith Lane (Mabberley) **2** 69
   (Rainow) **1** 145
Smith Lane Fm **2** 69
Smith's Almshouses **5:1** 34
Smith's Bridge (Altrincham) **2** 9
   (Dunham Massey) **2** 22
   (Timperley) **2** 32
Smith's Entry **5:1** 22, 24
Smith's Green (Crewe) **3** 8
Smiths Green
   (Lower Withington) **1** 91
Smith's Green Fm **3** 8
Smith's Meeting Ho, The **5:1** 34
Smith's Pentrey **4** 16
Smith St **1** 316
Smith's Walk **5:1** 20
Smithy Bank (Darnhall) **3** 170
   (Over) **3** 175
Smithybank Fm **4** 94
Smithy Cottage **2** 303
Smithy Fm (Buglawton) **2** 292
   (Eaton in Astbury) **1** 62
Smithy Fold **1** 280
Smithy Green
   (Bredbury, lost) **1** 265
   (Cheadle) **1** 251
   (Peover Inferior) **2** 90
Smithygreen (Bosley) **1** 56
Smithy Lane (Barnston) **4** 263
   (Barthomley) **3** 8
   (Cuddington) **3** 199
   (Lt. Legh) **2** 116
   (Overpool, lost) **4** 193

Thorncliff Hall **1** 309
Thorncliffe, Lt. **1** 313
Thorncliffvale **1** 309
Thorncliffwood **1** 309
Thorneycroft **1** 112
Thorneyfield **3** 25
Thorn Fm **3** 189
Thorngrove **1** 223
Thornhill Fm **1** 268
Thorn Ho **1** 223
Thornlaw Cottage **2** 303
Thornliebank **1** 123
Thorns, The (Godley) **1** 306
 (Greasby) **4** 292
Thornset Fm **1** 141
Thornsgreen **2** 11
Thornton Brook **3** 259
Thornton, Childer, *v.* Childer
 Thornton
Thornton Common Rd **4** 231
Thornton Cottage **4** 231
Thornton Grange **4** 231 (add.
 5:1 xlii)
Thornton Green **3** 259
Thornton Hall
 (Childer Thornton) **4** 197
 (Thornton Hough) **4** 231
 (Thornton le Moors) **3** 259
Thornton Heath **4** 197
Thornton Hough (township) **4** 230
Thornton Ho **4** 231
Thornton le Moors (par.) **3** 253
 (township) **3** 258
Thornton Lodge **4** 231
Thornton Mill (Ince) **3** 252
 (Thornton le Moors) **3** 258
Thorneycroft Hall **1** 85
Thornycroft Lodge **1** 79
Thornycroft Pools
 (Gawsworth) **1** 69
 (Henbury cum Pexall) **1** 79
 (Siddington) **1** 79

Thornyfields **3** 316
Thowler Lane (High Legh) **2** 48
 (Millington) **2** 55
Threaphurst **1** 288 (add. **5:1** xxii)
Threaphurst Lane **1** 288
Threapwood (extra–parochial) **4** 61
 (add. **4** xi, **5:1** xl)
Threapwood, Lower and Upper
 4 61
Threebrooks Wd **3** 88
Three Lanes End **4** 322
Threepers' Drumble **3** 54
Three Shires Heads **1** 162
Threethorne Cottages **1** 232
Three–Wells, The **3** 88
Throstle Bank Mill **1** 280
Throstle Bank St **1** 316
Throstlegrove **1** 286
Throstlenest **1** 155
Throstlenest Fm **1** 200
Throstles Nest **4** 49
Thurlwood **2** 309
Thurlwood Fm **3** 19
Thursbitch **1** 141
Thurstaston (par.) **4** 279
 (township) **4** 279 (add. **5:1** xii)
Thurstaston Common **4** 281
Thurstaston Hall **4** 279
Thurstaston Hill **4** 281
Thurstaston Rd **4** 278
Thwaite Lane **4** 312
Tidnock **1** 68
Tidnock End **1** 68
Tidnock Ho **2** 299
Tidnock, Lt. **1** 68
Tidnock Wd **1** 68
Tile Yard Cottage
 (Bromborough) **4** 243
Tileyard Cottage (Tushingham cum
 Grindley) **4** 49
Tilston (par.) **4** 53
 (township) **4** 58 (add. **4** xiii)

Vale Ho **2** 32 (add. **5:1** xxiii)
Valehouse Reservoir **1** 326
Valehouse Wd **1** 326 (add.
   5:1 xxiii)
Vale Mills **1** 326
Vale Pk **4** 327 (add. **5:1** xlv)
Vale Rd **2** 16
Vale Royal (Whitegate) **3** 179
Valeroyal (Rainow) **1** 145
Valeroyal Cut **3** 181
Valeroyal Pk **3** 179
Valewood Fm **2** 69
Valley, The **3** 27
Valley Brook **1** 37
Valley Fm (Crewe) **3** 8
   (Monks Coppenhall) **3** 27
Valley Ho **1** 232
Valley Lodge, The **4** 260
Valley Rd **3** 47
Valley Wd **3** 170
Vardentown **1** 102
Vauxhall **3** 39
Vauxhall Ho **3** 39
Verdon Bridge **1** 223
Verdon Ho **1** 223
Vernon Pit **1** 210
Verona **3** 151
Viaduct Wd (Lea) **4** 177
   (Gt. Mollington) **4** 178
Vicarage (Buglawton) **2** 292
   (Ringway) **2** 30
Vicarage Gorse and Lane **2** 16
Vicarage Wd **1** 163
Vicar's Cross (Gt. Boughton) **4** 125
   (Littleton) **4** 113
Vicar's Lane **5:1** 78
Victoria Rd **5:1** 67
Victoria St **1** 316
Victoria Wd **2** 81
Villa Fm **2** 62
Village, The
   (Lower Bebington) **4** 249

Village Fm (Daresbury) **2** 149
   (Wettenhall) **3** 167
Village Rd
   (Higher Bebington) **4** 247
   (Heswall cum Oldfield) **4** 278
   (W. Kirby) **4** 295
   (Oxton) **4** 270
Village, The Old (W. Kirby) **4** 295
Villaview **3** 183
Vinetree Fm **3** 47
Vineyard Fm, The **4** 252
Virjuice f.n. **2** 26

Wade Brook **1** 37
Wadebrook Bridge
   (Lostock Gralam) **2** 191
   (Witton cum Twambrook) **2** 196
Wade Green **2** 114
Wades Gate (Eastham, lost) **4** 188
   (Hooton) **4** 191
Wades Green **3** 156
Wades Green Hall **3** 156
Wadworth's Fm **1** 123
Waggonshaw Brow and Fm **1** 145
Wagg Rd and St **2** 299
Waidall **2** 3
Walby, Kiln **4** 305
Waldron's Lane **3** 25
Walfield, Hulme, *v.* Hulme
   Walfield
Walgherton (township) **3** 73
Walgherton Lodge and Pool **3** 74
Walker Barn **1** 145
Walker Brow and Fm **1** 111
Walkerfold **1** 280
Walker Lane **1** 280
Walkerley Mdw f.n. **3** 132
Walker Pit **1** 210
Walkers Bottoms **1** 74
Walker's Green
   (Kinderton cum Hulme) **2** 239
Walkersgreen (Pott Shrigley) **1** 134

Warburton Green **2** 30
Warburton Lane (Partington) **2** 27
   (Warburton) **2** 35
Warburton Mill and Pk **2** 35
Warburton Wd **3** 243
Warchew f.n. **1** 92
Ward Lane **1** 273
Wardle (township) **3** 322
Wardle Bank **3** 308
Wardle Bridge and Lock **2** 245
Wardlebrook Fm **1** 313
Wardle Covert **3** 323
Wardle Fm **3** 322
Wardle Fm Bridge **3** 322
Wardle Hall **3** 322
Wardle Old Hall **3** 323
Wardsend **1** 184
Wardsend Bridge (Adlington) **1** 184
   (Poynton with Worth) **1** 210
Wardsend Fm **1** 184
Ward's Knob **1** 155
Ward's Lane **2** 267
Warford, Marthall cum
   (township) **2** 82
Warford Cover **1** 105
Warford, Gt.
   (township) **1** 104 (add. **5:1** xv)
Warford Hall and Lane **1** 105
Warford, Lt. **2** 82
Warford Ho and Lodge **1** 105
Warford, Old **2** 83 (add. **5:1** xvi)
Wargraves **4** 242 (add. **5:1** xliii)
Warhill **1** 315 (add. **1** xxii)
Warihull **2** 245 (add. **5:1** xxxii)
Warkmoor Rd **1** 273
Warlow Pike **1** 326
Warmby f.n. **4** 279
Warm Hole **1** 326
Warmingham (par.) **2** 258
Warmingham
   (township) **2** 262 (add. **4** x)
Warmingham Bridge **2** 263

Warmingham Lane **2** 245
Warmingham Moss **2** 263
Warmingham Rd **3** 25
Warmingham Wd **2** 263
Warmundestrou,
   Domesday Hundred **3** 1
Warpoole **3** 149
Warps Lodge, Old **2** 144
Warrastfold Bridge **1** 315
Warren **1** 69
Warren Ho (Willaston) **3** 80
Warrenhouse
   (Frodsham Lordship) **3** 231
Warren Wd **1** 291
Warrens, The **4** 189
Warrilowhead **1** 129
Warrington Bridge **2** 144
Warrington Common **2** 225
Warrington Lane **2** 40
Warrington Rd (Hatton) **2** 150
   (Walton Superior) **2** 158
   (Witton cum Twambrook) **2** 196
Warringtons Bridge
   (Bidston cum Ford) **4** 311
Warrington's Bridge
   (Wallasey) **4** 334
Warrington St **5:1** 67
Warth Meadow **1** 268
Warton's Bridge **3** 2
Washes Lane **4** 195
Wash Fm **2** 93
Wash Fm, Lower **2** 143
Washford Mill, Higher **2** 292
Wash Hall **4** 206
Wash Lane (Allostock) **2** 219
   (Latchford) **2** 144 (add.
   5:1 xxix)
   (Timperley) **2** 32
Wash Lane Fm **2** 219
Wash, Lower **2** 143
Washpool **1** 145
Washway **1** 41

Wicker Ho and Lane
  (Guilden Sutton) **4** 127
  (Hale) **2** 25
Wickson Lane **3** 304
Wicksted Fm **3** 112
Wicksted Hall **3** 113
Widowhurst **1** 274
Widowscroft **1** 311
Widow's Home Fm **2** 219
Wiend, The **4** 249
Wiganshill **1** 242
Wigans Lake Fm **3** 243
Wiggin Clough **1** 326
Wigland (township) **4** 50 (add.
  5:1 xl)
Wigland Hall **4** 50
Wigwam Wd **1** 210
Wigsey Fm and Lane **2** 35
Wilacre Lane (Brereton cum
  Smethwick) **2** 277
  (Smallwood) **2** 317
Wilaveston (Willaston),
  Domesday Hundred **4** 167
Wilbrahams Almshouses **3** 39
Wilbraham's Walk **3** 61
Wilcott's Heath **3** 46
Wild Bank **1** 320
Wildboarclough (township) **1** 159
Wilderness, The (Adlington) **1** 184
  (Moreton cum Alcumlow) **2** 305
  (Sutton Downes) **1** 155
Wilderness Wd **2** 311
Wildersmoor **2** 40
Wildersmoor Fm and Hall **2** 40
Wilderspool **2** 145
Wilderspool Causeway **2** 144
Wild Forest Wd **1** 60
Wild Heath **3** 103
Wildmoorbank Hollow **1** 129
Wildmoor Edge **1** 164
Wildmoor Lane **3** 265
Wilkesley **3** 93

Wilkesley, Dodcott cum
  (township) **3** 92
Wilkesley Covert and Lodge **3** 99
Wilkynsons Soler **5:1** 35
Willaston (nr. Nantwich)
  (township) **3** 78
Willaston (nr. Neston)
  (township) **4** 232 (add. **5:1** xii)
Willaston (Wisterson)
  (township) **3** 41
Willaston Cottage **3** 80
Willaston Grange **4** 232
Willaston Hall **3** 78
Willaston Ho **4** 232
Willaston Mill **4** 233
Will Bank Fm and Ho **3** 144
Willey Fm **4** 9
Willey Moor (Bickley) **4** 9
Willeymoor (Tushingham cum
  Grindley) **4** 49
Willeymoor Cottage **3** 113
Willeymoor Lane **4** 49
Williamson's Bridge **4** 102
Willie's Wood **1** 93
Willington (extra–parochial) **3** 285
  (add. **5:1** xii)
Willington Corner (Delamere) **3** 212
  (Tarvin) **3** 283
  (Willington) **3** 286
Willington Hall **3** 285
Willington Lane **3** 212
Willington Mill **3** 285
Willington Mill Fm **3** 285
Willingtons, The **3** 286
Willington Wd **3** 285
Willis's Wd (Beeston) **3** 304
  (Peckforton) **3** 312
Willot Hall **1** 195
Willow Bank (Latchford) **2** 144
  (Mottram in Longdendale) **1** 315
Willowbank (Higher Whitley) **2** 126
Willowbed **2** 104

INDEX OF PLACE–NAMES IN COUNTIES OTHER THAN CHESHIRE

This index includes instances (in vols.**1–4, 5:1** [addenda and corrigenda and Chester only] and in **5:2** [addenda and corrigenda only]) of the quotation of 'out–county' place–names. These have chiefly been quoted for the drawing of analogy or comparison, but occasionally in connection with changes to the county boundary. In some cases new etymologies have been offered which differ from those in published EPNS volumes.

St. (Street) is here distinguished from St (Staffordshire).

NOTES ON THE DISTRIBUTION OF FIELD–NAME ELEMENTS

The corpus of material is provided in field–name lists for 505 townships of Cheshire and covers categories C and D in the index of elements (see **5:1** 85). In the Hundred of Macclesfield (M) there are 75 such townships, in Bucklow (B) 73, in Northwich (No) 66, Nantwich (Na) 63, Eddisbury (E) 66, Broxton (Br) 85, Wirral (W) 75.

When ranged in order of frequency of occurrence, in terms of the percentage of Cheshire townships in whose field–names they are represented, the elements which denote kinds of field and enclosure fall into groups.

I.   The most common els. in Cheshire f.ns. are **feld** (93%), **mǣd(we)** (84%), **croft** (83%), and **(ge)hæg** (72%);

II.   **land** and its variants (56%) and **æcer** (49%) occur in about half the townships;

III.   Between 50% and 25% of townships contain representatives of **butte, flat** (ON), and **ryding** (40%+), **inntak** (ON), **pingel/pingot**, **lēah (ley)**, and **geard** (30%+), **park/pearroc, pasture** and **scēat** (20%+);

IV.   Between 20% and 10% of townships present f.ns. from **outlet, pece, rūh,** and **stede** (15%+), **grēne**[2] , **pacche, mǣð, clos, slang** and **lǣs(we)** (10%+).

V.   Less than 10% of townships present **backside, (ge)dāl, eorðe, edisc, fald, furlang, hamm, holmr** (ON), **loom, pichel/pightel, plat**[2]**, rein** and **waroð** (5%+); **bing** (ON), **brǣdu, cae** (Welsh), **coetgae** (Welsh), **corner, crib, cryme/crymel, cryfting, cutting, eng, ersc, erðing, falh, feorðung, filand, gardin, garðr, gata, grund, hægen, haga, hēafod–land, hege–stōw/ hege–stall, hiche/hiching, hlinc, inheche, innām** (OE/ON), **lǣge, launde, leyne, loca, lot, maes** (Welsh), **orceard, oxgang, pale, paradis, part, penn**[2]**, place, plain, plek, plock, plot, poket, purs, pynd–fald, quarter,**

quillet, rand, rang(e), rāp, rod[1]**, rod**[3]**, root, rūm**[1]**, (ge)ryd(d), ryde, rye–land, scēo, scofl–brǣdu, slæget, sling, slippe, splott, spot, stall, sticce, stoccing, strīp, stubbing, styccing, swæð, þveit** (ON), **tilð, tir** (Welsh), **tunge–scearp, tyning, vǫllr** (ON), **walet, walk**.

The noticeable distribution patterns of the chief f.n. els., in terms of the percentage of townships in a Hundred which present representative f.ns., reveal that, of the four most common els. (group I), **feld** appears in 80–90% of townships in every Hundred; **mǣd(we)** is least frequent (60%) in Br and W, most frequent (80–90%) in M, E, Bu; **croft** is less frequent (60–70%) in No and E than the rest; **(ge)hæg** is less frequent in E (30%) and Na (50%) than in No (60%) and the rest (80–90%).

Of the elements in group II, **land** is less frequent in No, Na, E and Br (13–23%) than in M, Bu, W (32–43%), and **æcer** is more frequent in Bu, M, No (50–80%) than in the others (20–30%).

Of group III, **butte** is more frequent in M, Bu, Na and W than the others; **flat** (ON) is most frequent in M and least in Br; **ryding** is more frequent in M, Bu, Na and E than in Br and No, and it is comparatively infrequent in W; **inntak** (ON) occurs more frequently in Bu, M and Na than in the others; **pingel/pingot** are more frequent in M and Bu than in the others, the related **pichel/pightel** more frequent in Bu and Br than the rest, and rare in W; **lēah** occurs more frequently in E (60%) and M, Bu, Na and No (30–40%+), than in Br and W (15%); **geard** is rare in E compared with Bu (50%) and the rest (30%); **pearroc** is more frequent in M, Bu and Na than in Br, No, W and E; **pasture** is less frequent in No, Br, E than in M (50%), Na (40%), W and B (20%); **scēat** is less frequent in Br, E and W than in M (40%), Bu (30%), Na and No (20%).

Of group IV, **outlet** is less frequent in Br and W than in the rest; **pece** is more frequent in M than in the rest; **rūh** is more frequent in M, Bu than in the rest; **stede** is more frequent in M than in the rest, and least frequent in Na and Br; **grēne**[2] is more frequent in M and Bu than in the rest; **pacche** occurs more frequently in Na and M than in No, Bu, E, Br, and is rare in W; **mǣð** occurs more frequently in Na (30%) and No (20%) than in M (10%) and the rest; **clos** is more frequent in M

(30%) than in No, Br (10%) and the rest; **slang** is more frequent in Na and Br (20%) than in M (10%) and the rest; **læs(we)** is more frequent in Na (20%) than in M (10%) and the rest, being least in W.

Of group V, **(ge)dāl** occurs more frequently in M (30%) than the rest (10%); **eorðe** is more frequently found in M (42%) than in Bu (10%) and the rest, being least in W; **edisc** is more frequent in Br and Na than in the rest; **fald** in Na and M than in the rest; **rein** (ON) in W than in the rest, being least in Bu; (for **pichel/pightel** see under **pingel**, in III *supra*); **backside** is more frequent in W and E and Br than in the others; **holmr** (ON) is more frequent in M, Bu, W than in E, Na, Br, and least in No; **furlang** is more freqnent in Br (14%) and E (13%) than in No and Na (10%), W (9%), Bu (7%) and M (6%); **loom** is more frequent in W (18%) than in Br, No, E (5–10%), Bu and Na (2–3%), being rare in M; **waroð** appears more frequently in M (30%) than in Bu, No, E (under 10%) and is rare in Na, Br and W; **hamm** (**homm**) is likely to have been confused with **holmr** (**hulm**), but it appears to have been more frequent in Bu than in the rest, least of all in Br and W; **plat²** is more frequent in Bu, M and No than in Na, E, Br and W; **gata** (ON) is more frequent in Bu, M, E, W, than in Na, Br and No; **slæget** only occurs rarely, in M, Bu, No; **sticce** occurs in only 1% of Cheshire townships and not at all in M and Bu; **orceard** is more frequent in Na, E, Br, W than in M, Bu, No; **quillet** occurs in E, Br, W, Bu, not in M, No, Na; **oxgang**, rare, occurs only in No and E; **part** occurs occasionally in M, Na, E, W; **plain** (ME) occurs, rarely, in M and Bu; **plek** occurs more frequently in Na than in the rest, not at all in W; **plock** occurs occasionally in Bu, Br, W; **slippe** occurs 7 times each in M and Bu, elsewhere only once in E; **rūm²** occurs slightly more frequently in M and Bu than in the rest (rarest in Wirral); **ryde** and **(ge)ryd(d)** occur mostly in M and Bu.

Some further comments present themselves immediately. The distribution of **mǣd(we)** may be complementary to that of **mǣð** which is more frequent in Na and No than in M and the others. These els. and **pasture**, **grēne²** and **outlet** all signify aspects of a dairy–farming pastoral land–use. **Outlet** has to do with a pasture paddock into which cattle kept indoors for the winter can be turned out at the appropriate

times; perhaps in E. Cheshire there would have been more need for
indoor wintering, but **backside** (most frequent in W. Cheshire) often
signified an in–pasture adjacent to byre and yard for use similar to that
of an 'outlet'. A 'math' (**mǣð**) signifies the organized production of
hay (cf. **day–math**).

Some of the f.n. els. signify clearances of wood, waste and heath.
The distribution of **(ge)hæg** may indicate that there had been less
medieval assarting of ancient woodland in E and Na than in other parts
of Cheshire; that of **ryding** that W had been pretty well cleared of
ancient wood by late medieval times, leaving little scope for piecemeal
'riddings' such as were to be made elsewhere in Cheshire.

The el. **lēah** in f.ns. may be confused with **lǣge**, but generally in
f.ns. it indicates 'open ground', ModE *lea*, which, probably, had
originally been open–woodland country: the distribution is comparable
with that of **ryding**, **ryde** and **(ge)ryd(d)**, being less frequent in the
western Hundreds than in the eastern and central ones. Again, the el.
rūh[2], which relates to rough pasture or to uncultivated heathland or
former woodland, is less frequently seen in f.ns. in W and the
mid–Cheshire Hundreds than in M and Bu. The old woodland of
Cheshire has left its traces on such types of f.n.

The contrasting feature of the medieval Cheshire countryside must
have been the cultivated fields: **feld** in its best sense, the open
ploughlands of the medieval village. The distribution of **land** and
æcer reflects the disposition of enclosures and allotments of
ploughland selions out of the old open fields; as do **butte**,
hēafod–land, **dāl**, **eorðe**, **furlang**, **loom**, **quillet**, **rein** and **oxgang**.
Those who did well in the carve–up got 'looms' and 'acres'. The less
lucky got 'headlands', 'butts' , 'quillets' and 'shovel–brodes'. The
enclosure and allotment and subdivision of holdings produces the small
land–units indicated by **flat**, **pingel/pingot**, **pichel/pightel**, **geard**,
pearroc, **pece**, **pacche**, **clos**, **hamm**, **plat**[2], **sticce**, **part**, **plek**, **plock**,
and **slippe**. The distribution of the el. **rūm**[1] reflects the use of the term
'moss–room' for allotment of turbary in a Cheshire peat–bog.

The el. **flat** is originally ON, like **gata**, **inntak**, **holmr** and **rein**.
The distribution of these f.n. els. in Cheshire cannot be taken as a guide

to Scand. settlement; the words appear to have been part of the ME
vocabulary; but the fact that they occur more frequently in some
Hundreds than others is a reflection of varying strengths of
Scandinavian influence in the local field–nomenclatures of different
districts. The apparent scarcity of f.ns. in **gata** and **holmr** in No, a
Hundred associated with p.ns. in **holmr, hulm**, is remarkable.

The enclosure of waste, wood and common has been a constant
pressure on resources: **inntak** and **innam** bespeak it: the shortage of
enclosable ground led, in some districts, to the utilization of roadside
verges and stream–bank margins when all the plain ground had been
occupied — the occurrence of **slang** reflects an acute shortage of land.
Pressure on available, usable, land will explain in part the occurrence
of f.ns. in **waroð**, for this el. refers also to terrain and topography;
meadows in valley–bottom flood–plains would be attractive to farmers
in upland moorland regions where streams have a seasonal spate.

The significance of the distribution of els. such as **croft** (relatively
less frequent in No and E), **scēat** (relatively less frequent in Br, E and
W), **stede** (relatively less frequent in E, Na, and Br) is as yet
unexplained.

These questions, and much else that might doubtless be elicited,
would be the proper business of some other specialist, a historian,
maybe, of landscape or agriculture or field–names, to whom it is gladly
resigned by this hand.

LINGUISTIC NOTES ON THE PLACE–NAMES OF CHESHIRE

The representation of the OE and ME phonology of the place–names of Cheshire is here described in graphemic rather than phonetic terms. The notes are arranged in sections, **A.** §§ 1–19 OE vowels, **B.** §§ 20-27 OE, ME and ON diphthongs, **C.** §§ 29-51 Consonants, **D.** §§ 52-56 Phonetic processes, **E.** § 57 Grammatical notes, and **F.** § 58 Lexicographical notes.

A. OE VOWELS

1.1. OE *ǽ* is represented in spellings for p.ns. from **æċer, æppel** (Merc. **eppel**), **ærn, æsċ**, (Merc. **esċ**), **æspe** (Merc. **espe**), **bæċe**[1] (**beċe**[1]), **bær–** (**bere**), **bær**[1], **cærse** (**cerse, cresse**), **dræġ** (Merc. **dreġ**), **(ġe)fær, fæġer, gærs** (**græs, gres**), **glæs**[1], **hæċ(ċ)** (Merc. **heċ(ċ)**), **(ġe)hæġ** (Merc. **(ġe)heġ**), **Hæp* (p), **hæsel** (Merc. **hesel**), **hæslen, hætse, hætt, hæðel, læċ(ċ)** (**læċe, leċ(ċ), leċe**), **næss** (Merc. **ness**), **snæp, stæpe, wæfre, wær** (**wer**), **wæsse** (Merc. **wesse**), **weġ** (cf. § 8 and Campbell § 328) as follows:

1.2. usually by ME *a* or *e* (see Ekwall, NoB 51, 16ff., Arngart, SNPh 43, 433-4; for *ǽ* before *l, r* etc., see § 17);

1.3. by ME *ey, ei, ay, ai, i, y,* ModE *ee, ea,* before *ġ,* [ʃ], [ss], *ċ*;

1.4. before *p,* by ME *a,* ModE *o, i, ea.*

2.1. OE *ǣ*[1] (< WGerm *ai + i/j*) is represented in p.ns. from **ǣċen,** *Bǣ̇ge* (p), **brǣdu, brǣmel, cǣġ, clǣfre, clǣġ, clǣġiht, clǣm–, clǣne, clǣte, dǣ̇ge,** *–flǣd* (p), **flǣsċ, grǣdiġ, grǣfe, hǣddre, hǣmed, hǣs, hǣter, hǣð, hǣðiġ, hǣðiht, hǣðor, hlǣfdiġe, hlǣw** (**hlāw**), **hwǣġ, hwǣte, hwǣten, lǣt, mǣl, (ġe)mǣne–, mǣnnes, (ġe)mǣre,** *Mǣrela* (p), *–rǣd* (p), **rǣġe, rǣw** (**rāw**), **sǣ, snǣd, stǣġer, stǣne, stǣnen, stǣner, stǣniġ,** *Tǣta* (p), **twǣm–**:

2.2.1. usually by ME *a* or *e*;

2.2.2. also by ME *o* (< *a*), ModE *oa,* before *m, n, d,* and by ME *ea, ey, ei, ay, ai,* ModE *ai, ei, ee,* before various consonants.

3.1. OE $\bar{æ}^2/\bar{e}$ (< WGerm $\bar{a}$) is represented in p.ns. from **æl** (**ēl**), **bæl** (**bēl**), **brǣr** (**brēr**), **brǣriġ** (**brēriġ**), **grǣġ** (**grēġ**), **lǣġe** (**lēġe**), **lǣs** (**lēs**), **mǣd** (**mēd**), **strǣt** (**strēt**), **wǣl** (**wēl**), *Wǣr–* (p), **wǣt** (**wēt**):

3.2.1. usually by ME *a* or *e*;

3.2.2. and by ME *i*, *ee*, ModE *ey*, *ei*, *ai*, before *d*, *t*; ME and ModE *ey*, *ay* before *ġ*; ME *ea*, *ei* before *l*, *r*.

4.1. OE, ON *ă*, ME *ă* are represented in p.ns. from **afnām**, **alor**, **alren**, *Arnketil* (p), **bagga**, **capal**, *cark* < **carreg**, **carn**, **cwabba**, **flaġe**, **flasshe**, **gaġel**, **haga**, **hara**, **lacu**, **mal**, **market**, **marle(de)**, **park**, **plaga**, **rasse**, **raton**, **sċ(e)aga**, *smal–* < **smæl**, **staca**, **stapol**, *war–* < **wær**[1] and *blak–* < **blæc**, **lake**, **rake**:

4.2. usually by ME *a*, but also by ME *o*, *e*, cf. §§ 17-18;

4.3. by late ME, ModE *ea*, *ai*, *ay* before [k], OE *ġ*; ME *au* before ME *ht* < [–k–t], Claughton.

4.4. OE *a* before *l* in **alor**, **alren** > *oller–* has a characteristic development *al–* (*11-14*), *ol–* (*from 13*), *owl–* (*from 13*), *wool–* (*18*), *hool–* (*19*), *oyl–* (*19*); cf. § 12.

4.5.1. OE *a* before *g* is usually represented by ME *aw*, *au*, *ow*, and occasionally *ew*;

4.5.2. but **sċ(e)aga**, **haga** produce characteristic alternative ME and ModE spellings *–a(g)h*, *–ach*, *–ae*, *–a*, *–ay* (esp. in N. and E. Ch), *–ie*, *–ea*; cf. spellings for Baguley (**bagga**).

5.1. OE, ME *a/o* before nasals is represented in p.ns. from OE **banke**, **cran(uc)**, **furlang**, **hamm**, **hamol**, **hana**, **hand**, *Haneca* (p), **hangende**, **hangra**, **hramsa**, **lamb**, **land**, **lane**, **lang**, **man–drēam**, **mangere**, **maniġ**, **mann**, **oxgang**, **panne**, **sand**, **spann**, **standende**; ME *Alvand–* (p), **branderith**, *Lambert* (p), **named**; ON **dammr**, *Gamal* (p), **hvammr**, **skammr**, **trani**:

[For the *i*–mutation of *a* + nasal, see § 8.]

5.2. usually by ME *a*, *o*, *au*, *aw*;

5.3. but a characteristic over–rounding before *mb*, *mm*, *nd*, *ng*, *nk* and in reinterpreted forms from **hān**, and in originally open syllables as in **lane**, **hana**, is represented by ME and ModE spellings *u*, *ou*, *ow*, *oo*, etc. See § 12.

6.1. OE *ā*, ON *á* are represented in p.ns. from **āc**, **ān**, **āte**, **blāc**, **brād**, **crāwe**, **dāl**, *fāg–* < **fāh**, **gār**, **gāt**, **hlāw**, **kráka**, **(ġe)lād**, **lágr**, **rá**, **rāp**, **rāw**, **skáli**, **stān**, *–stān* (p):

6.2.1. usually by ME *a* and *o*; *a* persisting when shortened in cpds.; *o* regularly after *12*;

6.2.2. by various ME, ModE digraphs *au, aw, ou, ow, ouw, oo, oa, ooa*.

6.3.1. ME *ā* of whatever origin, before *l* + cons (cf. § 17) is represented in p.ns. from **ald–, ball–, cald–, calf–,** *Ceolm–* (p) (Cholmondeley **4** 21; Cholmondeston **3** 136), **halc–, hall–, salh–, salt–,** *Walh–* (p), **–wall**, by ME *o*, ME, ModE *au* (with [î]), and ME *u*;

6.3.2. by ModE *o* before *r* + cons. or between *w–r*, in p.ns. from *–arn* (< **ærn**), *war–* (< **wær**[1] etc.), cf. § 17.

7.1. ON *ǫ* is represented in p.ns. from **flǫt** (ME *flat*), **hǫgg, knǫttr, stǫrr, þing–vǫllr**:

7.2. by ME, ModE *a*, occasionally *o*.

7.3. ME and ModE *e* for **vǫllr** in Thingwall may be due to confusion with **wælla, wella**, but might possibly reflect the Scand plural *vellir* (cf. Þingvellir, Iceland).

8.1. OE, ON, ME *ě* is represented in p.ns. from *Bebba* (p), **bere–ærn, berned (brende), blesi, bred–, breden, brekka,** *Brett–* (p), *Cēnfrið* (p), **crew, denn, denu, ecg, edisċ, ende**[1], **erg, feld, fenn(ig), fersc, fleke, heċ (hæċċ), heċing, heġ, helde, hencg, henn, here–,** *Herestān* (p), *Herewīg* (p), **hesta–, kerlingr,** *Ketill* (p), **kettlingr,** *Lambert* (p), **melr, mere**[1,2], **mersc, nese, nesu, penn**[1,2], **persone, peru, pleġ–,** *Pleġmund* (p), **plek,** *Prǣn* (p), **sker, spenne, stede,** *Tegan* (p), **terfyn, teyntour, trendel, þel, þengel, þyrne,** *Verdon* (p), **weġ** (Merc. **wæġ**), **wella, wende, wer (wær), werned, west, (ġe)wind**[2], **wrenna**:

[OE *e* in **denn, denu, ende**[1], **fenn, hencg, henn, spenne** represents *i*–mutation of *a* + nasal, see § 5; in **helde, wella**, the *i*–mutation of *a/ea* before *l* + cons, see § 17.]

8.2. usually by ME *e*; also ME *i, y* in short syllables; ME *a* (> ModE [ei], [a]);

8.3. also by *e, a, i, y, u,* and *ay, ey, ei, ye, ee, ou* before *r*, and nasals. An unusual difficult development of (?) OE *ě* before *r* + cons. occurs in Kermincham.

8.4. OE *ě* before *ġ* is represented by ME, ModE *a, e, ey, ei, ai, ay*.

9.1. OE, ME *ē* is represented in p.ns. from **bēcen, brēċ, ċēd,** *Cēna* (p), *Dēw* r.n., **ēdre, ēsing** < OE **ēfesung, glebe, grēne**[1,2], **grese, pēl, prēst** < OE **prēost, smēðe,** *Swēta* (p), **swēte, wēfre**:

9.2.1. usually by ME, ModE *e*;

9.2.2. in shortened syllables by ME, ModE *i, y* and ME *a*.

9.3. ME $\bar{e}$ (< OE $\bar{e}$ or $\check{e}$) subsequently shortened or diphthongized, is represented by late ME, ModE *ee*, *ea*, *i*, *ey*, *ei*, *a* [ei]. Cf. § 8.

10.1. OE, ME $\check{\imath}$ is represented in p.ns. from **bica**, *Bicca* (p), **bicce, bigging, bil(l)ing, bing, bridd, brink, chiri, ciriċe, cis, clif, cniht, criu, drit, edisc, ermite, finn,** *Hichecok* (p), *Hild–* (p), *–hild* (p), **hind, hlid**[1], **hlinc, hlið, hring, hvin,** *Ida* (p), **–iġ, –iġn, iġen, impe, –ing(–), inġ(–), inntak, king** (< **cyning**), ON **kirkja, lind, lisso–,** *Lisote* (p), **micel, middel, mikill, miln(e)** (< **myln**), **mixen, pichel, piriġe, pise, risc, riscett, riscig,** ON *Sigriðr* (p), **slinu, smið, smiððe, spitel, spiwol, spring, stiġel,** *Tilla* (p), **timber,** *Titta* (p), **trinity, twisla, widu (wudu), wiht, wilde,** *Wil–* (p), **winn**[1], *Wine–* (p), *–wine* (p):

10.2.1. usually by ME, ModE *i*, *y*;

10.2.2. also by ME *e*, *u*, *o*;

10.2.3. in lengthened syllables also by ME *ey*, *ie*, *uy*, ModE *ea*, *a*, *ay*;

10.3. before *ġ*, *ġn* also by ME *i(e)*, *y(e)*, *e(y)*, ModE *ee*, *y*;

10.4. in spellings for **micel, mycel,** with alternative [ʧ] and [k], by *u* (with [k] *1200*, [ʧ] *14*); *y*, *i* ([k] *14*, [ʧ] *14*); *o* ([ʧ] *16*);

10.5. after *w*, before *d*, *t*, or *l*, sometimes by ME *o*;

10.6.1. before nasal, nasal + cons., usually by ME, ModE *i*, *y*, *e*, *u*;

10.6.2. in p.ns. from **slinu**, *Wine–* (p), also by ME, ModE *ey*, *ee*, *ai*, *oy*;

10.7. in spellings from **pise (peosu), hlið (hleoðu), smið (smeoða)** with back–mutated forms, by ME *ea*, *e*, *uy*, ModE *oy*, *ie*, *ei*. See § 18;

10.8. before *sc* [ʃ] also by ME, ModE *u*, *ui*, *ey*, *a*.

11.1. OE $\bar{\imath}$, ON *í* are represented in p.ns. from **bíc, cícen, díc, fínig, híd, híwan, hríðer, hwít, Íri, lín, píc, scíd, scír, scríc, síc, síd, síde, stíġ, svíri,** *Tíd–* (p), *Tída* (p), *Tír* (p), **wic, wíd,** *Wíġ–* (p), *–wíġ* (p), **wír, wíðeġn:**

11.2.1. by ME *i*, *y*, usually;

11.2.2. also by ME *e*; *a*, *u*, *o*;

11.3. by various digraphs ME *ui*, *uy*, *oi*, *ye*, *ei*, *ou*, *ow*, ModE *oy*, *oo*, *ee*, *ey*, before *l*, *n*, *r*, *d*, [ʧ], *st*.

12.1. OE, ME $\check{o}$, is represented in p.ns. from **boga, bola, bold,** *Ceolla* (p), **cnocc, cnoll, cocc, col, coningre,** *Copin* (p), *Coppa* (p), **cot,** *Cotta* (p), **croh,** *Doddel* (p), **fold, ford, gof, gorst, goter, hol**[1,2], **holm, holt, hop, hord, hors, mold, norð, ofer,** *Offa* (p), **pode, port, rod**[1], **shrogge, sogh, spor,** *Sprot* (p), *Steinolfr* (p), **stoc, stolpi,** *Thor–* (p), **þorn, tod, toll, tor, worð, worðiġ(n):**

12.2. by ME *o*; also *a*, *u*, *i*, *y*, *e*;

12.3. by ME, ModE *ou, ow, oe*, ModE *oo, oa, oy* before *r*, and nasals;
12.4.1. For ME, ModE *ŏ* in *ol, on* > *oul, oun*, cf. §§ 4, 5, and spellings for **alor, hana, hand, land, sand**.

12.4.2. OE *ŏ* before *l, l* + cons, is represented by ME *o, u*, ME and ModE *a, ow, ou*, cf. spellings from **alor** (*oller, owler*); **cnoll**; **hol, holh** (the dat. sg. **hole**, nom. pl. **holu** > ME *hōle*, pl. *hōles*, behave as OE *ō*, see § 13).

12.4.3. The development of OE *ō* and *ŏ*, ME *ō* and *ŏ* before *lm* is chiefly represented in the spellings of p.ns. ascribed to ON **holmr**, late OE **holm** and (the hitherto supposed) ODan ***hulm** (see **5:1** 237-9).

12.4.4. In Ch, the vowel in p.ns. from **holmr, hulm** is represented by *o* (*from late 12*, *13*), *u* (*from 12*), *uu* written *w* (*13*), *ou* (*15* (*17*), *16*) *au* (*19*); and *a* in unstressed final syllable (*1550* Kettleshulme **1** 110; cf. Oldham's **1** 102 (**5:1** xv) where confusion with –*hum*, –*hom*, –*ham* < **hamm** is possible). The principal feature in the Ch examples is the alternation of **holm** and **hulm** spellings, and the ModE dial. alternative forms [(h)ɔum, (h)oum] spelt *holm(e)*, and [(h)u:m, (h)ju:m] spelt *hulm(e)*, which gives occasion for supposing an ODan variant ***hulm** in the region. But there are numerous instances of alternations, in contemporary records, of *o* and *u* spellings for one and the same place–name, and this suggests that the reason may be a feature in the ME dialect of Ch, south La, north St. There is no evidence for [hju:m] for *hulm(e)* before modern times. We may be dealing with a sound indifferently represented by the ME spellings –*olm* and –*ulm*, and artificially fragmented after the spellings; perhaps **holm** > [o:lm] > [ou(l)m] and [u:(l)m] with characteristic WMidl rounding of vowel, and vocalisation of [l] (cf. §§ 14.5, 15.5). An alternative solution may lie in another direction: the alternation of *holm(e), hulm(e)* may arise from OE **hamm** (dat. sg. **hamme**), with vowel rounded *homm(e)*, over–rounded *humm(e)*, lengthened on simplification of consonant *hum(e)*, in the inflected form, *homm(e)* > *hu(m)m(e), hou(m)m(e)*, heard as [(h)uĩ m(ə), (h)oĩ m(ə)] as if **holm**. Not enough is known about the morphology and distribution of the element OE **hamm, homm**. An instructive model appears in the spellings for Holme Lacy, PNHe 95. It should be pointed out that we do not yet have enough information about medieval f.ns., also that *u* often appears in latinized forms. See further the discussion by G. Fellows–Jensen in SSNW 313-16.

13.1. OE *ō*, ON *ó*, are represented in p.ns. from **bōc**[1], **bóndi, bōs, bōsiġ, bōt**, *Bōta* (p), **bōth** (ODan), **brōc, brōm, clōh, crōh, flōcere**, flókari, *Frōd* (p), gōs, grōpe, hlōse, hōh, mōr[1], (ġe)mōt, mōtere, ōra, ōsle, pōl, rōd, skógr, sōt, spōn, stōd, stōpel, stórr, stōw, tōt, trōg; ME *ō* in p.ns. from **clos** and (from lengthened OE *o*) **hol, stoc:**

13.2.1. by ME, ModE *o* usually;

13.2.2. also by ME *ou*(*w*), *ow*, *oo*, *au*, *aw* when final;

13.2.3. by ME, ModE *u*, *a*, *e* in short syllables, *i* [i] before *d*; *ou*, *ow*, *oo*, *oa*, *au* before various consonants;

13.2.4. by *oe* before *r*;

13.3. by ME, ModE *oy*, *oi* before *h* [χ], *ð*, *l*; see § 12.4; cf. Holes **5:1** xxiv (2 41 Add.) for ModE *oe* < ME *ō* from OE **hol.**

14.1. OE *ŭ* is represented in p.ns. from **bucc(a),** *Bucc*(*a*) (p), *Budd*(*a*) (p), **bulluc, bult,** *Buna* (p), **bune, burh, burna, busċ, buskr, butt,** *Cudd*(*a*) (p), **cumb, Cumbre,** *Ducc*(*a*) (p), *Dudd*(*a*) (p), **fugol,** *Hucc* (p), **hulm** (but see § 12), **hulu, hund, hux, lumm, pull, sċucca (sċeocca), slump, spura, stubb (stobb), sumor, þurnuc, uferra, upp, wudu, wulf,** *Wulf–* (p), *–wulf* (p):

14.2. usually by ME *u*; also by ME *o*, *ou*, *ow* before various consonants and finally;

14.3. by ME *e*, ModE *a*, before [k], *d*, *l*, *m*, *n*, *r*;

14.4. by ME, ModE *i*, *y* before *d*, [v], *t*, cf. § 15.4; spellings *wed–*, *wid–*, *wyd–*, etc., for Woodford **1** 217, *Wodehouses–* **3** 268, may reflect **widu** (without back mutation). See § 10.

14.5. For ME *ŭ* and *ū* before *lm* in p.ns. from ?**holm,** ?**hamm,** see § 12.4.

15.1. OE *ū*, ON *ú*, are represented in p.ns. from **brū,** *Brūn*(*a*) (p), *Brúni* (p), **būr**[1], **clūd, crūc**[1], **cū, dūce, dūfe, dūn, fūl, hūder, hūs, mūga, mūl, mūs, plūme, rūde, rūh, rūm, sūr, sútari, sūtere, sūð, þrūh, tūn,** *Ūhtrǣd* (p):

15.2.1. by ME *u* usually;

15.2.2. by ME *o*, *ow*, *ou* before various consonants and finally;

15.3. by late ME, ModE *oy*, *oi* before *s* in p.ns. from **cū;**

15.4. by ME *e*, *i*, *y*, after shortening before *d*, *ð*, *n*, cf. § 14.4.

15.5. For ME *ŭ* and *ū* before *lm*, see § 12.4.

16.1. OE *ȳ* and *ẏ* are represented in p.ns. from **bryċe, bryċg,** *Brȳni* (p), **bý, byden, byġe**[1,2], **byht, bȳre, byrh, byriġ, byxen, cnycyn, cryc, cryfting, cryme, cryw, cyln,** *Cyne–* (p), **cyning, cyte, drȳġe, dyn(c)ge, (ġe)fyrhð, gylden,** *–gȳð* (p), **hryċg, hyġel, hyll, hyrdel(s), hyrne, hyrst,**

myċel, myċg, myln, myrġe, plȳme, pyrle, pytt, (ġe)ryd(d), ryding, ryġe, rysċ, sċylf(e), sċypen, sċyte, spyrt, stybbing, styde, synder, tȳning, þȳfel, þyrel, þyrne, þyrs, wylfen, wyrm:

16.2. usually by ME *i/y* or *u*, but also by ME *o, a, e*;

16.3. by various digraphs for diphthongs upon *i/y, e, o, u* before OE *ġ* [ʃ], *r, r* + cons., *ng, d, m(b), s, t*, and in p.ns. from **cryw**.

17. BREAKING of OE vowels before *l/r/*[χ] + cons.:

17.1. OE *a/ea* before *l/r/h* + cons. is represented in p.ns. from **ald**, *Ald–* (p), *Alh–* (p), *Bald–* (p), *–bald* (p), **ball, cald, calf, fald, falh, fall, halc, hald, half, halh, hall, salh, salt, stall, swalwe**, *–wald* (p), **wald, walh; bearu**, *Eald–* (p), *Ealh–* (p), *Earn–* (p), **earn, ears, fearn, ġeard**, *–heard* (p), **mearċ, mearð, nearu, orċeard**, *Pearta* (p), **sċeard, spearca, spearwa, sweart**, *–weard* (p), **weard, wearg, wearm; neaht, fleax**:

17.2.1. by ME *a* or *e* usually; occasionally by *ea*. Cf. § 4.5.2;

17.2.2. by ME *al* +, *ol* +, *oul* + cons.;

17.2.3. by ME *–ar* +, *–or* +, *–ur* +; *–er* +, *–ir* + cons.

17.2.4. In p.ns. from **niht–, neht–, næht–, neaht–** it is represented by ME *e, a*, ModE *i*.

17.3. The OE *i*–mutation of *a/ea* before *l/r* + cons. is represented in p.ns. from *Ælf–* (*Elf–*) (p), **fælġing (felġing), helde, wælisċ (welisċ**, < *lh*, see SMED 142, SNPh 48, 321–4), **wælm (welm), wællere (wellere), wella (wælla); derne, mercels**:

17.4.1. usually by ME *a* or *e*.

17.4.2. The vowel in **wella** is represented by ME *e* or *a* (ME *e* in *well* becomes ModE *i* [i], cf. § 8.2);

17.4.3. that in **helde** by *e* and prosthetic [j] diphthong spellings (cf. § 8.3).

17.4.4. P.ns. in **earn** have *ya–, ye–* spellings with prosthetic [j].

17.5. OE *eo* before *r* + cons. is represented in p.ns. from **beorc**, *–beorht* (p), *Beorn–* (p), *–beorn* (p), **ceorl, cweorn, deorc, eorl, eorðe, heorð, steort, weorc, weorf**:

17.6.1. by *e, o, u, i, y* usually; by ME *er* +, *ar* +, *or* +, *ur* + cons.;

17.6.2. in p.ns. from **eorl, eorðe**, by *ya–, ye–, yo–* spellings with prosthetic [j].

17.7. OE *i* (< WGerm *i*) with *r* + cons. followed by *i/j* (see Campbell § 154) is represented by p.ns. in **birċe, birċen, birċels, heorde**:

[Campbell § 154, n. 3 questions the relevance of **heorde** here, cf. ibid. § 202; also OE

birċe may be the smoothing of an OE ***bierċe** (ibid. § 228).]

17.8.1. before *rċ*, *rd* by ME *i*, *y*, *e*, *u*, *o*.

17.8.2. OE *–eord–* is represented by ModE *yeard–*, *yord–* with prosthetic [j].

17.9. OE *ī* / *ēo* before *ht* in p.ns. from **līht**, **lēoht** is represented by ME *i*, *y*, *e*.

18. BACK MUTATION. The representation in Ch p.ns. of OE back–mutated forms (Campbell §§ 205-21) is as follows:

18.1.1. OE *æ*, *ea* < WGerm. *a* is represented in p.ns. from *Beada* (p), *Beadu* (p), *Peada* (p), **stapol** (**steapol**):

18.1.2. by ME *e* or *a*; also by ME *y* [i] before *d*.

18.2.1. OE *eo* < WGerm. *e* is represented in p.ns. from **beofor, eofor, meolu, smeoru, seofon** by ME *e*;

18.2.2. in p.ns. from **heorot** by ME *a*.

18.3.1. OE *eo* < WGerm. *e* before *w* is represented in p.ns. from **eowu** (Campbell § 211) by ME *ow*, *ou*, *ew*;

18.3.2. also *yow–*, *yew–* with prosthetic [j].

18.4.1. OE *eo* < WGerm *i* is represented in p.ns. from **beonet** (< ***binut**), **clif** (pl. ***cleofu**), **endleofan, gleoda, hlið** (gen. pl. **hleoða**), **neoðera, pise** (**peosu**), **smið** (gen. pl. **smeoða**):

18.4.2. by ME *e*;

18.4.3. by ME *ou* in p.ns. from **neoþera**;

18.4.4. by ModE *ey* before *d* (< *d*, *ð*).

18.4.5. Spellings in *–e–* in p.ns. from **clif** represent ME *e* < OE *i* (see § 10.7). ME *cleve*, *clive* (cf. Clive **2** 234) can represent OE *clife* dat. sg. Derivation of ME *cleve* from back–mutated OE nom. pl. ***cleofu**, dat. pl. ***cleofum** would require topographical corroboration of the plural, or ME analogical nom. pl. *–es* forms.

19. DIPHTHONGIZATION AFTER PALATAL CONSONANTS

19.1. The representation of vowels and diphthongs after initial palatal consonants OE *ġ*, *sċ*, *ċ* is seen in p.ns. from **ġear, ġeat, ġeong, sċēad, sċ(e)aga, sċēap** (**sċēp**), **sċeorf, sċeort,** *Ċead–* (p), **ċeaster, ċēse** (Angl., ***cīese, cȳse** WSax) as follows:

19.2.1. OE *eo* after *ġ* by ModE *yo*;

19.2.2. after *sċ* and before *r* + cons., by ME *u*, *o*, *y*, *i*, *e*.

19.3.1. OE *æ/ea* after *ċ*, from *Ċead–* (p), **ċeaster**, by OE *æ, ea, e*, ME *e* or *a*;

19.3.2. after *ġ* by ME *e, a*;

19.3.3. after *sċ*, from **sċ(e)aga**, see § 4.5.2.

19.4. OE *ā/ēa* after *sċ*, from **sċēad**, by ME *a*.

19.5.1. OE *ē/ēa* after *sċ*, from **sċēap, sċēp**, by ME *e*, ModE *i, ee*;

19.5.2. after *ċ* from **ċēse** by ME *e*.

B. OE, ON and ME DIPHTHONGS

20.1. OE *ēa* is represented in p.ns. from *Bēac* (p), **bēam, dēad, dēaw, ēa,** *Ēad–* (p), **ēan, ēast, ġēac, grēat, hēafod, hēah** (wk. **hēa(n)**), **lēac, lēad, lēah** (dat. sg. **lēa**, etc.) **man–drēam, pēac, rēad, rēafere, sċēafa, sċēat, sēað, strēam, tēafor, þrēap:**

20.2.1. by OE *ea, æ*, ME *e, a, o, au, u, ea, eay, ey, ei, ie, i* (before [χ]);

20.2.2. also by ME *yei–, ya–*, ModE *yai–* from **ēa, ēan** with prosthetic [j].

21.1. The *i*–mutation of OE *ēa* is represented in p.ns. from **ēċels* (WSax **īeċels*), **hlēp(e)* (WSax **hlīepe**), **hēġ** (WSax **hīeġ**), **ēġ** (WSax **īeġ**):

21.2. by ME *e a, i, y*; ME *ey, ei, ea, ee*; ME *ya–* representing prosthetic [j].

22.1. OE *ēo* (including *ēo* < WGerm *iu + i*/[j]) is represented in p.ns. from **bēo,** *Bēofa* (p), **bēos, betwēonan,** *Ċēol–* (p), **clēow, dēop, dēor,** *Dēor–* (p), *Ēorēd* (p), **ēow (īw), fēond, fēower, flēot, frēo,** *Frēowine* (p), **grēot, hēope, hrēod(iġ), hwēol,** *Lēof–* (p), **mēos(uc), nēowe (nīwe), prēost, sċēot, swēora, þēof, trēo(w):**

22.2. by ME *eo, e, i, y, a, o, u*, ME *ee, ea, ei, ey*;

22.3.1. before *w*, by ME *u, eu, ew, ou, ow, iew, yw, aw*.

22.3.2. In p.ns. from **trēo(w)** some spellings reflect **trēow(–)**, ME *eu* (*el DB* Goostrey **2** 226), *u, ou, o*; some **trēo**, ME *e, ee, i*, ModE *ey, y*; cf. Campbell § 279.

23.1. ME *au* is represented in p.ns. from **daube** by ModE *o* [ɔ:], **launde** by ModE *ow, aw*.

24.1. ON *au* is represented in p.ns. from **haugr, laut, raun, rauðr,** *Rauðr* (p), **straumr:**

24.2. by ME *au, ow, ou, eu, a, u, o*.

25.1. ON *ei* is represented in p.ns. from **beit, deill, geit, grein, leirr, leið, rein, skeið, steinn,** *–steinn* (p), **sveinn, þveit:**

25.2.1. by ME *ey, ei, ay, ai;*

25.2.2. before *n* by ME *e, eh, ee;* by *a* before *d* (< ð), *r.*

26.1. ON *ja, ia* < *e* is represented in p.ns. from **bjarg (berg), hjallr,** *Ingiald* (p), **kjarr** (ME *ker*):

26.2. by ME *aa, ee, e, a, o.*

27.1. ON *jó* and *jú* are represented in p.ns. from **kjóss; djúp (dēop):**

27.2. ON *jú* by ME *u* (*Duphyard* **4** 248).

28.1. ON *jǫ* before *r* is represented by ME *e, a;* before *s* by ModE *i.*

28.2. ON *jǫ* (< *e*) is represented by *Ósbjorn* (p).

C. CONSONANTS

29.1.1. OE *w*, ON *v* are represented (other than in initial position and in initial groups *cw–, hw–, sw–, þv–, tw–*) in inflexional forms of els. such as **bearu, mæd, nearu,** and in p.ns. from **clēow, crāwe, dēaw, eowe, hlāw, īw, nīwe, spearwa, spiwol,** *Sprow–* (p), **stōw,** *–wine* (p):

29.1.2. by ME, ModE *w;*

29.1.3. by ME *u, v* initial, ME *u* in consonant groups from OE *cw, hw,* etc. and in inflexions.

29.2.1. ME *w* is lost from initial position: before *u(l), o(l);* of second el.; and in cons. groups *wr–, sw–, tw–, þw–;*

29.2.2. from final position: inflexional and post–consonantal; after OE *ā, ō, ēa;*

29.2.3. between *o* and *r.*

29.3.1. OE *w* initial, and initial in second el., is sometimes represented by ME *hw–, wh–, qu–, qw–, su–* [sw–] influenced by OE *hw* (see § 41.4).

29.3.2. OE *sw–* initial is represented by ME *scu–, scw–, squ–, swh–, szy–,* as if the *w* were *hw* [χw]; cf. § 30.2.2.

29.4. ME [w] is represented by 1. ME [χ] written *gh, ch;* 2. ME, ModE *l, r* [ḷ, ṛ]; 3. ModE *y* (*Oylershaw* **2** 318).

29.5. Prosthetic *w* appears in ME and ModE spellings for e.g. **āc, alor, āte, hār, īw;** cf. § 41.2.2, 54.

29.6. Unhistorical ME, ModE *w* appears 1. as substitute initial of second el., Stanney, *Heppales* **1** 299, Grappenhall; 2. as result of popular etymology Wigland, Etchells, Ringway, Shotwick Park, Stockport, Shurlach, Poundswick **1** 241, etc.

30.1.1. OE, ON *r* is represented (other than as initial; or second element in initial consonant groups *br, cr, dr, fr, gr, hr, kr, pr, tr, þr, vr, wr, scr, spr, shr*) in p.ns. from **alor, alren, bearu, beorc, beorg, berned, birče, burg, cærse, čeorl, Cumbre, eorðe, fersc, gærs, gorst, hangra,** *–here* (p), **hord, hyrdels, hyrne, hyrst, kjarr, mere, mōr**[1]**, nicor, norð,** *Orm* (p), **pearroc,** *–rǣd* (p), **smeoru, snōr, sparð, spor(a), spyrd, swēora, þorn, þyrel, þyrne, tyddring, wællere,** *Wær–* (p), **waroð, weorf, worð, worðig(n), wyrm:**

30.1.2. by ME, ModE *r* usually;

30.2.1. by ME, ModE *rh* initial, *Alde Rene* **4** 19, North Rode, Wrenbury, Rhodes **1** 197, 325, Rhuddall **3** 296; cf. §§ 29.3.2, 41.9.

30.2.2. OE *hr–, wr–* initial lose *h, w* in ME.

30.3. OE, ON *r* is represented by ModE *w* (< [r̥]): 1. final; 2. in the groups *ltr, rt, rl.*

30.4. ME *r* interchanges or is lost next to *l, m, n, r.*

30.5. ME *r* is represented by ModE *d*: 1. before [z], Gawsworth; 2. intervocalic, in *paddock* from **pearroc.**

30.6. ME *r* is frequently metathesised, e.g. in p.ns. from **berned, cærse, gærs, fersc,** and in cons. groups.

30.7. ME *r* is lost: 1. from cons. groups, (1) initial ME *wr–*, ModE *spr–, shr–* and (2) medial and final ME *rsl*, ME, ModE *rd, rn, rsb, rst,* p.ns. from **gorst,** ModE *rf, rl, rm*; 2. When final unstressed, Clemonga **2** 70, Gunco.

30.8. Unhistorical *r* appears: 1. anticipating *r* in next syllable, Corbishley, Wybersley; 2. after initial ModE *d,* p.ns. from **dumbel**; 3. intervocalic in ModE, Heire **3** 233; 4. in ME, early ModE, before *d, g, l, m, n, s,* cf. *1350* Handbridge, *1262* Runcorn; 5. for final *w* in ModE, Goodser **1** 113, Ollershaw; and for ModE [ou], Limbo **4** 262.

31.1.1. OE, ON *l* is represented (other than as initial; or second el. in initial consonant groups *bl, cl, fl, gl, hl, pl, sl, wl*) in p.ns. from *Ælf–* (p), *Ælle* (p), *Æþel–* (p), *Al–* (p), *Ald–* (p), **ald,** *–ald(r)* (p), **balc,** *–bald* (p), **ball, bold, bóli, bræmel, bulluc, bult, bytle, calf, calu,** *Čeol–* (p), **čeorl, cnoll, colt, cristel, dæl, dāl, dalr, dimpel, dingle,** *Doddel* (p),

dumbel, falh, feld, fugol, fūl, halc, halh, hall, hāðel, *–helm* (p), hol,
holh, holm, holt, hulu, hyll, *Ketill* (p), ketlingr, *Maccel* (p), mæl, mal,
marle, melr, mercels, molda, myċel, mylen, pingel, pōl, salh, salt,
sċylfe, *Sċyttel* (p), stall, stólpi, toll(r), twisla, wælla, *–wald* (p), wilde,
wulf, *Wulf–* (p), *–wulf* (p):

31.1.2. usually by ME, ModE *l*.

31.2.1. ME, ModE *l* represents [ī], see discussion of Meols **4** 296-7;

31.2.2. it is lost when final or before certain consonants;

31.2.3. it usually persists in spellings for **holm**, but cf. *Allom* **2** 275;

31.2.4. it is represented by *u, w* before various consonants, by ME,
ModE *–augh–, –ough–* from **halh, falh**, etc., (*o*)*w*, (*o*)*u* from **cnoll, dāl,
hol**[1], **stall**, etc., cf. §§ 31.5, 41.3, 41.8.

31.3. ME *l* interchanges with, and is lost near, *l, m, n, r*.

31.4. ME, ModE *l* is metathesised in cons. groups *lw, lsk, ld, dl, tl, gl*.

31.5. Unhistorical ME, ModE *l* appears: 1. anticipating a following *l*; 2.
for unhistorical *r*; 3. substituted for final *w*, cf. § 31.2.4, Goostrey,
Rainow, Stocia **2** viii, 263, Henshaw.

32.1.1. OE, ON *n* is represented (other than as initial, or as second el.
in initial consonant groups *cn, gn, hn, kn, sn*, or as an inflexional form)
in p.ns. from **ærn, atten, bean, birċen**, *Brūna* (p), **coningre, cyln,
fælging**, *–en* suffix forms, **flint, h̨ænep, hangra**, *–ign* / *–egn* suffix
forms, *–ing* suffix forms, **inntak, land, lang, man–drēam**, *–mund* (p),
myln, sand, stān, *–stān* (p), **þorn, þyrne, tráni, tūn**, *Win–* (p),
worðiġ(n):

32.1.2. by ME, ModE *n*;

32.2. by ModE *kn* (Mossnook **2** 81) by inverted spelling of [k] in OE
cn–, cf. § 34.7.1.

32.3. OE, ME *n* is lost: 1. initially, by aphaerisis from **næddre**; 2.
finally, after *l, r*, and in *–ign* (e.g. **worðiġn**); 3. before consonants, and
from final *–ng, –furluc* (< *furlang*) **2** 65 (**5:2** Add.); 4. in p.ns. from
–ingtūn after loss of *g*.

32.4.1. ME, ModE *n* interchanges with, and is lost near *l, m, n, r*.

32.4.2. OE, ME *n* in *ln* from **myln** persists in spelling to *18*, but is lost by
1237 Milton **3** 204; in p.ns. from **cyln**, *n* usually persists (cf. *1560 Killcroft*
4 12); but cf. ModE and dial. pronunciations [kil, mil].

32.5. Metathesis of *n* occurs, Tranmere **4** 257 (*Tramnol 1524*) Pownall **1**
229 (*Pownehale 1290*).

32.6. Unhistorical *n* appears: 1. by anticipation of following *n*, Cuddington **4** xii, 28, Tittenley, Dukinfield, Swettenham; 2. by analogy, e.g. Shrigley, Redacre, Hollowmoor, Gallantry; 3. by metanalysis in p.ns. from **atten.**

33.1.1. OE, ON *m* is represented (other than as initial and in inflexional forms) in p.ns. from **bēam, botm, boðm, brōm, Cumbre, hæmed, hamol,** –*helm* (p), **holm, līm, man–drēam,** –*mund* (p), **named, rūm, skammr, þrīm,** *Wœrma* (p):

33.1.2. by ME, ModE *m*.

33.2. ME *m* interchanges with *n*; cf. §§ 30.4.2, 31.3, 32.4.1.

33.3. In spellings for Warmingham **4** 262, *m* after *r* and before [ng̃], [ndʒ], [ntʃ] is replaced by *ch, b* (*Worchingham 1265, Werbincheam late 13*).

33.4. Unhistorical m occurs finally after [l̄], –*holme 1551* Bramhall.

34.1.1. OE, ME *c* [k], ON *k* (also OE *cc*, ON *kk*) are represented (other than as initial, or as second el. in the initial group *sk*) in p.ns. from **āc, bæc, bæc–stān, banke, blæc, bōc**[1]**, brōc, bucc,** *Bucca* (p), **cnocc, draca, duce, hafoc,** *Hucc(a)* (p), **kirkja, krókr, lēac,** *Maccel* (p), **pēac, pearroc, sċrīc, sċucca, slakki, staca, stoc, stocc(en), þæc, þicce,** and in inflexional forms of **dīċ, sīċ, wīċ:**

34.1.2. as ME [k] by various spellings, *c, k, ch, q(u), cc, ck, kc, kk, kh.*

34.1.3. ME, ModE *ch* appears in spellings for Coole, Coppenhall, Chrimes **3** 194, etc.

34.1.4. ME [k] spelt *q* appears in Frodsham St. (Chester).

34.2.1. OE *cw*, ON *kv* and ME –*k* + *w*– are represented by ME *qu, qw, cu, ku*;

34.2.2. by *c* [k], *q* [k] with loss of [w], Queastybirch;

34.2.3. by ME *wh*, ModE *w*, Whabmore **3** 228, Waggonshaw **1** 145, Wobs **3** 148.

34.3. ME –*k(e)s*– pl. or gen. sg. and –*k* + *s*– are sometimes represented by ME, ModE *x*, Croxton, Bexton, Macclesfield, Taxal, cf. § 34.10.

34.4.1. ME [k] when voiced to [g], is represented by ME, ModE *g, gg*, cf. §§ 35.8, 36.6;

34.4.2. by ME, ModE *ng* for *nk*, Bongs **2** 170, Woodbank.

34.4.3. ME [k] assimilates following [g], Kirket **4** 249.

34.5.1. ME [k] > [x] is represented by ME *h, gh, hg* between vowels, before *t, l, h,* and final after *r*, Boughton, Claughton, *Heyrekwyhenegreues* **4** 155 (**5:2** Add.), Leighton, Noctorum, Shocklach.

34.5.2. ModE *gh* *1694* for Higginbotham **1** 266 (**5:1** xxi) may represent [g] for [k].

34.6. ME [k] > [t] is represented by ME, ModE *t*, *d*, final after *r*, *l* (before [z]), *n*, *k*, or dissimilated from preceding *k*, or between vowels, or before *l*, *r*, e.g. Liscard, Drade Low **3** 108.

34.7.1. OE *cn*, ON *kn* is represented by ME *chn*, *cn*, ME, ModE *kn* (Knutsford, Nangreave, Noctorum).

34.7.2. *k* etc. is lost from the spellings in ME, Knowles **1** 150, Gorseyknoll **1** 118, and ModE Knutsford, Nabbs **1** 155, Nangreave.

34.8. Loss of ME [k] occurs: 1. by assimilation to ME, ModE *t*, [v], *g*, *p*; 2. from ME [ks] between vowels and before *t*, *l*, cf. § 34.10.2; 3. from initial ModE [sk] > [ʃ], Shambrooks **4** 328, and ME –*skb*–, Hesby **4** 311.

34.9. Metathesis of *k* occurs in Utkinton, Biskenwood **4** 103.

34.10. Unhistorical [k] appears: 1. in [st] > [kst] spelt *x*, by inversion of § 34.8.2; 2. spelt *q*, between [ks] and [w] in Foxtwist **1** 194 ; spelt *ck*, before [st] and anticipating a following [k]; 3. before *n*, *1847* Mossnook **2** 81, cf. § 34.7.

35.1.1. OE *ċ* is represented in p.ns. from **æċer, bæċe**[1] (**beċe**[1]), **bēċen**[1], **biċċe, birċels, birċen**[1,2], **brēċ, bryċe, ċeacca,** *Ċead*– (p), **ċeap, ċeaster,** **ċęd,* *Ċeofa* (p), *Ċeol*– (p), **ċeorl, ċese,** *Ċidda* (p), **ċiriċe, dīċ, ēċels, hæċ(ċ), hlenċ, hlinċ, læċ(ċ), laferċe, mereċe, miċel,** –*rīċ* (p), **sīċ, styċċe, styċċing, wīċ, winċel:**

35.1.2. by spellings for ME [tʃ] (by assimilation, voiced [dʒ]), [s] and [ʃ] (by AN influence), and [k] (by Scand influence or OE inflexion). Cf. OE *sċ*, § 47;

35.2.1. by OE *c*, Cheaveley; ME *c*, an AN spelling in *DB* forms;

35.2.2. by ME, ModE *ch*; and medial and final ME *cch*, *hch*, ModE *tch*;

35.2.3. by AN *tz*, *z* medial and final;

35.3.1. by spellings for [ʃ]: ME *sc*, *sch*, –*ssh*–, ME, ModE *sh*, ModE –*ss*–, cf. § 47;

35.3.2. by ME *s* [s] final and initial;

35.4. by spellings for [dʒ] < voiced [tʃ]: ME, ModE *dg(e)*, *(g)g(e)*, *gh(e)* final, ME *j* initial;

35.5. by ME *h*(*h*) for [χ] final or before *h*, Birkenhead, *Horeisyhengs* **2** 89, Sandbach, Northwich;

35.6. by spellings for [ks] < [ts] < [tʃ], medial and final: ME, ModE *x*, *cs* (Northwich, *Merexedale* **4** 123, Mickley, Shurlach), *ts* (Bache,

Smellage **4** 216);

35.7. by spellings for ME [k]: 1. ME, ModE *k* initial, usually due to Scand influence, **kirkja/ċiriċe**; 2. medial and final ME *c*, *k*, *kc*, *kk*, *ck*, *ch*, *cc*, due to OE inflexion or Scand influence, **dīċ/dík, sīċ, wīċ**;

35.8. by spellings for ME [k] voiced (§ 35.7), represented by ME and (mostly) ModE *g(g)* (§ 34.4.1), final, intervocalic, or followed by *l*, *g*, *f*, [k], *b*, *t*.

35.9. OE *ċ* is lost before *t* (Churton, Witton).

36.1.1. OE, ON *g* (velar), other than initial, is represented in p.ns from **beorg, boga, burg, carreg,** *clōg–* < **clōh,** *fāg–* < **fāh,** *falg–* < **falh, fugol, furlang, haga, hring, hugol,** –**ing** (cf. § 38), –*ing* (p), *Kolgrimr* (p), **lang,** *lēag–* < **lēah, muga, plaga (pleġa), plōg,** *rūg–* < **rūh, ryding, sċ(e)aga, sċ(e)agiht, skógr, spring, stigu** (originally velar, became palatal, see § 37), **sugu, þing, trōg, wearg; bagga, bugge, cogge, frogga, sugga, tagga.**

36.1.2. OE *g* (velar) initial becomes ME [g] plosive, written *g*.

36.1.3. ME [g] is represented by ModE *gu* initial (Gallows Fd **1** 118) and final (Hague, Tongue **1** 316);

36.1.4. by ModE *gh* initial (Ghorsty Fd **2** 235) and in *ng*, Thingwall;

36.1.5. by ME *gg* in *ng*, *Dunneiggeslond* **3** 5;

36.2. by ME *g* final, intervocalic or before consonants, in p.ns from **hēah, lēah, sċ(e)aga;** Bowdon, Fullhurst, *Mogeleghes* **1** 53, Trafford;

36.3.1. unvoiced to [k], by ME, ModE *c*, *(c)k*;

36.3.2. initial after vowels; next to *l*, *r*, *n*; final after *o*; in *ng* and in p.ns. from –**ing**, spelt ME, ModE *nk*, *nc(h)*, *ngk*, ModE *nck* (with loss of nasal, *Chepfaldefurluc* **2** 65 (**5:2** Add.)).

36.4.1. OE velar *g* becomes ME [x] represented *h*, *hc*, *ch*, *hg*, *gh*: intervocalic; final after vowel in p.ns. from **boga, haga** (cf. § 4.5.2), **sċ(e)aga, trog;** and after *r*, *l*;

36.4.2. before *t*, *f*, *l*;

36.4.3. ME [x] > [þ] represented by ME *th*, *ghth*, *gth* ; [þ] > [f] by ModE *gh*, Wedneshough.

36.5. OE *g* (velar) in palatal contexts is represented by ME *gy* (Corbishley), *ȝ* (*Leȝe* **4** 261) and [j] written *i*, *y* in spellings for *lēag–* < **lēah,** *hēag–* < **hēah, haga, fugol, wearg** + *h*.

36.6. OE, ON *g* (velar) is represented by ME [u,w] spelt ME *u*, *w*, *v*: 1. in p.ns from **boga,** *fāg–* (< **fāh**), **fugol, haga,** *hēge* (< **hēah**), **lágr,**

lēag– (< **lēah**), **mūga, plaga, sċ(e)aga, skógr, sugu, trog**; 2. after *l, r* in ME *lh, rh* > *lg, rg*; **beorg, burh, falh, salh**.

36.7. It is lost in ME p.ns. from **sċ(e)aga**; before ME *f, l, n*; from ME *ng* and in *–ing* p.ns. before *d, t*, and final; from ME *rg* final and before *t, h*; from ModE before *st*.

36.8. ME [g] > [d] is represented by *d*: 1. before ME [k], *l, s* [s], *s* [z] (this [dz] > [ʧ] spelt *tch*); 2. after *n*, spelt ME, ModE *nd, ngd*.

36.9. ME [g] is assimilated to following [g].

36.10. Unhistorical *g* appears after ME, ModE *n*, Beachin **4** 86, Handley, Siddington.

36.11.1. OE, ME *gg* is represented in p.ns. from **bagga, bugge, cogge, frogga, sugga, tagga**:

36.11.2. by ME *g(g)*, *(g)gh*;

36.11.3. by ME *gle*, ME, ModE *c, k, ck*.

37.1.1. OE *ġ* (palatal) other than initial is represented in p.ns. from *Bæġe* (p), **clǣġiht, dryġe, fæġer, flaġe, gaġel, hæġen, heġn, holeġn, hyġel**, *īfeġn*, *–iġn /–eġn* suffix formations, **mæġden, myrġe, ryġe**, *–sīġe* (p), **slæġet, stæġer, wiðeġn, worðiġn; stiġel, stiġu** (originally velar, palatalized in ME); **byr(i)ġ (burh), cæġ, clæġ, græġ, ēġ, (ġe)hæġ, hēġ**, *–iġ* suffix formations, **stiġ, weġ**, *Wīġ–* (p), *–wīġ* (p), **worðiġ**.

37.1.2. ME *g* [g] appears before *a, u* in p.ns. from **ġeat, ġeard**, due to pl. **gatu** and influence of Scand **gata, garðr**.

37.2.1. OE *ġ* is represented by ME *ge, i, j, h, yh, hy, y, Ꝫ* initial; and *y, i, g, gh, (c)h, –w–, –uu–*;

37.2.2. OE *–yġ–* by ME *y, uy, ui, oi*, ModE *oy*.

37.3. ME, ModE [j] is lost when final in first el. before *h, l, p, st, t* in cpds.; when intervocalic; before *n* in *–iġn, –eġn*.

38.1. Assibilation of OE *ġ* in OE *–ing* in final position is represented by spellings of Billinge **1** 138, **2** 198, **3** 194, 298, *Cristynch, Cruftinge, Cruftenche* **4** 110, 152, 162, Collinge **4** 173, Cutting **4** 42, Damage **3** 110, **4** 76, 178, 194, 197, Demmage **4** 176, *Dunneiggeslond* **3** 5, Dunsdale **3** 230, Gollinge 3 105, Kingsley, Lockinch 3 294, Riddings **3** 81, *Salingecroft* **3** 5, Sprinch **2** 179, Springe **1** 110, 147, 159, **3** 125, 136, 195 etc., Traffinch **3** 63, Wallange **2** 212, *Wyringe* **1** 54.

38.2. Assibilation in *–ing–* in medial position, as final part of first el. before second el. in *h–* (**hām, hyll, (ġe)hæġ**), is represented by spellings of Altrincham, *Babrinchull*, Benchill, *Codingeye* **4** 85, Dane in Shaw,

Iddinshall, Kermincham, Tushingham, Warmingham, Wincham.

38.3. Unhistorical reflexes of assibilated *ng* are represented in spellings for *Caryngfeld* **4** 147 (**5:1** xxiii), Orrishmere, Minshull **3** 154; Nogginshaw **3** 294; Alsager **3** 2; cf. § 47.4.

　　39.1.1. OE *cg* is represented in p.ns. from **brycg, docga (dogga), dyncge, ecg,** *Ecg–* (p), **hecg, hencg, hocg (hogg), hrycg, mycg,** *Wicga* (p):

39.1.2. by ME (*g*)*gh*, *gg*, ME, ModE *dg*, for [ʤ];

39.2. by ME, ModE *ch*, ModE *tch*, *sh*, for [ʧ].

39.3.1. Final and intervocalic *cg* is represented by ME, ModE *g*, [g] or [dg];

39.3.2. by ME *g* [g] and ModE *gh*, before *l*, *m*;

39.3.3. by ME *k* (cf. § 36.3) and ME, ModE *d* (cf. § 44.4), before *l*.

　　40. For the evolution of OE *–ing*: see §§ 10; 32.3.4; 32.6.1; 36.3.2; 36.7 and discussion § 38 and Ch **2** 8, **3** 142-3; for unhistorical *–ing*, see §§ 36.10, 38.3.

　　41.1.1. OE *h*, other than initial, occurs in p.ns. from **clōh, crōh, hēah, hōh, lēah, rūh, wōh**;

41.1.2. and in the groups *–hh–*, *–lh*, *–rh*, *–ht*, occurs in p.ns. from **pohha,** *Pohha* (p); **falh, halh, holh, salh,** *Walh–* (p); **burh, furh; cniht, feoht, leoht, niht, wiht,** *Wiht* (p), **sċeagiht.**

41.2.1. OE *h* initial before vowels is usually represented by ME *h*;

41.2.2. occasionally attracts prosthetic [w] or [j], see § 54; ME [hj] > [ʃ] written *sh*, Sheeping Stead **1** 189.

41.3.1. OE *h* is lost in ME initial before vowels, and initial of second el., and intervocalic;

41.3.2. from *hl, hn, hr, hw,* from *lh* before *b, t; hh* is simplified.

41.4. OE *hw*, ON *hv*, is represented by ME (AN) *ho*, ME *wh, qu, qw, cw*, ME (AN) *g*.

41.5. OE *–hh–*, in Pownall, is represented by ME *h, k; u, w*. OE *–h–h–* by ME *–c–h–* in *Hechavedland* **4** 38 (**5:2** Add.).

41.6. OE *–ht* is represented by ME (AN) *st, zt, x(s)t*; ME *ht, hc(t), c(h)(t); gt(h), ght*; ModE *x* (*Fexulfildes* **1** 74).

41.7. OE *lh, rh*, in which a glide vowel spelt *e, u* sometimes intervenes, is represented by ME *lh, lg(h), lc(h), lg, lx(h), lx(g)(h), lth, lph, lff, lw, l(e)wh* (Campbell §§ 412, 447, 574 (2) note 2), and *rh, rgh, rch, rth*.

41.8. OE *h* final after a vowel is represented by ME *g(h)*, *ch(g)*, *hc*, *xh*; *k*, *c*; *(g)th*, *ght*.

41.9. Unhistorical *h*, for aspiration or hiatus, appears 1. initial before vowels; 2. after initial *r*, cf. § 30.2.1.

42.1. OE, ME, ModE [x] in various spellings figures in §§ 20.2.1; 34.5.1; 35.5; 41.

42.2.1. *Edlagheston* *1288* (Edleston **3** 140) for OE *Ecglafes*– has *gh* for [w] < [v] by inverse analogy with the change [g] > [w], see §§ 29.4; 36.6; 51.1.2.

42.2.2. ModE spelling *gh* for [f] appears *late 16.*

42.3. ME [x] interchanges with ME [þ], and is replaced by ModE [k], ME, ModE [w], ModE [ʃ].

42.4. [x–l] > [kî] > [tî] is suggested by *Pyghall* **4** 175, *Rypuhhul* **1** 92, antecedents of ModE *pightle*, *pichel* [paitî, paikî].

43.1.1. OE, ON *t* is represented (other than as initial, or as second el. in initial consonant group *st*–) in spellings of p.ns. from *Bōt* (p), **cot**, **cristel**, **croft**, **ēast**, **feoht**, **flint**, **gorst(iġ)**, **hægtesse**, **heort**, **holt**, **hors**, **hyrst**, **lytel**, **mōt**, **port**, **preost**, **sċēat**, **sċēot**, –*stān* (p), –*steinn* (p), **steort**, **þistel**, **toft**, **twisla**, **wiste**:

43.1.2. by ME, ModE *t* usually;

43.1.3. sometimes by ME *th*;

43.2. by ME, ModE *d*; whence [r] between vowels (cf. § 44.3) (Bostock), before *b* (Mobberley) and *l* (Walkerley **3** 132);

43.3. by other voiceless stops, written ME *p*, *k*, *ck*.

43.4. OE *t* in *ht* and *nt* intervocalic > ModE [ks] written *x*, ME, ModE [ns], see Betchton, *Fexulfildes* **1** 74, Torkington.

43.5. OE *t* is lost: 1. before ME *b*, [k], *d*, *s*, *t*; 2. from ME, ModE *lt* in consonant groups; 3. after ModE [g], [k], ME and ModE [r], ModE [ʃ]; 4. from *st* in various positions (Snelson, Austerson, etc.) whether intervocalic or in consonant groups; 5. by confusion with def. art., Rocklost **1** 157.

43.6.1. Unhistorical *t* appears after ME *þ*, *h* [x], ME, ModE *f* [f], ModE [ʃ], *s*, *x*, *p*;

43.6.2. also by metanalysis or aphesis, in names with *saint*, St Olave's (Chester), St Edith's (Shocklach), and in **atte** p.ns.

44.1.1. OE, ON, ME *d* is represented (other than as initial) in p.ns. from *Ade*– (p), **ald**, *Ald*– (p), –*ande* pres. part., *Beadda* (p), *Beadu*– (p),

bold, bóndi, brād, bred, brende, cald, clūd, *Ēad–* (p), *–ede* pa. part.
adj., edisċ, feld, *–flǣd* (p), ford, *Frōd–* (p), ġeard, golde, hǣmed,
hēafod, heard, helde, hīd, hyrdel, (ġe)lād, lind, mǣd, merled(e),
–mund (p), sand, sīde, slæd, *Tīd–* (p), tyddrung, *–wald* (p), wind,
wudu:

44.1.2. by ME, ModE *d* usually;

44.2.1. by ME, ModE [t] written *t*, *th*, due to unvoicing (Altrincham,
Nantwich, Thornset, Turngate) or to assimilation to *t* (Clutton,
Peckforton);

44.2.2. by ME, ModE [ð, þ] written *th*, *tth*, *dh*, cf. p.ns. from **ford**, **geard**
(Handforth), and between vowels and semi–vowels (*Aldemethwe* **4** 107
(**5:2** Add.), Tytherington **1** 214 (**5:1** xx));

44.3. by ME *r* (cf. § 43.2), Bostock, Doddington, etc;

44.4. by ME *g* before *l*, *r*, *n*, *b*, [z] due to substitution of palatal for
dental stop, Mag Brook, Tagsclough; or to assimilation, Leggate.

44.5. ME [dj] > ModE [ʤ, ʧ], Marljurr **1** 211, see discussion of
Blackeyers **1** 265 (**5:1** xxi).

44.6. OE, ME *dl* is metathesised, Middlewich, Tilstone, Worleston.

44.7. OE, ME *d* is lost from consonant groups, before or after *b*, [k], *g*,
l, *n*, *r*, *m*, *s*, [z]; after *n*, loss of [d] from [nd] leaves the grapheme /nd/
with value [n], whereupon [nd] is written *nd–d*, Sandyford **3** 211.

44.8. Unhistorical *d* is introduced next to *l*, *r*, *n*, *m*, *b*, *s*, [ʃ].

45.1.1. OE, ON *ð*, *þ*, interchangeable symbols for [þ, ð] are
represented, other than as initial, in p.ns. from *Æðel–* (p), bōth, boðl,
boðm, brandreth, eorðe, *–frith* (p), hǣð, heorð, hlið, mearð, neoðera,
norð, *–rith* (p), sēað, skeiði, smēðe, stæð, sūð, *–þrȳþ* (p), waroð,
wīðeġn, worð, worðiġ(n):

45.1.2. by ME, ModE *þ*, *th*;

45.1.3. by ME final [þ] spelt *t*, *tht*; medial and final [ð] spelt *dth*, *dh*;

45.1.4. by ME *t*, *d*, *td*, *dt*, *dth*;

45.2.1. by ME [χ] spelt *ch*, *gh*, *h*;

45.2.2. by ME [f] written ME *f*, *ph*, *u*, *v*;

45.2.3. by ME *z* by AN influence, Rudheath;

45.2.4. by ME, ModE [w] spelt *u*, *w*, and [ĩ] written *l*(*l*) intervocalic or
before *l*, *f*, Halton, Rostherne, Bowfields.

45.3. OE, ME [ð, þ] are lost when final, Antrobus, Halton, Smeaton; and
from *rð*.

45.4. Unhistorical [þ] spelt *th* stands for [x], Ashley (*Ahselegth*) **2** 10, Baguley.

46.1.1. OE, ON *s* is represented, other than as initial, in p.ns. from **bōsig, hæsel, hrīs, hūs, inis, kjóss, lǣs, lūs, meosuc, ōsle, ros, twisla, wiste**:

46.1.2. by ME, ModE *s* for [s, z];

46.2.1. by ME *sc, sc(h)* for [s] as reflex of OE *sċ* > ME *s*;

46.2.2. by ME, ModE *c* [s], *ss*;

46.2.3. by ME *x* final, *Glasshowse, Glassehoux* **3** 244, Poole Hall **4** 192; and for *s* in *st* (this also by *sh* [ʃ]);

46.2.4. by ME, ModE *sh, ch, tch* for [ʃ, ʧ].

46.2.5. OE, ME, ModE [s] > [z] usually written *z, tz, zz*; [ʤ] written *dg, ge*, Bridgemere, Edgeley.

46.3. *s* is metathesised in *rs, ms, sk, st*.

46.4. *s* is lost from *st* initial: before [f, g, ʤ]; after [ʧ,d]; by assimilation.

46.5. Unhistorical *s* is introduced initial in ME before *t, d, th*.

47.1. OE *sċ* initial is usually represented by ME *sch–, sh–, ssh–*, but also by *ch–, s–*, and under Scand influence, by *sk–*.

47.2.1. OE *sċ*, other than initial, is represented in spellings for p.ns. from **æsċ(–), busċ, (ġe)bysċe, edisċ, mersċ, risċ(–), tonge–s(ċ)harp, Welisċ**:

47.2.2. by ME *sh, sc(h), ss(c)(h)* for [ʃ]; *(t)ch, hc*; *s, z*; also *sk, sc* [sk], *x, (c)hs*, through Scand influence and metathesis, see § 48;

47.3. in *–nsċ–* by ME *gh* ([ʤ] or [ʃ]), Church Minshull; when initial of second el. after *–n*, and when final after vowel, by ModE *g* [ʤ], Nogginshaw **3** 294, Oat Eddage **3** 71;

47.4. when initial of second el. after *–ng–* [ng] or [ŋ], by *ȝ* ?[z]: *Tunkezarppelond* **3** 158-9 (**5:1** xxxvi).

47.5. ME [ʃ] initial of second el. after [k] in p.ns. from **hafoc–sċerde** becomes [–ksj–], [sj], represented *–sy–, Haukeserd* **4** 11, *Haukesyerd* **1** 276; and after [t] in p.ns. from **sċeaga**, becomes [tj] spelt *ti*, [sj] spelt *ci, Stocia* **2** viii, 263.

47.6. Unhistorical eModE [ʃ] for [x] in [lx] is spelt *gh, sh*, Walgherton.

48.1. ME *sk* [sk] from ON *sk* or OE *sċ* under Scand influence, is usually represented by ME, ModE *sk, sc(h), schk*;

48.2. by *st*, Taxmere **2** 271;

48.3. by ME *sh, ch*, ModE *sh* for [sx], [ʃ], [(s)x], Scholar Green, Shambrookes **4** 328, Wedneshough, and in p.ns. from **flask, flasshe**.

48.4. Only in *Skippon Crofts 1573* (**3** 154) does *sk*– for [ʃ–] appear.

49.1.1. OE, ON *p*, other than initial, is represented in p.ns. from capel, ċēap(–), clympre, grōpe, hēopa, hlēp, lopt, mapel, maplen, sċēap, stapol, timper:

49.1.2. by ME *p*, *ph*(*p*);

49.2.1. by ME *b*, ME, ModE [f], [v].

49.3. It is lost by assimilation next to *b*, *m*, Shipbrook, *Chapmonswiche*.

49.4. Epenthetic *p* appears after *m*, Hampton, Nantwich.

49.5. ME *p* initial in second el. after *x* becomes [b], Flax Boughs **4** 49 (**5**:2 Add.).

50.1.1. OE *b*, other than initial, is represented in p.ns. from *Bebba* (p), **brembel, crumb, cumb, cumber, Cumbre, hobbe, lamb, timber:**

50.1.2. by ME *b* usually;

50.1.3. also by ME *v*, *f*.

50.2. ME *b* from the group *mb* is lost from pronunciation, sometimes from spelling.

50.3. Epenthetic *b* appears after *m*, *le Crymbe* **2** 171, Lumbhole, Plumley, Wilmslow.

51.1.1. OE *f* for [f] and [v] is represented, in positions other than as initial, in spellings for p.ns. from *Ælf*– (p), *Bēofa* (p), **calf**, *Ċeofa* (p), **clǣfre, clif, cnafa, cofa, croft,** (ġe)**delf, efes, efesung, fīf,** –*flǣd* (p), –*ġifu* (p), **grǣfe, hafoc, half–pening, hēafod, hlǣfdiġe, hræfn,** –*lāf*(p), *Leof*– (p), **ofer,** *Pofa* (p), **sċylfe, stæf, tēafor,** –*ulf*(p), **weorf,** *Wulf*– (p), –*wulf*(p):

51.1.2. by ME *f*, *ff*, *ph*; *th*; *v*, *u*, *fv*; *b*, *p*; *w*; *gh* [χ], *h*, *g*.

51.2. OE, ME [f,v] is omitted before certain consonants; between vowels; from the groups *lf*, *rf*, *nf*.

D. PHONETIC PROCESSES

52. Assimilation / dissimilation of consonants affects the sequences *l–n–r*, *n–m*, *g–k*, *t–d*–[ð]–[þ], *p–b*.

53. Voicing / unvoicing of consonants affects *d–t*; *f–v*; *k–g*; [tʃ]–[dʒ]; [ð]–[þ]; *s–z*; *p–b*. See §§ 35; 45.

54. Prosthetic [j] and [w] (cf. §§ 29.5; 41.2.2), usually written ME, ModE *y*, *yh*, *ʒ*, *g*; *w*, *u*; appear in forms of p.ns. from **āc, alor, ān, āte,**

ēa, ēan, earn, ēast, ecg, ēġ, ende, eofer, eorl, eorðe, eowe, erðing, hæðiġ, hafoc–sċerde, hār, hēafod, hēah, helde, hende, hēopen, hilder, holm (ModE [hju:m]), hyrde, hyrdels, hyrne, impa, īw, orċeard.

55. THE VOWEL IN UNSTRESSED SYLLABLES

55.1. In final position, this is represented in ME by –e universally:

55.1.1. in ModE as –ey;

55.1.2. by –er;

55.1.3. by –a;

55.1.4. by –ow.

55.2. In medial position (compare the forms of the inflexions –as, –es, –an, –um in §§ 57.9, 57.10, 57.5, 57.6, 57.12 infra; and on ME –i, –y in unstressed medial syllable see 3 143 s.n. Botterley), it is represented as follows:

55.2.1. ordinarily by ME, ModE –e–, the commonplace form, before t, d, s, m, n, r, l, [k];

55.2.2. by –er– (Wimboldsley 2 257, Sheepers 1 301;

55.2.3. by i/y before t, d, s, n, r, l, [k];

55.2.4. by u before p, b, s, m, n, r, l, [k] or [ks];

55.2.5. by o before m, n, r, l, [k] or [ks]; by –ou– before s or m;

55.2.6. by a before t, s, m, n, r, l, [k], [ks].

55.3. The OE ġe prefix is represented by ME, ModE i, y; *13*: *Stanilode* 1 40 from –(ġe)lād; *14*: *Eliuereslach* 2 201 from *ēl–ġefær, *Londymere* 4 266 from land–ġemǣre, *Stanidelf* 3 228 from –(ġe)delf; *15*: *Maryheye* 1 58 from –(ġe)hæġ; *19*: Broady Way 2 231 from –(ġe)hæġ, Watry Shead 1 71 from *wæter–(ġe)sċēad.

56. A GLIDE VOWEL is represented in Ch p.n. spellings as follows:

56.1. before a consonant following d, t, ð; r, l, m, n; s, [ʃ]; [f], [v], b, p; g, [k], [ks]; w;

56.2.1. before d after l, n, f [v], k; before t after n, [ʃ], [v]; before ð after r, l;

56.2.2. before r after d, t, ð, l, [ʃ], [v], b, g, [k], w; before l after d, t, ð, r, m, n, s, [v], b, g, [k], [ks]; before m after t, ð, l, s, [ʃ], p, [k]; before n after t, r, s, [v], [k];

56.2.3. before s, st, after l, n, [k]; before [ʃ] after r;

56.2.4. before [f] after l; before [v]; before b after r, l, s; before p after r;

56.2.5. before *ġ* after *r*; before [k] after *l*, *n*, *s*, *p*; before *ċ* after *r*; before [χ], *h* after *r*, *l*;

56.2.6. before *w* after *d*, *t*, *r*, *l*, *s*.

56.3.1. The glide vowel is represented as *u* before *r*, *l*, *m*, *n*, *h*, *w*:

56.3.2. before *r* after *d*, [k];

56.3.3. before *l* after *d*, *r*, *s*, *g*;

56.3.4. before *m* after *ð*, *r*, *l*, *s*, *k*: including p.ns. in **boðm, byðme**;

56.3.5. before *n* after *r*;

56.3.6. before *h* [χ] after *r*, *l*;

56.3.7. before *w* after *d*, *t*, *r*.

56.4.1. The glide vowel is represented as *o* before *ð*, *m*, *n*, *w*:

56.4.2. before *ð* after *r*;

56.4.3. before *m* after *t*, *ð*, *l*, *s*, [k]: including p.ns. in **boðm, botm, byðme**;

56.4.4. before *n* after *ð*, *r*: including p.ns. in **fearn(–), hyrne(–)**;

56.4.5. before *w* after *d*, *r*, *l*, *s*: including p.ns. in **mǣd (mǣdwe); bearu (bearwe); falh (falw–), holh (holwe–); lǣs (lǣswe–)**.

56.5.1. The glide vowel is represented as *a* before *r*, *l*, *m*, *n*, [k]:

56.5.2. before *r* after *w*;

56.5.3. before *l*, after *d*, *t*;

56.5.4. before *m*, after *ð*, *s*: including p.ns. in **boðm, byðme**;

56.5.5. before *n*, after *ð*, *r*;

56.5.6. before [k], after *n*.

56.6.1. The glide vowel is represented as *e* before *d*, *t*, *ð*, *r*, *l*, *m*, *n*, *s*, [ʃ], *b*, [k], *h*, *w*:

56.6.2. before *d* after *l*, *n*, [v], *k*;

56.6.3. before *t* after [ʃ], [f];

56.6.4. before *ð* after *r*;

56.6.5. before *r* after *d*, *t*, *ð*, *l*, [ʃ], [f] or [v], [k]; including p.ns. in **alren, elren**;

56.6.6. before *l* after *d*, *ð*, *r*, *m*, *n*, *s*, *f*, [v], *b*, *g*, *k*, [ks];

56.6.7. before *m*, after *ð*, *l*, *s*, [ʃ], *p*, *k*: including p.ns. in **boðm**;

56.6.8. before *n*, after *r*, *s*, [v], [k]: including p.ns. in **þorn, fearn, hyrne; hræfn,** *Hræfn*;

56.6.9. before *s*, after *l*, [k];

56.6.10. before [ʃ], after *r*;

56.6.11. before *b*, after *r*, *l*, *s*;

56.6.12. before [k], after *s*, *p*;

56.6.13. before *h*, [χ], after *l*;

56.6.14. before *w*, after *d*, *t*, *r*, *l*, *s*: including p.ns. in **mǣd (mǣdwe)**; **bearu (bearwe)**.

56.7.1. The glide vowel is represented by *i/y*, before *r*, *l*, *m*, *n*, *p*, *f*, [k], [tʃ], h [χ]:

56.7.2. before *r*, after *d*, [sk];

56.7.3. before *l*, after *d*, *t*, *s*;

56.7.4. before *m*, after *ð*, *p*, [k]: including p.ns. in **boðm**;

56.7.5. before *n*, after *t*, *r*: including p.ns. in **þorn**, **fearn**, **hyrne**;

56.7.6. before *p*, after *r*;

56.7.7. before *f*, after *l*;

56.7.8. before [k], after *l*;

56.7.9. before [ts], after *r*;

56.7.10. before *h* [χ], after *l*: including p.ns. in **halh**, **salh**.

E. GRAMMATICAL NOTES

57. Examples, in date order, are grouped under a century or '*DB*' code.

57.1. The representation of OE and ME inflexion in Ch p.n. spellings is affected by the development of the vowel in the unstressed syllable (cf. § 55).

57.2. Concord between sb. and adj. in gen. sg. *–es* appears in *Bradewey . . . Bradesweys nether ende c.1200*, **4** 115.

57.3. The standard ME inflexion of sb. and adj. as first el. of cpd. p.ns, is *–e–* which represents:

57.3.1. sb. and pers.n. OE *–an* > ME *–(e)n* gen.sg. (*DB*: Bostock **2** 202, Budworth **3** 184, **2** 107, Byley **2** 233, Cheaveley **4** 118, Coppenhall **3** 22, Shocklach **4** 63, Tabley **2** 60, Wrenbury **3** 119; *12*: Hankelow **3** 89; *13*: Bosden **1** 256, Checkley **3** 56, Swettenham **2** 283, Tattenhall **4** 97, Tittenley **3** 90, etc.);

57.3.2. adj. OE *–an* > ME *–e(n)* dat. sg. (*DB*: Newton **4** 145, Romiley **1** 292; *12*: Aldford **4** 77, Bradford **2** 210, Eastham **4** 187 (**5:1** xlii), Fowle Brook **1** 25, *Grenelache* **1** 171; *Horston Feld* **2** 54, *Sothebroc* **2** 51, Whitby **4** 198; *13*: Bradford **1** 95, Bradley's **1** 100, *Fodon* **2** 86, Harebarrow **1** 101, Holdings **2** 199, Newhall **3** 101, etc.);

57.3.3. other inflexions such as OE *–e*, *–a*, gen. sg. and pl.

57.4.1. The *–e–* of § 57.3 is associated with variants, in unstressed position:

57.4.2. ME *–a–*, sb., gen. pl., for OE *–a* (*DB*: Acton **3** 126; *17*: Pickmere **2** 120), OE *–e* (*13*: Dunham **2** 19), OE *–an* (*14*: Baguley **2** 12);

57.4.3. ME *–u–*, sb., gen. sg., for OE *–an* (*13*: Baguley **2** 12; *15*: Checkley **3** 56; *16*: Baddiley **3** 124);

57.4.4. ME *–o–*, adj., nom.? (Caldecott **4** 62);

57.4.5. ME *–i–*, *–y–*, sb., gen. (see discussion at Botterley **3** 142-3) (*12*: Baguley **2** 12, Calveley **3** 307; *13*: Baddiley **3** 124, Bulkeley **4** 17, Checkley **3** 56, Crossley **2** 290, Gatley **1** 244, Hadley **3** 106, Henshaw **1** 84, Matley **1** 312, Spurstow **3** 315, Tabley **2** 60; *14*: Audlem **3** 82, Bickley **4** 6, *Bothileghe* **3** 25, *Buddeley* **2** 60, Butley **1** 193, Dodcott **3** 92, Gatley **1** 97, Godley **1** 306, Midgley **1** 167, Reddyshaw **1** 233, Ridley **3** 313, Shocklach **4** 63, *Woluelegh'* **2** 117, *Wolvylegh* **2** 106); adj., dat. (*13*: Bradley's **1** 100, Romiley **1** 292; *14*: Bradley **3** 228, Brindley **3** 133; *15*: *Holybroke* **1** 29; *17*: Cadiell **4** 24; *19*: Cordiwell **4** 55).

57.5.1. OE *–an–*, gen. sg. inflexion of pers.n. or sb. as first el. in cpd. p.ns.:

57.5.2. appears as *–(e)n–* (*DB*: *Caluintone* **4** 2, Grappenhall **2** 140, Tattenhall **4** 97, *Tunendune* **2** 1; *12*: Catten Hall **3** 240, Pownall **1** 229, Runcorn **2** 176, Swettenham **2** 283; *13*: Bosden **1** 256, Capenhurst **4** 200, Coppenhall **3** 22, Ebnal **4** 40, Hankelow **3** 89, Hockenhull **3** 274, *Pylatenhale* **4** 43, *Stopinhul* **1** 159, Tittenley **3** 90, Wornish **1** 64; *14*: Carrington **2** 17 (**4** ix, xiv), *Copenhaleeuese* **3** 247, Drakelow **2** 198, Ox(*e*)*furth* **1** 137, Tidnock **1** 68, Yieldnow **2** 36 (**5:1** xxiii); *15*: Haveleyhey **1** 241);

57.5.3. appears as *–e(n)–* (*DB*: Butley **1** 193, Cheaveley **4** 118, Coppenhall **3** 22, Moulton **2** 207, Shocklach **4** 63, Wrenbury **3** 119; *12*: Hankelow **3** 89; *13*: Bosden **1** 256, Checkley **3** 56, Swettenham **2** 283, Tattenhall **4** 97, Tittenley **3** 90; *14*: Chadkirk **1** 292, Drakelow **2** 198, Haveleyhay **1** 241, Hockenhull **3** 274, Ox(*e*)*furth* **1** 137);

57.5.4. is lost through dissimilation (Cadding **1** 323).

57.6.1. OE *–an–*, dat. sg. inflexion of adj. as first el. in cpd. p.ns. is represented by:

57.6.2. *–an–* (*13*: *Sartandal* **2** 101);

57.6.3. *–en–* (*DB*: Blakenhall **3** 51, Handley **4** 90, Malpas **4** 38, Newton by Chester **4** 145, Siddington, **1** 84, Wettenhall **3** 166; *11*: Blacon **4** 168; *12*: Oulton **3** 185, Radnor **2** 318, Swettenham **2** 283; *13*: *Blakenhallbroc* **2** 163, *Bradenaker* **3** 82, *Hendenethebothum* **1** 287, Holdings **2** 199, Saltney **5:1** 58, *Siddall* **4** 97, Sunderland Hay **4** 331, *Syddenale* **2** 229, Sydney **3** 24, *Wetenhay* **2** 264; *14*: Blakeney **4** 32, *Bradenhale* **3** 176, *Fodon* **2** 86, *Holenden* **4** 70, *Longenhale* **3** 177, Sidney **3** 255, *Sydenalwro* **2** 109; *16*: *Bradnok* **1** 52; *17*: Widenor **2** 273; *18*: Newhall **3** 101; *19*: Blakeney **3** 11, Whittnall **3** 22, Widney **2** 225);

57.6.4. *–e(n)–* (*DB*: Newton **4** 145, Romiley **1** 292; *13*: Bradford **1** 95, Bradley's **1** 100, *Fodon* **2** 86, Harebarrow **1** 101, Holdings **2** 199, Newhall **3** 101).

57.7. Unhistorical ME *–en*, nom. pl., appears in p.n. spellings for: *14*: Chester **5:1** 5; *16*: Woodhouse **3** 230.

57.8.1. OE *–ena–*, sb., gen. pl. of first el. in cpd. p.ns. is represented by:

57.8.2. ME *–en(e)–* (*DB*: Cranage **2** 223); ME *–in(e)–* (*12*: *Holcineden* **2** 280; *13*: Dukinfield? **1** 276, *Knavenebrec* **4** 271, Nangreave **1** 297; *14*: *Knauenegreuehul* **4** 90); *–ing–* (Cadding– **1** 323).

57.8.3. Unhistorical ME *–en(e)–*, *–an–*, for 57.8.1, appears in some spellings for *13*: Grappenhall **2** 140, *Threlowenhet* **2** 323, Tittenley **3** 90; *14*: Preston **2** 156; *16*: Childer Thornton **4** 196.

57.9.1. OE *–as* sb., nom. pl., in final position is represented:

57.9.2. generally, by ME, ModE *–(e)s* ([s], [z]);

57.9.3. this [s] is occasionally written ModE *–ce* (*17*: Staneyland **1** 231, *Rylance* **1** 230; *19*: Filance **2** 109);

57.9.4. the [z] is occasionally represented by ME, ModE *–(e)z* (*14*: *Ackerez* **2** 23, *Downes* **1** 148, *Heppales* **1** 299, *Hersichecliffz* **3** 5, *Heyez* **2** 94; *15*: *Butter Shops* and *Darke Row* (Chester) **5:1** 23, Knutsford Booths **2** 76, *Lakez* **2** 179, Withins **3** 227; *16*: Leese **2** 229, Lymm Booths **2** 37, *Newfoxholez* **1** 71, Seven Oaks **2** 133, Two Fords **3** 195, *Walmez* **2** 194).

57.9.5. ME *–as* in *1488 Brocholas* **2** 155 probably represents *–us* rather than an OE survival.

57.9.6.1. ME *–es* nom. pl. (< OE *–as*) alternates with ME *–is*, *–ys* (*13*: Birtles **1** 72, **4** 22, Burley **2** 98, Cotton **4** 111, Danes Moss **1** 67, *Halis* **3** 50, *Heyeloundis* **1** 66, *Rylance* **1** 230, Somerford Booths **1** 63, Stublach **2** 255; *15*: Knutsford Booths **2** 76, *Langwallys* **3** 177; *16*: Birches **2** 185, Greaves **4** 44);

57.9.6.2. and with ME *–us* (*13*: Blake Low **1** 82, *Bruchus* **4** 69; *14*: Birtles
1 72, Cinder Hill **2** 310, Clays **3** 319, *Colhuppus* **3** 193, *The Crofts* **5:1**
40, *Downes* **1** 148, *Flaskus* **4** 168, *Foxecotes* **4** 38, *Harewodehacrus* **2**
319, *Hokes* **2** 315, *Knolles* **4** 43, Knutsford Booths **2** 76, Lymm Booths
2 37, *Plumlegh Plankus* **2** 94, Riddings **3** 81, Somerford Booths **1** 63,
Spittle Croft **3** 226, Stublach **2** 255, *Wallebuttus* **3** 67, Whatcroft **2** 41; *15*:
Burghess **2** 110, *Colletfyldus* **4** 37; *16*: Souche **3** 294).

56.9.7. Unhistorical ME *–es* sb., nom. pl., appears in spellings for p.ns.
(*13-14*) in **cot** and **stoc** and in Toft **2** 81. The inflexion of OE *cot*, pl. *cotu*,
in the spellings for Cotton **4** 111 is *chota* *1100* (< *cotu* nom. pl.); *cotun*,
coten *13* (< *cotum* dat. pl.); *cotes* *c.1200* (new ME nom. pl.); that of OE
stoc, pl. *stocu*, in Stoke **4** 181: *stok* *13* (< *stoc* nom.sg.); *stoke* *1260* (< *stocu*
nom. pl. or *stoce* dat. sg.); *stokes* *1284* (new ME nom. pl., as if *stoke* were
felt to represent *stocu* rather than *stoce*).

57.10.1. OE *–es* sb., gen. sg., is represented in Ch p.n. spellings:

57.10.2. usually by ME, ModE *–(e)s–* ([s], [z]);

57.10.3.1. as the inflexion of the first el. in cpd. p.ns. this alternates with:

57.10.3.2. ME *–is–*, *–ys–* (*DB*: Wincham **2** 136; *12*: Barnston **4** 263,
Greasby **4** 291, *Louingishey* **2** 280, Plemstall **4** 135, Thurstaston **4** 279,
Wirswall **3** 112, Wistaston **3** 45; *13*: Bidston **4** 308, Hapsford **3** 257,
Helsby **3** 235, Hurleston **3** 146, Huxley **4** 101, Minshull **3** 154, Worleston
3 151, etc.; *lo* *16*: *Harpisforth* **2** 42, *Magdalenis* **2** 157));

57.10.3.3. ME *–us–* (*12*: Plemstall **4** 135; *13*: Aldersey **4** 82, *Byrusbrok* **3**
158, Cogshall **2** 109, Fullhurst **3** 122, Hapsford **3** 257, Knutsford **2** 73,
Minshull **3** 154, Occlestone **2** 252, Shrewbridge **3** 131, etc.; *lo* *16*:
Hawkesyord **1** 166);

57.10.3.4. eModE *–os–* (*16*: Rostherne **2** 56);

57.10.3.5. ME *–as–* (*13*: *Seurydas Alfland* **4** 335, Worleston **3** 151 (**4** xi);
14: Alsager **3** 2, Rostherne **2** 56; *16*: Cholmondeston **3** 136; *17*:
Wimboldesley **2** 257).

57.10.4. Unhistorical ME *–es*, *–is*, etc., ModE *'s*, gen.sg., appears in final
position and, in cpd. p.ns., as inflexion of first el. which in some instances
(†) is an OE or ME fem. pers.n. (*DB*: Tittenley **3** 90; *12*: Budworth **2** 107;
13: *Chapmonswiche* **2** 86, †*Gunnyldiscrofte* **2** 166, †*Leuildeslewe* **4** 12,
†*Livildesforde* **2** 192, Marbury **2** 117, *Negtmereslond* **4** 70, †*Seurydas
Alfland* **4** 335; *14*: *Bradefordeswey* **2** 201, *Brodemoreshefd* **1** 75,
†*Denyldescroft* **2** 315, Hunger Hill **3** 321, *Knauenes Greue Hul* **4** 90,

Lady Hey **2** 200, †*Luysotesrudyng* **1** 137, Marl Fd **1** 87; *15*: Ringway **2** 28; *16*: *Roolegheslawne* **1** 88; *19*: Ladys Hey **4** 103, Leonard's **2** 119, Tagsclough **1** 162).

57.10.5. The second syllable of **eglēs**, in the p.n. Eccleston **4** 151, develops like a gen.sg. *–es*.

57.10.6. The unusual *–es* gen.sg. of OE *bōc* (fem., Campbell §§ 624-5) appears in *DB* Boughton **4** 123.

57.11. OE *–er*, *–or* sb., nom. and gen. sg., *–ru* sb., nom. pl., *–ra* sb., gen.pl., in cpd. p.ns with first els. such as **calf, ċild, hǣt, hūder, lamb,** are represented by ME *–er–*, *–ir–*, *–re–*.

57.12.1. OE *–um*, sb., dat. pl., is represented by ME *–um* (*12-14*), *–om* (*13-16*), *–am* (*13-19*), *–em* (*15*), *–im* (*13*), *–m* (*14-19*), in *Bothim* **2** 71, Cotton **2** 280, Hallamhall **2** 154, *Hallom* **2** 186, *Hulum* **3** 322, Lathamhall **2** 29, Mottram **1** 202, 313, Parme **2** 251, Statham **2** 38, Stockham **2** 179;

57.12.2. by ME *–un* (*13-14*), *–on* (*13-16*), *–an* (*15*), *–en* (*13*) in *Bacun* **3** 158, Cotton **2** 280, Mottram **1** 202, Organ **4** 195, Statham **2** 38, *Threlowen–* **2** 323.

57.13.1. ON inflexions are rarely represented:

57.13.2. ON *–ar*, sb., nom. pl. in *19*: Asker Dale **4** 260;

57.13.3. ON *–ar*, sb., gen. sg. in *13*: Marple Wood **1** 283; *19*: Langerlaths **2** 121, Pellerdale **4** 229;

57.13.4. ON *–ir*, sb., nom. pl. in *13*: Netherleigh **5:1** 56;

57.13.5. ON *–t*, adj., neuter (**þverr, þvert**) in *13*: *Tvertouercloh* **2** 323;

57.13.6. ON pres. part. suffix *–andi* (?*Rikandebrigge* **1** 140, xxi: see **5:1** xvi).

57.14. The ME pres. part. suffix is represented by *–ande* (*Fnastandestubbe* **1** 201-2 (**5:1** xviii), *Gaggand'thorne* **1** 201-2 (ib.), *Quakandlowe* **1** 125, *Rikandebrigge* **1** 140, xxi, **5:1** xvi); *–inde* (*Louyndgreues* **1** 88, *Rotindebroke* **1** 71, *Standing Stone* **1** 128); *–yng* (*Hyngyng Stones* **5:1** 61, Shady Brook **3** 206).

57.15. Latin inflexion affects the forms of Antrobus **2** 127 and Noctorum **4** 268, and the spelling *Routhestorum 1391* for Rostherne **2** 56. Latinity is evident in the development of the p.ns. Heronbridge and Roodee **5:1** 54, 62.

F. LEXICOGRAPHICAL NOTES

58. Contributions to ME and ModE lexicography from Cheshire place–names are discerned under the following references (see also the Elements Index **5:1** 85-396, items marked † and *):

approvement **2** 234

bache **2** 250
bark–house **1** 124, **4** 41
   (Löfvenberg *Contributions* 90)
baggard **2** 242
benty **2** 288
bike **4** 6-8 (see also **5:1** 104)
bodkin **5:2** Add. (**1** 90)
booth–hall **3** 35
   (Löfvenberg *Contributions* 90)
brick, brick–yard **3** 274
bullace–tree **1** 129
butt(–fish) **1** 116

cindered **2** 316
clay–pit **2** 78, **5:1** 134
cranberry **2** 145, 315
   (N&Q Mar 1968, 88-9)
crossed **4** x (**2** 27)
crim **2** 171, **5:1** xxx
crypt **5:1** 151
crinkle **4** 186

denez (*Sir Gawain* 2223) **2** 187
dodge, surnames *Dodge*, *Dodgson*
   1 158
dove–house **3** 317

eel–fare **2** 201

fair–weather **3** 118
field–land **2** 109

fish–yard **5:1** 179-80 (cf. Db **3** 730,
   Löfvenberg *Contributions* 86)
flay **3** 256
float **2** 13
fnastande **5:1** xviii
franklin **4** 87

gag **5:1** xviii–xix (**1** 201-2)
gate–house **2** 233
   (Löfvenberg *Contributions* 93)
golf **4** 12
gorse–tree **2** ix, 227

heading **4** 43
heath–cock **4** 153
heating–house **3** 40
hemp–yard **5:1** 221, **2** 41
hickwall **2** 319
Higginbottam, surname **5:1** xxi
   (**1** 266) (cf. Db **1** 146)
hilder **4** 72
hillocky **3** 129
hither **2** 313
hodge, hog; surnames *Hodge*,
   Hodgson **1** 158
hospitaller **3** 9
household **3** 259
hump **3** 165
hut **5:2** Add. (**1** 106-7)

jousting **4** 148, **5:1** 73

Kinsey, surname **2** 263

limepit **4** 253

marlpit **1** 75, 217, **3** 175, **4** 249-50
marly **2** 232
moorish **3** 289

nettly **4** 335

paved **3** 322
pear **2** 251-2
pear–tree **2** 289
peel **2** 218
penthouse, pentice **5:1** 32
pigeon **3** 311
pingot **5:1** 306
plek **3** 60
plock **5:2** Add. (**5:1** 309)

quick–dyke **2** 185

rand (*Sir Gawain* 1710) **3** 235

rasse (*Sir Gawain* 1570) **1** 278, **2** 25,
 4 ix–x
roadway **3** 241
root–fall, root–fallen **5:1** xxxix (**4** 6)
rope **3** 68, 226
rugged **3** 256-7
rye–land **2** 164
rykande (*Sir Gawain* 2337) **5:1** xvi
 (**1** 140, xxi)
 (see also *Names* 11 (1963) 213f.)

sharesmith (?*Shearsmith*, surname)
 2 63
shewell(s) **2** 85
sharp (*Sir Gawain* 424, 1593, etc.)
 v. tonge–s(c)harp
snatch **3** 146
snithe **1** 120, **3** 225
solein **2** 316, **3** 111
sty–way **5:1** 358

?tack **1** 172, **5:1** xvii
thistly **3** 267
threaper **5:1** 365
thrutch **2** 164
timperon **5:2** Add. (**2** 31)
toll, tolt **5:2** Add. (**1** 170, **3** 267,
 4 155, 317, **5:1** xvii, 368)
toll–gate **4** 65
toll–stock **3** 41
tolt, see toll
tonge–s(c)harp **5:1** xxxvi (**3** 158-9),
 368, **5:2** Add. (**1** 162-3, **4** 107)
turf–pit **1** 219, **5:1** 373
tush **4** 47, 50, 55

watershed **1** 71
wild–cat **3** 21, 46
wooden **4** 274
wrinkle **4** 331

yoking **3** 118

INTRODUCTION TO 'THE PLACE–NAMES OF CHESHIRE'

[The three following sections existed in final draft at the time of Professor Dodgson's death. They are supplemented by Appendixes I and II *infra*]

I. THE GEOGRAPHICAL SETTING AND GEOLOGY

CHESHIRE occupies a region which has been of crucial importance in the ethnic and political history of England. It saw the meeting of Angle and Briton, the rise of Penda's Anglian kingdom of Mercia and the fall of the Welsh kingdoms of Cadwallon of Gwynnedd and Cyndylan of Powys, the creation of the Norman palatinate of Chester, and the long Welsh–English confrontation in the Middle Ages. It coasts the Irish Sea which brought the Vikings from Ireland, and it extends inland towards the Danish borough of Derby and the territories of the Danelaw. It is as rich as any county in England in place–names which commemorate such things.

Cheshire occupies the geographical and geological interval between the Cambrian and the Pennine mountain ranges, usually spoken of as the Cheshire Plain, part of a lowland tract which extends northward beside the Irish Sea as far as Lancaster and southward far away into the Midlands. A detailed account of the geological features has been given with each of the Hundreds and a general review may suffice here. [See further: Broxton Hundred **4** 2, Bucklow **2** 1–2, Eddisbury **3** 161–2, Macclesfield **1** 51, Nantwich **3** 1, Northwich **2** 184, Wirral **4** 166–7; also, D. Kenyon in Appendix II, *infra*.]

In the eastern part of the county, the eastern half of Macclesfield Hundred, a mountainous moorland, the solid geology emerges with the millstone grit and coal measures which form the western edges and scarps of the Peak massif. The solid geology under Cheshire is a great trough or downfall. The coal measures reappear at Denhall in Wirral in the extreme west of the county. Alderley Edge marks an emergence of the successive Permian and Triassic sandstones and pebble–beds which lie parallel to the main Pennine massif. These series are largely overlaid, under most of mid–Cheshire, by the Keuper Marl beds. In Bucklow Hundred, Weston, Halton, Lymm, High Legh and Bowdon emerge from beneath these beds. In the Eddisbury and Broxton Hundreds of west Cheshire there are the broken sandstone plateau and escarpments of the Central Ridge in Delamere Forest, and at Frodsham, Helsby, Broxton, Beeston, Edge and Carden; and in Wirral Hundred there are the Sandstone and Pebble Beds which show up at Chester, Storeton, Bidston, Caldy, and the Irish Sea shore rocks called Red Noses and Yellow Noses **4** 327.

At two different levels in layers of the Keuper Marl beds, rock salt domes occur, and this gave rise to brine springs in various places upon which the ancient and modern salt industry was founded. So important was this industry in the economy of medieval Cheshire from before Domesday Book that the word *wich* (OE **wīc**) 'trading place, industrial site' came, in Cheshire, to be used already by 1086 almost exclusively for a 'salt–wich', as a place at which *the* local industry was conducted; hence the collective term *The Wiches*, or the DB term *in Wico* 'at the salt–works', or **wyche–hous** for 'salt factory', see **2** 192–4, 240–4, **3** 30–1, 37–9. Names from **salt(–)**, **wīc**, **wyche–**, **brine** occur in the following townships: Acton Grange, Aldersey, Alsager, Austerson, Baddington, Bowdon, Bradwall, Brereton cum Smethwick, Broxton, Dodcott cum Wilkesley, Dodleston, Eaton near Davenham, Hale, Hapsford, Hatherton, Helsby, Lower Kinnerton, Leftwich, Little Leigh, Macefen, Marbury, Marston, Middlewich, Mobberley, Nantwich, Newton by Frodsham, Northen Etchells, Northwich, Norton, Poole, Rope, Rudheath Lordship, Sandbach, Sproston, Weaverham cum Milton, Weston near Runcorn, Wigland, Witton cum Twambrook, Worleston, Wychough. The movement generated by the conveyance of salt to market created and revived routes, salt–ways, which channelled the traffic in and out of Cheshire throughout the Middle Ages; see **1** 49–50 (XXIX) and **saltere**.

Apart from where it is broken by the more prominent Sandstone outcrops in Wirral, Delamere Forest, and Alderley Edge, and west of the tremendous faulted profiles of the Millstone Grit in the east, the surface of Cheshire is made of a drift geology of Boulder Clay and Glacial Sand and Gravel.

The relief–map of Cheshire has critical contours at 100', 200', 400' and 600'. In Wirral and Broxton Hundreds, the 100' contour defines a ridge separating the valleys of the rivers Dee and Goyt and extending north–west as a low plateau from the foot of Beeston and Peckforton Hills to the north end of Wirral in which it remains generally flat and level, but rises occasionally to 200', culminating in prominent hills at Heswall (350'), Thurstaston (300') and Bidston (200'). It is traversed by a prehistoric river–bed, followed again by the Shropshire Union Canal from beside the R. Dee at the north–west corner of Chester to Wervin and Stoke where it opens upon the R. Gowy marshes.

In Broxton and Eddisbury Hundreds, the 200' contour defines the edge of a tilted plateau whose higher western side is called the central ridge, and forms a series of steep, scarped hills from Helsby (450') and Frodsham (above 400') in the north to Beeston (500'), Peckforton, Bickerton (above 600'), Broxton and Edge in the south. This ridge is broken by a gap at Tiverton (used by the A51 Nantwich – Tarporley – Chester route and the Shropshire Union Canal and the Crewe – Chester railway), guarded by Beeston Castle against medieval Welsh invasion.

In Bucklow Hundred, the 100' contour defines a plateau between to the north the valleys of the rivers Mersey and Bollin and to the south those of Weaver and Peover Eye. This plateau rises to 250' or more at Halton, Hull Appleton and High Legh, and in places presents a steep face to the Mersey and Weaver valleys.

In the middle of the county the basin of the R. Weaver, with its tributaries the rivers Duckow and Dane (with the R. Wheelock) and Peover Eye, is defined by the 200' contour in Bucklow, Northwich, Nantwich, and Eddisbury Hundreds. The basin crosses the south border of the county at Tittenley and the 200'–250' contours here form a gap followed by the Crewe – Shrewsbury railway, the Shropshire Union Canal and the road from Market Drayton via Audlem to Nantwich through the lower extremity of a ridge between Cheshire and Staffordshire running south–west from Mow Cop and Cloud End which guides the county boundary for part of its length.

Central Cheshire either side of the R. Weaver, then, is an undulating plain, deeply cut by rivers in some places, especially the upper Dane and the middle and lower Weaver, consisting of the Weaver basin at 100' to 200', in plan shaped like a fat carrot, the point at the extreme southern tip of Cheshire near Audlem, the broad end along the north slopes of the valleys of the Peover Eye to the east of Northwich and the Weaver to the west. To the north east of the Bucklow plateau and the Weaver basin, the 200' and 300' contours define the basin of the middle course of the rivers

Bollin and Dean with Wilmslow in the middle of it. To the east of this basin, the elevation rises across the East Cheshire plain gradually towards the 600' contour east of and above Odd Rode, Congleton, Macclesfield, Hurdsfield, Bollington, Shrigley, Adlington, Poynton, Marple, Romiley and Hyde, broken by the rivers Dane, Bollin, Goyt, and Etherow. This contour marks the edge of the mountain and moorland of the Peak and Pennine massif, rising steeply at Mow Cop (1050'), The Cloud (in Buglawton, 1125'), Yearns Low (in Rainow, 1213') and at Cats Tor (in Rainow, 1703'), etc. This plain's average profile is interrupted by a promontory at the 400' contour especially by the rock cliff and promontory at Alderley Edge (600') and Marple Ridge. The mountain area which constitutes the old region of *The Lyme* **1** 2–6 is broken by the rivers Goyt, Etherow and Dane. (The addition – *under Lyme* seems to be controlled by the 400'–500' contour of these Lancashire, Cheshire, Derbyshire, Staffordshire uplands.) West of the Goyt and Dane it consists of a series of steep–sided, flat–topped ridges roughly aligned north–south with peat bog or moorland cover. North of the R. Etherow the ground rises very suddenly from 600' to the high moors and peat bogs of the smooth summits of the Pennines proper at Featherbed Moss and Dun Hill (Tintwistle).

The blanketing glacial drift of clay and sand varies in thickness from a few feet to several hundred, indicating that it covers and fills many bold features in the solid geology rock landscape. The east side of the Delamere Forest plateau in Eddisbury Hundred, and a sporadic scatter of locations in Nantwich, Middlewich and Macclesfield Hundreds, reflect a great fan of sand and gravel left by the lake of melt–water escaping from a melt–water dam. The sands and gravels show mostly on the east slope of the central ridge (giving rise to such place–names as Sandyford [Delamere], Sandiway [Weaverham Lordship], *Sondiakes* [Weaverham cum Milton] **3** 210, **5:1** xxxvii, Martonsands [Marton], Sandicroft [Church Minshull], *Sondell* [Broxton Hundred] **2** 4, Sand Hills [Bickerton] **4** 6, Sandhills [Egerton] **4** 34, *Sondyhull* [Malpas] **4** 43), and in a broad band across the south and east of the county between the 400' and 600' contours (whence names such as Sandford [Newhall], Sound, *Sondes* [Barthomley] **3** 9, Sandbach, Sandiford [Church Hulme], *Sondul* [Capesthorne] **1** 75, *Sondifordestrete* [Lower Withington] **1** 92, *Sondyforth* [Goostrey] **2** 228, Sandy Lane [Peover Superior], Soond Field [Plumley] **2** 94, *Sondiflatte* [Witton cum Twambrook] **2** 197,

Sondfordley [Tabley Inferior] **2** 124, *Sondiford* [Tabley Superior] **2** 64).
See also **gravel, gravelly**.

Otherwise, the Boulder Clay is everywhere except for the alluvium in
the river valleys and the blown sand along the Irish Sea coastal plain of
Wirral (hence Meols **4** 296). The other distinctive surface features of the
Cheshire plain are the meres and the mosses. Hollows in the undulating
cover of boulder clay left behind by the melting of the last Ice Sheet filled
with water and those which occupied a viable catchment and were not
emptied by natural drainage persisted as lakes, such as The Mere,
Rostherne Mere, Bar Mere and Oakmere. But some of these lakes filled
with vegetation and sphagnum–moss peat and became bogs, 'mosses',
such as are found in many parts of the county (Bickley Moss, Carrington
Moss, Cracow Moss, Lindow Moss, Sossmoss, *Southmosse*
[Wildboarclough] **1** 164, etc.), see **mos**.

Although, in a general way, the distribution of names ancient and
modern containing the element **sand** coincides with the drift geology map
of glacial and blown sands, nevertheless, the variety in types of ground
does not fall into areas as clearly distinguished as the drift geology map,
or the general review just given, might suggest. A perusal of the
field–name lists in these volumes will show that in many townships all
three of the elements **mos** 'moss', **sand** 'sand' and **clæg** 'clay' occur.
Associated with this sequence of types of soil is the other common
feature of the old Cheshire plain landscape, the marl–pit (cf. **marle,
marle–pytt**). Many thousands of these pits were dug over some six
centuries at least, down to the nineteenth, in the arable lands of Cheshire,
from which clay was excavated from below surface sand or gravel and
spread as a top dressing to improve or replace the tilth and fertility of the
ground. The old pits filled with water and were colonized by fish; those
with steep sides above water level offered a foothold for tree and bush
colonization; they were a factor in the ecology of the environment. They
were useful for fishing, for water–supply, for withies, and for soaking
flax and hides, as a search of the field–name lists would reveal.

The predominant vegetation of this landscape when the Anglo–Saxons
arrived was the still extensive remains of a deciduous, largely oak,
woodland, except where interrupted by the bog or carr vegetation of the
lowland mosses, or the sparser birch, dwarf oak, wicken and peat of the
Pennine moors, or the lowland heath and moorland tracts such as
Rudheath. The place–names, ancient and modern, show evidence of a

frequent occurrence of oak (see **āc, ācen, ǣcen**), ash (see **æsc, æscen, askr, esc, eski**), alder (see **alor, *alren, elren, elri**), birch (beorc, birce, ***bircel, *bircen**[1], **bircen**[2], **birki**), hazel (see **hæsel, hæslen, *hæsling, hesel, hesli**), holly (see **holegn**), willow (see **píll, salh, salig, *salegn, salceie, *wilig, *wilegn, *wiligen, wīðig, *wīðigen**), and thorn (see **þorn** (–ig, –iht), ***þornuc, *þurnuc, þyrne**). Less frequent, in fact rather rare in some instances, were beech (see **bēce**[2], ***bēcen, bōc**[1], ***bōcen**), aspen (see **æspe, æspen**), box (see **box, byxen**), elm (see **elm, *elmen**), elder (see **ellen, ellern, elren, *hyldre**), mountain–ash or 'wicken' (see ***cwicen**), lime (see **lind, linden**), maple (see ***mapel, *maplen**), and yew (see **īw**). It is noticeable that names from the hazel and the yew become more frequent in modern record than they were in the medieval; that names from the hawthorn (see **hagu–þorn**) seem only to occur in modern minor–names. Here and there, names were taken from the rare exotics, the appletree (see **æppel, crabbe**), the plumtree and the bolace (see **plūme, plȳme, plūm–trēow, bolace**), and the pear–tree (see **peru, pirige**).

The prevalent oak and the pastoral economy dictated by the clay soils and the woodland produced the bark and the hides for a tanning industry which accounts for place–names and field–names containing **bark(e), barkere, bark–hous, tan, tan–bark, tan–hous, tan–pit, tan–yard** and for the eminence of Glovers and Tanners in the medieval trade of Chester.

Less dense tree coverage is indicated by names from ***busc, busshi, *buskr, *(ge)bysce, brēr** (–ig), **brōm, brōmig, *brōmuc, bruiere, fearn**(–ig), **gorst** (–ig), ***gorstage, *gorsting, *gorst–trēow, *hæddre, *hǣs, hǣð, *hǣðig, hǣðiht, hrīs, hrís, *hrīsen, *hvin, whin, launde, *līhte, llwyn, *rūh**[2], ***rūhet**. But it would require expertise different from this editor's to discern through geology, nature–study and archaeology whether these represent natural variations of tree–cover, or evidences of human tree–clearing reverted to scrub. These names have a less direct, but not less important, significance than those containing the various terms for deliberate tree–ridding such as **brende**[2], **brēc, bryce, *(ge)fall, fall, felling, rōd**[1], ***ryding, (ge)ryd(d), *ryde, *sænget, stubb, *stubbing, *stybbing, stocc** and ***stoccing**. The 'bush, scrub, gorse and heath' names, also, may represent districts in which human agency in Iron Age or Roman times had deforested the ground. This possibility, not yet tested for Cheshire, ought to colour our appreciation of the very common settlement–name element **lēah**. Reference to **5:1** 265–8 shows that more than a hundred of the major settlement–names contain this element and very many indeed (not counted) of the medieval and minor names. The significance of this kind of name is 'settlement in a woodland context' as well as 'tract of less dense woodland; glade in a wood'.

The distribution of **lēah** and **tūn** names recorded before 1500 shows us no exciting large scale opposition, but there are some more localized features which deserve notice. The element **lēah** is rare in Wirral, where woodland is signalled by occasional **skógr** or **hyrst** but frequent **wudu**. This may indicate a less dense, more fragmented, tree cover in Wirral — separate woods rather than continuous cover. Analysis of the names of the Wirral townships shows a ratio of about 8:5 between habitative names and nature–names; in coastal and estuarine locations, habitative and nature–names are in the ratio 1:1, but, inland the ratio is 5:2. The habitation–names are predominantly in **tūn** or **bý**. The forest in Wirral was no obstacle to settlement, by the look of it. Elsewhere in Cheshire, historical geography is challenged by different patterns of distribution which can be discerned in the **lēah** / **tūn** names.

II. THE DISTRIBUTIONS OF OE HABITATIVE AND NATURE–NAMES

Since the majority of settlement–names in Cheshire, whether or not township– and parish–names, are nature–names, and many of these are in OE **lēah**, there is interest in the distribution of habitative names in such OE elements as **tūn**, **burh**, **hām**, **worð**, and **worðign**; see Map of Hundreds, Parishes and Townships.

There is a group of adjacent townships in the east of Bucklow Hundred with habitative names in **hām** and **tūn** which we might call the 'Dunham group', comprising Dunham Massey, Altrincham, Ashton on Mersey, Carrington, Partington, Warburton, Oughtrington in Lymm, Agden, Bollington and Millington. These lie on a drift geology of alluvium, river gravel, blown sand and peat–moss and are surrounded by townships with names in **lēah** or some other nature–name element which lie on the boulder clay or Triassic sandstone outcrop.

In the west of Bucklow Hundred, there is another such group of townships, with names in **tūn**, which we might call the 'Halton group', comprising Weston, Halton, Norton, Stockton, Walton, Appleton, Newton by Daresbury, Keckwick, Daresbury, Hatton, Stretton, Clifton, Sutton, Aston by Sutton, Dutton, Bartington and Preston on the Hill. These lie in a region where there is a tract of blown sand and alluvial soils along the south bank of R. Mersey; and where, inland, the glacial drift clays are thin upon, or penetrated by outcrops of, the Keuper Marl and the Permian and Triassic sandstones which show at Halton Hill and Weston Point and Clifton.

Township–names of the habitative type, in **tūn**, etc., form clusters in other districts. About Northwich are Crowton, Acton, Weaverham cum Milton, Barnton, Anderton, Marbury, Great Budworth, Marston, Witton, Wincham, Lostock, Davenham, Whatcroft, Eaton, Moulton, Bostock and Wharton. These lie on sites based on the alluvium of the Weaver, the Dane and the Peover, and on interruptions of the boulder clay by sand and gravel and sandstone outcrop.

Similar, near Middlewich are Newton, Kinderton, Cotton, Ravenscroft, Wharton and Sutton. Again, near Warmingham are Elton, Tetton, Moston, Eardswick in Minshull Vernon, and Leighton.

In the Nantwich region is a numerous group: Cholmondeston, Stoke, Hurleston, Acton, Edleston, Baddington, Austerson, Hatherton, Buerton, Batherton, Hunsterson, Hatherton, Doddington, Walgherton, Wybunbury, Chorlton, Shavington, Wistaston, Alvaston, Worleston, Willaston, Wisterson and Aston iuxta Mondrem. These lie on sites based on the glacial sand beds which interrupt the boulder clay.

There is a group of place–names in **tūn** about Chester. These are Mollington, Moston, Upton, Chorlton, Croughton, Newton, Picton, Boughton, Guilden Sutton, Littleton, Christleton, Cotton Abbotts and Edmunds, Rowton, Saighton, Buerton, Eaton, Poulton, Eccleston, Claverton, Marlston, Dodleston and Kinnerton. Their sites are not so obviously controlled by features gross enough to be plotted on the drift geology sheets; but here again, we must look to alluvium, glacial sand and sandstone outcrop interrupting the glacial clays.

Less close, but still discernible groups, occur. In north–east Macclesfield Hundred are Brinnington, Bredbury, Offerton, Torkington, Norbury, Poynton and Adlington. Near Macclesfield are Bollington, Tytherington, Upton, Henbury, Gawsworth and Sutton.

In south–east Cheshire is a loosely ranged line of townships with names in **tūn**, **burh** and **æcer**: Buglawton, Astbury, Great and Little Moreton, Church Lawton, Haslington, Alsager, Batchton, Weston and Chorlton.

Near Swettenham and Kermincham are Lower and Old Withington, Marton and Siddington.

Elsewhere, in north–east Bucklow Hundred and north–west Macclesfield Hundred, there is a series of township–names in **tūn**, **burh**, **worð**, **worðign** and **port**: (*a*) Stockport, Brinnington, Offerton, Torkington, Poynton, Worth, Norbury, Adlington; (*b*) Newton in Prestbury, Prestbury, Henbury, Siddington, Withington, Snelson, Ollerton, Norbury by Knutsford, Tatton; and (*c*) Millington, Bollington, Ashton on Mersey and Northenden. These townships enclose an area about the basin of the R. Bollin within which all the townships except Wilmslow have natural–feature names. Wilmslow occurs upon and adjacent to a patch of glacial sand and peat (Lindow Moss **1** 230, *Sandhole* (Bollin Fee) **1** 223 and several *Sand–* names in the field–name lists). The other townships in the contained areas are upon the boulder clay, but the distribution of surrounding habitative names is in three patterns.

The first pattern is fairly simple: (*c*), the western and southern members of the perimeter, are townships of the 'Dunham group' and south of these (*b*) are townships lying on the edge of an arc of glacial sand beds which relieve the boulder clay to the south of the Alderleys.

The second pattern is less obviously controlled. There is a line of habitative names (*a*) from Stockport to Adlington, below but parallel to the 600' contour, whose location is apparently dictated by local anomalies in the boulder–clay cover — patches of sand or river–alluvium, or by a generally better drainage due to the elevation of the escarpment (to the east of their sites) of the coal–measure and mill–stone grit up–thrust at 600', or perhaps some advantage due to the underlying solid geology here, the parallel strata of Permian and Triassic sandstones which lie adjacent to the edge of the local measures in the triangle Bredbury, Macclesfield, Carrington.

Another encircling pattern appears in Nantwich Hundred, where a group of townships (Tittenley, Wilkesley, Coole, Broomhall and Sound), with natural–feature names from **lēah**, **halh**, **sand**, are ringed by townships with habitative names from **burh, cot, tūn, byrh–tūn** (Marbury (cum Quoisley), Smeaton [in Dodcott cum Wilkesley] **3** 97, Woodcott, Alvastbury [in Sound] **3** 123, Baddington, Austerson, Hatherton, Hunsterson and Buerton). It looks as though this distribution, also, reflects a clay / sand alternation in the glacial drift. Perhaps Sound (**sand**) ought to be categorized as a site apt for an habitative name in this particular analysis.

Again, in south–west Nantwich Hundred and south–east Broxton Hundred, a group of township–names, and old names of secondary settlements, in **lēah** (Burwardsley, Horsley [in Beeston] **3** 303, *Thorteleg'* [in Spurstow] **3** 317, Brindley, Stoneley, Baddiley, Chorley, Cholmondeley, Bickley) is surrounded by **tūn, burh** and **hām** place–names (Peckforton, Bunbury, Haughton, Hurleston, Acton, Edleston, *Alvastbury* [in Sound] **3** 123, Wrenbury, Norbury, Tushingham, Hampton, Egerton and Bickerton).

The interpretation of these circular patterns of distribution might be that they are the result of settlement exploitation of more immediately tillable soils in less densely wooded locations; habitative names in **tūn, hām, burh, cot, worð** and the like indicating the locations of strongest and earliest exploitation, in which the dominant feature is the human structure; the nature–names indicating the locations of the ground more resistant to colonization, in which the dominant feature is the natural setting and its control over subsistence and development. In some districts the habitative names lie round the edges of the more intractable nature–name areas; in others, a district of several townships with habitative names, in which a fairly complete settlement has been successful, is bordered or surrounded by tracts of less exploited country where the nature–names occur.

This view of the distribution of habitative names indicates a distribution favouring the areas where the glacial drift is relieved by sand or gravel or sandstone outcrop.

It is also notable that the habitative names cluster in west Bucklow Hundred, north Bucklow Hundred, in the middle reaches of the R. Dane in Northwich Hundred, in Nantwich Hundred around Nantwich, and around Chester. They extend in a series along the edge of The Lyme, along the south–west border and in Broxton Hundred and are widespread and predominant in Wirral.

It would seem obvious that the history of any settlement in Cheshire must be conditioned by the soil–conditions and the relief. The townships with nature–names, in general, lie on or among the stiffer clays, those with habitative names on the more amenable soils. The areas occupied by the habitative names might be regarded as the areas most attractive to development . . .

III. THE SCANDINAVIAN ELEMENT IN CHESHIRE PLACE–NAMES

The Scandinavian element in the place–names of Cheshire has been discussed by G. Barnes, 'The Evidence of Place–Names for the Scandinavian Settlements in Cheshire', LCAS 63 (1952–3), pp. 131–55; S. Potter, 'Cheshire Place–Names', LCHS 106 (1955), pp. 16–20; A. H. Smith, 'The Site of the Battle of Brunanburh', LMS 1, i (1937), pp. 56–9; F. T. Wainwright, 'The Scandinavians in Lancashire', LCAS 58 (1945–6), pp. 71–116, 'North–West Mercia, A.D. 871–924', LCHS 94 (1942), pp. 3–55 and 'Ingimund's Invasion', EHR 63 (1948), pp. 145–69; G. Fellows–Jensen, *Scandinavian Settlement Names in the North–West* (Copenhagen 1985), pp. 366–73 and passim; and by me in 'The Background of Brunanburh', *Saga–Book* 14, iv (1956–7), pp. 303–16, 'The English Arrival in Cheshire', LCHS 119 (1967), pp. 1–8 and 'Place–Names and Street–Names at Chester', CAS n.s. 55 (1968), pp. 29–61, esp. 50–7 [see *infra*, Appendix I, A–C].

The evidence of Scandinavian settlement is to be sought in the entries under the more than two hundred Scandinavian head–words of the Index of Elements **5:1** 85–396 and in the Old Scandinavian and Old Irish personal–names listed in the Personal–Name Index, Sections I.C and D, **5:1** 412–14 (corrections at **5:1** xxiii, cancels *Kári* p. 413, and at **5:2** Add., adds ON *Þengill*, *Þorbjorn* and *Ulfhildr* (fem.), and OIrish *Béollan*, to p. 414). This material can be augmented by consideration of that which may underlie the entries in Section I.E, **5:1** 414–20, esp. *Coll*, *Liulf*, *Orme*, *Oudfride*, *Reynald*, *Randolf*, *Roger*, *Simond* and *Story*; Section II, **5:1** 420–3, esp. *Kel*, *Kettle*, *Stenkel*; Section III, **5:1** 423–4, s.vv. **anddyri**, *Dennis*, *Thoraud*.

The first impression, that there is a great amount of Scandinavian material in the p.ns. of Cheshire, should be balanced by the observation that Scandinavian inflexions are rarely represented in the ME and later spellings (see *supra*, Linguistic Notes, §§ 57.13.1–6), and that the number of names for which an entirely Scandinavian linguistic composition can be postulated is not nearly so large as either that for which a hybrid origin is indicated, or that for which the Scandinavian element was in effect nothing more 'foreign' than a common ME loan–word; i.e. one of the Scandinavian elements in the Ch dialect of Middle English being used in the formation of a ME place–name. Such a p.n. is not evidence of Scandinavian settlement; it is evidence of a Scandinavian influence on the English language and nomenclature used in a locality. That influence may be due to the immigration and settlement of speakers of a Scandinavian language; it may be due to the cultural transmission of vocabulary. We must remember that many a modern Englishman who spoke no French, knew no Frenchman and never visited a French railway engine–shed, has, nevertheless, kept his motorcar in a 'garage' (in ModE ['gɑrɑːʤ] the French word is cultivated; in the other ModE ['gæriʤ] it has been absorbed into traditional English; compare *damage*).

The Cheshire place–names which contain the two hundred listed elements of Scandinavian derivation cannot without reservation be taken as evidence of a settlement of Scandinavians, or of the presence of speakers of a Scandinavian language, at the locations those names originally identified. Some of these place–names are only ambiguously 'Scandinavian'. There is a numerous class of place–names for which it would be difficult to choose on formal grounds whether to propose as etymon the Scandinavian element or an English cognate, e.g. **akr, bingr, bleikr, blindr, brún**[2] (OE **brūn**[1]), **elri, *finn, flag, flaga, flet, *flókari, fótr, gálga–tré, gangr, gor, grjót** (OE **grēot**), **hallr** (OE **hall**[2]), **hamarr, hamall** (OE ***hamol**), ***hegn** (OE **hægen**), **hengjandi, hesli** (OE Merc **hesel**), **hǫfuð, horn, hrís, hross** (OE **hors**), **hundr, hveiti, kál** (OE **cāl**), **kambr** (OE **camb**), ***kartr** (OE **cært**), **knottr, langr, lín, lítill, mosi, norð, selja** (OE **salig**), **skratti, smiðr, smiðja, smjǫr, snap, stafn, stíf, sútari, þorpari** (OE ***þorpere**), **vrangr**.

ON **kaldr** can be preferred to OE **cald** when there is another Scandinavian element in a compound, or a Scandinavian influence discernible in the place–names in the neighbourhood, e.g. Caldy 4 282, Cold Airs 4 189, *Colders* 4 248. It is difficult to choose between ON **dalr** and OE **dæl**; however likely the ON element may be it cannot certainly be identified in Dawpool 4 280, Dungeon 4 278 (**5:1** xliv), 4 219, Longdendale 1 2, *Flindow* 4 180, nor in Lingdale 4 270 which may have a ME first element. The forms of Mickledale **3** 229 and *Mickeldale* **4** 234 belong to a set of place–names which exhibit the effect of Scandinavian influence upon an English place–name. ON **mikill** is likely to be confused with OE **micel** in those forms where elision of *–e–* in oblique case inflexion of the OE word produced *micel* > *micl–* whence ME *mi(c)k(e)l(e)*, instead of ME *michel(e)*. In Cheshire place–names the ME spellings for OE **micel** mostly contain *–k–*, so the basis could be either ON *mikill* or OE *micl–*. No significant distribution has been plotted. But a Scandinavian character is more marked in the place–names Grisdale **2** 49, Helsdale **2** 39 (**5:1** xxiv), Crowsdale **4** 253, Pellerdale **4** 229, *Piledale* **4** 234, *Uluesdale* **4** 162, *Steyncolesdale* **4** 282.

ON **djúpr** and OE **dēop** look alike in Middle English spellings: *Duphyard* **4** 248 probably represents the ON element in a hybrid composition with OE **geard** (not ON **garðr**).

Lathegestfeld **4** 244 seems to have an ON compound as its first element, but the themes of the compound, **leiðr**, **gestr** have OE cognates **lāð**, **gest**.

The place–name *Liveschke* **2** 101 (in Appleton; whose name–spellings indicate that the pronunciation may have been influenced by ON **epli**) could represent either ON **hlíf–eski* or OE **hlīf–esce* under Scandinavian influence ([k] for [tʃ]).

The place–name Flookersbrook **4** xiv, 146 (**5:1** xli) contains ME **flokere* which could represent either ON **flókari* or OE **flōcere*.

ON **flet** and OE **flet** are equally appropriate possibilities for the first element of Flittogate **2** 122, with ON **haugr** and OE **hōh** respectively as second element.

It is not easy to separate ON **haugr** from OE **hōh** in Cheshire place–names unless there is a clear Scandinavian influence in the toponymic, historic or archaeological context. The place–name Harrow **4** 279 is ambiguous like Flittogate, but ON **haugr** seems more likely in the place–names Arno **4** 270 (with an OScand personal–name), Fornall **4** 301 (although recorded poorly and late it appears to contain ON **forn**) and *Wyt*– and *Wette Haves* **4** 287 (with characteristic *–au–* spelling).

ON **lind** and OE **lind** are indistinguishable. The late–recorded field–names Linn Lund **2** 265 and Limeric **2** 260 suggest, hazardously, compositions of ON **lind**, **lundr** and **brekka**.

It looks as though ON **skíð** replaced OE **scīd** in the form *Schit(h)raweford(e)* **3** 5, and the reverse occurred in *Shidgateswra* **1** 253.

The place–name Statham **2** 38 could be derived from the dat.pl.form of either ON **stǫð** or OE **stæð**.

ON **svartr** rather than OE **sweart** can be preferred for Black Rock (*Swarteskere*) **4** 326 (**5:1** xlv) and Swartins **4** 140.

Middle English spellings for ON **tún** would be indistinguishable from those for OE **tūn**. In some Cheshire place–names the ON element might be thought to be preferable where the first element of the name is Scandinavian, e.g. Claughton **4** 316, Gayton **4** 275, Larton **4** 300, Storeton **4** 253, Thurstaston **4** 279, Anderton **2** 95, Croxton **2** 236, and *Thorston* (*Thorstonessuice*) **3** 195. But in such place–names the first element may be rather a ME derivative or loan–word than the original Old Scandinavian word. The place–name Claughton **4** 316, in Wirral, certainly seems to contain ON **klakkr** as first element. There are two instances of this type of place–name in Lancashire (PNLa 167, 178) in districts subject to Scandinavian influence. It could probably be regarded as an entirely Scandinavian place–name if we could be sure that it was not representative of a type of name produced when an Anglo–Saxon tradition of toponymy using OE denominators acquired a new repertoire of qualifiers drawn from the vocabulary of the Scandinavian immigrants.

The type of place–name which appears to be the composition of an Old Scandinavian first element (personal–name or common substantive) and an Old English second element (typically OE **tūn**, but cf. OE **twisla** in Tintwistle **1** 320) is really to be seen as an English place–name reflecting a stage in the process of absorption of Scandinavian vocabulary into an English–language onomasticon. Such place–names have been regarded as Scandinavian–English hybrids, most notably the kind known as the 'Grimston–hybrid' in which the first element is a Scandinavian personal–name and the second element is an Old English habitative name–element such as **tūn**.

Thurstaston, Anderton, Croxton and *Thorston* **3** 195 appear to be of the 'Grimston–hybrid' type. The latter three give rise to various degrees of uncertainty about the personal–name element. In Anderton and Croxton the personal–names could be the Middle English derivative rather than the original Old Scandinavian form. Not every modern British *Simon* is Hebrew, nor every *Derek* Breton, *Karl* German, *Bridget* Irish nor every *Julie* French. In the place–name *Thorston* the personal–name may be the late Old English personal–name *Thurstan* which is represented in the spellings of Thurstaston as an alternative to its original

ON *Þorsteinn*.

ON **hlíð**[2] is sometimes indistinguishable from OE **hlið**[1] but it is to be preferred in explanation of the place–name Arclid **2** 264 with a Scandinavian personal–name as first element.

There is another numerous set of Cheshire place–names which are derived from elements which were originally Old Scandinavian words but became part of the common or the dialect vocabulary from which Middle English and Modern English place–names were composed. Such place–names are at least as likely to have been created by Cheshire native speakers of the North–West Midland regional dialect of English as they are to have been created by Scandinavian immigrants. In this category are place–names from such elements as **beit, bing, blesi, flat, fleke, gildi, gildri, hemp, hinder, hǫgg** (ModE dial. **hag(g)**), **hvammr, inntak, kapall, karl, kjarr, kráka, lágr, lǫg, marr**[1], **maðra** (eModE **mather**), **mȳrr, rotinn, skinn, skinnari, stakkr, stolpi, svíri, werre**.

Afnames **4** 198 obviously represents ON **af–nám** or the derivative ME *afnam*. *Offenomes* **1** 125 may be similar; but it could represent an OE **of–nām* the reciprocal of OE **inn–nām**.

Old Norse **bóndi** obviously persisted in Middle English; in Cheshire place–names the Middle English and Modern English instances, always with English second elements, occur in Bucklow and Northwich Hundreds.

Old Danish **bōth** and Old Norse **búð** cannot be formally distinguished from each other in the material. Most of the relevant place–names should be explained as from ME *both(e)*, ModE *booth* 'a booth, a stall, a herding camp', especially when the element is suffixed to a place–name. They are evidence of a system of out–pasture and transhumance husbandry and a consequent pattern of seasonal, secondary dependant settlement in early medieval and post–Conquest times rather than evidence of the settlement of a Scandinavian population. Nevertheless, the distribution of the place–names which contain this element and which are recorded before 1500, a distribution predominantly in the Hundreds of Macclesfield, Bucklow and Northwich, might indicate that both aspects of the anthropology ought to be borne in mind.

ON **brekka** appears to have been current in the ME dialect in Runcorn and Wallasey in the 14th century. The definite article appears for *le Breck* **2** 179 and Breck Rd **4** 333. It is as likely that *Breccotes* (Norley) **3** 251, *Knavenebrec* (Oxton) **4** 271, and *le Brecfeld* (Wallasey) **4** 333 are ME compositions as that they are ME modifications of Scandinavian simplex place–names in **brekka**. Cambrick (Liscard) **4** 328 may contain as first element either OE **camb** or ON **kambr**. Yet the distribution of the examples recorded before 1500 is in the north part of the Hundreds of Wirral, Eddisbury and Bucklow. The element does not appear, even after 1500, in the place–names in the Hundreds of Nantwich and Broxton, a regional limitation which must be an isolectic effect rather than a topographical one.

Old Danish **brink**, the cognate of Old Norse **brekka**, may lie behind a number of Cheshire place–names, but it would be difficult to distinguish from the putative cognate OE *****brince**, see **5:1** 115. The ME form *brink(e)* might be derived from either. However, allowing that *Babrinchull* **2** 79 may contain an –**ing**² formation rather than **brince** or **brink**, the instances first recorded in sources dated before 1500 are *le Brynk* (at Finney in Kingsley) **3** 240, Brinkshaws (in Etchells) **1** 243, 245 and *leȝ Brenk'* (Runcorn) **2** 179, places which lie in the north parts of the Hundreds of Eddisbury, Bucklow and Macclesfield. Instances first recorded in later records are for places in a similar distribution except for Brink Hay (Thurstaston, Wirral) **4** 281. The restricted distribution, again, might reflect a linguistic as well as a topographical controlling factor. In medieval Cheshire the ME word *brink* may have been more usually current in the vernacular vocabulary and the nomenclature alike, in a region whose dialect had been subject to Scandinavian influence.

The place–name Cracow **3** 58 is derived from the ME derivative *crake* rather than from the original ON word **kráka**.

ON **fiski–garðr** might lie behind the name of *Halton Fyshgarth* **2** 171, but no sign of it appears in the forms recorded for *Fys(s)h(e)yord–* names in Wirral, a Scandinavian settlement area, at **4** 244, 250, 316; and ME *garth* (from ON **garðr**) was part of the common ME word–stock. In the place–name *Brende Yearthe* **2** 155, ME *garth* alternates with ME *earth* (from OE **eorðe**).

ON **fit** 'grassland on the banks of a river' is the origin of ModE dial. *fitty* (Lincs.) 'marshy, marshland', which suggests that the word had a continuous currency throughout the ME period, represented in the names *Braderfitlond* (Caldecott) **4** 63, *Fittie Carr* (Rainow) **1** 147.

ODan **flask** became ME **flasshe** which is too common to be seen as a distinctively Scandinavian signal. However, the distinctly Scandinavian form with *sk* may be discerned in spellings for Flaxmere **3** 249, Flash **1** 319, Flash Wood **1** 56, *le Flaskus* (Wirral Hundred) **4** 168, Flashes **2** 300.

ON **flat** survived into ModE dialect and because it is a common element in Cheshire place–names medieval and modern it cannot be used as a distinctive Scandinavian place–name indicator. It is remarkable that this field–name element occurs frequently everywhere in Cheshire except in the Hundreds of Broxton and Wirral. In the latter, a word of Scandinavian origin might have been expected. So the distribution must have something to do with the significance of ME *flat* (< ON **flat**) rather than with that of ON **flat**; most of the instances first recorded at dates before 1500 are probably post–Conquest Middle English place–names rather than pre–Conquest ones. However, *Halwarte Flatte* (Odd Rode) **2** 315 has an Old Scandinavian personal–name as first element.

ON **gap** is the origin of ME **gappe** but it seems likely that the ME word is the element found in most of the Cheshire place–names for which the element is adduced. The instances first recorded in sources dated before 1500 are Gap House (Kettleshulme) **1** 112, *Lodelegapp* (Macclesfield Hundred) **1** 53, *le Kyngesgap* (Halton) **2** 172, *le Nethergap* (Hooton) **4** 191, and *Emmotesgape* (Poulton cum Spital) **4** 253. These all lie in or near areas where place–names reflect a Scandinavian influence. The f.n. Horn Nips (Rowton) **4** xiii, 115 appears to be a special case.

ON **gata**, as ME *gate*, became part of the common ME vocabulary. However, it is notable that this appears as an element in street–names only in Macclesfield and Stockport, not in the other Cheshire towns.

Golacre (Liscard) **4** 328 contains either ON **góligr** or its ME form *goli(k)* as first element; the second element could be ON **akr** or OE **æcer** or their common ME form *acre*.

ON **gríss** gave rise to ME *grise*, ModE dial. *grice*; but the place–name Grisdale **2** 49 is of a type *Gris(e)–*, *Grizedale* used in NCy areas (PNLa 166, 220, WRY **6** 135, 261, We **2** 223) whose place–names show signs of Scandinavian influence.

Gremotehalland(Storeton) **4** 256 contains ON **grið** 'truce, protection, sanctuary', but that word had already been adopted into English legal terminology by the end of the eleventh century, so *grith–mōt* might be regarded as a ME or a late–OE compound. However, the location of this Cheshire instance in an area where there is a discernible Norse influence in the place–names lends emphasis to the Scandinavian factor in the history of the element and might account for the formation of the name, although Cleasby–Vigfusson contains no evidence of an Old Norse compound *griða–mót*.

ON **holmr** was the origin of the late OE loan–word *holm*; both are the origin of ME *holm(e)*, which appears as a common element in place–names and field–names in many midland and northern counties with much the same significance as the element ME *ham, hom* from OE **hamm**. It is usually impossible to distinguish between the ON form and the ME form. The element appears with Scandinavian characteristics in only three instances; Kettleshulme **1** 110 with the ON personal–name *Ketill*, Grinsome (Ince) **3** 252 with the pers.n. ON *Grímr* if not OE *Grīm(a)*, and *Routheholm* (Wallasey) **4** 335 with ON **rauðr**. But the distribution of instances recorded before 1500 shows ME *holme* a common element in north and east Cheshire and in Wirral, absent or rare in the Hundreds of Broxton and Nantwich. For names first recorded in sources dated after 1500 the element is absent from the Hundred of Nantwich, it is rare in the Hundreds of Northwich, Eddisbury and Broxton, it is more frequent in the Hundreds of Macclesfield, Bucklow and Wirral. The two categories together produce a distribution in which *holme* appears most frequently in the Hundreds of Wirral, Northwich, Eddisbury and Macclesfield, not often in the Hundreds of Bucklow and Nantwich, not at all in the Hundred of Broxton. See further, *supra*, Linguistic Notes, §12.4.4; **5:1** 232 (**holmr**) and 237 (**hulm**); also G. Fellows–Jensen, *Scandinavian Settlement Names in the North–West*, Copenhagen 1985, 313–16.

ON ***hvin*** becomes ME, ModE *whin*; but it may appear in a Scandinavian context in *Tyrwhin* (Congleton) **2** 301, Wimbricks (Greasby, Saughall Massie) **4** 293, 323.

ON **karl** becomes ME *carle*. *Carlecotes* (Romiley) **1** 294 can be regarded as a ME formation composed of two ME words, one of them of Old Scandinavian origin, the other of Old English. In *Carlisboth* (Macclesfield Hundred) **1** 52, both elements are of Old Scandinavian origin, but both are part of the common vocabulary of the ME dialect, so it is difficult to say that this is a Viking–age place–name rather than one coined in the late Anglo–Saxon or post–Conquest eras. These names in *Carle–* are evidence of a Scandinavian influence on the vocabulary of the English language in a district.

ON **kjarr** becomes the common ME *ker*, ModE *carr*, and its only distinctive Scandinavian appearance in Cheshire place–names occurs in Gunco (Macclesfield) **1** 115 composed with a Scandinavian personal–name.

ON **kerling** becomes Northern ME *kerling* 'a carline, an old woman', and it is the ME word which appears in *Karlingescroft* (Capesthorne) 1 75 composed with OE, ME **croft**. *Carlingkeslowe* (Plumley) **2** 94, with OE **hlāw** rather than ON **haugr**, looks like a ME formation but the archaeological and anthropological significance of the name are not known: it may represent the replacement of the first element of the Old English name of an old burial mound or it may mark the re–use of such a mound for an un–Christian, late Anglo–Saxon, post–Viking burial.

Old Danish **klint** gave rise to ME, ModE dial. *klint, clint*. The place–name Clinton **1** 100 could be a Scandinavian–English hybrid, with either OE **tūn** or OE **dūn**; but it could be a ME formation coined after **klint** had been absorbed into the common ME vocabulary. Instances of place–names for which ODan **klint** is proposed, none recorded from sources dated earlier than the 15th century, occur in Wirral (The Clints, *le Clyntes*, *the Clynsse*, see **4** 182, 196, 243, 334) where the cognate ON **klettr** might have been expected. The Vikings who settled in Wirral in the tenth century may not yet have lost the nasal consonant from their pronunciation of the word (see the remarks on Frankby at **4** 287 (**5:2** Add.) and in Gillian Fellows–Jensen's article 'Anthroponymical specifics in place–names in *–bý* in the British Isles', *Studia Anthroponymica Scandinavica: Tidskrift för nordisk personnamnsforskning* I (1983), p. 51); or there may already have been a Danish element in the Scandinavian population of Wirral (see Denhall **4** 220); or the word *clint* may have already become a common substantive in the local dialect of English by the time these names were formed.

ON **lyng** becomes ME, ModE dial. **ling**, seen as a common substantive in *Pultonling* (Poulton cum Seacombe) **4** 331. In the place–name Lingdale (Oxton) **4** 270 this first element is in composition with ME *dale*, which would represent either ON **dalr** or OE **dæl**; it is, therefore, difficult to determine whether Lingdale represents a ME place–name formed of elements of mixed or of entirely Scandinavian origin, or represents a place–name coined in the Scandinavian language of the Norse settlers in Wirral.

ON **mjúkr** becomes late OE, eME **mēoc**, ME **meke**, ModE **meek**; but only if ON **á** is discerned as final element in the place–names Micker Brook **1** 32, Mecca Brook **4** 290, should the ON form be proposed in the etymology, for it is not apparent that the ON word **á** passed into the English dialect of Cheshire (cf. **ēa**, Peover Eye **1** 33). The usual word for a river was OE **ēa**, ME *ee*, *eye* as in the river–names Mersey **1** 31 and Peover Eye; ON **á** may be seen in the river–name Croco **1** 19, but it is otherwise rare.

ON **rein**, 'a boundary strip' later 'a ploughland strip', becomes ME and ModE dial. *rean*, *rain*, *rhene*, etc. The instances of this element in place–names recorded in sources dated before 1500 all lie in the Hundreds of Wirral and Broxton. The significance of the distribution is not obvious. None of them appears to be a particularly Scandinavian composition. Perhaps there was a technical difference between the kinds of selion signified by OE **land** and ON **rein**, or some feature of land–tenure and partition, which made it likely that there would be a greater number of reans in West Cheshire than elsewhere.

ON **skáli** 'a temporary hut or shed' produces place–names in *–scholes*, *Schole(s)*. The instances recorded at dates before 1500 show it simplex, or in composition with OE and ME elements or place–names, or with OE personal–names; but never in a Scandinavian collocation. The distribution of these instances shows up in the Hundred of Macclesfield (3x), Bucklow (5x), Northwich (2x) and Eddisbury (1x). Instances for dates after 1500 occur in the Hundreds of Macclesfield (3x) and Bucklow (1x). It is notable that the element is not seen in Wirral and is not frequent in Cheshire. In that Hundred ON **erg**, and in the rest of the county ODan **bōth**, may have been the preferred terms for out–pasture arrangements.

ON **slakki** 'a small shallow valley, a hollow in the ground' becomes ME and ModE dial. *slack*; the distribution of the material, early and late, is dictated more by topographical than by ethnographical or dialectal effects.

Place–names such as Drysike **1** 323, Oaksike **1** 325 may be hybrids composed of an English element and ON **sík**; but the form of the second element may represent the cognate OE **sīċ** modified either by oblique case inflexion (compare the forms of place–names from OE **wīċ**, pl. **wīcu**), or by analogy with the ON word. Again, the final element in those place–names may be the ME derivative *sike* rather than the ON word.

The place–names Queastybirch (in Hatton) **2** 150 and Quiesty (in Higher Whitley) **2** 127 present problems of choice between ON **kví** or kvíga (both produce ME *qui*) and between ON **stía** or OE **stigu** (both produce ME *sty*). These place–names could be composed entirely of Scandinavian elements, *kvíga–stía* or *kvía–stía*; or they could be hybrid formations in ME from *qui* (< **kvíga**) and *sty* (< OE **stigu** or ON **stía**). There is, at least, a strong Scandinavian influence in the vocabulary of these names. They are to be associated with the compound place–name *Kybull* **5:1** xxviii (2 142–3), from ON *kvía–ból*. The element ON **ból**, ODan **bōle** is very doubtfully distinguished from ON **boli, bolr** and ME *bole* 'a bull' (< OE *bula) in the place–names *Bolehul* **2** 314 (**5:1** xxxii), *Boughmoor* **2** 291, *Bolewik* **3** 55, Bellmarsh **2** 223, 227, where the final elements are English words.

Twerslondes (Newton by Chester) **4** 148, a hybrid formed with OE **land**, suggests that ON *þvers* had entered into the ME dialect. The place–name Toft **2** 81, close to Knutsford, looks like a Scandinavian place–name but the ODan word **toft** was borrowed into late OE, and was in fact a common ME substantive in the areas subject to Scandinavian influence, and it should be borne in mind that Toft might be more accurately described as an Anglo–Scandinavian or a Scandinavian English place–name.

There are some Cheshire place–names which may be thought to have a Scandinavian character, for which, however, the history is not well recorded and the ascription of Scandinavian elements is less than confident. Into this category fall the place–names ascribed to ON **bjarg** **5:1** 105; Hillbark **4** 288, Stoneby **4** 327, Stone Bark **4** 334 are late–recorded, hybrid or anglicized, and the second element shows confusion with ON **by(r)** and **berg**.

Also open to doubt are the place–names Bootherson **3** 27, *Bottynbrydge* **4** 331 and Witherwin **2** 97 and place–names ascribed to the elements **deill; erg; kjóss** only adduced for modern minor names in instances where there is evidence neither for Scandinavian settlement in that vicinity nor for the Middle English tradition of the name; **nabbi** seen only in place–names of recent record; **vað** (> *wath*) not clearly distinguished from OE **waroð** (> *warth*), see Wharford **2** 174 (**5:1** xxx).

The place–name Lathamhall (Ringway) **2** 29 might be derived from the dative plural of ON **hlaða** 'a barn'; but the name may represent the manorial transfer of a family surname rather than an original toponymic. Hickershaw **1** xxi, 70 may be a Norse–English hybrid, but there is only a typological analogy to rely upon, not an early record. The Scandinavian first element in Capesthorne **1** 73 and *Cappis feld* **4** 256 lacks historical or archaeological verification.

Holdhaly **4** 248 may well contain ON **hǽli**, but uncertainty about the first element casts doubt on the second.

ON **munnr** may provide the first element in a hybrid compound *Munstel–* in the place–name *Munstelmor* (Willaston near Nantwich) **3** 80, not a remarkably Scandinavian district. ON **skammr** has been discerned as the first element in field–names in Wirral with English second elements, at **4** 248, 290, 328 (*le Schamforlong*, Scamblants, *The Shambrook(e)s*); but the two latter instances are only late recorded.

All these reservations having been made, there yet remains a significant number of examples which are clearer evidence of a Scandinavian influence or a Scandinavian element in the place–names of Cheshire.

Ballgreave **1** 127 and *Balgreave* (Odd Rode) **2** 314 are Norse–English hybrids in which the first element is ON **bál**. OE (WSax) **bǽl** for OE **bēl** would have been a formal alternative, but the dialect geography rules against that supposition. Perhaps originally these two place–names have been analogous with Belgrave **4** 149, and have been modified to the Scandinavian cognate of the first element.

The place–names Berks **3** 259, Birkill **2** 182 involve the similarity of ON **birki** and OE **beorc**. The latter name may be a hybrid of ON **birki** and OE **hyll**, but the first element may have been originally Old English **birce** 'birch'. Birkin (in Rostherne) **2** 58 and Birkenhead **4** 313, show evidence of a Scandinavian–influenced pronunciation of the first element, originally Old English **birce** and **bircen**.

The hybrid place–name *Hinderle* (ON **hind** and OE **lēah**), in the composite place–name *Hinderleklow* the old name for Marple Wood **1** 283, retains evidence of the ON gen.sg. inflexion, *–ar*, of the first element; a feature also observable in Pellerdale **4** 229 and Langerlaths **2** 121.

The form of ON **meðal** influences that of ME **middel** in the field–name *Medylfylde* (Caldy) **4** 286. The first element in *Swaynescroft* (Etchells) **1** 240 and *Swaynesrudinge* (Newton by Daresbury) **2** 156 (**5:1**

xxix) is either ON **sveinn** or the Scandinavian personal–name *Sveinn*.

Rostherne **2** 56 has an OScand personal–name as first element but the second element is more like Old English **þorn, þyrne** than ON **þyrnir**; this is either a Scandinavian–English hybrid or an anglicized Scandinavian place–name.

The ON element **kirkja** becomes ME and ModE dial *kirk*; and the form influences or alternates with those of OE **cirice**, ME *chirch(e)* etc. as element or affix in eleven Cheshire instances recorded before 1500, and in thirty recorded after 1500; occurring most frequently in the Hundreds of Macclesfield and Wirral in both eras, next most frequently in those of Bucklow and Northwich in the later era. ME and ModE *Kirk–* does not occur in the place–names of the Hundred of Nantwich, and only rarely in those of the Hundreds of Eddisbury and Broxton. ON **kirkju–býr** is a different subject; it is a special kind of place–name in **bý**.

The place–name *Leyt Yate* (Storeton) **4** 256 has ON **leið** as first element, but OE **geat** not ON **gata** as second el. This looks like an English place–name with a Scandinavian element in it. Similarly *Schuplendyngis* (Frodsham) **3** 227 has ON **lending** as its second element, but has OE **scip** not ON **skip** for the first element. *Routlothefeld* **4** 75, from ON **rauðr** and ON **laut** may offer an example of an Old Scandinavian place–name being modified into a ME field–name. The location, in Farndon township, is unexpected for a Scandinavian name, and the etymology is therefore suspicious.

The spellings for Spuley Bridge **1** 140–1, **5:1** xvi and ME **rykande** (*Sir Gawain* 2337) are derived from the form of the ON pres. part. *rjúkandi* rather than from that of OE *reocende*.

Schraytefeld (Cotton Abbotts) **4** 112 may be a ME hybrid, with OE or ME **feld** as final element, ON **skreið** as first element; but the ON element may well have been already a part of the ME dialect vocabulary when the place–name was coined.

Tintwistle **1** 320 has proved an awkward place–name (see the various Addenda in **3** xiv, **5:1** xxii and **5:2** *supra*); whilst the final element is clearly OE **twisla**, the first element has been misleading. Yet, the ON pers.n. *Þengill* would make better sense as first el. than the archaic and poetical OE *Þengel*.

Cheshire place–names in the characteristic Scandinavian element **bý** are found in the Hundreds of Wirral, Eddisbury (the northern part) and Bucklow (the western part). They fall into categories classified according to their formation and the difficulty of their interpretation.

The place–names Greasby **4** 291, Helsby **3** 235, Whitby **4** 198, Irby **4** 264 and perhaps Pensby **4** 271, exhibit an alternation, in the second element, between OE **burh, byrig** and ON **bý**. This alternation was observed in PNNth (xxii) as a replacement of an original OE element by an ON one in such Northamptonshire place–names as Badby, Naseby, Thornby, Kirby in Gretton Nth 10, 73, 74, 167 respectively, and in PNCu 219 and 106 for Lazonby and Scaleby respectively. Of these instances, only Badby is reliably attested and even so the *–byrig* form in the tenth–century Anglo–Saxon charter is never repeated in later references. In this series of place–names, the phonetic equation is not easy to reconstruct; if **burh** or **byrig** in final position were reduced to *–bur, –byr* there might ensue a phonetic or graphic coincidence with some representation of **bý(r)**. But some of the Cheshire place–names in which alternations have been discerned exhibit typical spellings *–bery, –beria* nearly contemporary with *–bi, –by, –bia*. On the face of it, these would represent fairly disparate phonemes. Consideration should be given to the possibility that these spellings in the Cheshire p.ns., and those in the Nth and Cu p.ns. as well, represent a scribal substitution. They tend to appear in DB or in (copied) cartulary entries or in later contexts, and they tend to be occasional (unsupported by any further independent tradition of forms from **burh** in spellings from other documents). The occasional *–beria, –bery* spellings might well be due to the similarity of the medieval abbreviations *–b̄i, –b̄y, –b̄ia* (for *–beri, –bery* and the Latinate *–beria*) for **byrig**, to *–bi, –by* and Latinate *–bia* for **bý**. No doubt some of the supposed instances of alternation or substitution represent scribal practice rather than phonetic fact; put simply, for a place–name pronounced [bɪ], the written forms *–bi, –by, –bia* might be misread *–beri(a), –bery* by scribes more accustomed to the crossed *–b* abbreviation sign than they were to Scandinavian place–name elements.

Until this doubt is resolved, we would be well advised to make judgements provisional. In view of the fact that the first element in the place–name Greasby appears to be English, we may suppose it originally had for second element OE **burh, byrig** and was analogous with Bromborough (**Brunanburh* **4** 237). This place–name, however, shows no tendency of the second element to be substituted by the Scandinavian element. The place–name Whitby may have been originally OE *æt Hwītan byrig*; but alternatively the name might well have been originally

ON *Hvíta–by*(*r*). In either case the first element may be a pers.n. Conversely, in the place–names Helsby and Irby, which have Scandinavian first elements, the second element ought to be read as being originally **bý**, for which, occasionally, –*bery* has been substituted by scribal error. The first element of Whitby being either OE **hwīt** or ON **hvít**, the preference between ON **bý** and OE **byrig** for second element cannot be decided.

In the case of Pensby **4** 271, the evidence for the substitution of OE **burh** for ON **bý** is poor. For the time being the place–name can be regarded as an instance of ON **bý** suffixed to a Celtic, or a Celtic–English hybrid, hill–name *Penn(–*hill*). Stoneby **4** 327 represents a modern substitution of –*by* in a different category from the foregoing examples.

In addition to Helsby and Irby, in the category of place–names which can be regarded as truly Scandinavian, are West Kirby **4** 294, *Kirkby in Waleye* **4** 332, Raby **4** 228, Hesby **4** 311 and the late recorded examples Storeby **2** 127, Raby **2** 135 (**3** xv), Stromby **4** 281 and Warmby **4** 279. The place–name Storeby clearly appears to be derived from ON **stǫrr**[2], and ON **storð** looks clear in *Dygisturht* (Kingsley) **3** 244, but the elements appear confused with one another in the place–names Storeton **4** 253 and *le Stor*(*te*)*greues* (Woodbank) **4** 209 (**5:2** Add.).

The first element of Haby **4** 264 is unidentified, so this late–recorded place–name might be originally Scandinavian in both elements, or the final element may be due to substitution of **bý** for **burh**. *Assheby* (Higher Whitley) **2** 127, Ashby **2** 48 (**3** xv) may be instances in which ON **bý** has been substituted for OE **tūn** (see Nth xxii–iii), or which exhibit an anglicization of an original *aska–bý* in which ME *asshe* (< OE **æsc**) has been substituted for the first element. Nevertheless, these two place–names may represent hybrid formations resulting from a continued use of the element **bý** into ME times, if not as a common noun, then as a toponymic element. Comparable with this would be the instances Kiln Walby **4** 305 and Frankby **4** 287, which indicate that the element **bý** continued to be an active, formative element for new place–names in post–Conquest times.

The characteristic ON **hesta–skeiði** is discerned in four late–recorded place–names; and in one from before 1500, *Haskethay* (Lt. Budworth) **3** 187.

ON **eng** is very rare in Cheshire place–names, perceived once, doubtfully, among the names recorded from before 1500, in *Horeisyhengs* (Peover Superior) **2** 89, and in three modern f.ns.

The place–name Ellen's Rocks **4** 248 contains ON **hella**, but the second element could be OE **land** rather than ON **lundr**, for these elements and ME **launde** could be confused in ME *londe, lound*, etc. The ON element appears clear enough in *Lund* etc. (Church Lawton) **2** 323, and *Lundrys* (Lower Withington) **1** 92 (perhaps with ON **hrís** rather than OE **hrīs**, but the form is ambiguous), and *Linseath* (Middlewich) **2** 243 (which is either a hybrid place–name, or exhibits OE **sēaδ** suffixed to a Scandinavian element simplex name). Linn Lund **2** 265 is not a reliable instance of **lundr**.

The element ON **þveit** is rare in Cheshire, occurring in field–names in Bidston in Wirral **4** 312 and in the place–name Morphany (Newton by Daresbury) **2** 154.

ON **skógr** is not frequent either. The pre–1500 material comprises five place–names in the Hundreds of Wirral and Eddisbury: *Grescow* (Bidston cum Ford) **4** 312 (in which the first element is not clearly identified), *Ascow* **4** 286, *Schowakyr* (Frodsham) **3** 228 (in which the other element might be either OE or ON although the ON one might be preferred), and Taskar **4** 317 (**5:2** Add.), Tolske **3** 267 (**5:1** xxxviii, **5:2** Add.) (in which the first element is OE). The instances of **skógr** adduced for Otterspool **1** 263, Wednesough **1** 309, Foscoe **2** 130, Ridding Scow **2** 151, are not well recorded. Swanscoe **1** 108 represents a late phonetic substitution for a different element.

The place–names Meols **4** 296, 299, Tranmere **4** 257 and *Melse Land* (Liscard) **4** 328 contain the characteristic ON element **melr**.

Norman's Hall (Pott Shrigley) **1** 134 (from OE **Norδmann**) and Ransel (Storeton), Roundsill (Bromborough) **4** 256, 237 (from **raun**) contain ON **sel**; the latter of these place–names is Scandinavian in both elements, the former has an OE first element which itself signifies a Scandinavian presence. That presence is also revealed by OE **Norδmann** in the place–names Normanwood (Taxal) **1** 173 and *Normonwode* (Kettleshulme) **1** 113; and by OE **Dene** and ON **Danir** in Denhall (Ness) **4** 220; by ON **Íri** in Irby **4** 264 (and see also Noctorum **4** 268); and by ON **Brettas, Bretar** in the place–names Britland (Tintwistle) **1** 321 and *Bretlandes* (Gt. Sutton) **4** 195.

Steniber (Hatton) **2** 151 represents a place–name Scandinavian in both elements, ON **steinn** and ON **berg**. *Stenris*(*h*)*iche* (Cheadle) **1** 253 is composed of ME *siche* (OE **sīċ**) and a dithematic place–name *Stenris* which looks like a compound of ON **steinn** and ON **hrís** (rather than OE **stān** and **hrīs**, which would have produced *Stanris–). *Stainfeld* and *Stanedelfe*, both in Frodsham **3** 228, show ON **steinn** influencing OE **stān** in place–names formed in English.

The elements ON **stǫrr**[1] and **storð** become alternatives in the place–names Storeton **4** 253 and *le Stortegreues* (Woodbank) **4** 209 (**5:2** Add.); spellings for **stǫrr**[1] predominate in the forms of Storeton. ON **storð** also appears in *Dygisturht* (Kingsley) **3** 244.

ON **strengr** is clearly the first element in Stringhey **4** 327. ON **þing–vǫllr** is clear in Thingwall **4** 273, and **vǫllr** in Langwall **3** 177.

ODan, ON **þorp** is rare in Cheshire place–names and the instances are not well recorded. Thorpe (Gawsworth) **1** 71 (**3** xiv) and Throps Mdw (Moston) **2** 260 are not recorded before the 19th century; Etrop (Ringway) **2** 30 and Okenthorpe (Eaton nr. Davenham) **2** 205 not before the 16th century; Thorp Wood (Bosley) **1** 58 is recorded from 1305. Alternatively the four last could represent OE **þrop**.

The following place–names have as their first element a personal–name of an Old Scandinavian type or origin, or a second element which is or could be Old Scandinavian: Antrobus **2** 127, Arno **4** 270, Arclid **2** 264, *Aynesargh* (Macclesfield Hundred) **1** 51, Gunco **1** 115, *Halwarte Flatte* (Odd Rode) **2** 315, Kettleshulme **1** 110, *Steyncolesdale* (Thurstaston) **4** 282, *Thurberneswra* (Foulk Stapleford) **5:2** Add. (**4** 107), Tintwistle **1** 320 (**3** xiv, **5:1** xxii, **5:2** Add.). With these may belong *Grymesbothum* (Newton in Mottram in Longdendale) **1** 317; in which the second element is **bōth**, dat.pl. **bōthum**. The first element here could be ON *Grímr* or OE *Grīm*, personal–names. But these are also by–names of the god Odin / Woden, and since, in Cheshire place–names except this one and Grinsome **3** 252, the theme *Grim–*, *Grym–* is only found with the elements OE **græfe** and OE **dīc**, the significance of the element may be somewhat more archaeological or cultural than personal.

Cheshire place–names recorded for dates before 1500 which have to be considered in pursuit of the Scandinavian element are: *Afnames* (Childer Thornton) **4** 198, Antrobus **2** 127, Arnold's Eye (Lt. Meols) **4** xvi, 300, Arrowe **4** 261, *Ascow* (Caldy) **4** 286, *Aynesargh* (Macclesfield

Hundred) **1** 51, *Blake–Hereye* (Wigland) **4** 52, Caldy **4** 282, ?*Colders* (Higher Bebington) **4** 248, R. Croco **1** 19, Crowsdale (Poulton cum Spital) **4** 253, Golacre (Liscard) **4** 328, Helsdale (Lymm) **2** 39 (**5:1** xxiv), *Kybull Croft* (Grappenhall) **5:1** xxviii (**2** 142–3), Organ (Gt. Sutton) **4** 195, Pellerdale (Raby) **4** 229, *Schowakyr* (Frodsham) **3** 228, *Steyncolesdale* (Thurstaston) 4 282, *Uluesdale* (Claverton) **4** 162.

APPENDIX I

Reprinted Articles on Cheshire Place–Names
by
†John McN. Dodgson

A. 'The Background of Brunanburh' [1957]
B. 'The English Arrival in Cheshire' [1968]
C. 'Place-Names and Street–Names at Chester' [1968]
D. 'Alliterative Place–Names' [1973]
E. 'The Welsh Element in the Field–Names of Cheshire' [1985]

The articles below, reprinted here by kind permission of the copyright holders, were building–blocks in the preparation of the 'Introduction' to the Survey of Cheshire Place–Names which Professor Dodgson was in the event sadly unable to complete. They form an important body of material which supplements the three completed sections of the 'Introduction', 220–247, *supra*. Some additional notes have been inserted here at the end of A, B, C, and E; these are indicated in the text by†.

A. THE BACKGROUND OF BRUNANBURH

[Reprinted from *Sagabook* XIV: 4 (1957), 303–16]

One of the places which have been suggested as the site of the famous battle fought A.D. 937 *ymb Brunanburh*, is Bromborough on the Mersey shore of Wirral, in Cheshire.[1] As long ago as 1937, A. H. Smith[2] demonstrated that the place–name Bromborough must be derived from the OE form *Brunanburh* 'the stronghold of a man called *Bruna*'. Recent collections of place–name spellings for this district[3] have not produced any evidence to upset Smith's argument; indeed, two spellings which support it can be added to the examples he quoted then.[4] But, as Alistair Campbell pointed out at the time, the identity of place–name does not prove that this *Brunanburh* in Wirral is the same as that near which the battle took place.[5] There is no available information which would, in fact, make proof possible; there are no recorded place–names in the vicinity of Bromborough which would support any of the traditional alternative forms of name for the battlefield as listed by Campbell and Smith, and there is no further record of the sea–name *Dingesmere*[6†] — the water over

---

[1] The proposed locations are listed in Alistair Campbell, *The Battle of Brunanburh* (1938), 57–80. Bromborough is marked on the map by the lower of the two crosses below the letter B on the Wirral shore of Mersey, see p. 253 *infra*.

[2] 'The Site of the Battle of Brunanburh', *London Mediæval Studies,* I, part 1 (1937), 56–59. Bromborough was identified with *Brunanburh* by Gibson in his edition of the Anglo–Saxon Chronicle in 1692, and by R.F. Weymouth in *Athenæum*, 15th August 1885, p. 207.

[3] *The Place–Names of Cheshire* (EPNS).

[4] *Bruneburgh* 1153 (1285) Cartulary of Chester Abbey, *Bronebur'* 1291 Eyre Roll.

[5] Campbell, op. cit., 59, note.

[6] Anglo–Saxon Chronicle 'A' and 'C' texts (ASC 'A', 'C') — altered to *Dinnesmere* in the Otho MS — *Dyngesmere* ASC 'B', *Dynigesmere* ASC 'D'. Agreement between 'A' and 'C' establishes *Dinges–* as the original form.

which the defeated Anlaf fled to Dublin. The place–name Wargraves[7] in
Bromborough parish,[†] which marks the site of the battle in the six–inch
Ordnance Survey Map, may be an old place–name of purely local usage
but it may also be a name more recently inspired by local antiquarianism.
There have been, as yet, no archæological discoveries there which might
lead to a certain identification.

In spite of the lack of conclusive evidence, however, it is possible to
show that the place Bromborough, once bearing the name *Brunanburh,*
is situated in a district likely to have been the scene of the battle.
Bromborough lies on the edge of an area of Norse settlement, which was
part of the larger territory of North–West England over–run by Norse
immigrants from Ireland and Man in the early–tenth century.[8] Details of
this settlement in Wirral are available in two sources, documentary
history,[9] and place–names.[10]

Apart from the Viking kingdom at York, the Wirral settlement is the
only Norse movement into England that is documented. The prime
document is *Annals of Ireland. Three Fragments,*[11] which though of
dubious tradition, is corroborated and supplemented by other Irish and by
Welsh annals. From these accounts, the following course of events
appears:[12]

---

[7] *Wargraves* does not appear in old records, so there are no early spellings for it.
It may derive from ME **werre** (OF **werre**) 'war, battle' and ME **grave** (OE **græf**) 'a
trench, a pit, an earthwork'.

[8] Eilert Ekwall, *Scandinavians and Celts in the North–West of England* (1918);
F.T. Wainwright, 'The Scandinavians in Lancashire', *Transactions of the Lancs. and
Cheshire Antiquarian Society* 58 (1945–6), 71–116.

[9] F.T. Wainwright, 'North–West Mercia, A.D. 871–924', *Transactions of the
Historic Society of Lancs. and Cheshire* 94 (1942), 3–55; and 'Ingimund's Invasion',
English Historical Review 63 (April 1948), 145–169.

[10] The Scandinavian settlements in Cheshire, as illustrated by place–names, lie
in defined areas, Danish east of R. Weaver, Norse in Wirral and district; see G.
Barnes, 'The Evidence of Place–Names for the Scandinavian Settlements in
Cheshire', *Transactions of the Lancashire and Cheshire Antiquarian Society* 63
(1952–3), 131–155; and S. Potter, 'Cheshire Place–Names', *Transactions of the
Historic Society of Lancs. and Cheshire* 106 (1955), 16–20 with map (fig. 3).

[11] Edited by John O'Donovan for the Irish Archæological and Celtic Society
(Dublin, 1860) from *Fragmenta Tria Annalium Hiberniae* (Bibliothèque Royale,
Brussels, MS. 5301–5302). This Brussels MS. is a nineteenth–century copy made by
O'Donovan of a copy made in 1643 by Duald Mac Firbis of a vellum manuscript
since lost.

[12] *v.* F.T. Wainwright, 'Ingimund's Invasion', loc. cit.

In A.D. 902 the Norsemen were expelled from Dublin. Led by one Ingimund they went to Britain. They landed in Anglesey where they were resisted by the king of the Britons,[13] who defeated them in battle and drove them out. Thereupon Ingimund and his people sought out Æþelflæd lady of the Mercians, her husband Æþelred being a sick man,[14] and requested land of her, in which to settle, being weary of war. She granted Ingimund land near Chester,[15] and there for a time he lived quietly, until he began to envy the English their better lands around Chester, a rich city.[16] Ingimund had secret consultations with the leaders of the Norsemen and the Danes, who agreed to join him in a bid for land. They would first ask for, and then fight for, the lands Ingimund coveted. They assembled secretly at Ingimund's house. Æþelflæd heard tell of the plot, and she garrisoned Chester,[16] and when the Danes and the Norsemen attacked the city, the garrison made a stout resistance. The siege being vigorous, the defenders sent messengers to Æþelred, then at the point of death (he died A.D. 911), to ask his advice and that of his lady. They advised upon a stratagem which was successful up to a point. But when the Norsemen began to undermine the city wall, Æþelflæd and Æþelred tried to draw them off by splitting the enemy forces; they persuaded the Irishmen who were among the Norsemen, and who were disaffected towards the Danes, to massacre the Danes. The Norsemen went on mining and were stopped only when all the beehives in the city were thrown down upon them from the wall, and they were so badly stung that they had to withdraw. But it was not long after that before the Norsemen came to do battle again . . .

The important features of this story are (a) the date — ranging from A.D. 902 to c. 910 (a lost continuation of *Three Fragments* presumably dealt with later attacks by the Norsemen upon the English); (b) the

[13] *Three Fragments* calls this king 'the son of Cadell son of Rhodri'; J.E. Lloyd, *A History of Wales*, I, 332, says Cadell son of Rhodri Mawr did not die until c. 909, and that his sons were Hywel and Clydog; Wainwright, op. cit., 167, note 4, suggests that *Three Fragments* should read 'the brother of Cadell . . .' to refer to Anarawd ruler of Gwynned and Anglesey until A.D. 916. Wainwright's correction is not necessary, for the *Three Fragments* scribe uses the term 'king' loosely, and the leader of the British force need not have been a reigning monarch: cf. note 14 *infra*.

[14] *Three Fragments* calls her 'Edelfrida Queen of the Saxons', and her husband 'Edelfrid the King.' He was *aldorman* of Mercia from 883 until his death in 911; she was married to him by the end of 889 and ruled Mercia after his death until she died in 918.

[15] *Three Fragments* reads 'Castra'.

[16] ASC 'A', 'B', 'C', 'D', has the Danes arrive on *anre westre ceastre in wirhealum* in 893; the Mercian Register embodied in the ASC (see note 35 *infra*) records the rebuilding of Chester. In ASC 'C' this is dated 907.

character of the settlement — the creation, by arrangement with the Mercian government, of a Norse community in North–West Mercia, which, once established, was liable to be rebellious, and which had apparently been settled in second–rate land upon which it wished to improve; (c) the relationship of various peoples in the new community — a mixture of Norsemen and Irishmen, entering into warlike political arrangements with the Danes who were at that time the enemies of the English state.

The characteristics and the distribution of the Norse element in the place–names of Wirral and district bear this analysis out,[17] as the following survey will show.

The place–names NOCTORUM ('the dry hillock', OIr **cnocc** 'hillock', OIr **tírim** adj., 'dry') and IRBY ('the farmstead of the Irish' ON *Íra–býr*) indicate, respectively, the location of Irish–speaking inhabitants and of the habitation of a community from Ireland.[18] In the place–name IRBY, as in GREASBY and WHITBY, there is an exchange of ON **býr** 'farmstead' and OE **byrig**, dative singular of OE **burh** 'stronghold, fortified house'.[19] In GAYTON, ON **geit** 'a goat' rather than OE **gāt** 'a goat' is the first element.[20] GAYTON is one of a number of place–names in Wirral where a Norse first element is combined with the ending *–ton*.[21] This ending may represent either OE **tūn** 'enclosure, farmstead' or ON **tún** 'farmstead, farm enclosure, enclosed in–field', which cannot be

---

[17] *v.* note 10, *supra.*

[18] ON *Íri* as a by–name usually denotes a man who has sojourned in Ireland.

[19] Irby is *Erberia, Irreby* c. 1100 (1280) Chester Cartulary, where OE **byrig** is an occasional substitution for original ON **býr**. Greasby is *Gravesberie* 1086 DB, *Grauesbyri, –biri, –beri* c. 1100 (1150 and 1280) Chester Cartulary, *Grauisby* c. 1100 (1280), c. 1153 (1280) ibid., and Whitby is *Witeberia* c. 1100 (1150), 1150, *Witebia* c. 1100 (1280), *Witebi* c. 1190 (14th) ibid.; in these two place–names original OE **byrig** is replaced by ON **býr**.

[20] *Gaitone* 1086 DB, *Geytona* 1238 Pipe Roll; there is no record of a ME form *Gatton* that would be expected from OE *gāt–tūn*.

[21] Claughton (ON **klakkr** 'a hill'), Storeton (ON **stórr** adj., 'great'), Larton (ON **leirr** 'clay'), and possibly Neston (? ON **nes** 'headland', though ME spellings in *Nas–* indicate OE Mercian **næss** (OE **ness**) 'a headland'). Thurstaston contains the ON personal–name *Þorsteinn*, spelt in the English fashion *Thurstan*; Barnston probably contains the personal–name ON *Bjǫrnúlfr* or OE *Beornwulf* as mediaeval spellings show.

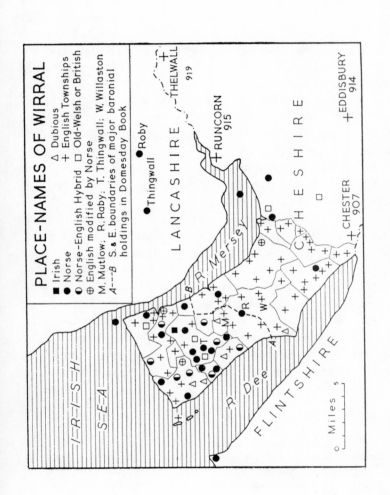

Figure A 1 : Place-Names of Wirral.

distinguished from each other formally.[22]

These place–names may safely be regarded as the creation of a mixed Anglo–Norse community predominantly Norse in speech; some of them may as well be purely Norse. Place–names which are assuredly Norse are MEOLS (ON **melr** 'sandbank'), TRANMERE ('the crane–frequented sandbank', ON **trani** 'a crane, a heron', ON **melr** 'sandbank'), THINGWALL (ON *þing–vǫllr* 'field where the Thing meets'), and certain other place–names, which end in *–by* (ON **býr**). WEST KIRBY and *Kirby in Waley* (the old name for Wallasey village as distinct from the parish of Wallasey in which it lay) are derived from ON *kirkju–býr* 'the church hamlet'; PENSBY contains Welsh **pen–** (British ***penno–**) 'a hill'; FRANKBY is 'the Frenchman's farmstead';[23] RABY is 'the boundary farmstead' (ON **rá** 'boundary mark'); HELSBY (outside Wirral, on the south side of Mersey in Eddisbury Hundred) is 'the farmstead on the ledge' (ON **hjalli** 'a ledge') and lies on the side of a steep and prominent hill overlooking the Mersey estuary.

Many of these places were not of sufficient importance to be entered in Domesday Book by name. If we subtract those place–names which show hybrid characteristics, from the place–names which do appear there,[24] there remain only MEOLS, THINGWALL, RABY and HELSBY that point decisively to Norse settlement, with NOCTORUM indicating an associated Irish settlement. Of these only RABY and HELSBY are habitative names. The minor character of the Norse habitative place–names in Wirral is shown by place–names in *–by*, many of which only appear in late records, while some are, so far, only known from nineteenth–century Tithe Award field–names which preserve the memory

---

[22] *v.* A.H. Smith, *English Place–Name Elements,* EPNS 26 (1956), s.v. **tūn** OE, para. (10).

[23] From ME *Frank* (OE **Franca**) 'a Frenchman'. In Domesday Book, fo. 264b, in the entry for Caldy, is the note 'et unus Francigena cum uno serviente habet duas carucas'. This Frenchman held an estate worth noticing as a separate item for taxation purposes, but the place had no separate name. The place–name emerges as *Frankeby*, 1230 *Harl. MS.*, 1304 Chester Fines. This place–name obviously does not contain ON *Frakki* 'a Frenchman'. Danish *Franki* would be unexpected here; though the place–name Denhall in Ness parish might derive from both ON *Dena* (gen. pl.) and ON *Dana* (gen. pl.) 'of the Danes', with ON **vǫllr** (dat. sg. **velli**) 'field' confused with OE **wella, wælle** 'a spring, a stream'.

[24] Noctorum, Greasby, Gayton, Storeton, Neston (and Ness), Thurstaston, Barnston, Meols, Thingwall, Raby, Helsby.

of their location — Syllaby (Gt. Saughall), Haby (Barnston), Hesby (Bidston), Stromby (Thurstaston), Kiln Walby (Upton near Woodchurch; *Gildewalleby* 1321 Cheshire Sheaf series 3, No. 24, p. 40). Another Norse place–name for a minor settlement is ARROWE, which also appears late in record (*Arwe* c. 1245 Chester), and derives from ON **erg** 'shieling', a word borrowed from MIr **airge**, Gælic **airigh**.[25†]

This word **erg** also appears in field–names, especially in Arrowe parish itself. Norse elements in the field–names of the area are widespread and pervasive.[26] Furthermore, there is a good number of Norse names of natural features in the area, e.g. ON **dalr** 'valley' in Crowsdale (ON **kross**), Lingdale (ON **lyng**), and *Steyncolesdale* (1298 Plea Roll, in Thurstaston parish; containing the ON personal–name *Steinkell*), and ON **sker** 'reef, sandbank' in Score Bank in the Mersey Estuary (called *Swarteskere* 1308 Black Prince's Register, 'the black reef'), and a lost *Le Skere* (1275 Cheshire Sheaf) off Wallasey.

The conclusions to be derived from this place–name evidence are, that Norse village–names begin as the names of minor and insignificant farmsteads that are subsidiary settlements in hitherto unused land within the framework of English townships and parishes; that the nature and distribution of Anglo–Norse hybrid place–names (see Figure A 1) as compared with the distribution of English place–names, indicates a Norse settlement beginning in north–west Wirral and spreading south and east across the peninsula from more exposed to more fertile and developed country; and that the prevalence and persistence of Norse field– and minor–names throughout the peninsula, and, at the same time, the persistence of English parish–, township–, field– and minor–names even in the Norse northern area of it, bespeak a deliberate and non–disruptive integration of Norse and English people into one Anglo–Norse community.

The Norse element must have remained dominant for some time; at least long enough to impress its consciousness of identity upon the pattern of regional government over and above the parochial level, as the

---

[25] On the possibility of this place–name's derivation directly from MIr **airge**, rather than from ON **erg**, *v.* Christian Matras, 'Gammelfærosk *ærgi*, n., og dermed beslægtede ord', *Namn och Bygd*, Årgang 44 (1956), 51–67. Also *v.* A. H. Smith, *English Place–Name Elements*, EPNS 25 (1956), s.v. **erg** ON.

[26] *v.* F.T. Wainwright, 'Field–Names', *Antiquity* 17 (1943), 57–66; also *English Historical Review* 63 (April 1948), 162.

distribution of certain place–names in Wirral indicates. The place THINGWALL is in the Norse northern end of the peninsula, and can only be the meeting–place of a Norse organisation. In Domesday Book, what is now the Hundred of Wirrall was known as the Hundred of *Wilaveston* (OE *Wīglāfes–tūn* 'Wiglaf's farmstead') which met at Willaston. Half–way between Thingwall and Willaston is RABY, 'the farmstead at the boundary–mark'. It looks as though the Norse colony had a defined boundary, within which it owned its own jurisdiction.

This special jurisdiction is commemorated also in the feudal arrangement of north Wirral in post–Conquest times. In 1182 the Pipe Roll names a minor hundred in Wirral *Caldeihundredum* 'the Hundred of Caldy'. This minor hundred, attached to the manor of Gayton, survived until recently.[27] The origin of this jurisdiction lies in the Norman re–organisation of the Anglo–Saxon shire of Cheshire. The feudal allocation of lands in Cheshire was made by the Earl of Chester to his own barons, whose baronies centred upon Halton, Mold (Flintshire), Rhuddlan (Flintshire), Malpas, Nantwich, Shipbrook, Dunham Massey, Kinderton and Stockport.[28]

In Domesday Book, Robert, baron of Rhuddlan in Flintshire, also held a block of lands in Wirral, which apart from Gt. and Lt. Mollington, all lay in the north and west of the hundred:[29] in Leighton, Thornton Hough, Gayton, Heswall, Thurstaston, Gt. and Lt. Meols, Newton, Larton, Wallasey, Neston, Hargrave, Hoose, West Kirby, Poulton and Seacombe. This estate is the origin of the minor hundred; it is approximately co–terminous with it. Apart from the Rhuddlan barony, the lands of north Wirral were held by the barons of Dunham Massy, Halton and Mold (Moreton, Claughton, Tranmere, Saughall Massey, Bidston; Barnston and half of Raby; Caldy; respectively). The greater part of the north of Wirral, therefore, was held in compact parcels by four of the most powerful Norman barons of Cheshire; by contrast, in the rest of Wirral the

---

[27] G. Ormerod, *History of Cheshire,* ed. T. Helsby (1882), II, 518, traces its feudal descent down to 1819 when some of its privileges were still observed. He lists the extent of the minor hundred as being then comprised of Thornton Hough, Leighton (in Neston), Gayton, Heswall, Thurstaston, West Kirby, Gt. and Lt. Meols, Hoose, Newton, Larton, and Poulton–cum–Seacombe.

[28] *v.* Ormerod, op. cit., I, 55; 56, 58 note; 520; 688; II, 245; 592; III, 187; 788, respectively.

[29] Ormerod, op. cit., I, 55; II, 353.

Domesday holdings are dispersed.

The treatment of this area of north Wirral, which is approximately co–terminous with the Norse settlement area, by the Norman administration, is paralleled elsewhere in Cheshire. The present Hundred of Bucklow, the northern hundred of Cheshire that marches with Lancashire along Mersey, was in Domesday Book two hundreds, *Tunendune*, the western one, meeting at an unidentified place, and *Bochelau*, the eastern one, whose name now applies to both, meeting at Bucklow Hill (*OE Buccan–hlaw* 'Bucca's mound') in Mere parish. In two mediæval lists[30] of the vills and manors of the barony of Halton (the minor hundred called *Haltonshire* was its jurisdiction), it is apparent that this barony was co–terminous with the Domesday Book Hundred of *Tunendune*.[31] Nantwich Hundred,[32] at the other end of the county, was one hundred in Domesday Book, *Warmundestreu* (OE *Wærmundes–treow* 'Wærmund's tree'), the meeting–place of which is unidentified. An inspeximus in 1438 of an inquisition made in 1342 lists the vills of the Nantwich barony held by William de Maubanc, baron of Nantwich,[33] and shows that this barony coincided rather with the Domesday Hundred of *Warmundestreu* than with the reformed Hundred of Nantwich. The townships of Church Minshull, Betchton, Hassall and Alsager were transferred from the Hundred of *Warmundestreu* (Nantwich) to that of Northwich (DB *Mildestuic* i.e. Middlewich), at some date in the twelfth century. Although they were then no longer in Nantwich Hundred, they remained in the Nantwich barony.

In these examples the Norman feudal estates with their own jurisdictions were based upon the Anglo–Saxon hundreds, and so preserved the shape of the old administrative pattern after the twelfth–century reorganisation of the major hundreds. Since this happens

[30] National Register of Archives (Historical MSS. Commission), Report No. 3636 (*Tabley Muniments*), entry No. 1063, a list of date c. 1300 *tempore* Henry Lacy, baron of Halton; Ormerod, op. cit., I, 704 and note, a list for a date c. 1360 at the death of Henry duke of Lancaster, baron of Halton.

[31] All the land of the present Bucklow hundred west of a line excluding Lymm, Grappenhall, High Legh, Mere, Tabley Superior, Pickmere and Marston.

[32] Ormerod, op. cit., III, 421.

[33] Enrolled in Chester Recognisance Rolls, *Report of the Deputy Keeper of the Public Records*, No. 37, Appendix II, p. 478. The barony was divided in 1342 among the daughters of Wm. de Maubanc.

in these other parts of Cheshire, it is not unreasonable to suppose the same process in Wirral, and to assume that the baronial minor Hundred of Caldy and the lesser block–holdings in north Wirral, represent a Norman adaptation of an administrative pattern that already existed when the Norman earls took over the shire. It looks as though the Norse enclave in Wirral was so politically distinctive that it justified a special feudal administration.

If the deductions made from place–names and from this excursion into Norman feudal history are added to those drawn from the historical account presented in *Three Fragments,* it becomes obvious that in Wirral there was throughout the tenth and eleventh centuries a recognised Norse colony, deliberately established in a definitely bounded area, and with a conscious identity sufficient to support and warrant a distinctive local administration. The situation was apparently repeated to some extent across Mersey in South–West Lancashire,[34] where there is another Thingwall (near Liverpool), the nucleus of a Norse enclave there whose inland boundary was likewise marked by a *rá–býr*, ROBY. The Wirral colony began a programme of vigorous, and occasionally, armed, expansion almost immediately after its establishment, towards the better lands of the English districts to the south. It is therefore proper to suppose that at any date shortly after A.D. 902–910, there would exist on either shore of the Mersey estuary a community of Norse settlers upon whose sympathy, at least, any Norse expedition passing up or down that river would be able to rely. There was here a route by which a ship–borne attack could have been delivered far into the mainland of Mercia, a route flanked by the territory of Norsemen who were not themselves averse to attacking the English. It would have been attractive to any Viking adventurer. It may have been the route of Sihtric's raid in 920, to Davenport in South–East Cheshire, the market–place (OE **port** 'market') on the R. Dane (*Daven*) which served the Danish area of the county; it will be recalled that there is a record of disaffection towards the Danes on the part of the Irish element in the Wirral settlement, in the *Three Fragments* account.

Of the state of affairs near the Mersey estuary the Anglo–Saxon Chronicle has little to say in a direct fashion. The affairs of North–West

[34] *v.* F.T. Wainwright, 'The Scandinavians in Lancashire', *Transactions of the Lancs. and Cheshire Antiquarian Society* 58 (1945–6), 71–116.

Mercia tend to be overshadowed by the events leading to the re–conquest of the Danelaw. However, the 'Mercian Register' included in the B– and C–texts of the Chronicle[35] records the building, between 907 and 919 of a series of fortresses along the west and north frontiers of Mercia. In 907 it records the rebuilding of Chester (a probable reason for this has been alluded to). In 909 (D–text) or 910 (C–text) it records the building of *Bremesburh,* in 912 *Scergeat* — these are unidentified so their strategic purpose is unknown — and in 914 Eddisbury (Cheshire), presumably to support Chester in guarding against incursions from the North and the Mersey estuary. In 915, the Register informs us, the frontier with mid–Wales was secured by a fort at Chirbury (Salop), and the head of the Mersey estuary was guarded by a fort at Runcorn (Cheshire). It also records, in the same year, the building of the unidentified fort *Weardbyrig* (there is no place–name evidence to assure an identification with Warburton in N. Cheshire, though such a location would be attractive). Finally, the 'Mercian Register' records Eadweard's building a fort at *Cledemuða* in 921 — probably at the mouth of the North Welsh River Clwyd, near Rhuddlan.[36] Meanwhile, according to another annal, not in the 'Mercian Register', he had fortified Thelwall (Cheshire) and Manchester in 919 (ASC 'A' *sub anno* 922). By 921 therefore, there was a line of five, possibly six, fortresses established to hold the frontier from North Wales to Manchester.

This great effort to secure the north–west frontier of Mercia was called forth by the steady build–up of Norse power in the north–country which culminated in the establishment of the York kingdom. The urgency of the need for fortification on this frontier cannot have been lessened by the existence upon the frontier itself of restless Norse colonies, whose territories would serve as excellent beach–heads for any expedition striking down into Mercia along a short, direct and strategic route from Mersey.

It is impossible to connect in any detailed way the facts known about *Brunanburh* with this context of political and geographical factors. The main tradition of the campaign derives from the Anglo–Saxon poem

[35] J. Earle and C. Plummer, *Two of the Saxon Chronicles Parallel* (1892), I, 92, note 7.

[36] F.T. Wainwright, 'Cledemuða', *English Historical Review* 65 (April 1950), 203–212.

(ASC 'A', 'B', 'C', 'D'), William of Malmesbury's two accounts — his own twelfth–century report[37] and his quotation of a mid–tenth–century Latin poem[38] — and from the account of Florence of Worcester,[39] also twelfth century. From these sources we learn that an alliance was made in the north–country[40] between Anlaf the Norseman and Constantine king of the Scots. They crossed the English frontier[41] or landed in the estuary of the Humber.[42] The English king gave way before them for a while according to plan[43] during which time they made great inroads and took much booty. Upon the king's taking the field against them, the enemy abandoned their booty and fled away towards their own country.[44] The English force of West–Saxons and Mercians under Athelstan and Edmund his brother utterly routed them in a fight around *Brunanburh*, pursuing them[45] throughout the day.[46] After the battle, Anlaf and his surviving companions returned by ship to Dublin across *Dingesmere*.[47]

All that emerges from this, is that the invasion was planned in the north–country, and reached 'a long way' into England; the enemy was defeated by a combined West–Saxon and Mercian force; the survivors of

---

[37] *De Gestis Regum Anglorum* ed. W. Stubbs (1887–89), I, 142.

[38] ibid., I, 151.

[39] *Chronicon ex Chronicis* ed. B. Thorpe (1848–9), I, 132.

[40] William of Malmesbury, Latin poem, lines 4–7; quoted by A. Campbell, *The Battle of Brunanburh* (1938), 154.

[41] William of Malmesbury; *v.* Campbell, op. cit., 152.

[42] Florence of Worcester; *v.* Campbell, op. cit., 147.

[43] William of Malmesbury; *v.* Campbell, op. cit., 152. The Latin poem, lines 11–18, *v.* Campbell, op. cit., 155, is more descriptive.

[44] William of Malmesbury, Latin poem, lines 26–33, *v.* Campbell op. cit., 155.

[45] Campbell's note (op. cit., 104) on *on last legdun* in line 22 of his text of the Anglo–Saxon poem, is important. He interprets it 'they pressed on behind'. This indicates pursuit upon and from the battlefield, rather than a long chase; see note 46 *infra*.

[46] The duration of the battle and its relevance to site of the battlefield is discussed by A.H. Smith, 'The Site of the Battle of Brunanburh', *London Mediæval Studies*, I, i (1937), 58. Note that William of Malmesbury parallels the OE poem's phrase *ondlongne dæg* (line 21, Campbell's edition) with *tota die usque ad vesperam* (Campbell op. cit., 153). If Bromborough be *Brunanburh,* we should have to assume that the battle took place after the invaders had withdrawn to the coast from their deep penetration inland. In that case, they may have begun to retreat as soon as the king turned out, as William of Malmesbury says (*v.* note 44 *supra*), their retreat culminating in a day–long disaster in the battle.

[47] OE poem, Campbell's edition, lines 53–56.

the enemy's defeat went off home, some of them taking ship to Dublin. Although this sea–borne escape to Dublin need not imply a direct Irish Sea passage, the only evidence against the location of *Brunanburh* on the North–West coast that comes from the traditional accounts, is the statement of Florence of Worcester that the landings took place in Humber.[48] His source for this statement is not known, and its authority can neither be attacked nor defended.

Unless Florence's statement is to be considered dependent on reliable tradition (and the OE poem and the Latin poem do not elucidate this), Bromborough in Wirral would appear to be the most eligible place for the battlefield. In no other locality does the context of geography, politics and place–names accord so well with the few facts we possess concerning the battle.

Additional Notes [A.R.R.]

Professor Dodgson's identification of the *Brunanburh* battle–site with Bromborough, Ch, has recently been supported by a new consideration of the historical context by N.J. Higham, 'The Context of Brunanburh', in *Names, Places and People: an Onomastic Miscellany in Memory of John McNeal Dodgson*, ed. A.R. Rumble and A.D. Mills (Stamford, 1997), 144–56.

p. 248 and n6, *Dingesmere*. See **4** 240 and **5:2** Add. Cf. *infra*, p. 263, n11.

p. 250 and n7, Wargraves. However, the el. **werre** here is probably a derogatory epithet and nothing to do with a battlefield. See **4** 242, **5:1** xliii.

p. 255 and n25. On ON **erg**, see further, G. Fellows Jensen, 'Common Gaelic *áirghe*, Old Scandinavian *ǽrgi* or *erg*?', *Nomina* 4 (1980), 67–74.

---

[48] It might be pointed out that the point of exit after the defeat may not have been the point of entry at the beginning of the campaign. It is not known whether the ships Anlaf fled in were his own; nor whether he found them where he had left them.

B. THE ENGLISH ARRIVAL IN CHESHIRE

[Reprinted from LCHS 119 (1967), 1–37]

The subject of this paper has been discussed by K. Jackson,[1] G. Barnes[2] and Dorothy Sylvester[3]. Other relevant statements have been made by E. Ekwall[4] and F.M. Stenton.[5] In this paper an attempt is made to demonstrate the likelihood that the date and manner of the arrival of the English in Cheshire was a sixth century[†] infiltration into a British territory. The exercise will consist of an attempt to synthesise the evidence from place–names and that from documentary history into a coherent sequence of unrecorded events. It will appear that the significance of the recorded history of the English in Cheshire is almost as inferential as that of the place–name forms.

For comparison and contrast with these evidences for the English arrival, it is useful to consider these evidences in respect of that other immigration at a later epoch, the Scandinavian settlements. This later process had a different outcome — whereas the English immigrants took over and henceforth completely controlled the British territory they had entered, the Scandinavian immigrants who settled amongst the English community in Cheshire were absorbed into that community, and did not achieve political control of it or of its territory. This difference is political: the English immigrant formed a government of his own for lack of a strong opposing British establishment,[†] whereas the Scandinavian

---

[1] *Language and History in Early Britain* (Edinburgh, 1953), 210–15.

[2] 'Early English Settlement and Society in Cheshire from the Evidence of Place–Names', *Transactions of the Lancashire and Cheshire Antiquarian Society* 71 (1961), 43–57.

[3] 'Cheshire in the Dark Ages', *Transactions of the Historic Society of Lancashire and Cheshire* 114 (1962), 1–22.

[4] *The Place–Names of Lancashire* (Manchester, 1922), 227–33; *English Place–Names in –ing* (Skrifter utgivna av Kungl. Humanistiska Vetenskaps–samfundet i Lund 6, 2nd ed., Lund, 1962), 79, 99.

[5] *Anglo–Saxon England* (2nd ed., Oxford, 1947), 77–8; cf. *Transactions of the Royal Historical Society,* 4th series, 22, 21, commented upon by K. Jackson, *Language and History in Early Britain*, 215–16.

immigrant found a firm English establishment in control of the territory he entered — even, in fact, controlling his immigration.[†] The evidence for the Scandinavian immigration is well known. It has been spoken of by G. Barnes,[6] S. Potter,[7] A.H. Smith,[8] F.T. Wainwright[9] and me.[10] There is no need to rehearse all this, nor spell out the details of the Norse and Irish place–names in Wirral which are memorials of the age of Ingimund's invasion and the battle of *Brunanburh* (Bromborough)[11] A.D. 937. But although the presence of the Norsemen in Wirral has been reported by history and illustrated by place–names, the Scandinavian presence in Cheshire as a whole is more pervasive than might have appeared from previous studies; it is illustrated in Figure B 1. Danes are recognised from their characteristic place–names, in the several places called

[6] 'The Evidence of Place–Names for the Scandinavian Settlements in Cheshire', *Trans. Lancs. Ches. Antiq. Soc.* 63 (1952–3), 131–55.

[7] 'Cheshire Place–Names', *Trans. Hist. Soc. Lancs. Ches.* 106 (1955), 16–20.

[8] 'The Site of the Battle of Brunanburh', *London Mediæval Studies*, I, part 1 (1937), 56–59; cf. A. Campbell, *The Battle of Brunanburh* (1938), 57–80.

[9] 'The Scandinavians in Lancashire', *Trans. Lancs. Ches. Antiq. Soc.* 58 (1945–6), 71–116; 'North–West Mercia, A.D. 871–924', *Trans. Hist. Soc. Lancs. Ches.* 94 (1942), 3–55; 'Ingimund's Invasion', *English Historical Review* 63 (1948), 145–69.

[10] 'The Background of Brunanburh', *Saga–Book* (The Viking Society for Northern Research) XIV, part 4 (1956–7), 303–16 *supra*, Appendix I: A].

[11] In the light of my argument hereafter about the importance of the *–ing*–suffix formations in English place–names, it is of almost ironical interest to note that such a formation appears as clinching evidence for the identification of *Brunanburh* with Bromborough. In the *Saga–Book* review of this historical problem I committed myself to A. H. Smith's identification of the battle–site and the Wirral place–name as against the identification with Burnswark in Dumfriesshire: but there remained a loose end — there was no explanation of the sea–name *Dingesmere* (*Saga–Book* loc. cit. 303 note 6 [= *supra*, p. 249, note 6]), a water across which the defeated Norsemen escaped back to Dublin. I now think that *Dingesmere* is a poetic and figurative invention of a name for the Irish Sea, from OE **mere**, 'a lake, a body of water', here 'the sea', compounded with a form *Dinges* which is the genitive singular of a name–form *Ding*. This form is not explicable as any known Old English personal–name, but it would be quite easily explicable as a kind of place–name form, i.e. as an OE *–ing*–suffix derivative of the river–name *Dee* (OE *Dēing > Ding*), so that *Dingesmere* would mean 'the water of *Ding*', and *Ding* would mean 'that which is named after or is associated with or which belongs to, R. Dee'.[†]

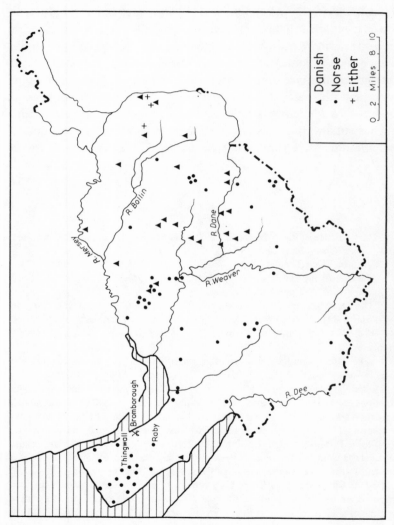

Figure B 1: Scandinavian Place–Names in Cheshire.

Hulme,[12†] and at *Toft* [13†] near *Knutsford,*[14†] etc., and even at *Denhall*[15†] in Wirral; but a Norwegian presence in the county at large tends to be obscured by its testimony appearing only in minor place–names, a number of which have been long lost from use. In Bucklow Hundred there is a concentration of Scandinavian place–names: there is a Danish element here, but the Norwegian predominates. Examples are, in Higher Whitley, *Colstonstoke*[16†] (from the OSwed personal–name *Kolsten*), *Assheby*[17] and *Storeby*[18] (from ON **býr**, 'a farmstead'; the latter also from ON **storr**, 'great, big', as in *Storeton* in Wirral); in Cogshall, *Colswaynesoke*[19] (from the ON personal–name *Kolsveinn*); in Seven Oaks, *Frandley*[20] (from the personal–name ON *Fráni,* or more obviously ODan *Frændi*); the first element in *Keckwick*[21] is the ON personal–name

---

[12] *Cheadle Hulme, Kettleshulme, Hulme* in Allostock, *Holmes Chapel, Hulme* near Kinderton, etc., from ODan **hulm** (as distinct from ON **holmr**), 'a marsh, a water–meadow'.

[13] *Tofte* 12th (17th), 1210; from ODan **toft**, 'a building site, a curtilage, a housestead'.

[14] *Cunetesford* 1086, *Knut(es)ford(e)* 1294, 1332; from the ODan personal–name *Knut* and OE **ford**, 'a ford'.

[15] *Danewell* 1184, 1238, *Danewall* 1302, *Denewell* c. 1240 (1293) (17th), c. 1268 (1400), 1308, *Denewale* 1288–90, *Dennewalle* late–13th, *Denewalle* 1343, 'the Danes' spring', from the genitive of OE **Dene**, ON **Danir**, 'the Danes', and OE **wella** (Mercian **wælla**), 'a well–spring'. This may refer to those Danes who helped Ingimund's Norsemen to attack Chester c. 902–10, *v. Saga–Book* XIV, 305, 308 note 23 [= *supra,* pp. 251, 254 note 23].[†]

[16] *Colstonstok(e)* 1479, 1504, *Colstonshok* 1481, *Colstansock* 1483, *Colstonsoke* 1484, *Colstanehok* 1486, *Colstansoke* 1556; a surname in the Higher Whitley district derived from a lost place–name, from the OSwed (perhaps also ODan) personal–name *Kolsten* (obviously anglicized *Colstān*) and OE **āc**, 'an oak'.

[17] *Assheby* 1507, 1514 (perhaps the same as *Assebe* 1287 (R. Stewart–Brown, *Calendar of the County Court, City Court and Eyre Rolls of Chester, 1259–1297,* Chetham Society (New Series) 84 (1925), 74 no. 178) if this is not in fact Ashley near Bowden), 'ash–tree farm', from ON **askr**, OE **æsc**, and ON **býr**, ODan **bý**, 'a farmstead'.

[18] *Storeby* 1507, a surname from a lost place–name.

[19] *Colswaynesoke* 1397, 1398, a surname from a lost place–name 'Kolsveinn's oak', from OE **āc**, 'an oak'; *cf. Colstonstoke* note 16 *supra.*

[20] *Franley* 1514, *Frandley* 1663; no great confidence is placed upon this derivation however.

[21] *Kekwic* 1154 (1329), *Kekewyc* early 13th, 'Kekkja's dairy–farm', from OE **wīc**, 'an industrial–, a trading–settlement; a dairy–farm'. The personal–name appears in the place–name *Kekmarsh* (North Riding of Yorkshire); see A.H. Smith, *The*

Kekkja†; in Hatton near Daresbury, *Queastybirch*²² is from ON **kví** 'a sty', and the equivalent OE **stigu**, 'a sty';† *Pillmoss*²³ is ON **píll**, 'a willow', and **mos**, 'a bog, a moss'; *Steniber*²⁴ is ON *steinn–berg,* 'stone–hill'; in Newton by Daresbury, *Morphany*²⁵ contains ON **þveit**, 'a meadow', and *Swaynesrudinge*²⁶ is from the ON personal–name *Sveinn.*†

This medley of East and West Scandinavian traces is consonant with the nearby appearance of the pair of place–names *Anderton*²⁷ and *Antrobus*²⁸, the former from OE **tūn**, 'a farmstead', the latter from ON **buskr** (replaced by the cognate OE **busc**), 'bush, scrub–land; a bush', both having as first element a personal–name ON *Einðriði, *Anðriði,* or ODan **Endrithi*, as in *Enderby* (Leicestershire, Lincolnshire) and *Ainderby* (North Riding of Yorkshire). It is possible that the one man gave his name to *Anderton* and *Antrobus.*†

There is another concentration of Norse nomenclature, with the familiar Irish connexion, in south–east Cheshire. The well–known *Scholar Green*²⁹ in Odd Rode (from ON **skáli**, 'a herdsman's shed; an out–pasture settlement', and OE **halc, halh**, 'a nook, a corner, a

---

Place–Names of the North Riding of Yorkshire, EPNS 5, 84, E. Ekwall, *The Concise Oxford Dictionary of English Place–Names,* 4th ed., s.v. *Keckwick, Kenswick,* A. Mawer, F.M. Stenton, F.T.S. Houghton, *The Place–Names of Worcestershire,* EPNS 4, 147, s.v. *Kenswick*; much of this is now useless.

²² *Quisty* 1216–72, *Kuysty* 1306.

²³ But this is late in record — *Pill Moss* 1831 (Bryant's Map of Cheshire).

²⁴ 13th (17th) Tabley MSS, (National Register of Archives Report 3636); only the one recorded instance.

²⁵ *Mortwayt* 13th (17th), *Morthwayt(e)* late 13th, 1285, *Morfanny* 1673; 'meadow at a marsh or moor', from OE **mōr**, 'a marsh, a moor', and ON **þveit**, 'a meadow', see the place–name *Moorthwaite* (Cumberland; A.M. Armstrong, A. Mawer, F.M. Stenton, B. Dickins, *The Place–Names of Cumberland* 1 (EPNS 20), 79, 2 (EPNS 21), 335). The modern form is similar to that of the Thelwall field–name *Marphany Meadow* 1842 (*Little Marfeny* 1748), from OE **mōr** or ON **marr**, 'a marsh', OE **fenn**, 'a fen, a marsh', and OE **ēg**, 'a water–meadow, a marsh'.

²⁶ Late 13th (17th), *Swaynisruding* late 13th, 'Sveinn's cleared–land', from OE **rydding**. It is remarkable how often a Scandinavian personal–name appears in the name of an assart or intake.

²⁷ *Andrelton* 1182, *Aldreton* 1183, *Anderton* 1184, *Henderton, Enderton* 1185, 1186.

²⁸ *Entrebus* 1086, 1281, *Anterbos* c. 1247 (17th), *–bus* c. 1250, *Anderbusk(e)* 1295, 1306, *Andrebusk(e)* 1305, 1307, *Antrobus* 1457.

²⁹ *Scolehalc, –haleth* (for *–halech*) 1272–1307, *Scol(e)halg(h)* 1286, 1300, 1307.

side–valley'), is accompanied by *Mekenisley*[30] (from the OIrish personal–name *Maicín* and OE **lēah**, 'a woodland'); in Somerford Radnor there was *Eycanecroft*[31] (from OIrish *Eachán* and OE **croft**, 'a croft'); there was another OIrish personal–name, *Gillurán*, in the place–name *Kelerondesweye*[32] in Aston–iuxta–Mondrum.[†]

This same pervasive Scandinavian element is seen in the place–names *Scows*[33] in Tiverton (from ON **skáli**); perhaps also *Tiresford*[34] in Tiverton;[†] *Wivercote*[35] in Macefen (which, despite E. Ekwall's analysis, is from OE **cot**, 'a cottage', with the ON personal–name *Viðfari*); *Blake Hereye*[36] in Wigland (from ON **erg** (< OIrish **airidh**), 'a shieling', as in *Arrowe* in Wirral); *Tarporley*[37] (from OE **lēah**, 'a woodland glade', added

---

[30] *Meken(en)isley* c. 1300, *Mekenaslegh* 1327, *Mekenesleg(h)* c. 1330, 1340, 1350.

[31] 13th; only one mention.

[32] 1297, *Kele–*, *Kilerondiswei* late 13th, *Kelrondesweye* 1297, *le Kelerondeswey* c. 1300, 'Gillurán's road', from OE **weg**, 'a way, a road'.

[33] A field–name in the Tithe Award of 1839; taken to be the same as *Scales* 13th (14th).

[34] *Tirisford* 1180–1220, *Tyrefford* early 13th, *Tireford* 13th (14th), *Teyresforth* 1351; OE *ford*, 'a ford', and either the ON form *Týrr*, or the rare OE form *Tīr*, of the god–name usually appearing as OE *Tīw* as in the day–name *Tuesday*.

[35] A lost place; *Wyuercote* 1289, *Wyvercote, Wevercote* 1290, *Wi–, Wyvercote* c. 1300. A document in the Cholmondeley MSS, Box J, (Cheshire Record Office), locates the c. 1300 reference in Macefen. The other references, presumably also relating to this parcel of the St Pierre family's share of the Malpas Barony (see R. Stewart–Brown, op. cit. note 17 *supra*, 150, no. 306; G. Ormerod, *History of Cheshire* (ed. Helsby, 1882), II, 254 (lit. *Wyner–*); *Report of the Deputy Keeper of the Public Records* 26, 41 (lit. *Wyner–*); *Calendar of Inquisitions Post Mortem* II, 463, 459) are identified by E. Ekwall (*The Concise Oxford Dictionary of English Place–Names*, 4th ed., s.v. *Weavercote;* followed by A.H. Smith, *English Place–Name Elements* II (EPNS 26), s.v. **wǣfre**) as a place–name *Weavercote* associated with the place–names *Weaverham, Weaver,* and derived from the river–name *Weaver*. This *Weavercote* does not exist, that form of the place–name is not known to my collections, and Macefen, hence *Wivercote*, is not near R. Weaver.

[36] 1312, 'the black or dark out–pasture or herdsman's shed', from OE **blæc**.

[37] *Torpelei* 1086, *Torperley* 1198–1216, *Torpereleye* 1307; a difficult place–name by previous derivations. E. Ekwall, *The Concise Oxford Dictionary of English Place–Names*, 4th ed., s.v., flounders about to suggest this place–name is 'pear wood near a hill called the *Torr*', from an original English place–name *Perley* (OE **peru** 'a pear (tree)', or **pyrige**, 'a pear–tree', and OE **lēah**, 'a wood') modified by a prefixed hill–name from the OE Celtic loan–word **torr**, 'a tor; a rocky hill'. He compares *Tormarton* (Gloucestershire), cf. op. cit. s.v. Didmarton (Gloucestershire).

to an OE word *þorpere, 'one who lives in a hamlet', a loan–word from ON þorpari, comparable with the term OE *bōthere, 'one who lives at a bōth', based upon ODan bōth, 'a herdsman's shelter', which is likely in Bootherson[38] in Monks Coppenhall).[†]

This passing review of the less obvious Scandinavian element among the place–names of Cheshire[39] indicates a complexity which is not historically recorded. First, it evidences an infiltration of English territory by Scandinavian settlers in areas and to an extent which historical record

This is not a well–attested type of place–name, and A.H. Smith, *English Place–Name Elements* I (EPNS 25), xxiii, and *The Place–Names of Gloucestershire* 3 (EPNS 40), 56, undermines and demolishes Ekwall's explanation. The explanation which I now suggest for *Tarporley* avoids the formal difficulties, but raises one as to the historical significance of the place–name. The spellings suggest OE *þorpera–lēah, ME *thorpere–legh, from OE lēah, 'a woodland', and the genitive–plural of an OE word *þorpere, 'a man who lives in a hamlet'; this would be borrowing from ON þorpari, 'a peasant, a cottager', the basis being ON þorp, 'a hamlet, a dependent settlement'. The Scandinavian basis of this place–name suggests that in the Tarporley district at some juncture there may have been an ethnic minority of Scandinavians to whom their English neighbours had given the nickname 'the Thorpers'.

[38] A field–name in the Tithe Award 1840; probably from an earlier unrecorded place–name *Bootherston (cf. the –s–ton > –son development in the place–names *Austerson, Snelson*, etc.), from OE *bōtheres–tūn, ME *botheres–ton.

[39] One or two further notes of interest may well be inserted here, to add to these observations upon the Scandinavian element. It explains the affix *Dennis* in *Lach Dennis,* and possibly also the affix *Andrew* in *Mottram St Andrew*. Correctly, neither place–name should have a *Saint,* but even *Lach Dennis* gets one by courtesy from time to time. *Lach Dennis* is part of the Domesday Book manor of *Lece* (DB fo. 267b). Another part of this manor was the lost *Lache Maubanc* (DB *Lece* fo. 266). The *Dennis* part was held in 1066 by one *Colben,* a personal–name representing ON *Kolbeinn* or ODan *Kolben.* If this *Colben* were a Danish *Kolben,* his part of the manor could have been distinguished from the other one by the adjective 'Danish', OE **Denisc**, ME *denshe, danais, denez, deneys,* which would easily be confused with the ME personal–name *Denis.* At *Mottram Andrew* there is no record of a manorial family or a manorial lord called *Andrew*; and there is no record of a notable church dedication; so this is not a straightforward affix. It can be explained if it is taken to be a descriptive or allusive affix, referring to some distinctive feature which would set this *Mottram* apart from the other place of that name, and which was called by a noun which could be confused with the personal–name *Andrew.* This elusive word appears first in the form *Motromandreus* 1351, and as *–andrew(e), –andreu* 1362. A form *–andreus* has been interpreted by popular usage as the genitive of the personal–name *Andrew.* Such a form could be derived from a compound of ON **anddyri**, 'a porch' and ON **hús**, OE **hūs**, 'a house', meaning 'a house with a porch', referring to some architectural feature of Mottram long ago.

does not indicate; second, by the appearance of hybrid place–names in which Scandinavian and English elements are combined, and by the distribution of these Scandinavian name–types in amongst the English place–names, it indicates a social relationship between the two populations in which the infiltration of Scandinavians into an English society created an Anglo–Scandinavian society and language, or, rather, an English society and language with a Scandinavian complexion. This reflects the political history of the ninth and tenth centuries in Cheshire, during which the English government did not lose control of the north–west Midlands. It also reflects the ethnic and linguistic relationship of the English and the Scandinavians which made the fusion possible. This contrasts with the ethnic and linguistic distance between Briton and Angle, and with the opposite political history resulting from the English arrival — that the British did not retain a government control of the area, and the social status of the two elements of the population at that epoch, immigrant English and resident Welsh, was opposite to that of the two elements of the population in the later period, immigrant Scandinavian and resident English. We must also remember that the evidence of place–names is valid evidence of social relationship and territorial settlement not recorded in documentary history: the Scandinavian settlement in Cheshire is shown by the place–names to be a more subtle and complex process, 'chronic' rather than 'critical' in effect, than is recorded by the chronicles. Similarly, the social relationships, the historical processes, and the long–drawn–out effects, of the English settlement in Cheshire among the resident Britons, can be expected to be more complex than the simple narrative of the records would describe: it can be expected, confidently, that the place–names relating to the arrival period will provide evidence from which inferences may be drawn which are both independent of and supplementary to the inferences which may be drawn from the record of history.

The use of both kinds of evidence, recorded history and the meaning of place–names, requires a reconstruction of the context in which the political events of history and the philological form and the social significance of place–names are not only intelligible in themselves but also consonant with each other. In this examination of the English arrival, the place–name material under consideration will consist of the Welsh place–names and the early stratum of English place–names in Cheshire. The recorded history under consideration will consist of the known series of political events which mark the establishment of English kingdom and authority in various directions by various parties at various times in the district of Cheshire. This kind of history is that of kings and battles, i.e. of politics in contemporary terms, but not necessarily that of populations; but its inferences as to the social scene are usable if they are controlled by the inferences which may be drawn from the English and Welsh place–names. The relationship between the early English place–names of Cheshire and the surviving or recorded British and Welsh place–names in the county can be used as an image of the relationship between the English settlers and the indigenous Britons. The philological form of the place–names, related to the history of the two languages, English and Welsh, can be used to define epoch and era in the history of politics and society. This delicate balancing of evidence and inference about social, political and linguistic history has to be adjusted to the further pressures of geography and archaeology if the whole exercise is to form a place–name study of the requisite integrity. All these matters will be entered into the case. But the balance most particularly sought in this essay will be, essentially, no more than that which can be struck by a particular application to Cheshire of the general thesis proposed in K. Jackson, *Language and History in Early Britain,* poised against an analysis of the early English place–name types. My observations upon the Welsh place–names are guided by Jackson. Particular references will be made to this work, but there would seem to be no need of a general rehearsal here, for G. Barnes and Dorothy Sylvester have already covered the principal necessary allusions.[40] It is sufficient, but important, to note again, that in Jackson's work, at pp. 220–24, Cheshire is found to lie in Area II and Area III (map, op. cit. 221) of a zoned increasing–frequency diagram of British river–name distribution, in which Area II 'appears to agree pretty well with the movement of expansion of the Anglo–Saxon occupation which took place in the second half of the sixth century in the South and the first half of the seventh in the North', and Area III is identified with 'the third and final stage of the Anglo–Saxon conquest; in the middle or third quarter of the seventh century in the North, the middle and second half of the seventh century in the Welsh Marches, and the middle of the seventh to the earlier part of the eighth century in the South–West'. The boundary between Area II and the more westerly Area

---

[40] Op. cit. under notes 2 and 3 above.

III, in Cheshire, is drawn approximately along the line of R. Gowy, or, as alternatively identified, along a line from Tarvin to Macefen which will be noticed hereafter.[41]

I. THE EARLY ENGLISH STRATUM IN THE PLACE-NAMES OF CHESHIRE

The phase of relationship between the English and the Welsh place–names in Cheshire which would be the most relevant to the business in hand, is that which reflects a phase of social relationship at which a point of equilibrium was reached between the English and the Welsh as influential elements in society. Before this epoch, one would expect English place–names to be less numerous in use, and after it more numerous in occurrence and general usage, and respectively less and more widespread in distribution. The converse will be held for the Welsh place–names.

There is a very interesting and special, if difficult (even dangerous), combination of exquisite scholarship and sweeping speculation required in the definition of the earliest stratum of English place–names in Cheshire as illustrated in Figure B 2. The county does not produce simple examples of the place–name types in OE **–ingas, –ingahām**,[42] 'the folk of –, the folk named after –', and 'the village of the folk of –, – the folk named after –', which are usually sought out as marking the territorial location and the identity of the primitive English communities in a newly taken country. The problem of this phenomenal deficiency can be evaded by the resolution of another problem, as will be seen hereafter; and the absence of OE **–ingas, –inga–**, place–names may be a false embarrassment anyway, for such place–names are not necessarily relevant to the first stage of English settlement in any one area,[43] but rather to some secondary stage.[44] But serious problems remain, which arise from

---

[41] See pp. 299, 303 below.

[42] See A.H. Smith, *English Place–Name Elements*, I (EPNS 25), s.v., E. Ekwall, *The Concise Oxford Dictionary of English Place–Names*, 4th ed., s.v. *–ing*; *English Place–Names in –ing*, 2nd ed., *passim*.

[43] Cf. K. Jackson, *Language and History in Early Britain*, 216.

[44] The case is outlined in J.McN. Dodgson, 'The Significance of the Distribution of English Place–Names in *–ingas, –inga–*, in South–East England', *Medieval Archaeology* 10 (1966), 1–29.

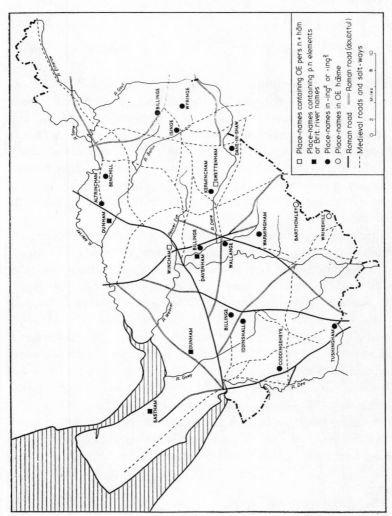

Figure B 2: Early English Place–Names in Cheshire.

the lack in the county area of any considerable corpus of English pagan burial archaeology — that other prime evidence of Dark Age English settlement.[45] The absence of archaeological material may be due to any one or more of several causes: that the English were already Christian when they reached Cheshire so that instead of creating pagan burial sites they used Christian churchyard burials; that they were still pagan when they arrived and did indeed create pagan burial sites, but these have by accident escaped discovery or recognition because they were few in number and small in size or content.

It is historically unlikely that the first English in Cheshire were Christian — it was necessary to send missionaries to Mercia in 653, Peada, the son of the heathen king Penda of Mercia, having married a daughter of the Christian king of Northumbria, Oswiu. This suggests that the first English in Cheshire, though probably pagan and likely to create heathen burials, did not leave detected burial sites. This supposes not many sites, and those not large (which supposes sites not long in use); or no sites at all. If the pagan English immigrants were few in number amongst a Christian Welsh population, it might be expected that the English pagan burial sites would be small and few. Further, the cultural minority represented by such a pagan–burying English community might quickly find itself adopting the customs of the majority in such matters — certainly, after the first generation in the new land, one might expect an assimilation of burial custom by the minority to that of the majority in a society in which English and Welsh lived side by side. If the pagan burial sites contained few burials they would be hardly noticeable under the plough or the spade of later ages. By the time that the pagan burials in Cheshire might have reached the large extent attained by some sites in south east England, the custom had been abandoned in favour of Christian (church–yard) burial. The lack of archaeology, in short, is the result of an historical sequence in which a minority population of pagan English did not persist in their distinctive burial customs for long enough for their pagan cemeteries to become noticeable. This lack of persistence is due to either or both of two causes — their rapid assimilation to the custom of their majority neighbours the Christian Welsh, or to their being

---

[45] There is no entry for Cheshire in Audrey Meaney, *A Gazetteer of Early Anglo–Saxon Burial Sites* (London, 1964).

overtaken by conversion to Christianity not long after their arrival in Cheshire, a conversion either at the hands of their Welsh neighbours or the hands of English missionaries. From the contemplation of these possibilities it might appear likely that the first English immigrants in Cheshire soon found themselves part of an Anglo–Welsh population, adopting certain Christian Welsh social customs quite quickly. If the balance of status between the Welsh and English elements in this Anglo–Welsh population shifted in favour of the English before their conversion to Christian practice, one would expect at least some trace of pagan procedure. Perhaps in the days of Penda there would be an English custom of pagan burial. The politically dominant Englishman, if pagan, would feel no need to accommodate himself to Welsh custom even if he had begun to do so during the era of his numerical and social inferiority. Moreover, one suspects that, when *The Place–Names of Cheshire*[46] is finally available for the inspection of the archaeologist, he might discover, in place–names like *Wilmslow* (OE **Wīghelmes–hlāw,* 'Wīghelm's mound') or *Gorse Stacks* (at Chester) formerly *Hunwaldeslowe* (OE **Hunwaldes–hlāw,* 'Hunwald's mound'), and in allusions like the place–names *Deadman's Suck* (Frodsham Lordship),[47] or *Dedemonnes Greue* (Storeton)[48] and even in references to discoveries such as those at Bartomly Farm (Wincle) and Saxfield (Northenden) reported in G. Ormerod, *History of Cheshire* (ed. Helsby, 1882), III, 769, 611 — grounds for suspicion that some traces of the pagan burials of the first English in Cheshire may have been discovered indeed, but not recognised. The archaeological situation can be argued in different ways; it need hardly be weighed against the place–name evidence further than the necessary reservation about the short period in which pagan burial may have been used in Cheshire, and the social implications of this in respect of the relations between English and Welsh. The point may be deferred until the conclusions of the study are drawn.

After the remark upon the lack of –**ingas**, –**ingahām** place–names, it might seem that the only ostensibly early English place–names —

---

[46] J.McN. Dodgson, EPNS 44 *et seq.*

[47] 1740, *Deadmans Such* 1677, 'dead man's watercourse', from ME **dede–man**, 'a corpse, a dead man' and OE **sīc**, 'a watercourse'.

[48] 1323, 'dead man's wood', from ME **dede–man** and OE **grǣfe**, 'a grove, a wood'.

denoting that group– or communal–entity which has been supposed to represent the pioneering English settlement — in Cheshire, would be *Barthomley*[49†] and *Wrinehill*[50†] which contain OE **hǣme**[51] 'the dwellers at –; those who are at home at –'. These place–names, *Barthomley*, 'the woodland of the dwellers at *Berton*', and *Wrinehill*, 'the hill at the place called after the dwellers at the river–bend(s)', are at the Staffordshire boundary, and may belong rather to the settlement of that inner region of Mercia than to that of Cheshire. It is also noticeable that *Barthomley* is a derivative place–name, based upon and representing colonisation from another place and place–name. Perhaps *Wrinehill* is no more reliable as an evidence of initial–phase immigration. Unless that immigration were supposed to be a matter of the colonisation of Cheshire from older settlement in Staffordshire.

The place–names in OE **hǣme** are of questionable value for our purpose. Nor can the Cheshire place–names in *–ington* be used as evidence of early English immigrant groups. They are not OE **–ingatūn**

[49] *Bertemeleu* 1086, *Bertamelegh* 13th, *Berthoneleg'* 1287, *Bertonelegh* 1289, a difficult place–name for which A.H. Smith, (*The Place–Names of the West Riding of Yorkshire* 1 (EPNS 30), 248, discussing *Mortomley* (West Riding) and *Marchamley* (Staffordshire), which is analogous with *Marchington* (Staffordshire)), suggests 'woodland of the dwellers at a **bere–tūn**', from OE **lēah**, 'woodland, a woodland glade', with a composition of OE **hǣme** with a lost place–name *Berton* (< OE **bere–tūn**, 'a barley–farm; a dependent farmstead').

[50] *Wrynehull* 1225, from OE **hyll**, 'a hill', and a name *Wryme* which appears in *Wriman ford* 975 (W. de G. Birch, *Cartularium Saxonicum,* No. 1312), *Wrimeford* 1240–50, *Wrineford* 1322, *Wryneford* 1686, with OE **ford**, 'a ford'; in *Wryme* 1299, *the Wryme* 1563, *the Rimes* (a field–name) 1842; and in *Wryme Syche* 1429, with OE **sīc**, 'a watercourse'. *Wryme* 1249 was the name of the district of Wrinehill in Cheshire and Staffordshire. W.H. Duignan, *Notes on Staffordshire Place–Names,* (London, 1902), 176, proposes a personal–name OE *Wrim(a)* for the first component of *Wriman ford.* However, the spellings and forms of this series of place–names suggest analogy with *Wryoheme* (W. de G. Birch, op. cit. No. 606); *v.* A.H. Smith, *English Place–Name Elements*, II (EPNS 26) s.v. **wrēo**; E. Ekwall, *The Concise Oxford Dictionary of English Place–Names,* 4th ed., s.v. *Wrington* (Somerset)), which is from OE **hǣme** and the river–name *Wring.* This river–name *Wring* represents OE **wrīo–ing,* 'that which is characterized by a **wrīo** (i.e. by a twist or turn); that which is awry'. The Cheshire–Staffordshire place–name *Wryme* would, without difficulty of phonology, represent an OE **Wrīo–hǣme,* (locative–dative **Wrīo–hǣmum* > **Wrīo–hǣman*), 'dwellers at the (river–) bend(s), – at the twisting river'.

[51] See A.H. Smith, *English Place–Name Elements*, I (EPNS 25), s.v.

types, in which OE **tūn** is compounded with the genitive of a plural OE
–ingas folk–name. They are OE **–ingtūn** types.[52] The original and the
analogical *–ington* place–name can appear any time, even quite late, in
the Anglo–Saxon period. These names cannot be used as a chronological
determinant. They and the place–names in OE **worðign**, 'a curtilage, a
(private) enclosed site', that characteristic Mercian element, such as
Northenden,[53] *Kenworthy*[54] in Northenden, *Arden*[55] in Bredbury,
Larden[56] in Faddiley — *Carden* is a special case [57] — seem more likely
to belong to an era in which Cheshire had been completely taken over by
Mercian colonisation. They are the place–names of the Mercian
establishment rather than of the English arrival.

It is evident that the English place–names of Cheshire are of the
Mercian dialect of Old English. The characteristics of that dialect are
illustrated in terms of south Lancashire place–names in E. Ekwall, *The
Place–Names of Lancashire*, 227–30. In Cheshire, the form OE
(Mercian) **wælla**, in place–names like *Bradwall, Heswall, Denhall*, etc.,
instead of or alternative to common Anglian OE **wella**, 'a well–spring',
is clear enough;[58] as also is the form *ol–* (> later dialect *owl–*) in such

---

[52] *The Historical Atlas of Cheshire*, ed. Dorothy Sylvester and G. Nulty (Chester,
1958), map on p. 17, *Place–Names*, by A. Oakes, puts OE **–ingatūn**, being misled
in this point by E. Ekwall's traditional analysis — *The Concise Oxford Dictionary
of English Place–Names*, 4th ed., s.v. *–ing* which is to be rejected in view of A.H.
Smith, *English Place–Name Elements* I (EPNS 25, 1956) s.v. **–ing**-[4], **–ingtūn**, and
even of E. Ekwall, *English Place–Names in –ing*, 2nd ed., 223.

[53] *Norwordine* 1086, 'the north settlement', from OE **norð** and **worðign**.

[54] *Kenworthin* 13th (17th), 1286, *Keneworthei* 1287, 'kingly, or royal, settlement',
from OE *cyne–* and **worðign**, **worðig** (see A.H. Smith, *English Place–Name
Elements* II (EPNS 26), s.v. **worðig, worðign**).

[55] *Hawardene* 1286, *Haurthyn* 1337, 'the high settlement', from OE **hēah**, 'high'
(as an adj.), 'high up' (as an adv.), 'a high place' (as a noun), and **worðign**.

[56] *Laurthyn* 1341, 'the low enclosure', from ME **lah**, ModE **low** (< ON **lágr**),
adj., 'low', and **worðign**; a place–name which may date from the tenth century or
after — the adjective *low* for English *nether* is a Scandinavian loan–word in English
— although it is possible that the form recorded is a later modification of an older
simplex usage **Worthin* < OE **worðign**.

[57] See p. 291 below.

[58] The fact that there are numerous instances of ME *–welle* spellings for the
Cheshire place–names in *–wall* (< OE **wælla** Mercian) does not imply a Mercian
overlay upon an original Northumbrian Anglian **wella**. It is rather to be explained as
the interference of a common English tradition in OE *–wella* > ME *–welle* with the

place–names as *Ollerton* (compare Lancashire *Allerton*) from OE **alor**, 'an alder tree', for this is a ME dialect characteristic of the Mercian area and supposes some distinctive characteristic in the OE Mercian pronunciation of the OE word. With these we may take the palatalized *ċ* of OE **æcer**, 'an acre, a plough–land' preserved in *Alsager* (compare Lancashire *Cliviger*) where the *g* is pronounced *–dg–* by voicing of the pronunciation *–tch–* from OE *ċ*; also the maintenance of the sound and spelling *ch–*, not *c–* (*k*) in the place–name *Chester* (compare Lancashire *Ribchester*, *Lancaster*); and numerous ME spellings in *u* in place–names in *–brugge*, *–bruche,* from OE **brycg**, 'a bridge', **bryce**, 'an intake; land broken–in from the waste'. Again, the appearance of the characteristic Mercian place–name element **worðign** in Cheshire is matched by that of the characteristic Mercian element–form **bold**,[59] 'a house, a dwelling', as in the place–names *Newbold* in Astbury and *Lea Newbold* and the lost places *Newbold* near Handbridge and *Newbold* near Nantwich.

There is no evidence of specifically Northumbrian dialect features in Cheshire place–names; if there was a Northumbrian Anglian settlement in the county, all traces of that particular dialect have been erased by Mercian form. It is inferred from this that the Northumbrians did not settle in Cheshire, or that any Northumbrian settlement was transitory or of impermanent identity. The English place–names of south Lancashire between Ribble and Mersey, on the other hand, show both Mercian and Northumbrian dialect features. E. Ekwall[60] interprets this as evidence of an original Northumbrian settlement as far south as R. Mersey with a later Mercian overlay as far north as R. Ribble. He ascribes the Northumbrian settlement to a time at or before the battle of Chester (613–616), and the Mercian intrusion to the days of Penda, king of Mercia (c. 626–54). The Mercian expansion under Penda carried Mercian power into Yorkshire in 633, whence the Mercian element in the place–names south of R. Wharfe in the West Riding.[61] This matter of Mercian characteristics in Cheshire,

---

local dialect tradition in OE –**wælla** > ME –*wall* — an interference almost commonplace in the recorded spellings of official documents. Bureaucratic method is not new.

[59] See A.H. Smith, *English Place–Name Elements*, I (EPNS 25), s.v.

[60] *The Place–Names of Lancashire*, 231–232.

[61] See A.H. Smith, *The Place–Names of the West Riding of Yorkshire* 7 (EPNS 36), 33–36, 39–42.

Lancashire and Yorkshire is relevant to the recorded course of Mercian history. On the face of it, the evidence of the –ingtūn, –worðign, place–names of Cheshire is part of the evidence of a wider distribution of these types, i.e. of a wider distribution of Mercian colonists and their nomenclature, in south Lancashire, south–west Yorkshire, Derbyshire, Staffordshire, Salop, Flintshire and Denbighshire. This would represent the era of the eighth century Mercian supremacy under Offa just as well as the seventh century Mercian expansion under Penda.

If, as it seems, it is advisable to reject the foregoing name–types as candidates for inclusion in the earliest stratum of English place–names in Cheshire, there are nevertheless two kinds of Cheshire place–names capable of being classified as that ancient. The first is the type of place–name in which OE **hām**, 'a village, a homestead', appears in composition, with a personal–name or a simple modifier. In *Swettenham*[62] and *Frodsham* [63]† it appears in composition with an OE monothematic personal–name. It appears in *Eastham* (*Estham* 1086, 'homestead or village in the east (of Wirral);† the east village') with OE **ēast**, 'east' (either as adj. or adv.); and in *Dunham on the Hill* (*Doneham* 1086) and *Dunham Massey* (*Doneham* 1086), both of which mean 'hill–village; homestead or village on a hill', it appears with OE **dūn** (dative–singular *dūne*), 'a hill'. In *Davenham* it appears with the British river–name *Dane*.[64] Such place–names can be among the earliest English place–names in the county. The simple construction of element or personal–name or river–name + **hām** would appear to be, in many counties, in geographical and archaeological contexts which suggest that such names belong to an epoch marked by the emergence of a recognition of social permanence in a territorial possession by the English community.[65] Certainly, in south east England, such a place–name formation seems to be more frequently incident in districts which would have been attractive to early English settlement than do the –**ingas**, –**ingahām** types.

---

[62] *Suetenham* late 12th (14th), 1220–30, 'Swēta's homestead or village', from the OE personal–name *Swēta*.

[63] *Frotesham* 1086, *Frodesham* 1096–1101 (1280), 1150 (14th), *Frodessam* 1175, 'Frōd's homestead or village', from the OE personal–name *Frōd*.

[64] See p. 292 below.

[65] See J.McN. Dodgson, 'The Significance of the Distribution of English Place–Names in –*ingas*, –*inga*–, etc.', *Medieval Archaeology* 10 (1966), 5.

More significant than these, however, is the second type of Cheshire place–name which may (indeed) be early; the place–name in which the OE noun–forming suffix –*ing*[66] appears in a specialised form, a palatalized and assibilated form with the pronunciation –*indge*, –*inch*, which represents an archaic locative–inflected form of a common–noun or place–name containing the –*ing* suffix.[67] In the place–names *Altrincham*,[68] *Benchill*[69] (in Northen Etchells near Northenden), *Wincham*,[70] *Kermincham*,[71]

[66] See A.H. Smith, *English Place–Name Elements*, I (EPNS 25), s.v. –**ing**, –**ing**[1], –**ing**[2], –**ing**[3], –**ing**–[4], –**ingas**, –**ingahām**.

[67] This special form is discussed by A.H. Smith, op. cit. s.v. –**ing**[2], and by E. Ekwall, *English Place–Names in –ing*, 2nd ed., 174–223 (Chapter III, 'Names in –*ing* (sing.) and –*inge*'), who do not quite see the point; and it is very thoroughly and industriously (and tediously) shaken out in J.McN. Dodgson, 'The –*ing* in English Place–Names like *Birmingham* and *Altrincham*', *Beiträge zur Namenforschung, Neue Folge* 2 (1967), Heft 3, 221–45; 'Various Forms of Old English –*ing* in English Place–Names', op. cit. Heft 4, 325–96, 'Various English Place–Name Formations containing Old English –*ing*', op. cit. 3 (1968), Heft 2, 141–89.

[68] *Aldringeham* 1290, *Altrincham* 1321, *Altringcham* 1547; OE *hām*, 'a village, a homestead', with an assibilated OE –*ing*–suffix formation upon the OE personal–name *Aldhere*. It means 'the **hām** (called) *Aldheringe*', in which *Aldheringe*, which is a locative form and should be pronounced –*indge*, means 'at *Aldhering*', and *Aldhering*, which is a nominative form and should be pronounced –*ing*, means 'that (thing, place, or, for that matter, where relevant, that person) which is called after, or associated with the name of, the man *Aldhere*'.

[69] *Baginchul* 13th (17th), *Bangengehull* 1289, *Baynchull* 1302 (17th), *Benshall* 1669; OE **hyll** 'a hill', with an assibilated OE –*ing*–suffix formation upon the OE feminine personal–name *Bēaga*. It means 'the hill (called) *Bēaginge*', with the same evolution as in *Altrincham supra*, from a proper–noun *Bēaging*, 'that which is called after the woman *Bēaga*'.

[70] *Wimundisham* 1086, *Wymundham* 1281; *Wy–*, *Wimingham* late 12th (17th), 1209 (17th); *Wymminchama* c. 1270, *Wymincham* 1306, *Wymyngcham* 1353; *Wemecham* early 13th (17th), *Wimesham* 1234 (17th), *Wymmycham* 1501 (17th); *Wyningham, Wynincham* 1281; *Wyncham* 1435, *Winsham* 1651; OE *hām* with the genitive–singular and the uninflected form of the Old English personal–name *Wīgmund*, and with an assibilated –*ing*–suffix formation upon that personal–name. The spellings represent three forms of name for this one place, 1. OE **Wīgmundes–hām*, 'Wīgmund's village', 2. OE **Wīgmund–hām*, 'the Wīgmund village' (as one might nowadays say 'the Dodgson house'), 3. OE **Wīgmundinge–hām*, 'the **hām** (called) *Wīgmundinge*', in which *Wīgmundinge*, a locative form, evolves similarly to *Altrincham supra* from a proper–noun *Wīgmunding*, 'that which is called after the man *Wīgmund*'.

[71] *Cerdingham* 1086, *Cherdingham* 1278, *Kerthyngham, –ing–* 1275, 1288, *Kerthincham, –ynch–* 1345, 1350; *Kermincham, –ynch–* 1286, 1341, *Kermyngham*

Dane–in–Shaw [72] (near Congleton), *Warmingham,* [73] *Tushingham,* [74] and

1312, *–ing–* 1564, *Kyrmingham* 1451; *Kernincham* 1286, *–yngham* 1310, *Kernycham* 1307, *Kernicham* 1422; *Kerincham, –yn–* 1353, *Keryngham* 1394, *Karingham* 1520; *Keryngeham* 1401; OE **hām** with an assibilated OE *–ing*–suffix formation upon an OE personal–name **Cēnfrið*. *Kermincham* means 'the **hām** (called) *Cēnfriðinge*', in which *Cēnfriðinge,* a locative form which leads to the pronunciation *–indge,* means 'at *Cēnfriðing*', where *Cēnfriðing,* a nominative form with the pronunciation *–ing,* means 'that which is called after the man *Cēnfrið*'.

[72] *Danehynchill* 1407, *Davenynsale, Daveninsale* 1593, *Daningschow,* c. 1610. *Dane Inch* 1610, 1621 (1656), *Dane–in–Shaw* 1843, *Dane Henshaw* 1831, *Dane–en–Shaw* 1842; of these, the forms dated 1593, c. 1610, refer to *Dane–in–Shaw Brook* and may represent a stream–name derived by back–formation from the place–name *Dane–in–Shaw.* The place–name *Dane–in–Shaw* is OE **hyll** 'a hill', OE **hōh,** 'a promontory, an eminence', and OE **halh** (dative–singular *hale*), 'a nook, a corner, a valley, land in a confluence', added to an OE assibilated *–ing*–suffix formation upon the river–name *Dane.* The basic formation appears as the name of *Dane–in–Shaw Brook* in *Dane Inch* 1610, 1621 (1656), and no doubt *Dane–in–Shaw* as a place–name means 'the hill etc., at (the stream called) the *Dane–Inch*'. The original form of *Dane–Inch* would be OE **Dæfeninge,* a locative form leading to the pronunciation *–indge > –inch,* and meaning 'at **Dafening*; at the **Dæfening*', where **Dæfening,* a nominative form with the pronunciation *–ing,* means 'that which is called after R. Dane'.

[73] *Warmincham* 1259, *Wermincham* late 13th, *–yncham* 1315; *Wermingham* 1260, *Warmingham* 1488; *Werningham, –yng(e)–* 1290, 1291; *Wernycham* 1478; *Warmengeham* 1306, *Wermynge–* 1342, *Warmynge–* 1492, *–inge–* 1574; *Werminsham* 1489; *Warringham* 1554; *Warmisham* 1629; *Warmincsham* 1656; *Warminckham* 1669; OE **hām** with an OE *–ing*–suffix formation, both assibilated and non–assibilated, upon the OE personal–name *Wǣrmund* or its short–form *Wǣrma.* The *–insh–, –ish–,* spellings represent the assibilated pronunciation (*–ing > –indge > –inch–*) and the ME *–inc–, –ing–,* spellings represent the uninflected unpalatalized (so non–assibilated) OE *–ing,* pronounced *–ing > –ink* by ME north–west–midland dialect. A compromise between the two forms is represented by *Warmincsham* 1656. The ME spellings *–inge–, –ynge–, –enge–,* can represent either the assibilated pronunciation *–indge* from the locative form, or the non–assibilated pronunciation *–inge–* from OE dative–singular *–inge* or genitive–plural *–inga–.* This place–name has undergone a partial assimilation to the OE *–ingahām* type of place–name. It is basically OE **Wǣrminge–hām* and **Wǣrming–hām,* in which OE **Wǣrminge,* a locative form leading to the pronunciation *–indge,* means 'at **Wǣrming*', and **Wǣrming,* the uninflected nominative form, with the pronunciation *–ing,* means 'that which is called after the man *Wǣrma (Wǣrmund)*'.

[74] *Tusigeham* 1086; *Tussinhgham* 1260; *Tussincham* 1272–1307; *Tussingham* 1288, *Tusshyngham* 1543, *Tushingham(e)* 1632, 1633; *Tussinham* 1311; *Tussigham* 1314; *Tussigcham* 1315, *Tussicham* 1316; *Tussingcham* 1315, *–yngcham* 1492; *Tussingeham* 1383, *–ynge–* 1392; *Tussyncam* 1416; *Tussynsham* 1472; OE **hām** with an alternatively assibilated and non–assibilated OE *–ing*–suffix formation upon an

Iddinshall,[75] the medial *–ing–* component is, or was formerly, pronounced *–indge–*, *–idge–* (often becoming *–insh–*, *–ish–*). Such place–names belong to what may well be called the 'Brummadgem' type, after the true and ancient pronunciation of the place–name *Birimingham*. In this kind of place–name the ME spellings *–insh–*, *–inch–*, and a frequently surviving pronunciation *–indge–*, *–insh–*, reveal the assibilation of the medial *–ing–* element. This same phenomenon may also have occurred in the lost place–name *Codingey*[76] in Coddington. All of these Cheshire place–names consist of an *–ing–*suffix formation with assibilated *–ing* (*–indge*), to which a further element has been added. The basic type of assibilated–*ing*–formation place–name without the addition of a further element, would appear as a place–name ending in *–inge, –indge*. Such a form is observed in the Cheshire place–names *Billinge*,[77] *Wallange*[78] (near

---

OE personal–name **Tūnsige*. *Tushingham* represents OE **Tūnsiginge–hām* and **Tūnsiging–hām*, in which **Tūnsiginge*, a locative form leading to the pronunciation *–indge*, means 'at **Tūnsiging*', and **Tūnsiging*, the nominative form with the pronunciation *–ing*, means 'that which is called after the man *Tūnsige*'.

[75] *Etingehalle* 1086; *Hedinchale, Edinchale* 1096–1101 (14th), 1150 (14th); *Idighala* c. 1150 (1285); *Idinchale* 1188–9 (14th); *Idinghale* 1233–7 (14th), *Ydinghall* 1270–1 (14th), *Idinghal(l)* 1287, 1288; *Idingham* 1270 (17th); *Idingehalle* 1272–90, *–hale* 1287; *Ydonehale, Ydonekale* 1291; *Idynshaw* 1535; *Idenshall* 1583; OE **halh**, (dat. sg. *hale*), 'a nook, a corner', with an assibilated OE *–ing–*suffix formation upon the OE verb *ettan*, 'to graze, to pasture'. The basis is an OE noun **etting*, 'a pasturage, a grazing; a grazing–place', which appears also in the place–name *Ettingshall* (Staffordshire). In the Staffordshire name the *–ing–*formation is compounded in the genitive–singular form of the non–assibilated *–ing*. The assibilated form in the Cheshire place–name demonstrates that *Iddinshall* contains the locative form of the OE noun **etting*, i.e. **ettinge* (leading to the pronunciation *–indge*). *Iddinshall* means 'the **halh** (called) *Ettinge*', in which *Ettinge* means 'at *Etting*', and *Etting* means '(the place called) the *etting* or pasturage; that which has to do with pasturing or grazing'.

[76] *le Codyngeheye* 1284–7, *Codyncheheye* 1284, *Codingey* 1296, 1300–7, *Codingeye* c. 1300; OE **(ge)hæg**, 'a fenced–in enclosure', and an *–ing–*suffix formation upon the OE personal–name *Cotta* which also forms the first component of the place–name *Coddington* of the township within which this lost place–name occurred. The ME *–ynche–* spelling suggests that the assibilated OE *–ing–*suffix formation was alternative to the non–assibilated–*ing* form, even if not the basic one.

[77] There are several instances of this name in the county: 1. *Billinge Hill, Billinge Head* and *Billinge Side* in Rainow, *le Bellyng'* 1503, *Bellendge, Bellendge* (*Carr*), *Billinge(s) Carr(e)*, *Billinge* 1611, 1620, *Billinge Head, Billinge Side* 1831; OE **hyll**, 'a hill', **sīde**, 'the side of –; a hillside', ON **sker**, 'a rocky cliff', with a hillname *Billinge* (pronounced *–indge*); 2. a place in Romiley (at Ordnance Survey Grid Ref.

Stanthorne and Middlewich), *Wyringe*[79] (a lost place–name in

942913 near Top o'th'Hill at Werneth Low), latterly called *Werneth Farm, Werneth House* (old O.S. 6–inch maps), was *Billings Green* in 1831 Bryant's map; 3. *Billinge Green* (pronounced –*indge*) in Rudheath, *Bellynge* (lit. *Mell–*) 1534–47 (Dugdale, *Monasticon,* IV, 242), 16th (Public Record Office, *Augmentation Office Miscellaneous Books,* Vol. 397, fo. 32: this volume and *Land Revenue Office Miscellaneous Books,* Vol. 200 deserve the attention of local historians and topographers in Cheshire), *Billings Greene* 1650, *Billing(e) Greene* 1650 (18th), *Billing Green* 1831, from OE **grēne**, 'a grassy space; a village–green', added to a place–name *Billinge* (pronounced –*indge*); 4. *High Billinge* (pronounced –*indge*) in Utkinton, *Belynge* 1503, *High Billinge* 1831; 5. *Billinge Meadow* 1839, a field–name in Acton near Weaverham; 6. *The Billings* 1838, a field–name in Harthill. This series should be taken with such place–names as *Billing Hill* (West Riding of Yorkshire), *Billinge* (Lancashire), *Billingshurst* (Sussex), *High Billinghurst* (Surrey), *Billings Hill* (East Riding of Yorkshire), *Billington* (Bedfordshire, Lancashire), *Bellington Hill* (Derbyshire), *Billing* (Northamptonshire), *Billingbank* (West Riding of Yorkshire). In this type of place–name (more minutely scrutinized in my 'Various Forms of Old English –*ing* in English Place–Names' *Beiträge zur Namenforschung,* Neue Folge 2 (1967), Heft 4, 326–32) an OE –*ing*–suffix formation **billing,* based upon OE **bill**, a sword; an edge; a bill; a prominent hill', appears sometimes assibilated (pronounced –*indge*) and sometimes non–assibilated (–*ing*). In the Cheshire examples the assibilation is clearly marked by –*ings* spellings for the pronunciation –*indge* and by –*ings* spellings for the pronunciation –*ingz* < –*inz* < –*indz* < –*indge*. The name–type OE **Billinge,* a locative form leading to the assibilated pronunciation –*indge,* would mean 'at **Billing*; at the **billing*', in which OE **Billing,* a nominative form with the pronunciation –*ing,* would represent the proper–noun use of OE **billing,* nominative, 'that which is named from or looks like or is associated with a *bill*'. G. Barnes, 'Early English Settlement and Society in Cheshire from the Evidence of Place–Names', *Trans. Lanc. Ches. Antiq. Soc.* 71 (1961), 45–47, erroneously analyses the type, and his deductions therefrom, op. cit. 45, need qualification since *Billinge* is not an OE –**ingas** folk–name type of place–name; also, *Bullingham* 1560 *Cheshire Sheaf* 3rd series, 23, No. 5392, is a hopelessly botched form, probably for *Bollington* near Macclesfield, and is not an OE –**ingahām** place–name.

[78] *Walleng Bridge* 1619, *Wall–inch–bridge* 1643, *Wallange Farm* 1842, *Wall Inch* 1883; perhaps 'well–bank', from OE (Mercian) **wælla**, 'a well, a well–spring', and OE **hlinc, hlenc**, 'a hill–slope, a bank', but far more likely to be an OE –*ing*–suffix formation upon OE (Mercian) **wælla**, i.e. OE (Mercian) **wælling,* equivalent to standard OE **welling,* 'a well–place, a place where water wells up', as in the place–name *Welling* (Kent). In the Cheshire place–name the –*ing* is assibilated: the origin is OE **Wællinge,* a locative form meaning 'at **Wælling*; at the **wælling*'.

[79] *boscus de Wyringe* 1357 (1620), probably 'place where the bog–myrtle grows', from an OE –*ing*–suffix formation upon OE **wīr**, 'bog–myrtle' — the word which appears as first element in the name *Wirral.*

Macclesfield Hundred, location unknown), and *Isinge*[80] (a lost place–name near Macclesfield). To these we might add *Collinge*[81] in Backford, but the history of this name eludes the record.

In the examination of the 'Brummadgem'–type place–names to which reference has been made,[82] it has been observed that the assibilated medial or final *–ing–*, *–ing*(e) (pronounced *–idge–*, *–indge*, etc.) represents an archaic OE locative–singular–inflected form (< Primitive OE *–ingī*) of the commonplace OE noun–forming suffix *–ing.* Here the locative–singular inflexion *–ī* has prevented the normal reversion of OE palatalized *ġ* to velar *g*, with the consequence that the OE palatalized *ġ* has undergone assibilation to *ǧ* (pronounced *–dg*).[83] It is to be supposed that in the oldest form of English the distinctive locative inflexion in *–ī* would be used by routine in the conversion of a noun into a place–name. The place–names *Tiverton*[84] (Devon) and *Silverton*[85] (Devon) contain a form OE **fyrd* for OE **ford**, 'a ford', which can only be the result of a mutation of the stem–vowel caused by an old inflexional *–ī*, so that beside the OE noun *ford* (< Primitive OE **furd*, cf. OHG *furt* (and place–names like *Frankfurt* (Germany), etc.) < West–Germanic **furdu–z*), there was a specifically toponymic form, the locative–singular–based OE **fyrd*

---

[80] *Esyng* 1274, 1467, *Hessyng'* 1467, 1471, *Hesyng'*, *–inge* 1508, 1560, *Eselyng* 1471, *Esynger* 1508, *Esingar* 1560, *The Isinge* 1620; from ME **ker** (< ON **kjarr**), 'brushwood, marsh', and an *–ing–*suffix formation upon an unidentified first element, perhaps OE **hǣs**, 'brushwood, heath'. The assibilation of the *–ing–*formation is obscured by the *k* of the suffixed *–ker,* but it emerges in the *–inge* spelling of the simple unsuffixed form *Isinge* 1620.

[81] *Collinge Farm* and *Wood* old O.S. 6–inch map, *Big* and *Little Collinge* 1839 Tithe Award field–names; perhaps an assibilated OE *–ing–*suffix formation upon OE **coll**, 'a hill', **col**, 'charcoal', or the OE personal–name *Col(l)a*.

[82] 'The *–ing* in English Place–Names like *Birmingham* and *Altrincham*', note 67 above.

[83] See A. Campbell, *Old English Grammar,* (Oxford, 1959), §§ 426–42.

[84] J.E.B. Gover, A. Mawer, F.M. Stenton, *The Place–Names of Devon* 2 (EPNS 9), 541; *æt Twyfyrde* 880–5 (c. 1100), *Tuuertone, Tovretona* 1086, *Tuiverton* 1141–55; OE **tūn**, 'a farmstead', added to an OE locative form **twīfyr d.*

[85] Op. cit. 569, xiv (addenda), and J.E.B. Gover, A. Mawer, F.M. Stenton, *The Place–Names of Nottinghamshire* (EPNS 17), xxxvii (addenda); *Sulfretona, Suffertona* 1086, *Seluerton* 1179, *Silfreton(e)* 1246; OE **tūn** added to a locative form OE **sulh–fyrd.*

(< Primitive OE *furdī*), 'at the ford'.[86] So, OE *twī-ford* would mean 'the double ford', and the locative of this, which would be the grammatical form used (so long as the distinctive locative inflexion persisted in use) when *twī-ford* was used as a place–name or when a location at a *twī-ford* or at a place called *Twī-ford* was to be denoted, would be OE *twī-fyrd,* 'at the *twī-ford;* at *Twī-ford*'. Similarly, the *Billinge* place–names commemorate an ancient locative–singular *Billingī,* 'at the *billing;* at *Billing*'.

Now, the distinctive locative in –*i* is an archaic feature in Old English.[87] The idiom of classical Old English as seen in the literary and inscriptional remains of that language from the late seventh century onwards, expresses location not by a simple locative inflexion but by a paraphrase — by the use of a preposition with the dative inflexion, which, by the gradual elision of the preposition, led to the locative use of the simple dative inflexion! Modern English follows this usage. So, in Bede's works, early eighth century, we find place–names which consist of a prepositional phrase, OE *æt,* 'at', or *on,* 'in', with the dative–inflected form of a proper–noun or a name.[88] It looks as if the distinctive locative inflexion was being ousted from current use by the dative inflexion as the grammatical locative form from about 650 onwards — a process which may well have begun to operate even earlier than this, although there is no documentation for the beginning of it. The inflexional –*ī* of the locative is written in the runic inscriptions *on rodi* (Ruthwell Cross), 'on the Cross', and *in Rōmæcæstri* (Franks Casket), 'in Rome–city'. These are poetic texts and may embody an archaism. But in these instances, and

---

[86] The locative–inflected toponymic form may also explain the mutation in OE *wyrð* for OE **worð**, 'a curtilage', see A.H. Smith, *English Place–Name Elements* II (EPNS 26), s.v. **worð**.

[87] This –*ī* locative (< Indo–European *–ei*) is well authenticated and attested in Old English and Primitive Germanic; see O. Ritter, *Vermischte Beiträge zur englischen Sprachgeschichte, Etymologie, Ortsnamenkunde, Lautlehre* (Halle, 1922), 117–118; K. Brunner, *Altenglische Grammatik nach der angelsächsischen Grammatik von Eduard Sievers neuarbeitet* (Halle, 1942), § 237:2; A. Campbell, *Old English Grammar* (Oxford, 1959), §§ 571, 572; E. Prokosch, *A Comparative Germanic Grammar* (Philadelphia, 1939), § 79:f; E. Ekwall, *English Place–Names in –ing,* 2nd ed., (Lund, 1962), 214–216; A. Meillet, *Introduction a l'étude des Langues Indo–Européennes,* 8th ed., (Paris, 1937), 322 f.

[88] See A.H. Smith, *English Place–Name Elements* I (EPNS 25), s.v. **æt**.

in such a form as Bede's *in loco qui dicitur Adtuifyrde id est ad duplex vadum* ('in the place which is called *Adtuifyrde,* that is to say at the double ford') in *Historia Ecclesiastica* IV, chapter 28, the idiom using the distinctive locative with a preposition may be seen as a transition from simple locative place–name–formation to prepositional–dative place–name–formation.[89] This transitional phase is recorded in texts from the late seventh century Ruthwell Cross and the early eighth century History. By Bede's time it is already formulaic — his *Adtuifyrde*[90] already shows a dative–singular inflexion in *–e,* a re–inflexion, after the OE preposition *æt* (which he renders by Latin *ad*), of the already locative–singular toponymic form OE **fyrd,* as if the locative **fyrd* were a basic nominative. The runic inscriptions reveal a confusion between a new idiom and an old grammatical form. The dative inflexion has not quite ousted the locative inflexion, but the locative form is to be seen here rather as a persisting obsolescent form than as a living and self–sufficient inflexion — it is not effective without the preposition. In Bede the locative form is not seen as a locative but as a toponymic nominative. So one might estimate that by 700 the distinctive locative–inflected form was a fossil, and that a place–name in the locative–inflected form is rather more likely to belong to a phase of the English language current before 650 than to have been formed after that time. Allowance must be made, of course, for the chance that an archaic inflexional form may have had a persistent effect on place–name formation down to a time after its loss in the language at large. It would be hard to draw a measure of the rate of obsolescence here. The habit of assibilating a consonant or mutating a vowel in order to create the specifically toponymic form of a noun may have outlived any memory of the grammatical *–i* inflexion which originally justified such a change. Allowance must also be made, when considering the distribution of such forms about the country, for the chance of differing degrees of conservatism in the idiom of the various dialect–regions of the Anglo–Saxons. But these commonplace bugbears of place–name study only limit, they do not invalidate, a general proposition that place–name forms which embody the effects of locative–singular inflexion in Primitive OE *–ī* ought in the first instance

---

[89] See A. Campbell, *Old English Grammar,* § 587.
[90] Some unidentified place on R. Alne in Northumberland.

to be thought of as examples of a type of place–name which would be current pre–650. They could be much earlier than this; and some could be analogical constructions from a later date.

Place–names of the *Billinge* and 'Brummadgem' types are archaic in form. Indeed, save for the controlling facts of history and archaeology and geography, such forms might reach back to the age of the earliest English speakers in Britain, for the *–ī* locative inflexion appears in the more archaic strata of continental Germanic place–names (e.g. *Groningen* (Holland) has a 'Brummadgem' pronunciation *Grinz < *Groninğe < *Groningi*) as may be seen from, say, the lists in E. Ekwall, *English Place–Names in –ing*, 1st ed. (Lund, 1923), 174–77, or C.I. Ståhle, *Studier över de Svenska Ortnamnen på –inge* (Skrifter utgivna av Kungl. Gustav Adolfs Akademien 16, Lund, 1946), 156–61, 558–9.

The 'Brummadgem' type of place–name has been identified, in a review of only the more obvious place–names in the material available for study,[91] in fifty–odd instances of place–names with assibilated medial *–ing–*.[92] The distribution of these names appears haphazard. It may be

[91] In my 'The Various Forms of Old English *–ing* in English Place–Names', note 67 above; see also E. Ekwall, *English Place–Names in –ing*, 2nd ed., 169–73.

[92] They are: *Abinger* (Surrey), *Altrincham* (Cheshire), *Atcham* or *Attingham* (Salop), *Atchen Hill* (Worcestershire), *Ballinger* (Buckinghamshire), *Ballingham* (Bedfordshire), *Bellingham* (Northumberland), *Benchill* (Cheshire), *Bengeo* (Hertfordshire), *Bengeworth* (Worcestershire), *Billingham* (Durham), *Birmingham* (Warwickshire), *Bobbingworth* or *Bovinger* (Essex), *Brangehill* (Ely), *Bullingham* or *Bullinghope* (Herefordshire), *Corringales* (Essex), *Cressingham* (Norfolk: a doubtful example), *Dane–in–Shaw* (Cheshire), *Dinchope* (Salop), *Drungewick* (Sussex), *Dungee* (Bedfordshire), *Dungewood* (Wight), *Ealingham, Edlingham, Eglingham, Ellingham* and *Eltringham* (Northumberland), *Fingest* (Buckinghamshire), *French Hay* and *Frenchhurst* (Kent), *Fringford* (Oxfordshire), *Habergham* (Lancashire), *Horningsheath* or *Horringer* (Suffolk), *Iddinshall* (Cheshire), *Kensham Green* (Kent), *Kenswick* (Worcestershire), *Kermincham* (Cheshire), *Millichope* (Salop), *Mongeham* (Kent), *Mongewell* (Oxfordshire), *Ovingham* (Northumberland), *Pattingham* (Staffordshire), *Peckingell* (Wiltshire), *Ratlinghope* (Salop), *Tetchwick* and *Tingewick* (Buckinghamshire), *Tushingham* (Cheshire), *Uckinghall* (Worcestershire), *Warmingham* (Cheshire), *Watchingwell* (Wight), *Whicham* (Cumberland), *Whittingham* (Northumberland), *Wiggins Hill* (Warwickshire), *Wilmingham* (Wight), *Wincham* (Cheshire). This list takes no account of similar names in Scotland and the Welsh Marches in Wales, e.g. *Burlingjobb* (Radnorshire), *Berchelincope* 1086, OE **hop** with an assibilated *–ing*–suffix formation, a place–name in an area which Offa's Dyke excluded; see also F.M. Stenton, *Anglo–Saxon England*, 2nd ed., (Oxford, 1947), 212–13.

incompletely discerned on account of the varied degree of detailed examination to which the place–names of the several counties have been subjected; more such names may come to light as the Survey of English Place–Names proceeds. But it would seem to be significant that the West Midlands (from Lancashire down to Herefordshire) contain 22, Cumberland, Northumberland and Durham contain 10 (Northumberland 8 of these), and south east England (below a line from The Wash to the mouth of Severn) contains 23 — Norfolk, Suffolk and Ely 3, Essex and Hertfordshire 3, Kent, Surrey and Sussex 6, Bedfordshire, Buckinghamshire, Oxfordshire and Wiltshire 8, Wight 3. This suggests a currency of the type all over England, with a preponderance as we move away from the south–east. But it is in that quarter that the unsuffixed –*inge* type of name is prevalent (e.g. *Ruckinge, Sellinge* in Kent), and, significantly, the OE –**ingas**, –**inga**–, folk–name types which appear to mark a secondary phase of the English settlement history. There has probably been a fairly thorough conversion of the assibilated singular –*ing* locative type of place–name to the pattern of the more modern plural –**ingas**, –**inga**–, type, in the south–eastern parts of the country, which accounts for the apparent unbalance of the distribution of the assibilated type. From the distribution of the surviving 'Brummadgem'–type place–names, it can be argued that such a pre–650 form in such a distribution indicates a pre–seventh century or early seventh century context in which the English had appeared in small or great numbers, powerfully or in a socially insignificant degree, at places all over south Britain. This is not unlikely. But it requires the assumption of English arrivals at the north west coast and the Welsh Marches earlier than history records and without the (as yet) traceable pagan burial clue.

The Cheshire region offers a suitable laboratory for the investigation of this situation. For it will be seen that whereas the history of the English in Cheshire begins early seventh century, the early English place–name forms could be pre–seventh century. The list of Cheshire place–names which may be supposed eligible to belong to an era ending c. 650 is not long. The Cheshire –*inghams* are distributed in relation to the Roman road system, except for Kermincham, Benchill and Dane–in–Shaw, which, like the –*inge* types lie near or upon salt–ways or other medieval routes. These non–Roman routes are not recorded before medieval times, but there is no evidence against their being ancient: they could well be at least as old as the Roman roads, for people travelled before the Romans came, and salt from the Cheshire field must have travelled somehow in very ancient days. The Cheshire *–ingham, –inge,* place–names lie in land which might have attracted early English settlement, as may well be observed from the excellent survey in Dorothy Sylvester's 'Cheshire in the Dark Ages',[93] in districts relatively free of dense woodland, i.e. either in non–forested places or in clear, or cleared, patches in the woodland. The Roman road context of the *–ingham* place–names is of importance here. Some of these early English *–ingham* place–names may lie in ground opened up in Roman times. The Roman road system in Cheshire appears to be the organic structure which dictates the pattern of distribution of these early English place–names, hence of the settlements which bear them. Thus we arrive at the conjecture, from the form and the distribution of these OE *–hām, –inge–hām* and *–inge* place–names, that the English arrival in Cheshire was made along Roman roads and before 650 at latest, and that on formal grounds the place–names are sufficiently archaic in style to have been coined in the sixth century.

II. THE WELSH PLACE–NAMES IN CHESHIRE

The clues necessary for the solution of the chronological uncertainty about the earliest English place–names in Cheshire are not yet all in hand. The next ones will be sought in another kind of evidence, from the Welsh place–names in the county, which will show the state of the Welsh language in use at the time when the English population adopted the current Welsh name–forms in use by the Celtic population. In the compilation of this body of evidence, it has not been found necessary to invent putative Welsh etymologies for ordinary–seeming English place–names;[94] only such place–names as have unmistakable Welsh elements or allusions have been brought forward. They are illustrated in Figure B 3. Nor has it been thought necessary, in an essay already attaining tedious length, to recite the numerous instances of medieval field–names etc., which contain Welsh personal–names, e.g. *Howeliscloutht* 1287 (an

---

[93] See note 3 above.

[94] A fault in Dorothy Sylvester's paper, note 3 above.

unidentified place in Macclesfield Hundred, from the OWelsh personal–name *Houel* and OE **clōh**, 'a clough, a dell'), *Brangaynland* c. 1295 (a selion in Chorlton near Wybunbury, from the OWelsh personal– name *Brangwain* and OE **land**, 'a land, a selion, a strip of plough–land'),[†] *Ouwanis Ruding* 1271 (in Faddiley; OWelsh personal–name *Oue(i)n* and OE **rydding**, 'cleared–ground'), *Maleres rudyng* 1339 (Tarporley; OWelsh *Meilyr*, OE **rydding**). Such place–names as this, and the Modern Welsh field–names commonplace in the nineteenth century Tithe Award lists for south west Cheshire — extending as far east as the Tithe Award field–name *Cae Hyn*, 'the old(er) enclosure',[†] in Weston near Barthomley — may be taken by allusion as evidence of a persistent if unemphatic and subordinate Welsh influence upon and within Cheshire society through medieval and modern times, an extension of that Celtic sub–stratum which Dorothy Sylvester[95] rightly and clearly realises.

The more important Welsh place–names in Cheshire are listed hereunder:

1. *Barhill* (Tushingham); *Barellesgreue* 1394, *Barrel* 1397, *Barhull* 1513, Welsh **bar**, 'a top, a summit', and OE **hyll**, 'a hill', with OE **grǣfe**, 'a wood, a grove'. The English word *hill* has been added as an explanatory suffix (a kind of translation added) to a Welsh hill–name *Bar*.

2. *Beam Heath* (Nantwich); *Creche* c. 1130, from OE **cryc* or **cric* < Primitive Welsh **crūg* < British **cruc**, 'a hill, a mound, a tumulus'. With this place–name should be taken *Church Leys* (a lost place–name in or near Hankelow; *Chircheleges* 13th, *–leghe* 1293) and *Churton* (near Aldford and Farndon; *Churton* c. 1170), which would appear to be OE **lēah**, 'a woodland, a glade in a wood', and **tūn**, 'a farmstead, an enclosure', with the same English borrowing from Primitive Welsh — OE **cric, *cryc* 'a hill, a mound'. There is neither trace nor record of an ancient church (OE **cirice**) at either place. The interest in these place–names lies in the nature of the English form used to express the original Celtic one. The substitution of OE *y* for the PrWelsh *ū* to produce OE **cryc,* would be a seventh–to–eighth century feature, whereas the substitution of OE *i* as in OE **cric* for PrWelsh **crūg* would be a sixth–to–seventh century feature.[96] It is not possible, from the forms recorded in the Cheshire names, to decide which OE form, **cric* or **cryc,* should be taken as the basis. In fact, there may have been an alternation, but it would seem as though the OE **cric* form, with *i* substitution, is the more obvious choice for these Cheshire place–names.

[95] Op. cit.
[96] K. Jackson, *Language and History in Early Britain,* 310.

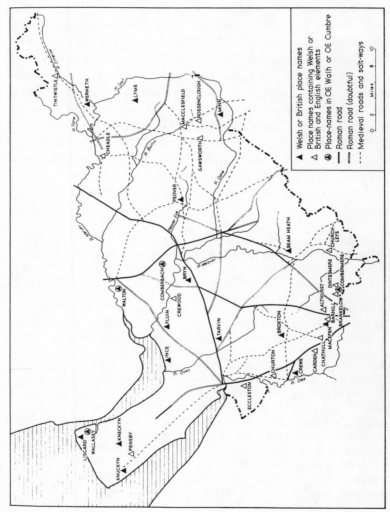

Figure B 3: British and Welsh Place—Names in Cheshire.

3. *Brankelow* (Dodcott cum Wilkesley); *Bromkelawa* c. 1130 (1479), *Brankelow* 1133 (18th), *Bronchelau* 12th, *Branchehillaue* 1540; related to this is the adjacent lost place–name *Branch of Wood* 1831. In these the elements OE **hlāw**, 'a hill, a mound, a tumulus', and OE **wudu**, 'a wood', have been added to a Welsh formation. The alternating *–ch–, –k–* spellings suggest that *k* replaced an earlier *ch*, and that the Welsh component in *Brankelow* and *Branch of Wood* would be PrWelsh **bron–cēd*, from **bron(n)**, 'a hill', and **cēd** (< British **cēto–**, cf. Welsh **coed**), 'a wood'. The process *ch > k* may even reflect a continuous Welsh speech tradition here down to the time of the Welsh sound–change which converted PrWelsh *cēd* to OWelsh *coid*, an evolution which took effect early– to mid–eighth century.[97] The PrWelsh *cēd* form of British *cēto–* appears in *Cheadle* and *Chathull*, below.†

4. *Brynn* (Cuddington); *le Brynne* 1391, Welsh **bryn**, 'a hill'.

5. *Carden*;[98] *Kauerthin* 1230, *Kaurdin* mid 13th, *Caerden* 1462; OE **carr**, 'a rock', and **worðign**, 'a private curtilage'. OE **carr** is an early loan–word from Welsh, from Welsh **carn** or **carrec**, 'a rock'.

6. *Chathull*; see under *Cheadle* below.

7. *Cheadle*; *Cedde* 1086, *Chedle* 12th; from PrWelsh ****cēd** (British **cēto–**, cf. Welsh **coed**), 'a wood', and OE **lēah**, 'a woodland'.[99] There is another *Cheadle* in Staffordshire. A similar compound is *Chathull* (a lost place–name in Malpas), *Chathull, Nant Chathull* 1333, from PrWelsh *****cēd** and OE **hyll**, 'a hill', with the further modification of Welsh **nant**, 'a wood'. This is an interesting stratification of elements: a PrWelsh place–name form is modified by an English element, and this fossilised into an English place–name then needs an explanatory affix to make it intelligible to the Welsh. The element PrWelsh **cēd** is also supposed for *Brankelow*, above.

8. *Church Leys*; see under *Beam Heath* above.

9. *Churton*; see also under *Beam Heath* above.

10. *Crewe* (near Barthomley); *Creu* 1086;

11. *Crewe* (near Farndon); *Creuhalle* 1086, *Cryu* late 11th;

12. *Crewood* (in Crowton); *Crewode* c. 1240; from Welsh **cryw**, 'a ford', with OE **hall**, 'a hall', and **wudu**, 'a wood'.

---

[97] K. Jackson, op. cit. 328–30.
[98] See p. 276 above.
[99] See K. Jackson, op. cit. 327.

13. *R. Dane; Dauene* 12th; whence *Davenham*[100] (*Deveneham* 1086, *Davenham* 1178) and *Davenport* (*Deneport* 1086, *Devennport* c. 1130, *Daven(e)port(e)* 1188, early 13th); derived by E. Ekwall[101] from MWelsh *dafn,* 'a trickle', but by A.G.C. Turner[102] from PrWelsh *Daṽen* < British **Damĭnā,* 'the river of the ox–goddess'. Here we would see a PrWelsh nasal bilabial consonant *ƀ, v* or *μ* (the transitional form between British *m* and Welsh *f* by lenition), rendered by English *f, v,* rather than by *m.*

14. *R. Dee*; British *Deva* 4th, English *Dee* 1043, *De* 1086, Welsh *Duiu* 10th, *Dwy* 14th, 'the holy one, the goddess' (cf. Welsh *Ærfen,* 'war–goddess'). Here the English form is evidence of the adoption of the river–name into English from PrWelsh prior to the development in Welsh of the diphthong *ui* in the second half of the seventh century.[103]

15. *Dintesmere* (a lost name at Combermere in Dodcott cum Wilkesley); *Dintesmere* 12th (18th century copy), *Duntsmere* 12th; OE **mere,** 'a mere, a lake', added to the anglicised genitive–singular of a form *Dint, Dunt,* which could represent the PrWelsh personal–name **Dūnod* (< British Latin *Donatus*) — the same personal–name as that borne by the abbot of Bangor Iscoed whose name Bede spells *Dinooth,* who was leader of the British delegation at the conference with St Augustine in 603. The personal–name form in Bede is discussed by K. Jackson.[104] It is a pre– or early seventh century form, probably contemporary with the historical date 603. The form in the Cheshire place–name (which probably refers to an arm of Combermere lake or to the lake itself) is identical.

16. *R. Duckow*; *Douclesbrooke* early 12th; OE **brōc,** 'a brook', affixed to a British river–name anglicized *Doucles–,* from Brit **Duboglassio–,* 'black water, black stream', i.e. a *Douglas* type of river–name. The English form here shows the retention of Welsh *g* as English *k,* a retention of *g* here is a relative archaism, for Welsh *g* was steadily weakened during the seventh century,[105] so this is a seventh century borrowing at latest.

17. *Eccleston*; *Eclestone* 1086, *Ecclestona* c. 1188; PrWelsh ***eglēs** (< Brit **eclēsia**), 'a church', and OE **tūn,** 'a farmstead, an enclosure'.

---

[100] See p. 278 above. Also here should be mentioned *Dane–in–Shaw,* pp. 279-80 above.

[101] *English River–Names,* (Oxford, 1928), 112.

[102] *Bulletin of the Board of Celtic Studies* XII, part 2, 111–114.

[103] K. Jackson, op. cit. 334.

[104] K. Jackson, op. cit. 295.

[105] K. Jackson, op. cit. 438.

18. *Fluin Lane* (Frodsham); *Fluhen* c. 1290; Welsh **llwyn**, 'a bush'. This name is a Middle English borrowing from some thirteenth century Welshman; at any rate, Welsh *ll*–, expressed as English *fl*–, *thl*–, is unlikely before about 1050.[106]

19. *Gawsworth*; *Govesurde* 1086; OE **worð**, 'an enclosure', with the anglicised genitive–singular of PrWelsh or OWelsh **gof**, 'a smith', perhaps used here as a personal–name.

20. *R. Gowy*; 1577; a late Welsh name for the river anciently called *Tarvin*.[†]

21. *R. Goyt*; *Guit* early 13th, *Gwid, Gwyth* 1285, *Goyt* c. 1251. Probably OE **gyte**, 'a rush of water', but A. G. C. Turner[107] derives it from PrWelsh **Gwuið* (cf. Modern *gwydd,* 'wild'). He observes[108] that PrWelsh *–ui–* was developed by the second half of the seventh century[109] and PrWelsh *gw–* was fully developed by c. 700. This could be a seventh century borrowing from Welsh into English.[†]

22. *Holtridge* (Norbury near Marbury); *Althurst* 1380; Old Welsh **alt** (> Welsh **allt**), 'a hill', and OE **hyrst**, 'a wooded hill'. Here again an English element of similar meaning is affixed to a Welsh place–name.[†]

23. *Ince*; *Inise* 1086; PrWelsh **inis** (> Welsh **ynys**), 'an island'.

24. *Knukyn* 1307–23 (a lost place–name in Irby); *Kne(c)kyn* 1454 (a lost place–name in Caldy); and *Knight Mosse* (a lost place–name near Macclesfield towards Sutton and Gawsworth), *Knuche* 1286; these are related, the latter being from Welsh **cnwc**, 'a hill', the two former from Welsh *cyncyn,* diminutive of *cnwc,* meaning 'little hill'.

25. *Landican*; *Landechene* 1086; OWelsh **lann** and an OWelsh personal–name *Tegan*. The *d* in *Landican* indicates that the original personal–name form was *Tegan* not *Degan,* which rules out an identification of this *Degan* with the Irish saint *Dagan,* bishop of *Inverdaile* (i.e. Ennereilly, co. Wicklow) c. 600, died 640. The place–name *Landican* is an inversion–compound, a type which develops in Welsh in mid– to late sixth century.[110]

---

[106] K. Jackson, op. cit. 479.
[107] *Bulletin of the Board of Celtic Studies*, XXII, part 2, 114–16.
[108] Op. cit. 115.
[109] Cf. *R. Dee* above.
[110] K. Jackson, *Language and History in Early Britain*, 226, note 2.

26. *Liscard*; *Lisnekarke* 13th, *Lisnecaryc* late 13th, *Lisenecark* 1260, 'house at the rock', Primitive Cumbrian **liss–en–carrec* as distinct from PrWelsh **liss–yr–carrec.*

27. *The Lyme*; *–lime* 1086 (in the place–name *Audlem*), *Lima* 1121. Probably 'the district named from an elm–grove', OE **Lim, *Līn,* < Pr Welsh **Liv, *Livn* < Brit **lemo–, *lemano–*; but A.G.C. Turner[111] takes it to mean 'bare place', OE **Līm* < Pr Welsh **Lïm(m)* > Brit **Lummịo–,* although this involves some fancy phonology. The significance of the form of the place–name, regardless of the meaning, is that it shows English *m* substituted for PrWelsh lenited *m*, as contrasted with the substituted English *v* in *R. Dane* (*Davenport, Davenham*) and *Tarvin.*

28. *Macclesfield*; *Maclesfeld* 1086; OE **feld**, 'open country', with an OE personal–name *Maccel*, probably an *–el* diminutive from a Celtic personal–name theme *Mag–, Macc–,* but this is problematical.

29. *Macefen*; *Masefen* 1170, *le Masefen* 1260; Welsh *maes–y–ffin,* 'the field at the boundary'.

30. *The Minn* (in Bosley and Wincle); *le Miyen* 1363, *le Mynde* 1471; OWelsh **minid**, 'a mountain'.

31. *R. Peover* or *Peover Eye*; *Peuerhee* 13th; OE **ēa**, 'a river', suffixed to a river–name *Pever*, whence *Peover Superior* (*Pevre* 1086), *Nether Peover* (*Pevre* 1086) and *Peover Inferior* (*Pefria* c. 1200), representing a PrWelsh form **Pebr* (< Brit **Pebro*, cf. Welsh *Pefr*), 'bright; bright river; the bright one'. English *v* here represents PrWelsh *ƀ*, the lenition–form of Brit *b* developed fifth century and later.

32. *Rossen Clough* (Sutton Downes near Macclesfield); *Rossyndale* 1360; from OE **dæl**, 'a dale, a valley', and an OWelsh **rosinn, –enn,* diminutive of OWelsh **ros** (ModWelsh **rhōs**), 'a moor, a heath', as in *Rossendale* (Lancashire) *Rossington* (West Riding).

33. *R. Tame*; *Tome* 1292; British **Tāma,* 'dark water'. Here the form with English *m* indicates that this river–name was adopted from British **Tāma* or from a PrWelsh form **Taµ–* in which the lenited *–m–* was heard as *m* rather than as *v.*

[111] *Bulletin of the Board of Celtic Studies* XXII, part 2, 116–19.

34. *Tarvin*; *Terve* 1086, 1239, *Teruin* 1222, *Teruen* 1185, *Terne* 1152; PrWelsh *terμin* (< British Latin *terminum*) cf. the Welsh place–name *Terfyn* (Flintshire); 'a boundary'. The English *v* for Primitive Welsh *μ* indicates that this Primitive Welsh sound was heard as *ƀ* rather than as *μ*.

35. *Tintwistle*; *Tengestuisie* 1086, *Tengetuesile* mid 13th; from OE **twisla**, 'a fork (in a river, etc.)', added to a British river–name of the type *Teign*.[†]

36. *Werneth*; *Warnet* 1086; a type discussed by K. Jackson,[112] from British *verneto–*, 'a place growing with alders'; similarly *Werneth* in Lancashire.

37. *R. Wheelock*: *Quelok* c. 1300, whence the place–name *Wheelock* (*Hoiloch* 1086, *Weloc* early 13th, *Quelok* late 13th); OWelsh **Chwelog, *Chwylog* (cf. Welsh *chwel, chwyl*, 'a turn, a rotation') < British **Suilāco*. The name was adopted by the English in a late sixth or a seventh century Welsh form, for British *su–* became OWelsh *hw–* in mid– to late sixth century.[113]

If we take the date–schemes proposed by K. Jackson in *Language and History in Early Britain*, it will be found that *Beam Heath, Church Leys* and *Churton* contain a Welsh element which has achieved a seventh century form; that *Brankelow, Cheadle* and *Chathull* contain a Welsh element in a form which has not undergone an eighth century Welsh change; that *Wheelock* contains a Welsh form which developed in the late sixth century; that *Duckow* contains a Welsh form rather more unlikely after the seventh century; that *Dintesmere* contains a Welsh personal– name with a sixth century development which would become less likely after the seventh century; that *Dane* and *Tarvin* show English *v*, whereas *Tame* and *Lyme* show English *m*, for a Welsh sound which was proceeding from *m* to *v* over a long period, sixth to tenth centuries, being heard by the English as *m* down to the tenth century, and as *v* as early as the late sixth century, with an overlap and alternation of English *m, v*, sound–substitution in the seventh century;[114] that *Dee* is a form which did not undergo a seventh century Welsh change; that *Goyt* may contain Welsh sounds developed in the seventh century;[†] that *Landican, Liscard* and *Macefen* are compositions of a type developed in the sixth century.

[112] *Language and History in Early Britain*, 555.
[113] K. Jackson, op. cit. 526.
[114] K. Jackson, op. cit. 491–3.

In general, it may be seen that these names were finally fossilised as English place–names in a form which indicates a continuous tradition of Welsh speech and sound–change down to the seventh century. These place–names are, for the most part, borrowed in a seventh century Welsh form. There arises here a question of dates. If the date of evolution of the Welsh philological forms is to be measured by the sound–substitutions used by the English immigrant who adopted the Welsh place–names, the date of the English immigration needs to be known first. Professor Jackson works on the basis of an English arrival in Cheshire in the seventh century — the date suggested by the documentary history — and uses this in his formal chronology. But it ought to be considered, that some of the place–names listed above could possibly be ascribed, on formal grounds, to a somewhat earlier — late sixth century — date, i.e. *Brankelow, Cheadle, Chathull, Duckow, Dintesmere, Dee, Dane, Tarvin, Tame, Lyme,* could, as a series, be late sixth century adoptions into English. There is a significant possibility here. Some aspects of the Welsh element in Cheshire place–names could indicate a late sixth century date of adoption, others a seventh century and later adoption: and there is evidence of Welsh place–names subject to Welsh language changes down into the seventh century, in Cheshire, before these names were fossilised by the English adopters. It is thus possible to suppose that the Welsh place–names were being borrowed by English speakers over a period late sixth to seventh centuries: that some forms represent sixth century adoptions — place–names borrowed at that stage and, upon being taken into English, immunized against Welsh speech changes — while some others were not finally removed into English usage until they had been subjected to the changes taking place in the Welsh language down to the end of the seventh century. The picture thus drawn would show a progressive borrowing of Welsh place–names by the English in Cheshire from the late sixth to the late seventh century; but a persistence in the county area of an active and living Welsh vernacular throughout that period, and possibly later.

We can suppose such a continuous Welsh speech–community in Cheshire from this construction upon the seventh century place–name evidence. We can put this supposition against that which we draw from the evidence of the early English name–forms, that there is an English element which is pre–650 and could well be much earlier. We should then find that we are dealing with a set of name–forms which, both English and Welsh, belongs to a late sixth century to seventh century formal sequence, and requires a mixed population of English and Welsh speakers in the population of Cheshire down to a period c. 650, and possibly from an epoch in the sixth century. This period would be that during which Cheshire was changing from a predominantly Welsh area to a predominantly English area. The place–names listed above exhibit two other manifestations of this Welsh > English overlap. First, a large proportion of them[115] are hybrid place–names, in mixed language, in which an English element qualifies, or explains, a Welsh element, or in which a Welsh personal–name appears with an English element. One does not find English personal–names with a Welsh element added. These features indicate the adaptation by the English of existing Welsh names, or recognitions by the English of a surviving Welsh social personality. It is important to recognise in these place–names an English emphasis: they are English place–names with a Welsh basis. They bespeak a time at which the English have taken over a Welsh country, with whose nomenclature and population they are not unfamiliar. The second manifestation of the Welsh > English social overlap to be seen from the place–names of Cheshire may be introduced from the place–names *Landican, Liscard, Brankelow* and *Dintesmere*, with which we should associate the place–names *Combermere,*[116] *Comberbach,*[117] *Walton*[118] and *Wallasey*[119]. These four names are 'Indian Reservation' types. *Combermere* and *Comberbach* are 'the lake' and 'the valley' of the *Cumbre*, i.e. of the OE equivalent of Welsh *Cymry: Walton* and *Wallasey* are 'the farmstead or village' and 'the island' of the *Walas*, i.e. of the OE

---

[115] E.g. *Barhill, Church Leys, Churton, Brankelow, Carden, Cheadle, Crewe* (near Farndon), *Crewood, Dintesmere, Duckow, Eccleston, Gawsworth, Holtridge, Macclesfield, Rossen Clough, Tintwistle.*

[116] *Cumbermere* 1119–1128 (1285), *Combermere* c. 1130, *Cumbremara* 1181; 'the Welshmen's lake', from OE **Cumbre** (genitive plural *Cumbra*) and OE **mere**, 'a lake, a mere'.

[117] *Cambrebech* 1172–81, *Combrebeche* 1190; 'the Welshmen's valley–stream', from OE **Cumbre** and OE **bece**, 'a stream in a valley, a valley with a stream in it'.

[118] *Waletun* 12th, 'the Welshmen's –, the serfs' farm', from OE **walh** (genitive plural *wala*) and OE **tūn**.

[119] *Walea* 1086; *Waleyesegh* 1351; 'the isle of *Waleye'*, from OE **ēg**, 'an island', suffixed to the place–name *Waleye* which is itself OE **ēg** with the genitive plural, *wala,* of OE **walh**, 'a Welshman; a serf'.

word for 'the foreigners; the inferior race; the serfs', which was applied to the Welsh. The significance of such place–names is social: these were places recognised by an English community as especially associated with, even reserved for, a Welsh population. They are names given at a time when the identification of a Welsh element in the population with a particular district is distinctive, not commonplace; i.e. when a predominantly Welsh district in Cheshire has become a remarkable survival. With *Combermere* one takes the place–names *Dintesmere* and *Brankelow*. In this Welsh enclave the Welsh names show evidence of seventh century Welsh survival. It is noteworthy that in *Combermere* and *Comberbach* the English use their version of the Welsh national name, *Cumbre* for *Cymry*. There is in this recognition of a proper and not necessarily inferior social status. But in *Walton* and in *Wallasey* — with which we might take not only *Liscard,* which is in Wallasey, but also *Landican* nearby in north Wirral — the national name, the Welshmen's own word for the Welsh nation, is not used. Here the English name is not quite so respectful of Welsh sentiment. There is a social degeneration implied.[†] In the *Comber–* place–names the Welsh are accorded a polite recognition of their personality as a race: in the *Wal–* names the recognition is less polite. The *Combermere* enclave is most interesting: it suggests an enclave of Welshmen speaking their own language down into the seventh century, with a certain amount of respectful recognition from the predominant English population.

In summary, then, it can be said that the Welsh place–names in Cheshire, and the English place–names which refer to the Welsh, show forms and meanings which refer to a state of the Welsh language which had been evolved by the sixth and seventh centuries, and which belong to a period in which the English and Welsh languages and nationalities existed side by side in Cheshire. The varieties of place–name under observation illustrate a change from a purely Welsh population, with place–names in Welsh, through a mixed population, with English adoption of Welsh place–names in a progressive and active state of Welsh phonology, with English modification of Welsh place–names; and then with an English distinction of the Welsh as 'different' or special groups in the community, which marks a point at which the established existence of a confident and predominant English community is probable.

III. THE EARLY HISTORY OF THE ENGLISH IN CHESHIRE

The framework of documented historical events in which the English arrival in Cheshire has been seen is really the fragmentary and episodic record of political events in a period c. 603 to c. 780. It has much to do with the emergence of an English establishment in Cheshire: it is only inferential about the English arrival. In 603 Dinooth (= Donatus), abbot of Bangor Iscoed, was president of a synod of British bishops which handled the negotiations with St Augustine. In 613–616 king Æðelfrið of Northumbria attacked the Welsh at Chester in a battle which visited an awful and proper divine revenge upon the monastery of Bangor. At this juncture, in the first decade of the seventh century, it looks as if Chester was in Welsh territory. It may well be that the Primitive Welsh place–name *Tarvin*, 'the boundary', on R. Gowy, is a true parallel with the Welsh place–name *Terfyn*, 'the boundary', near *Prestatyn* in Flintshire, at the north end of Offa's Dyke, and that it may be taken with the Welsh place–name *Macefen*, 'field at the boundary', near Malpas, as commemorating a line along R. Gowy and the Broxton Hills which formed a sixth or seventh century boundary line between the Welsh and their eastern neighbours, just as *Terfyn* in Flintshire commemorates the eighth century and later boundary at Offa's Dyke. The Tarvin–Macefen line may even have been the Welsh frontier which Æðelfrið penetrated in 613–616.

In 689, according to a lost annal recited by Henry Bradshaw, monk of St Werburgh's Chester, in his *Life of St Werburge*,[120] Book I, ll. 2317–2324, Æþelræd king of Mercia (674–704), Penda's son, founded a church at St John's Chester.[121] By 689 we might thus discern Chester as within the English sphere of influence. Æþelbald king of Mercia (716–757) is thought to have built Wat's Dyke, and Offa king of Mercia and the English (757–796) is known to have built Offa's Dyke. Wat's

---

[120] *The Life of St Werburge of Chester, translated into English by Henry Bradshawe*, ed. C. Horstmann *Early English Text Society*, 88, (1887).

[121] There is neither need nor reason to query this tradition: it is unnecessary to suppose with Helsby, in his edition of G. Ormerod, *History of Cheshire*, I, 306–7, 192 that this should in truth be a reference to Æþelræd, ealdorman of Mercia (died 911), Æþelflæd's husband, Ælfred's son–in–law.

Dyke firmly seals the English domination of Cheshire by 757. The endowment of a church in Chester by a Mercian king in 689 shows the accomplishment of some sort of effective take–over, as far as R. Dee at least, by that date. It can be said, then, that the English took over Cheshire between 613–616 and 689.

In the interval between 613 and 689 lie the reigns of Penda, king of Mercia (626–654), the rule over Mercia of Oswiu king of Northumbria (654–657), and the reign of Wulfhere, king of Mercia (657–674). Of these periods, it is the reign of Penda which is most significant. Penda was the founder of English political domination in the midland empire of Mercia. He is seen in alliance with Cadwallon, king of Gwynedd, in 633, to defeat Eadwine, king of Northumbria (616–633), Æðelfrið's successor. Here, he is bearing a hand in the feud between the Northumbrians and the Welsh, first noticed in the battle of Chester, and doubtless exacerbated by Eadwine's reduction of the kingdom of Cerdic of Elmet (near Leeds) c. 616–620.[122] In 642 the Northumbrians struck into Mercia, and their king Oswald (633–642) was killed by Penda's folk at *Maserfeld* (Oswestry). This location suggests that the invasion was directed into the Welsh Marches area of Mercia, and that it might have been aimed against the same English–Welsh alliance.[†] Again, in 654, Penda with Welsh allies attacked Oswiu, king of Northumbria (642 (Bernicia), 645 (Deira)–670), who defeated Penda, killed him, and ruled Mercia until 657. The subsequent history is a process of recovery and consolidation and expansion of the Mercian power in southern England, and a holding operation by Mercia against the Northumbrians. The period 603–689[†] shows a shift of Welsh influence away from Chester and the extension of English influence as far as Chester. The part of this period occupied by the reign of Penda shows the emergence[123] of Mercian English

---

[122] The whole business of the feud between Northumbria and the Welsh should be seen as a result of the friction between the northern English and the British, caused by the Northumbrian political expansion in the late sixth and early seventh centuries across the north country, into territory formerly controlled by the Welsh of Cumbria, Elmet, Gwynedd and Powis.[†] The battle of Chester should be seen as a major operation by the Northumbrians to make by war a political situation which could relieve their settlement of Lancashire from interference.

[123] The process of this emergence is carefully described in F.M. Stenton, *Anglo–Saxon England*, 2nd ed., 81–82: Penda's kingship effectively dates from the death of Eadwine and of Cadwallon, 633.

military–political power as an ally of the Welsh against the Northumbrian English, and then as the enemy of the Northumbrian English with Welsh allies assisting. There is no English record of strife between Welsh and Mercian English in these years.[†]

IV. CONCLUSIONS

Inferences which may be drawn from three bodies of evidence — early English place–names, Welsh place–names, and early English history, in Cheshire — can now be collated. Certain English place–names of a potentially pre–seventh century type appear sporadically all over the county, but along Roman roads and similar ancient ways. Welsh place–names appear sporadically all over the county, some of which could have been adopted by the English in a pre–seventh century form, others in a later form. Certain types of hybrid place–name, and the English place–names which embody a social and racial distinction (especially when taken with the early English and the Welsh place–names), show a continuous juxtaposition of Welsh and English populations. It is also seen that there appears to be evidence of a Welsh frontier along R. Gowy down to the seventh century; that the Mercian English and the Welsh are in political harmony, and in alliance or co–operation against the Northumbrians, during a period in which English political influence is replacing Welsh political influence at Chester and in Cheshire.

This collation of inferences implies that the English take–over from the Welsh in Cheshire was accomplished between 613–616 and 689 without political strife — that it was only a reflection in political organisation of a change in the balance of society which had already taken place. The emergence of Penda and the political power of the Mercian English in Cheshire would thus be seen as the result of a social situation which had already been created. The English take–over made his career possible: his accession to power did not precipitate, although doubtless it confirmed and gave impetus to, that take–over.

It is quite possible to construe events in this way. At first one may suppose the infiltration of British Cheshire by small groups of Mercian Englishmen in the latter part of the sixth century, settling in scattered sites along Roman roads, i.e. settlement of English immigrants in a British context, unobtrusively. These English would either assimilate their customs quickly to those of their neighbours or they would remain numerically negligible for so long that, by the time they had multiplied to noticeable numbers, they had gradually or by conversion adopted Christian funeral habits, and so we do not find (or recognise) their pagan burial sites. In the Welsh–English population created by this quiet immigration, a gradual build–up of the numbers of the English element would pass unnoticed by history or even place–names, until a point was reached at which the English achieved numbers sufficient to give them a social preponderance over the Welsh, and the Welsh became a minority which eventually lost its social status of parity. This shift from a Welsh–English to an English–Welsh weighted society is marked in the place–names, and in the political events of the seventh century. But the absence of any record of political strife between Mercians and Welshmen at this period,[†] and the converse record of Anglo–Welsh alliance — beginning with a Mercian involvement in a Northumbrian v. Welsh feud — suggests that the political change marked by the obsolescence of the Tarvin–Macefen frontier, the ascendancy of Penda, and the English foundation at St John's Chester in 689, was an inexorable but quiet and uncontested transition. These historical events occurred in a society whose English complexion had been peaceable and steadily intensified as its Welsh complexion waned. It is necessary, I think, for us to allow a generation, perhaps more, before Penda's day, in which the English element of the population of British Cheshire could develop enough weight and status to sustain a take–over bid and the assumption of the Welsh feud against the Northumbrians. The fact that this social take–over was associated with the assumption by Penda of the military leadership of the war against Northumbria need not be taken as evidence that English mercenaries arriving at that juncture made the first English settlements. No doubt, in Penda's time, new English population would be attracted into Cheshire. But Penda's assumption of the leading role after the death of the Welsh king Cadwallon, asserting the political supremacy of the English over the Welsh in Cheshire (in common with that of the Mercians over the other English of the midlands), is just as likely to indicate the political realisation and expression of a social situation already existing.

Again, there is an inference — no more, but unavoidable — that the English arrival must antedate the Mercian establishment. This inference requires an English arrival in Cheshire before the seventh century, while the region was still Welsh; i.e. in the sixth century. Here the possible significance of a Welsh frontier at Tarvin–Macefen is important. If this were an *ethnic* boundary — and it is almost (if not exactly?) co–incident with the boundary between K. Jackson's zones II and III[124] — there should be no early English place–names west of it. *Tushingham* and *Dunham on the Hill* adjoin it, *Eastham* and *Codingey* are within it. If it were a Welsh *political* frontier, and if the initial English settlement were, as it seems indeed to be, a peaceful and scattered immigration, then early English place–names might well appear west of the line and adjacent to it. These would represent a process of settlement by leave and allowance (a parallel, maybe, with Æþelflæd's handling of the Norse immigration into Wirral),[125] i.e. a social and ethnic minority not affecting the political arrangements of the Welsh majority. The probable explanation of the Tarvin boundary is that it represents a determination, by a Welsh political entity in Chester and west Cheshire, of a line up to which its jurisdiction was either effective or supposed or claimed, at a time when the power of disposition in the rest of Cheshire had been resigned to some other power. At a guess, it might be said that down to about 613–616 the Welsh were politically and socially dominant west of this line, but east of it by that time they were not predominant in a mixed English–Welsh population. The Tarvin boundary would become obsolete upon a political change, since it appears to have been a political rather than an ethnic boundary. This boundary had already been infiltrated, by the English immigrants who created the early place–name settlements, by the time that the Welsh political frontier shifted to R. Dee and westward.

To sum up, the evidence indicates that the English would arrive in British Cheshire by peaceful infiltration as a minority element of the population in the latter part of the sixth century; they would multiply as part of a mixed Welsh and English population until they became the preponderant element in that population; at this point, and hardly before this point, this preponderance would be converted into a predominance expressed politically by the Mercian assumption under Penda of the war between the Welsh and the Northumbrians — a predominantly English

[124] See p. 270 above.
[125] See J.McN. Dodgson, 'The Background of Brunanburh', *Saga–Book* XIV, 305–6 [= *supra*, pp. 251–2].

mixed population assuming political liabilities previously contracted by that predominantly Welsh population out of which it had developed. The tradition of the place–names suggests the gradual emergence of English Cheshire out of British Cheshire by a quiet social progression in which the social status of the Welsh diminished as that of the English magnified — a social progression whose culmination is the basis of the political events recorded in seventh century history. Here the historical record and event provide a kind of rear–view mirror, in which we see the image of a scene farther back along the road. It is the place–names which enable us to reconstruct the significance of that image, with its mirror–like inversion of the status of the Welsh and the English by the time the seventh century English history opens.

Additional Notes

Notes, *infra*, which are followed by '(J.M.D.)' are taken from manuscript addenda and corrigenda added by Professor Dodgson in 1988 to his copy of the article, prior to his intended subsuming of the main thrust of the argument into the 'Introduction' to the Cheshire survey.

For Welsh names in Ch, see also Appendix I: E, *infra*; for Old English names, see also Section II of the 'Introduction', *supra*, and Appendix I: D, *infra*; for Scandinavian names, see also Section III of the 'Introduction', *supra*, Gillian Fellows–Jensen, *Scandinavian Settlement–Names in the North–West*, Navnestudier 25 (Copenhagen, 1985) and *eadem*, 'Scandinavians in Cheshire: a Reassessment of the Onomastic Evidence', in *Names, Places and People: an Onomastic Miscellany in Memory of John McNeal Dodgson*, ed. A.R. Rumble and A.D. Mills (Stamford, 1997), 77–92.

Figure B 1. The rivers shown in the extreme north-east of the county are the Tame, Etherow and Goyt. (J.M.D.) Some names shown on this map as 'Danish' would now be shown as 'Either' (Danish or Norse) in the light of the reassessment reflected in the additional notes, *infra*, to p. 265. (A.R.R.)

Figure B 2. On this map, Frodsham (**3** 221) should be added, Barthomley (**3** 5, **5:2** Add.) and Wrinehill (**3** 56) should be deleted. (J.M.D.)

p. 262, l. 5. *For* sixth century *read* seventh century. (J.M.D.)

p. 262, l. 19. *For* for lack of a strong opposing British establishment *read* after the failure of a strong controlling British establishment (J.M.D.)

p. 263, l. 2. *For* even, in fact, controlling *read* which was able to retain control of (J.M.D.)

p. 263 n11, *Dingesmere*. See **4** 240 and **5:2** Add. (A.R.R.)

p. 265 (*Hulme*) and n12. *hulm* is not a reliable touchstone of ODanish any more, = **holmr** (J.M.D.). See further, **5:1** 237–9; Linguistic Notes, *supra*, § 12.4.4; and Gillian Fellows–Jensen, *Scandinavian Settlement–Names in the North–West*, Navnestudier 25 (Copenhagen, 1985), 313–16. (A.R.R.)

p. 265 (*Toft*) and n13. See **2** 81. The el. **toft** was, however, an early loan–word into OE and the Ch p.n. need not be a Danish coining, cf. Gillian Fellows Jensen, *Scandinavian Settlement Names in Yorkshire*, Navnestudier 11 (Copenhagen, 1972), 75. (A.R.R.)

p. 265 (*Knutsford*) and n14. See **2** 73. Note, however, an alternative etymology, from the scandinavianization of an original OE *cnotta–ford* 'ford at a hillock', suggested by Gillian Fellows–Jensen in *Anglo–Saxon England* 19 (1990), 15–16. (A.R.R.)

p. 265 (*Denhall*) and n15. See **4** 220. This p.n. may possibly confuse OE *Dena–wælla* 'Danes' spring' with ON *Dana–vollr* 'Danes' meadow'. (J.M.D.)

p. 265 (*Colstonstoke*) and n16. See **2** 127. *Colstonsoke* (1484) is the better form. (J.M.D.)

p. 265–6 (*Keckwick*) and n21. See now **2** 152 where the pers.n. is identified as the ON by–name *Keikr*. (J.M.D.)

p. 266 (*Queastybirch*) and n22. See **2** 150. Cf. also the *TA* f.n. Quiesty (**2** 127) in Higher Whitley. (J.M.D.). See also *supra*, 240.

p. 266 (*Swaynesrudinge*) and n26. See **2** 156. Alternatively, the name may contain the common sb. **sveinn**; cf. *Swaynescroft* 1290 Court (p) in Etchells **1** 240. For some other Scand pers. nn. appearing in the name of an assart or intake in Ch, see: *Hawardisruding* **2** 323, *Hosebarnisruding* **1** 83, *Saxiruding* **3** 226 and *Thurberneswra* **4** 107 (**5:2** Add.). (J.M.D.)

p. 266. Both Morphany (**2** 154) and *Swaynesrudinge* (**2** 156) are hybrids. (J.M.D.)

p. 266. Note also Tintwistle which may contain the ON pers.n. *Þengill*, see **5:2** Add. to **1** 320–1, rather than the archaic OE **þengel** 'prince' suggested **3** xiv. (J.M.D.)

p. 267 (OIrish personal–names). Note also *Rugonnyscroft* **2** 316, which may contain OIr *Ruadacán*. (J.M.D.)

p. 267 (*Tiresford*) and n34. This should be deleted. It contains the OE pers. n. *Tīr*, see **3** 320 (J.M.D.)

p. 268 (*Bootherson*). It is not safe to rely on an OE ***bōthere**, as Bootherson (**3** 27) is only a *TA* f.n. (J.M.D.)

p. 275 and nn49, 50. Note, however that Professor Dodgson later decided that neither Wrinehill (**3** 56) nor Barthomley (**3** 5, **5:2** Add.) can be accepted as containing OE **hǣme**. (A.R.R.)

p. 278 and n63. Frodsham (**3** 221) might, however, be from OE **hamm** not **hām**, see **5:1** xxxvii (J.M.D.)

p. 278. Eastham (**4** 187) probably contains OE **hām** alternating with **hamm**, see **5:1** xlii. (J.M.D.)

p. 289. For *Brangaynland* see further **3** 60 and **5:1** xxxiv. (A.R.R.)

p. 289. For Cae Hyn (**3** 75), see further, *infra*, Appendix I: E, no. 24. (A.R.R.)

p. 291, no. 3 (*Brankelow*). However, note Professor Löfvenberg's alternative etymology from OE ***brōmuc** referred to at **3** 94. (A.R.R.)

p. 293, no. 20 (*R. Gowy*). However, note Professor Jackson's comments, at **3** xiv. (J.M.D.)

p. 293, no. 21 (*R. Goyt*). See, however, **1** 27–8, where Turner's etymology is rejected. (J.M.D.)

p. 293, no. 22 (*Holtridge*). However, note Professor Jackson's comment at **3** xvi. (J.M.D.)

p. 295, no. 35 (*Tintwistle*). For the first el. see now **5:2** Add. to **1** 320–1. See also **3** xiv. (A.R.R.)

p. 295 (*Goyt*). The theory that R. Goyt may contain Welsh sounds developed in the seventh century has now been rejected, see **1** 27–8. (J.M.D.)

p. 298, l. 17. *For* degeneration *read* derogation and demotion (J.M.D.)

p. 300, l. 20 'against the same English–Welsh alliance'. *Query* 'or against Powis' (J.M.D.)

p. 300, l. 25. *For* 603–689 *read* 613–689. (J.M.D.)

p. 300 n122 'and Powis'. Perhaps not. Would control Staffs, Salop but not Ch nor Fl. (J.M.D.)

p. 301, ll. 3–4 'There is no English record of strife . . . in these years'. Here should be mentioned the Mercia–Powis war and the death of Cyndylan in the mid seventh century. (J.M.D.)

p. 302, ll. 13–15 'the absence of any record of political strife between Mercians and Welshmen at this period'. Note, however, the Mercia–Powis war. (J.M.D.)

C. PLACE–NAMES AND STREET–NAMES AT CHESTER

[Reprinted from CAS NS 55 (1968), 29–61; read 2 March 1968]

It is not the purpose of this paper to recite all the history of the names of the streets of Chester as recorded in the last 700 years or more. The detailed material for an historical gazetteer will be more concisely presented in my forthcoming *The Place–Names of Cheshire*.[1] Furthermore, much of the available information is already displayed adequately in the articles by W.E. Brown and G.W. Haswell,[2] and by the countless notes and queries from various contributors scattered about in *The Cheshire Sheaf*; and by the admirable map by Mary E. Finch and F.H. Thompson, No. 51 in *The Historical Atlas of Cheshire* (Chester 1958), which should be compared with Fig. C 1.

The present purpose is restricted to the exhibition of some of the more general problems which various local names raise, and to examine some particular aspects of local history which are either illustrated or even further obscured by place–name and street–name evidence.

Although this approach depends upon the safe assumption that the history of the city and its parts is already known to this Society, certain background commonplaces need to be stated at the outset for the sake of convenient reference. We are, at Chester, dealing with a Roman legionary fortress which grew into a medieval city. Archaeology and the town street–plan together exhibit the shape of the Roman town, the rectangle enclosed by the north and east city–walls, by Pepper Street, White Friars, Weaver Street, Linenhall Street and St Martin's Fields. The name of Chester is a figurative model of the change. It appears first as *Deva*,[3] called by the Romans after the holy river, *Dee* (Lat. *diva* 'the goddess'), on which it stood. It was called *Carlegion* in British, reported by Bede in

---

[1] Volumes 44–48, 54 in the EPNS's *A Survey of English Place–Names.*

[2] 'Chester Street–Names Past and Present', CAS, 10 and 12, 1905, 1907.

[3] Δηουα 150 Ptolemy, *Deva* 4 Antonine Itinerary. In the presentation of dates, dating by centuries A.D. is given in simple figures; e.g. 150 here represents the date 150 A.D., and 4 represents the fourth century A.D.

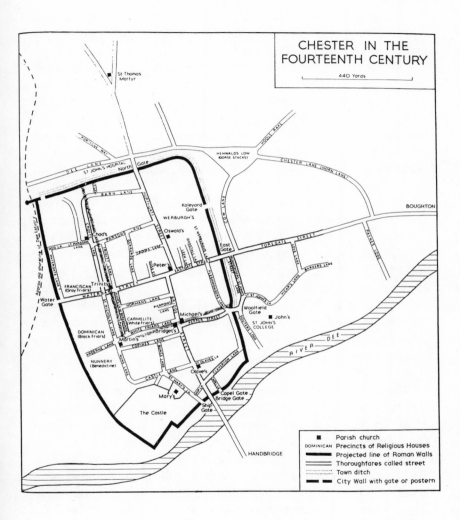

Figure C 1: Plan of Medieval Chester.
Thoroughfares known as *streets* are drawn in heavy line.

734 who translates it *civitas Legionum* in Latin, *Legacæstir* in Old English. The Anglo–Saxon name *Legacæstir* arises from the addition of their word **ceaster** 'a Roman city', to the name *Lleon*, which they took from *Carlegion, Caerlleon*. The English name means 'the Roman city called *Legion*', a translation of *Caerlleon*. In the eleventh century the *Legion* theme, the *Lega–* element of the English name, was dropped. *Legaceaster* gave way to simple *ceaster*, Chester: otherwise the modern form of the city–name would have been something like *Leicester*. There was no need to identify which *chester* this Chester had been in British times, it was to the English *the* chester. Similarly, in Welsh, Chester was *y Gaer* '*the* city'. As the capital of the north–west and of Wales, and as lying more westerly than less distinguished *chesters* elsewhere in the land, it was sometimes called *West–chester* 'the Chester of the west'. It can be estimated from historical record that the Romano–British city *Carlegion* became the English *Legaceaster* during the period 616 to 689, i.e. between the battle of Chester in 616 between Æthelfrith of Northumbria and the forces of Gwynedd, and the foundation in 689 of St John's church by Æthelræd of Mercia, a period during which Penda's Mercia assumed the political responsibility for containing the Northumbrian power and asserted for itself a status more independent than that of a mere ally of Cadwallon's Welsh power; a period in which began that withdrawal of the Welsh frontier, from a line along R. Gowy between Tarvin and Macefen, back to the line established by Offa's Dyke.[4]

The stages by which the typical legionary fortress plan was expanded into the shape of medieval Chester is one of the most interesting and annoying problems which remain unsettled. It is doubtful whether place–name study will provide the answer to the question of how and when this was done; the spade will be the more likely tool for that task. But it seems likely that some toponymic suggestions, mere straws in the wind, may lead the archaeological investigation. In the course of this paper, a number of archaeological and historical inferences will be drawn from place–name forms and the topographical location of the named places in the city, which may, by accident of phrase, look like assertions of fact: it must be remembered that a place–name etymology is significant

---

[4] This sequence is described in my paper 'The English Arrival in Cheshire', LCHS, 119, 1967 [*supra*, Appendix I: B].

only in terms of that human and environmental context which attended the invention of the name, and that philology can at best indicate some possible significances which need the support and proof of historical record or archaeological discovery. The arguments presented in this paper, therefore, will be in some measure inferential as well as deductive: the inferences and deductions drawn will be such as may interest the inferences and deductions drawn from the other kinds of evidence of past time. That sort of philological archaeology provided by place–names eventually requires the control of the other kinds of archaeology, documentary and material. This statement provides a sufficient insurance against any damage to history and archaeology that might be caused by a place–name student running amok along the lanes of Chester.

BERWARD STREET AND ST CHAD'S CHURCH

The first subject for examination is historical. We have to challenge the accuracy of a part of that tradition of our knowledge of the street–names of medieval Chester which depends upon the survey of the city *tempore* Edward III (1327–77) which was copied into the first *Assembly Book* of the Corporation of Chester in Richard Dutton's mayoralty 1573–4.[5] It is upon this Elizabethan tradition of the survey of Edward III's time that all subsequent treatments of the street–names of the city depend: and whereas for the most part it seems accurate enough, there is now some documentary evidence of error in this tradition of the names and layout of the north–west part of the medieval town, in the streets and buildings near *The Crofts*. In particular, there is something wrong with the received tradition of the location of the lost *St Chad's church* and the identification of *Berward Street* with Linenhall Street.

The Crofts is a name usually associated with the open ground, unoccupied until the old city gaol and the infirmary finally swallowed it, in the north–west corner of the medieval city. But it must originally have applied to the whole extent of the ground inside the west wall of the city, from the castle to the north wall: as if, in expanding beyond the Roman wall, the city had included within its greater circuit allotments of unbuilt

[5] Published in Morris (R.H. Morris, *Chester in the Plantagenet and Tudor Reigns*, Chester, 1894, 254–257.

ground. The medieval wall is not the result of a necessary inclusion and protection of developed suburbs; it is a project by some authority or other allowing for future and subsequent, perhaps immediate, expansion beyond the Roman town. *The Crofts* in their later extent appear to be referred to, by the middle of the thirteenth century, as *le Croftis*,[6] *le Croftes*.[7] Individual allotments of ground, *the croft, a croft,* are frequently referred to, but all the ground inside the west wall, west of St Martin's Fields, Linenhall Street, Nicholas Street and Castle Esplanade, from the north wall of the city to the castle, appears to have been occupied by allotments in early medieval times. The site for the foundation of *St Mary's nunnery* was described in 1128–53 as 'those crofts (*illas croftas*) which Hugh son of Oliver held'.[8] The *Black Friars' chapel* was described in c. 1217–26 as 'St Nicholas's chapel founded in the crofts of Chester (*in croftis Cestrie*)'.[9] These two religious houses occupied the space between the castle and Watergate Street. From the middle of the thirteenth century onwards, *The Crofts* is the name of the ground north of Watergate Street. King Street was formerly *Barn Lane*, called after St Werburgh's Abbey's barn in the crofts.[10] These northern crofts were called 'the crofts of Northgate Street' in 1348,[11] as though the allotments were appurtenant to a particular part of the town. The encroachment upon this northern part of *The Crofts* was under way by the middle of the thirteenth century, with the establishment of the *Grey Friars'* house. Their east precinct–wall (still standing in 1574) was along Linenhall Place, and Linenhall Street was *Gray Friars Lane* 1480 to 1775, whereas it was *Crofts Lane* or *Street* 1345 to 1574. But north of the *Grey Friars* there seems to have been little permanent building until

---

[6] c. 1252–3 Sheaf 3, 33, No. 7453, from a Talbot deed. Sheaf 3, represents *The Cheshire Sheaf,* 3rd Series.

[7] 1265–91 (14) Chester II, 617n. Chester represents J. Tait, *The Chartulary of Chester Abbey,* Chetham Society (New Series) Vols. 79, 82. The bracketed date (14) indicates the date or century of the actual document in which a record appears.

[8] 1128–53 (1400) *Calendar of Patent Rolls,* cf. CAS 13, 91; G. Ormerod (ed. T. Helsby), *History of Cheshire,* 1882, 346, hereafter referred to as Ormerod.

[9] c. 1217–26 a charter among the miscellaneous documents in the records of the Corporation of Chester, City Record Office.

[10] *grangia in croftis* 1249–65 (14) Chester II, 617 n1.

[11] *le croftes de Northgatestrete.* Vernon MSS., Box 3, C1. No. 39, in Cheshire County Record Office.

modern times. The extension of the infirmary in 1963 occupied the last remnant of The Crofts at their north end, formerly *Lady Barrow's Hey*.[12] South of this was *Kitchen Croft*,[13] part of The Crofts lying in St Martin's parish, whence the street–name St Martin's Fields; and also *Gaol Fields*[14] and *Infirmary Field*,[15] named after the *City Gaol* (1706) and the *Infirmary* (1706). The gaol was south of Bedward Row, contiguous with the *Grey Friars'* site. The Linen Hall was built upon the site of the *Covent Garden*[16] of the Grey Friars. The site of their house was partly occupied by an inn called *The Yacht*,[17] whence *the Grey Friars Close or the Yacht Field*.[18]

Into this area of *The Crofts* we are required by tradition to fit the location of *St Chad's church* and *Berward Street*. The identification of *Berward Street* with Linenhall Street is suggested by the place of the entry for *Berward Street* in the 1574 Assembly Book copy of the Edward III survey. *Berward Street* there has a paragraph to itself among a list of streets leading off Watergate Street, as if it might well have been a lane off the north side of Watergate Street; but the sixteenth–century scribe was preserving his options by putting it separately because his old text did not clearly inform him. His arrangement certainly indicates that *Berward Street* was a lane off Watergate Street, but it strongly suggests that there might have been some special reservation about it in his mind, requiring a reserved manner of entry. It will appear that by 1574 the location and identity of *Berward Street* had in fact been forgotten, and that the 1574 transcript has been interpreted, wrongly, as identifying *Berward Street* with Linenhall Street because that transcript suggested by

[12] *the Ladie Barrows Hey* 1620 Sheaf 3, 4, No. 633, an enclosure belonging to the *Barrow* family, said to have been wealthy merchants in Chester in the sixteenth and seventeenth centuries, Sheaf 3, 32, No. 7184, cf. 'the close next unto the New Tower now on the holding of my lord Barro' 1533–4 Sheaf loc. cit.

[13] 1724 NotCestr (F. Gastrell, *Notitia Cestriensis, or Historical Notices of the Diocese of Chester,* Vol. I, Cheshire, ed. F.R. Raines, Chetham Society (Original Series) 8, 1845), 104.

[14] 1860 White (F. White & Co., *History, Gazetteer and Directory of Cheshire,* Sheffield, 1860).

[15] 1844 Tithe Award, Tithe Redemption Commission No. 5/308; 1848 Tithe Award T.R.C. No. 5/100.

[16] 1540, Ormerod, I, 350.

[17] 1749 Sheaf 3, 10, p. 72, c. 1772 Sheaf 1, 1, p. 25.

[18] 1775, CAS 24, 63.

its drafting that *Berward Street* was the most westerly lane running northward off Watergate Street in the medieval town–plan.

The names of Linenhall Street have been 'Crofts Street' or 'Crofts Lane' 1345 to 1574,[19] 'Gray Friars Lane' 1480 to 1775,[20] 'Manx Lane' 1665–1691,[21] 'Lower Lane' 1714 to 1830,[22] and 'New Linenhall Street' and more shortly 'Linenhall Street' from 1782.[23] It was first named as the street running along and to *The Crofts* from Watergate Street; then as the lane which ran from the *Grey Friars;* then as the home of a community of Manxmen living in this quarter in the seventeenth century;[24] then as the lane lower down Watergate Street than the other lanes leading northward and as the lower of the only two thoroughfares leading to the north wall of the city (Northgate Street was the other, of course, along the top of the hill on which the Roman city stood); and the modern name is taken from the Linen Hall.[25]

In 1574, coinciding with the Assembly Book transcript, Linenhall Street is called *lez Croftez Streete or St Chaddes Streete*[26] and in 1728[27] it appears as *Lower Lane formerly called Berwards Street.* The first of these equations indicates a site of *St Chad's* on Linenhall Street which could cause *Crofts Street* to be called *St Chad's Street.* The point will be

---

[19] *regia strata del Croftes* 1345 Portmote Rolls (MR/42) in Chester City Record Office; 1389 Br. Mus. Additional Charter 50202; *venella vocata le Croftes* 1459 Portmote Rolls MR/98; *Crofts Lane* 1396 CAS 24, 61, *lez Croftes Streete or St Chaddes Streete* 1574 Corp. (= Deeds of the Corporation of Chester, in the City Record Office).

[20] *Gray Fryars Lowne* 1480 CAS 24, 61; *le Grayfrerelane* 1510 Sheriffs Books (SB) in City Record Office; *Grey Friars Lane* 1775 CAS op. cit., 45–6.

[21] *Manks Lane* 1665 Sheaf 3, 44, No. 9164; *Mancks Lane* 1691 op. cit., No. 9225.

[22] *Lower Lane* 1714–27 Corp. C/Ch 8A/5, — *formerly called Berwards Street* 1728 Sheaf 3, 45, No. 9238–9, — *or Linenhall Street* 1830 loc. cit.

[23] Sheaf 3, 45, No. 9238–9.

[24] Sheaf 3, 44, No. 9228.

[25] Built 1774–1778 on *Yacht Field* in *The Crofts,* and the site of *Grey Friars*: a market hall for the Irish linen trade, also used as a cheese–market; *Linen Hall and Cheese Fair* 1848 Tithe Award Map, Tithe Redemption Commission No. 5/100; *Cheese Mart* 1860 White. In 1782 it was *New Linenhall* (cf. Linenhall Street *supra*) superseding *the old Linen Hall* 1831 Hemingway (J. Hemingway, *History of the City of Chester,* Chester, 1831) II, 12, which stood on the east side of Northgate Street near the Cathedral.

[26] See note 19 *supra.*

[27] Sheaf 3, 48, No. 9740.

taken up again. The 1728 reference identifies Linenhall Street (as *Lower Lane*) with *Berward Street* because of the 1574 transcript tradition.

This identification, received from, or rather, read into, the 1574 Assembly Book transcript, is incorrect, as is clearly proved by a series of ancient deeds[28] which deal with a property down Watergate Street opposite Holy Trinity Church, in *Alvenis–, Aluineslone. Aluineslone* is Weaver Street, for in 1405[29] property in *Aluineslone* was described as between *Alueneslone* to the east, *le Blakefrerelone* ('Blackfriar Lane', i.e. Nicholas Street) to the west, and Watergate Street to the north. Weaver Street is called *Alban Lane* in the 1574 transcript, and *Albane Lane now Weever Lane near to the Trinity Church* in a sixteenth century reference[30] which locates it at the west end of Watergate Street Row South. In 1656[31] it was called *St Alban's–lane. Alban* for *Alven* looks like the commonplace confusion and substitution, phonetic as well as orthographic, of *b* and *v*.[32]

From these Vernon deeds and the 1574 transcript we now see Weaver Street as *Aluenislone* c. 1260, *Aluinislone* 1291, *–es–* 1292, *Alueneslone* 1405;[33] *Aluenelone*;[34] *Alban Lane* Edward III (1574),[35] *Albane Lane* 16,[36] *St Alban's–lane*;[37] *Weaver Lane* 16,[38] *Weavers Lane* 1712,[39] *Weaver–street, formerly named St Alban–lane* 1831.[40]

Now, in the same series of deeds[41] there are documents dealing with the same or an adjoining property, a messuage in Watergate Street,

---

[28] Vernon MSS., Box 3, C1, Nos. 5, 3 and 8.

[29] *Ibid.*, Box 3, C2, No. 2.

[30] Sheaf 3, 32, No. 7173, to be dated either 1533–4 or 1556.

[31] Ormerod, I, 188.

[32] Although it is interesting to note that the abbot of St Albans visited Chester in 1362 to examine the affairs of Chester Abbey (CAS 13, 32) it need not be relevant to *Alban Lane*: for that matter, there was a certain *Alban Minur* at Chester in c. 1185 witnessing a grant to St Mary's Nunnery (CAS 13, 96, 3), and Stephen *de Sancto Albano* (of St Albans) was Chamberlain of Chester c. 1242–3.

[33] Vernon MSS., Box 3, C1, Nos. 5, 6, 8, and C2, No. 2, respectively.

[34] *Ibid.*, Box 3, C1, 36.

[35] Assembly Book, cf. Morris, 256 (corrigenda), Sheaf 1, 1, p. 239.

[36] *v.* note 30 *supra.*

[37] *v.* note 31 *supra.*

[38] 1533–4 Sheaf 3, 32, No. 7173, cf. note 30 *supra.*

[39] Assembly Book of the Corporation of Chester, City Record Office, AB/3, ff. 192, 202v.

[40] Hemingway, II, 10.

[41] Vernon MSS., Box 3, C1, Nos. 2 (date 1290), 30 (date 1342) and 4 (date 1294).

opposite Holy Trinity Church and on the corner of *Berewardeslone*. One of them,[42] dated 1342, conveys a messuage in *Watergatestrete civitatis Cestrie super le corner' de Berewardeslone ex opposito ecclesie Sancte Trinitatis* 'in Watergate Street, city of Chester, upon the corner of Bereward's Lane, opposite the church of Holy Trinity'. Another of them[43] describes *Berewardeslone* in 1294 as *venella que extendit se a domo fratrum Carmelitarum Cestrie usque ad ecclesiam Sancte Trinitatis et que venella vocatur Berwardeslone civitatis Cestrie* 'the lane extending from the house of the Carmelite Friars of Chester to the church of Holy Trinity, and which lane is called *Berwardeslone,* city of Chester'. This lane from White Friars to Holy Trinity is exactly on the site of Weaver Street. Another of these documents,[44] a deed dated 1292, of property in *Aluineslone* (i.e. Weaver Street), bears an endorsement *Berwardislone* which I think is in a fourteenth–century hand. This proves an old identification of *Aluineslone* and *Berward Street*. A document in a different collection[45] records that c. 1240 John son of John son of Norman held land in *Bereward Lone*. The family of Norman lived in Commonhall Street[46] which runs into Weaver Street.

It is now obvious that *Berward Street* was Weaver Street. *Berward Street* appears as *Bereward Lone* c. 1240,[47] *Berwaselone* 1290,[48] *Berwardeslone* 1294,[49] *Berwardislone* 14,[50] *Berewardeslone* 1342,[51]

---

[42] *Ibid.*, Box 3, C1, No. 30.

[43] *Ibid.*, Box 3, C1, No. 4.

[44] *Ibid.*, Box 3, C1, No. 8.

[45] Br. Mus. Add. Charter 49979, cf. CAS 10, 23, No. XIII; the correct date may be *ante* 1238.

[46] *Normanslone* 1295 Br. Mus. Add. Charter 50058; *Mothal–, Mothallelone* 1342 ib. 50149–52; *le Comen Hall Lane* 1468–9 Treasurer's Account Rolls, Chester Record Office, 1/3; the later name was taken from the ancient moot–hall of the city (*communis aula* 1337 Add. Charter 50142) which stood on the south side of Commonhall Street and the north side of Pierpoint Lane. Cf. 'a lane anciently called Norman's–lane and many yet call it Common–hall–lane because it was situate at a great hall, where the pleas of the city, and the courts thereof, and meetings of the mayor and his brethren were there holden' 1656 Ormerod, I, 188.

[47] Br. Mus. Add. Charter 49979, *v.* note 45 *supra*.

[48] Vernon MSS., Box 3, C1, No. 2.

[49] *Ibid.*, No. 4, *v.* note 43 *supra*.

[50] Endorsement on Vernon MSS., Box 3, C1, No. 8, of *Aluineslone, v.* note 44 *supra*.

[51] *Ibid.*, Box 3, C1, No. 30.

1351,[52] *Benewardeslone* 1280–1,[53] *Berward Street, – Strete* Edward III (1574),[54] *Berward Street* 1656.[55] The name means 'the bear–keeper's lane', from Middle English **bere–ward** 'a bear–ward, a bear–keeper'. The surname is recorded in Chester as lately as that of Agnes *Berward* t. Edward IV.[56] Bearward Streets existed in medieval London,[57] Nottingham[58] and Northampton.[59] The identification of *Berward Street* with *Alban Lane,* both now Weaver Street, raises an interesting example of a street with two names. What is now Weaver Street would appear to have been *Bereward Lone* down to mid–14, *Alvens Lane* (later *Alban Lane)* from mid–13 to sometime before 1534, *Weaver Lane* from 1534 onwards. By 1574 the name *Bereward Lone* was so ill remembered that its identification was uncertain: the name had been ousted by *Alvens Lane.* It is now only an idle speculation whether the *bere–ward* in the name *Bereward Lone* c. 1240, might have been the man *Alvin* (< Old English *Ælfwine*) in the name *Aluenislone* c. 1260.

If the transcript is shown by other documents to be imprecise about *Berward Street,* it is not so vague about *St Chad's Lane* and *Dog Lane.* It allots these now–lost street–names to two lanes touching upon the lost *St Chad's church.* The 1574 transcript indicates that *St Chad's Lane* (called *Sant Chadde Layne*) was at the end of *Parson's Lane* (i.e. Princess Street) along *Crofts Lane* (i.e. Linenhall Street); that *St Chad's church* was on *St Chad's Lane;* and that, from *St Chad's Lane* end, a lane called *Dogge Lane* ran westward to the city wall. The 1574 transcript keeps *St Chad's Lane* and *Dog Lane* distinct; it seems to know its way about the town at this point; we ought to think of two streets, and that, *tempore* Edward III, *St Chad's Lane* and *Dog Lane* were not identical but both touched *St Chad's Church.*

---

[52] Ormerod, I, 349.

[53] Miscellaneous deeds, Chester Record Office.

[54] Assembly Book, cf. Morris, 256, 257; Sheaf 1, 1, p. 239.

[55] Ormerod, I, 188.

[56] Morris, 333.

[57] *Berewards Lane* (London, All Hallows Barking by the Tower), *Berewardeslane* 1285; and *Hog Lane* (London, Bishopsgate). *Berewardelane* 1279; see E. Ekwall, *Street–Names of the City of London,* Oxford, 1954, 112–113.

[58] Mount Street (Nottingham), *le Berewarde Gate* c. 1240, see J.E.B. Gover, A. Mawer, F.M. Stenton, *The Place–Names of Nottinghamshire,* EPNS 17, 19.

[59] Bearward Street (Northampton), *Berewardstrete* 1281, see J.E.B. Gover, A. Mawer, F.M. Stenton, *The Place–Names of Northamptonshire,* EPNS 10, 7.

The location of St Chad's Church has been variously stated. In *The Cheshire Sheaf*, 1st Series, 2, 116, no doubt of the location is allowed: it was at the bottom of Princess Street, on the north side, opposite the road leading to the City Gaol; it was standing as late as *tempore* Henry VII; a chapel and well in *Little Parson's Lane* was given to Chester Abbey by Richard Fitton *tempore* Henry III (1217–72), no doubt St Chad's. Of this, we may say that the prescribed location is only a street's width off the mark. The *Little Parson's Lane* location is right enough, but *Little Parson's Lane*[60] is not *Parson's Lane* (i.e. Princess Street). Princess Street was first 'the lane opposite the abbey gate',[61] and then 'Parson's Lane' from mid–13 to 1817[62] because in it was a dwellinghouse for the vicars of St Oswald.[63] *Little Parson's Lane* was connected to *Parson's Lane*: presumably its westward extension across *Crofts Lane* (i.e. Linenhall Street). There is a more or less vague agreement in all historical discussions, that St Chad's church stood somewhere along the line of Bedward Row.[64] But the location had in fact been lost or forgotten by the seventeenth century.

The location of St Chad's can now be recovered from a series of allusions: upon the premise that St Chad's stood on *Little Parson's Lane* and that this was off the west end of *Parson's Lane* (i.e. Princess Street). In c. 1252–3 we find mention[65] of land near *The Crofts* and the lane towards St Chad's church. In 1336 we find mention[66] of a plot of land *between* St Chad's lane (leading to the town wall towards Bonewaldesthorne) and the land of Hugh Mody; here also we note the

[60] *petit Parsone lone* 1242 (17) Br. Mus. Harleian MS. 7568, f. 119, cf. Sheaf 3, 19, No. 4643; *vicus qui vocatur Petit Personeslone* 1291–1323 (14) Chester II, 877.

[61] early 13 (no date) Sheaf 3, 36, No. 7962; c. 1284 (14) Chester II, 463.

[62] *Personeslone* c. 1249–65 Chester II, 614 to *Princes Street* 1817 Ormerod, I, 180.

[63] R.V.H. Burne, *The Monks of Chester,* S.P.C.K., 1962, 46.

[64] 1724 NotCestr notes that there was formerly a chapel in *Little Parson's Lane,* almost as if he knew and used that street–name, *v.* Chetham Society (Original Series) 8, 95. Gastrell also cites (op. cit., 122), as does Ormerod, I, 354, the location given in the Shakerly of Hulm MS. 95, i, 11, 'St Chad–Chapell in the field near Watergate on the north side, now ruinated, anno 1662', cf. also Br. Mus. Harleian MS. 2125, f. 267b, 'it stood in the croft over against the Black Friers, on the north side the Watergate Street, next the Watergate'.

[65] Sheaf 3, 33, No. 7435.

[66] *Ibid.*, No. 7504.

emergence of a lane behind the church of St Chad. In 1448 we have a deed[67] for 'a garden in the Crofts at the end of the lane leading from the church of St Chad as far as the stone wall of the city'. But most precisely, we find a deed[68] dated 1389 which describes a garden upon The Crofts, bounded on one side by the lane extending from The Crofts to St Chad's church, on the next side by the land of Richard Geve, on the third side by *regia strata del Croftez* (i.e. *Crofts Lane* now Linenhall Street and St Martin's Fields), and on the fourth side by St Chad's church. This shows that St Chad's church in *Little Parson's Lane* (i.e. the east end of Bedward Row) was one boundary of a garden between *Crofts Lane* (Linenhall Street — St Martin's Fields) and *the lane from The Crofts to St Chad's church*. Thus, St Chad's stood at the north–west angle of the intersection of Linenhall Street and Bedward Row opposite the end of Princess Street, directly across the road from the location proposed years ago in *The Cheshire Sheaf*. The plan suggested in this construction is represented by Fig. C 2, which is a diagram of the situation in 1389 (Add. Ch. 50202).

This plan shows St Chad's church abutting upon three thoroughfares, 1. the continuation of *Parson's Lane* (Princess Street), i.e. *Little Parson's Lane*, 2. *Crofts Lane* (Linenhall Street — St Martin's Fields),[69] 3. a lane behind the church.[70] It would seem quite possible that the name *St Chad's Lane* might be applied to any of these thoroughfares. Certainly it seems to have been applied to *Little Parson's Lane*[71] and to

---

[67] Vernon MSS., Box 3, C2, No. 36.

[68] Br. Mus. Add. Charter 50202.

[69] Mistakenly identified with *Berward Street* by the 1574 transcript.

[70] This was *the lane extending from The Crofts to St Chad's church* in 1389 (Add. Ch. 50202). It ran northwards from the west end of St Chad's. Presumably this was the lane which is mentioned in 1336 (Sheaf 3, 33, No. 7504) and 1343 (Sheaf 3, 40, No. 8491) as 'St Chad's lane leading to the town wall towards Bonewaldesthorne'. Hemingway (I, 357) noted in 1831 a blocked–up arch in the north wall of the city in the north–west angle near Bonewaldesthorne's Tower west of the postern leading to the canal wharf. He thought it was 'probably of ancient date', to give access to ships in the old haven. Such a postern would have been approached by the little lane behind St Chad's.

[71] In 1656, Ormerod, I, 188: 'out of Berward Street in ancient time went a lane to St Cedd's church now ruined and gone called Chadd's Lane'. This follows the implications of the 1574 transcript which gave *Crofts Lane* the name *Berward Street*.

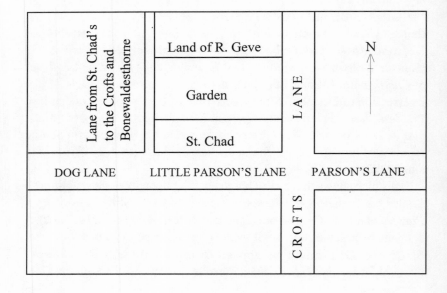

Figure C 2: The Site of St.Chad's Church in 1389
as indicated by Br. Mus. Additional Charter 50202.

Crofts Lane.[72] It seems fairly certain that *Dog Lane* [73] ran to the west wall[74] from the end of *St Chad's Lane*, i.e. *Little Parson's Lane,* i.e. the east end of Bedward Row.

STREET–NAME TYPES IN CHESTER

The names of the medieval thoroughfares of Chester fall into types, in many respects similar to the types distinguished for medieval London in E. Ekwall, *The Street–Names of the City of London,* Oxford, 1954. The medieval thoroughfares are named after a building standing upon them or to which they gave access, or after a person or a family to whose residence or property they led, or after some trade or activity followed at the place.

Named after buildings were Bridge Street, Eastgate Street, Watergate Street and Northgate Street;[75] these were principal thoroughfares; minor lanes also appear in this type, e.g. Castle Esplanade (*Nones Lane* Edw. III (1574) Assembly Book (cf. Morris, 256), 'Nun's Lane', named from St Mary's Nunnery); Castle Street (*Casteleslone* 13 (14) Chester I, 407, 'lane to the castle'); Commonhall Street (*v.* note 46); King Street (*Bernelone* 1265–91 (14) Chester II, 618, 'the lane near the abbot of Chester's barn' 1238 Br. Mus. Add. Charter 49985, *v.* note 10); Linenhall Street (*v.* p. 314 *supra*); Nicholas Street (*viculus Sancti Nicholai* 1297 Portmote Rolls (MR/3), Chester Record Office, 'the lane of St Nicholas'; *Blakeffrer Lane* 1398 Sheaf 3, 43, No. 8974, *le Blakefrerelone* 1405 Vernon MSS., Box 3, C2, No. 2, 'the Black Friars' lane'; named from the Black Friars and their chapel of St Nicholas); St Mary's Hill (*Sant Marye*

---

[72] *Croftez Streete or St Chaddes Streete* 1574 Corp., see note 19 *supra,* cf. Sheaf 3, 19, No. 4574. The same identification should he made for *alta via que ducit ad ecclesiam Sancti Cedde* 1505–6 Morris, 167.

[73] *Dogge Lane* Edward III (1574) Assembly Book (cf. Morris, 254–7, Sheaf 1, 1, 239); *(le) Doglone* 1413 Portmote Rolls MR/75; Morris, 351.

[74] At the west wall *tempore* Edward III it may have met another lane coming up from the Watergate, but this is not mentioned or named until *venella vocata Watergate Lane* 1547 (Public Record Office, Ministers Accounts, S.C.6/Edw. VI/61) and 1554 (*ib.,* S.C.6/P&M/45), and the actual location of this *Watergate Lane* is not known to me.

[75] Also Foregate Street which means 'the street before, i.e. outside, the gate'.

Lane Edw. III (1574), after St Mary's on the Hill); St Olave Street (*venella Sancti Olavi* 1216–72 Ancient Deed C3659 in Public Record Office; 'the lane which leads to the church of St Olavus the king' 1321 Portmote Rolls, MR/24); St Werburgh Street (*vicus Sancte Werburge* 1265–91 (14) Chester II, 607); Trinity Street (*venellum Sancte Trinitatis* 1281 Br. Mus. Add. Ch. 50013); and so forth.

The lanes of the city are in many instances named after a person. Black Friars was *Arderne Lane* Edw. III (1574),[76] from the surname *de Arderne,* cf. 'tenements which sometime belonged to Katherine de Arderne in the lane which leads from Watergate Street towards the Friars Preachers' 1345,[77] i.e. houses in Nicholas Street. Bunce Street was *Buncelone* in 1328,[78] from the surname *Bunte, Bunce*; Andrew *Bunte* c. 1260 gave Dieulacres Abbey land in Castle Street which had belonged to Richard his brother.[79] Richard *Bounz* was sheriff of the city 1243–4.[80] Commonhall Street was *Normanslone* 1295.[81] Crook Street is the site of both *Gerardislon* c. 1230[82] and *Crokeslone* c. 1220–50.[83] These names are taken from the Middle English personal–names *Gerard* (from Old German *Gerard,* Old French *Gerart*) and *Crok* (from Old Norse *Krókr*). *Crokeslone* led off Northgate Street, *Gerardislon* led off Watergate Street. Presumably they met, and the name of *Crokeslone* was extended to both of them. Cuppin Street was *Copineslone* 13,[84] from the Middle English personal–name *Copin,* a pet–form of *Jacob* (cf. Old French *Jacobin*), subsequently anglicized by analogy with the Old English personal–name *Cupping.*[85] Godstall Lane was *Sant Goddestall Lane* Edw. III (1574). This name has been rationalized to *god–stall,* as it were *god–stow,* 'God's place'. Its original form appears in *Goddescalles Lane*

[76] Assembly Book, *v.* Morris, 256.

[77] Vernon MSS., Box 3, C1, No. 37.

[78] *Ibid.,* No. 20.

[79] Morris, 568.

[80] His nieces Agnes and Alice inherited his land in *Parson's Lane* (Princess Street) *v.* CAS 10, 50, LXVIII and note.

[81] *v.* note 46. *Norman* is a Middle English pers.n. from Old English **Northman** 'The Norwegian'.

[82] CAS 10, 20, IX.

[83] (14) Chester II, 866.

[84] (c. 1311) Chester II, 311; 1286 CAS 10, 40, XLVI.

[85] Hemingway, II, 31 (cf. Morris, 255) speculates needlessly about 'licensed bagnios or cupping houses'.

1574,[86] *Godscall–Lane* (lit. *Inodscall–*) 1656,[87] *Godescalk's–Lane* 1706. [88] It contains the Old French personal–name *Godescal* (Old German *Godasscalc, Godescalcus,* appearing in Old English as *Godesscalc* 931),[89] which means 'the warrior of God'. Only the north end of this lane survives as a street, the south end being covered by Eastgate Street Row North since at least 1574.[90] The prefix 'Saint' in the Edward III survey alludes to the Chester legend of *Godescal* the hermit of Chester,[91] supposed to have been Henry, emperor of Germany, who retired to Chester to end his days as a hermit. This Henry is supposed by the medieval tradition to have been that emperor who in 1114 married Matilda daughter of Henry I of England. That emperor was Henry V (1106–1125) and he died at Nimegen. It was the emperor Henry IV (1056–1106) who assumed the name *Godescallus*; he died at Liege. The origin of this legend cannot be ascertained: it is likely that a recluse called *Godescalc,* installed near St Werburgh's churchyard in the twelfth century, became the subject of romantic speculation and a majestic rumour has associated his name with an emperor of the same name. A similar glorification attended a hermitage at St Johns, to which Harold Godwinsson is supposed to have retreated after Hastings. Leen Lane was *viculus Hugonis le Lene* 1325,[92] *Hulone* 1396,[93] *Leen Lane* Edw. III (1574).[94] This is 'Hugh de Lene's lane'. Hugh de *Len* granted his wife land in Eastgate Street c. 1240.[95] His son Robert de *Lene* renewed the grant c. 1270.[96] Reginald de owned land in Newgate Street in *Leen(e)* 1292[97] and 1295[98] and in *le Cokesrowe* (Pepper Alley Row) in

[86] Corp., C/Ch/3. 7, Chester Record Office.

[87] Ormerod, I, 188.

[88] Hemingway, I, 344.

[89] W. de G. Birch, *Cartularium Saxonicum* Nos. 680, 681, cf. T. Forssner, *Continental Germanic Personal–Names in England,* Uppsala, 1916, 121.

[90] Cf. 'land where Goddescalles Lane crossed from Eastgate Street to the churchyard of St Werburgh's' 1574 Corp., C/Ch/3. 7, Chester Record Office.

[91] Rehearsed in Hemingway, I, 343, 48, cf. Morris, 255; Ormerod, I, 188; Sheaf 3, 48, Nos. 9711, 9703, 8935, 8939.

[92] Portmote Rolls (MR/25), Chester Record Office.

[93] Sheaf 3, 44, No. 9211.

[94] Assembly Book, cf. Morris, 255.

[95] CAS 10, 26.

[96] CAS 10, 31; No. XXIX wrongly dated 1274.

[97] CAS 10, 48.

[98] Br. Mus. Add. Ch. 50057.

1330.[99] Reginald's surname is written *de Lene* 1300,[100] *de Thlen* 1315,[101] *de Thlene* 1330.[102] This surname, occasionally confused with Middle English *le Lene* 'the lean, the thin', is almost certainly derived from the Welsh place–name, Lleyn, of the district of Caernarvonshire. Leen Lane was originally a thoroughfare from the north side of Eastgate Street to St Oswald's churchyard. The northern end of Leen Lane exists behind the St Nicholas Chapel grocer's–shop. The southern end is built over and the name Leen Lane has been extended to the passage leading from Leen Lane into Northgate Street.[103] Pierpoint Lane, *Perpoynts Lane* Edw. III (1574),[104] contains the surname *Pierpoint*. Richard Pierpoint was sheriff of Cheshire early–13,[105] Alice de Pierpoint was abbess of St Mary's Nunnery late–13.[106] Shipgate Street was *Rabyeslone* 1420,[107] named after the *Raby* family — from Raby in Wirral — who were sergeants of Bridgegate from c. 1300 onwards.[108] Weaver Street was called after a certain *Alvin* and someone called 'the bear–keeper'.[109] White Friars was *Fulchardeslone* c. 1200,[110] from the Old German personal–name *Fulcard*. It was *vicus Alexandri Harre* 1258 to 1291,[111] named after Alexander Harre c. 1258[112] who owned land in Bridge Street. Members of the same family, Roger and Hamo Herre, took part in the transaction of land in St Olave's 1230–34 mentioned *infra*. It was subsequently *viculus Sancte*

---

[99] Vernon MSS., Box 3, C1, No. 22.

[100] CAS 2, 161, 166.

[101] Loc. cit.

[102] Vernon MSS., Box 3, C1, No. 22.

[103] Cf. Sheaf 3, 43, No. 8952, which states that what was known as *Smith's Passage* in 1892 was misnamed *Leen Lane* in 1948.

[104] But *Dirty Lane* 1831 Hemingway, I, 25.

[105] *Tempore* Philip de Orreby, Justiciar of Cheshire 1209–28.

[106] *Tempore* Edward I, 1272–1307.

[107] Vernon MSS., Box 3, C2, No. 16.

[108] Ormerod, I, 356.

[109] *v.* p. 317 *supra*.

[110] (14) Chester II, 475.

[111] 1258 Sheaf 3, 13, p. 6, c. 1260 Sheaf 3, 33, No. 7449; *Alysaundres Lone harre* 1291 Sheaf 3, 43, No. 8971; *Alexander lone Harre, Alexandreslone harre, –endres–*, CAS 2, 154, 10, 47, Sheaf 3, 34, No. 7641; *Alexandreslone* 1291 Br. Mus. Add. Ch. 50036.

[112] Vernon MSS., Box 3, C1, No. 13.

Brigide 1286,[113] and *Whytefryers Lone* 1286,[114] after St Bridget's and the White Friars. Dee Lane at The Bars was 'a gayte that goythe downe to the water of Dee that is namyd *Paynes Loode*' Edw. III (1574).[115] Hugh Payn was sheriff of Chester 1287–8, 1288–9, 1292–3, Nicholas Payn was sheriff of Chester 1289–90, 1293–4.[116]

The normal range of medieval customs and trades is represented in the names of the streets and Rows.[117] Goss Street,[118] Pemberton Street,[119] and Frodsham Street[120] refer to the townsmen's livestock, herding, stalling and droving. Goss Street would be a goose pen or market, *Oxe Lane* would be a stall for draught or plough oxen, Frodsham Street would be the way for the citizens' cattle to be driven from town to *Chester Field,* out past Gorse Stacks towards Flookers Brook. Lower Bridge Street was 'the beastmarket' in 1533.[121] *The Cornmarket* was Eastgate Street from 1279 to 1439[122] and Northgate Street from 1533 to 1610.[123] Newgate Street was 'flesh–mongers' lane', 'butchers' lane', from the twelfth to the

---

[113] Br. Mus. Add. Ch. 50025.

[114] Morris, 254, but I have not seen the original of this. There is *Whitefrerelone* 1351 Ormerod, I, 349, *Whytefrerelone* 1393 Vernon MSS., Box 3, C1, No. 50.

[115] Assembly Book; cf. Morris, 255. *Gayte* here is Middle English *gate* (Old Norse **gata**) 'a road'. *Loode* (from Old English **(ge)lād**) is 'a passage, a river–passage, a right of way'.

[116] Cf. Vernon MSS., Box 3, C1, No. 2.

[117] *v.* p. 341 *infra.*

[118] *Goselone* 13 (14) Whalley II, 339 (*The Coucher Book of Whalley Abbey* ed. W.A. Hulton, Chetham Society (Original Series) 10, 11, 16, 20, 1847–1849); *Goselane* c. 1230–40 Bunbury MSS., E18/710/13/2, West Suffolk Record Office, Bury St Edmunds.

[119] Or some thoroughfare near it from King Street to the north wall — *Oxe Lane* Edw. III (1574) Assembly Book, cf. Morris, 257, 570, Ormerod, I, 188, Sheaf 1, 1, p. 240, CAS 13, 36.

[120] 'Cow Lane' from 1290 (*Qu Lone* Court (R. Stewart–Brown, *Calendar of County Court, City Court and Eyre Rolls of Chester 1259–1297* Chetham Society (New Series) 84 (1925) 165) to 1817 (*Cow Lane* 1817 Assembly Book AB/5/378, Chester Record Office). I am obliged to the Hon. Editor for the latter reference.

[121] Sheaf 1, 1, p. 191, cf. Sheaf 1, 2, p. 147, Sheaf 3, 43, No. 8983, and Morris, 258.

[122] c. 1279 (n.d.) Sheaf 3, 36, No. 7940; 1288 (18) Sheaf 3, 40, No. 4812; 1289 (17) National Register of Archives Report 3636; 1439 CAS 2, 182.

[123] Sheaf 1, 2, p. 147, Morris, 257, 262, 267, 299, 300. Speed's Map (1610) shows it here; CAS 13, 36 locates it at the end of Princess Street; Morris, 298 describes the history in the sixteenth century.

eighteenth century,[124] becoming Newgate Street in 1745.[125] Love Street, off Foregate Street, was *Love Lane* Edw. III (1574)[126] and hardly needs explaining, unless we should put it at the head of our list as referring to the oldest trade of all. White Friars was written *Foster's Lane* and *Fustard's Lane* Edw. III (1574),[127] which is reported as *Forster's Lane, Forster Lane,* in 1656,[128] rather as an antiquarian allusion than as a living street–name. This 1574 transcript form is probably an attempt to make sense of an illegible version in the Edw. III original, of the old name of White Friars, *Fulchardeslone* c. 1200,[129] written *Folcardes–* and *Fulcardes–*, but there was a Middle English surname *Fuster* meaning 'a saddle–tree maker'. St John Street was *Irnmonger Strete* 1228–40,[130] 'ironmongers' street'; it settled down as 'St John's Lane' after *vicus Sancti Johannis* 1238.[131] Souters Lane appears as *Souterlode* 1272,[132] apparently 'the shoemakers' river–passage', from Old English **sūtere** (cf. Modern English dialect *sowter*), Old Norse **sútari**, 'a shoemaker'. Castle Drive is the site of *Mustardhouses* 1415[133] to 1597.[134] Mustard makers at Chester are mentioned in 1392–3.[135] In 1544 this property was called *Gloverhouses*,[136] a name persisting until 1713[137] and alternating with the name *Skinners Lane*[138] and *Skinners Houses*.[139]

---

[124] *Flesmongerlone* 1100–60 (14) Chester I, 371, to *Newgate Street or Fleshmonger's Lane* 1747 Land Revenue Office Miscellaneous Books (Public Record Office) Vol. 257, ff. 33–39, and *Fleshmongers Lane* 1781 Sheaf 3, 15, p.11.

[125] Sheaf 3, 15, p.11.

[126] Assembly Book; *v*. Morris 255.

[127] Assembly Book, *v*. Morris 256.

[128] Ormerod, 1, 188.

[129] (14) Chester II, 475.

[130] Chester II, 458.

[131] Br. Mus. Add. Ch. 49988.

[132] Morris, 254.

[133] Chester Recognizance Rolls, Public Record Office (Reports of the Deputy Keeper of the Public Records 37, p. 370).

[134] Morris, 297.

[135] Crownmote Rolls, QC/R10, Chester Record Office; Sheaf 3, 20, No. 4945, and Br. Mus. Harleian MS. 7568, f. 165a, report that one Robert *Mustard* lived here and gave name to the property.

[136] Corp., C/Ch/2/8, Chester Record Office.

[137] *the Glovers Houses* 1713 Assembly Book, AB/3 f. 208.

[138] 1545 Corp., C/Ch/2/10, to 1801 Corp., C/Ch/2/88, 1831 Hemingway, I, 366 — he calls it *Skinner Street* in II, 267.

[139] 1685 Assembly Book AB/3, f. 2v., to 1712 *ibid.*, f. 196.

The glovers and skinners were important craftsmen in medieval Chester. They may well be the reason for the curious place–name *Gloverstone*. This is first noted as *Gloueriston* 13 Br. Mus. Add. Ch. 49971; it means 'the glover's stone' or 'the glovers' stone'. It was the name of an irregular polygon of ground outside the castle gate and north–west of St Mary on the Hill churchyard, containing part of the top end of St Mary's Hill, and a short street which led from Castle Street opposite Bunce Street to the Castle Ditch and the Outer Gate of the castle. Most of the area is now occupied by the castle barracks block. This patch of ground enjoyed the status of a manor, township and village in 1678.[140] It was a township of Broxton Hundred. It was named from a large stone which stood in front of the castle gate and which marked the limit of the city jurisdiction down to at least 1879.[141]

This stone is no longer to be seen. It was described in 1625 as 'a (greate) stone called Glovers' Sto(u)ne, . . . a grey stone of marble standing in the street, . . . a blewe marble stone, . . . the meere(stone) called Glovers Stone'.[142] Other *Gloverstones* at Chester are recorded.[143] *Glouerstan* 1194–1211, *Glouerston* 14,[144] appears in the context 'a messuage between ~ and Eastgate'. *Glouerstanes* 1194–1211[145] appears in the context 'that part of a messuage next to St Michael's church which is farther away from the church towards ~'. *Le Gloverestones* 1345[146] appears in 'two adjoining messuages in Watergate Street next to ~'. Other instances are *Glouerstanes* 13[147] and *le Gloverstones* 1302–3,[148] which have not been identified but are probably those in Watergate Street. It can be seen that there were *Gloverstones* in Watergate Street, and near the Eastgate, and near St Michael's in Bridge Street, as well as that at the castle–gate.

[140] Ormerod, III, 581.
[141] Sheaf 1, 1, 268.
[142] Morris, 108–110; CAS 5, 175–206.
[143] Morris, 111.
[144] Whalley I (Chetham Society (Original Series) 10), xviii. This seems to be the same as *Gloverstone* 1190–1211 (17) Ormerod, II, 401.
[145] Whalley I (Chetham Society (Original Series) 10), xvii.
[146] Morris, 226, CAS 2, 176, cf. Morris, 111.
[147] Whalley II (Chetham Society (Original Series) 11), 343.
[148] Portmote Rolls MR/7, cf. Morris, 254.

These various stones, it is supposed, derived their name from their use by glovers to dress their leather upon. It has been suggested that they may have been used especially by glovers not guilded in the city.[149] Glovemaking was an important business in medieval Chester, the Glovers and Skinners holding the staple trade of the city down to the eighteenth century.[150] The *Gloverstone* near Eastgate may well have been associated with Walter son of Gerard *Cirotecarius* ('Glover; glove–maker') c. 1253, and Ameria daughter of Gerard *Cirotecarius* c. 1267–8, landowners in Eastgate Street and Foregate Street.[151] Another interpretation might be that these stones in the principal streets may have marked the limits of the medieval fairs of the city, the duration of which was marked by the elevation of an effigy of a gloved hand on a pole at St Peter's church, and that 'glover' in *Gloverstone* may not mean 'a glove–maker' so much as 'one who is associated with The Glove', i.e. 'a Glover — one who comes to The Glove Fair'.[152] There are two aspects of these stones which require emphasis. The stone at the castle gate was described as a 'blue' stone. There were other stones about the city which were 'blue' and which were boundary marks. In Handbridge township there was a field called Blue Stone Field in 1839.[153] There was a 'blue stone' in St John's parish near Boughton, *the Blewe Stone by Spittle* 1620,[154] which marked the boundary between Cheshire and the city, and another, *the Blewe Stonne at Blacon* 1671,[155] was the boundary mark of the rights of Great Saughall manor to fish in R. Dee from this point to Woodbank. The *Blewe Stone by Spittle*

---

[149] Sheaf 1, 1, 153; CAS 10, 53–66; 5, 175–206; Morris, 111.

[150] Morris, 111.

[151] Sheaf 3, 33, No. 7454.

[152] This would be a variant of the type of surname discussed in G. Fransson, *Middle English Surnames of Occupation 1100–1350*, Lund, 1935, 190–202.

[153] Tithe Award, Tithe Redemption Commission No. 5/103. The field–name is also recorded in 1779 Sheaf 3, 32, No. 7191, as *the Jeffreys Faugh now the Blue Stone Field*. The older name was *Geffreishale* 1259 Chester Plea Rolls, Public Record Office (Deputy Keeper's Report 26, p. 37); 1260 Court 16 (written *Geffeishale* Ormerod, II, 821); *Gefreis Halc* c. 1150 (1353, 1383, 1400 inspeximi) CAS 13, 93 and Calendar of Patent Rolls, 1400, cf. Sheaf 3, 7, No. 1205, 'Geoffrey's nook'. This was part of Claverton manor's holdings of Saltney, in Marlston cum Lache, and belonged to the Nuns of Chester. The blue stone probably marked a manorial boundary.

[154] Sheaf 3, 4, No. 619.

[155] Sheaf 3, 22, No. 5183.

in 1620 may be the very stone referred to in an early form of the place–name Boughton, i.e. *Bochtunestan* 1096–1101 (1280), 1150,[156] *Bochtuneston* 1096–1101 (1280),[157] 'the stone at Boughton, the Boughton stone', i.e. a stone marking the boundary between the Cheshire manor of Great Boughton, which belonged to St Werburgh's since before Domesday Book, and the Chester Hundred part of Boughton, Spital Boughton. In this connection, 'blue–stones' and boundaries, it may be noted that J. Wright, *English Dialect Dictionary*, s.v. *blue* (adj.) quotes only R.O. Heslop, *Northumberland Words. A Glossary of Words used in the County of Northumberland,* English Dialect Society, 1892–4, 'Blue Stone, a long stone of granite placed on the east footpath of the old Tyne Bridge, to mark the division between the Durham and Northumberland portions of the structure'.

'Blue' in these constructions has its ancient Old English and Old Norse meaning 'dark–coloured, dark grey, slate–coloured'. The Chester ones would probably be Welsh slate stones. A blue or slate–coloured stone would be very distinctive against the local red sandstones of the Chester district, and so very suitable for a boundary–marker. The principal *Gloverstone* at the Castle–Gate was a blue–stone and marked a limit of jurisdiction. It is possible that the other *Gloverstones* were blue–stones too, marking some kind of limit, but this supposition leads to no useful extrapolation. What would be more probable, would be to suggest that a slate–stone would make a better and more convenient leather–dressing block than would a sandstone, and that a series of blue–stones standing in the town might well have been taken into use by the glove–makers as a matter of convenience. The questions raised by these references are whether these *Gloverstones* were all 'blue–stones', whether they were all boundary marks, whether they were all *in situ* before the glovers began to use them as work–blocks.

This digression around the *Gloverstones* led from *Skinners Houses*. From the same street in its older name *Mustard Houses,* a further digression might be made, to contemplate the name Pepper Street. This

---

[156] Chester I, 3 and 56.
[157] Chester 1, 3, n39.

appears as *Peperstrate* 1251–5 (17)[158] and *Peperstrete* c. 1258,[159] and has never changed its name. Adjacent to it, if not identical with it, was *venella de Pepurstreete* 1374,[160] *the lane of Peper Street* 1458 (17).[161] The name *Pepper Street* probably means what it says and indicates a thoroughfare redolent of pepper, a street where spicers did their trade. It is very likely that of all their spices, only pepper would be pungent enough to be discernible through the stench of a medieval thoroughfare.

Other medieval towns have Pepper Streets: there is one at Middlewich[162] another at Nantwich,[163] there is one at Nottingham,[164] and there is Pepper Alley in Southwark.[165] This sort of name is credible in a medieval town. But the name–type Pepper Street also appears as a road–name in the countryside. For instance, Pepper Street, a road in Appleton, Pepper Street Farm in Hatton near Daresbury, Pepper Street Farm in Bramhall near Stockport,[166] Pepperstreet Moss in Hunsterson;[167] *Pepper Street* was a road in Ince in 1584[168] and 1671;[169] *Pepper Street*

---

[158] Dieul (*The Chartulary of Dieulacres Abbey*, ed. G. Wrottesley, William Salt Society's Collections (New Series) 9, 1906), 325.

[159] Vernon MSS., Box 3, C1, No. 13.

[160] Portmote Rolls MR/48, Chester Record Office.

[161] Sheaf 3, 20, No. 4764, citing Br. Mus. Harleian MS. 7568, f. 141. Here it is also called *Peper Alley or Lane* (17th century), and appears to be a footpath from Bridge Street to Newgate over the open ground south of Pepper Street. The *Pepper Alley* 1781 Sheaf loc. cit. may be that at Pepper Alley Row.

[162] *Pepperstreete* 1463 (17) MidCh (J. Varley, *A Middlewich Chartulary*, Chetham Society (New Series) 105, 108, 1941–1944) II, 304; *Peper Lane* 1487 (17) op. cit., I, 151.

[163] *Peper Strete* 15 National Register of Archives Report No. 1085, 287.

[164] *Pepirstrete* 1315, *Peperlane* 1395, J.E.B. Gover, A. Mawer, F.M. Stenton, *The Place Names of Nottinghamshire*, EPNS 19, 19.

[165] *Peper Alley* 1439, J.E.B. Gover, A. Mawer, F.M. Stenton, A. Bonner, *The Place–Names of Surrey*, EPNS 11, 31.

[166] On an old road thought to be Roman (Ormerod, III, 536n.) first named as *Bramhall Pepper Street* 1649 (J.P. Earwaker, *East Cheshire*, London, 1877, I, 455 and note). The Appleton and Hatton instances are also on an ancient line of road, associated with sections of a Roman road exposed during the construction of motorway M6 and examined by the Lymm Historical Society.

[167] First noted in 1842 O.S.; probably commemorating an ancient road from Nantwich to Woore in Salop, by way of Bridgemere and Doddington. The surname *le Streteward* 'streetkeeper' appears at Doddington nearby, in 1312 (Chester Plea Rolls, Report of the Deputy Keeper of the Public Records 37, 10).

[168] Rental in Public Record Office, S.C.12/26/65.

[169] Sheaf 3, 49, No. 9873: here it is apparently a hamlet.

was the name in 1831 (Bryant's Map) of Pickmere Lane, in Pickmere and Wincham; *Pepper Street* was the name in 1842 (Ordnance Survey Map) of Hawthorne Street in Wilmslow; *Pepper Street* was the name in 1842 (Ord. Surv.) of the main road through Henbury, that from Northwich to Macclesfield.

In such place–names, which seem in almost every instance to be associated with a road, there is a choice between two explanations. J.K. Wallenberg suggested[170] that Pepperness[171] near Sandwich, Kent, contained Old English **pipor** 'pepper, peppercorn', by allusion to the nature of the sand or fine gravel here. On this basis, a 'Pepper Street' would be a dusty or gritty road. The other possibility, which would only apply to modern names, i.e. those not given before about 1700, would be to construe 'pepper' in its figurative modern slang and dialect sense, as 'a hot–tempered, fiery, rowdy fellow; a brawler'. Some dialects use this of an itinerant pedlar or horse coper as if these were all rowdies. Then a *Pepper Street* would be the sort of road used by rowdy pedlars and such–like travelling folk. One may note here the slang use of the Southwark street–name *Pepper Alley* cited in the Oxford English Dictionary, for any rowdy alley, or for any pugilistic affray. One of the Rows of Chester was called *Pepper Alley Row,* perhaps a hot spot in the town.

STREET–NAMES AND THE MEDIEVAL TOWN–PLAN

It has been observed[172] that until 1800 there were only five or six *streets* so called in Chester: Bridge Street, Watergate Street, Northgate Street, Eastgate Street and Pepper Street within the walls, Foregate Street without. The lesser thoroughfares were lanes. However, a survey in 1728[173] states 'the number of the streets in this city are ten . . . . Lanes there are thirty–four . . .' In 1831 Hemingway[174] complained that a few

---

[170] J.K. Wallenberg, *The Place–Names of Kent,* Uppsala, 1934, 593.

[171] *pipernæsse* 1023, J.M. Kemble, *Codex Diplomaticus Ævi Saxonici,* London, 1839–48, No. 737; *pepernessa* 1016–35 op. cit., No. 1328.

[172] Cf. Morris, 254–5.

[173] Sheaf 3, 48, No. 9774.

[174] II, 410–11, note.

years previously the city authorities had dignified all the *lane*–names out of existence and there was only Dee Lane left.

If we ignore the commonplace snob–effect which marks social pretension in street–names, King Street for *Barn Lane,* Princess Street for Prince's Street for *Parson's Lane,* Park Street for *The Nine Houses,* and so forth, we find that a *street* in medieval Chester was something different from a *lane,* and that the terminology of medieval street–names appears to be exact. Some thoroughfares do in fact come to notice as *streets* and then degenerate into *lanes.* In this category are Linenhall Street and St John's Street. Linenhall Street was *Crofts Lane,* but it is first recorded as *regia strata del Croftes* 1345.[175] St John's Street was *Irnmonger Strete* 1228–40[176] and *vicus Sancti Johannis* 1238,[177] *Sent Johans Stret, Sent Jones Street* Edw. III (1574),[178] but *Sent Joneslone* 1337[179] to *St John's Lane* 1880.[180] Conversely, *Bereward Lane* c. 1240 had been dignified to *Berward Strete* by Edw. III (1574).[181] Duke Street was 'Claverton Lane' from early–13 to 1782,[182] but is named *Clavirton–, Claverton Street* in 1288 and 1289.[183] If allowance is made for various kinds of evolution, it is found that those thoroughfares in medieval Chester to which such terms as *alta via, alta strata, regia strata, regia via, vicus, magnus vicus,* and the term *street,* have traditionally or originally been applied, are distributed in an interesting way. Bridge Street, Watergate Street, Northgate Street, Eastgate Street, and Foregate Street are especially dignified, as the principal axes of the city. This is not unexpected. The other thoroughfares which were dignified by the style *street* were those at Linenhall Street (*Crofts Lane* originally 'Crofts Street'), and Weaver Street (*Berward Strete* originally *Bereward Lone* and *Aluineslone*). Pepper Street has been a *street*

---

[175] *v.* note 19 *supra.*
[176] (14) Chester II, 458.
[177] Br. Mus. Add. Ch. 49988.
[178] Assembly Book, cf. Morris, 255, 256.
[179] Br. Mus. Add. Ch. 50143.
[180] Sheaf 1, 2, p. 139.
[181] *v.* p. 317 *supra.*
[182] *Clauertunel'* 1202–14 *Facsimiles of Early Cheshire Charters* ed. G. Barraclough, Oxford, 1957, No. 12; *Clavertonelane* 1208–29 (17) Dieul 333; *Clauertunelane* c. 1217–32 Miscellaneous deeds in Chester Record Office; *Clayton Lane* 1782 Sheaf 3, 37, No. 8117.
[183] Court 155, 158.

throughout its recorded history, as befits the street leading to a wall–gate, Newgate. St John's Street is outside the medieval wall, but it deserved its original dignity of *street* as an approach to the same wall–gate, to St John's and to the river–side landing–place at *Souter's Lode. Claverton Lane* (Duke Street) may have deserved its occasional promotion into a *street* because it led from Bridge Gate to Newgate, and because it had an originally distinctive status as a city colony of a manor of the county, i.e. it was a manorial hamlet as well as a thoroughfare. In general, the medieval *streets* are the main public thoroughfares. The *lanes* were rather more private in nature, as if in theory these were accommodation–roads leading to, and belonging to the property which they served. *Lanes* may even have originated as access–ways over private ground; distinguished from *streets* which were public. If the medieval *streets* are drawn upon a plan of Chester, (as indicated by heavy line in Fig. C 1), it is found that they are approximately relative to the plan of the Roman town. The principal *streets* of the Roman town meet at The Cross, by St Peter's, and they have remained *streets* down to this day. But it will be seen that the term *street* was also applied to the thoroughfares lying along the site of the Roman west wall and of the Roman south–east wall.

Now, if we plot the limit of the Roman city circuit against the sites of the medieval parish churches, we note that whereas St Chad and St Martin stand a few yards outside the line but quite near it, Holy Trinity, St Bridget (original site) and St Michael stand upon it. It was long ago suggested[184] that the three latter might have been sited as they are, in some real archaeological relationship with the Roman wall, because *The Two Churches,* the name in 1831 for that part of Bridge Street at St Michael's and St Bridget's, was the approximate site of the Roman south gate. Holy Trinity should then mark the site of the Roman west gate. St Peter's occupies a prætorian site as befits its maternal and senior status. St Oswald is a special case as the abbey parish church. St Mary's is really the parish church of a parish in Broxton Hundred. St John's is not a city parish either, being the focus of a distinct episcopal enclave as far back as Domesday Book. St Olave's is quite extraordinary.

It would be possible to construe the Roman–wall sites of Holy Trinity, St Bridget's and St Michael's, and the sites of St Chad's and St

---

[184] Sheaf 3, 24, No. 5468 (March 1927), cf. Hemingway II, 26 (1831).

Martin's near to the Roman–wall site, in a certain way: that Holy
Trinity, St Bridget's and St Michael's were built where and while a
wall–site was available, and that St Martin's and St Chad's came a little
too late for this and had to be placed outside that line because it was all
occupied by the date of their foundation. The relationship between the
sites of these churches and the expansion of the city walls from the
Roman line to the medieval one cannot be discerned with accuracy or
assurance. It would be of great interest to know whether there is
archaeology or co–incidence in this relationship. And, of course, such
a supposition of relationship brings up the further problem of the degree
of difference to be supposed between the date of actual foundation and
the date of first record. Holy Trinity emerges in 1188, St Bridget's in
1224, St Michael's in 1178–82, St Martin's in 1195, St Chad's in
1252–3, yet St Olave's in 1119! It may well be that by some accident of
documentation, the emergence of these churches into exact record
during the twelfth century does not relate to archaeological fact. They
and their priests are not mentioned in Domesday Book, and it is to be
supposed they were not then built. Perhaps this means that sites in the
place of the Roman wall were free for development in the twelfth
century. Perhaps that would mean that the Roman wall had been
dismantled then, or by then.

The fate of the Roman circuit cannot be speculated upon. But there
are some circumstances in the place–names of the city which might be
relevant to the problem of the development of the south–east corner of
the medieval city outside the Roman circuit, and so to the date and
process of this development. The names to be discussed in this
connection are those of Newgate and of Duke Street.

Duke Street is so named in 1795[185] after Thomas Duke, sheriff of
Chester 1722–3, mayor 1740–1, died 1764, who lived in Lower Bridge
Street nearly opposite this lane. Its name before that was 'Claverton
Lane' which appears early–13,[186] and occasionally 'Claverton Street' in
late–13.[187] Claverton is a township of St Mary's parish in Broxton
Hundred south of the city liberties. The only obvious reason for calling
this street after Claverton is that it probably alludes to land belonging

[185] Sheaf 3, 37, No. 8117.
[186] v. note 182 supra.
[187] v. note 183 supra.

to Claverton. The Domesday Book entry for Claverton records that to this manor appurtained eight burgages in the city and four across the river. It is important to note that these eight burgages were 'in the city', *in civitate*. It is a fair inference that by 1086, and probably by 1066, *Claverton Lane* was *in civitate,* within the city, and that by that time the city limits were those of the medieval city wall not those contained by the Roman wall. In Domesday Book the manor of *Redcliff,* which contained St John's, was not *in civitate* but is entered as in the *Hundred* of Chester. Between *Claverton Lane* and St John's, by 1086 or 1066, lay the boundary between the city proper and its liberties: i.e. the line of the medieval wall at the south–east of the town was already the boundary of the city by Domesday Book.

Obviously there is something anomalous in the history of the south end of Chester. Perhaps here, as at *The Crofts,* we observe the result of an inclusion into the city of ground originally outside it. There is here, as at *The Crofts* to the west side, some evidence of open ground within the medieval wall. Apart from Pepper Street, St Olave's Lane, Bridge Street and *Claverton Lane* (Duke Street), there was no development of building until modern times. In fact, Park Street, until the Nine Houses appear there in 1690,[188] was only a lane joining Duke Street and Newgate,[189] and it had not a name of its own. It is *Nine Houses* from 1690 to 1789, *Newgate Street* by mistake of Lavaux's map in 1745,[190] *Park Street* and *Mr Hamilton's Park* 1789,[191] being the edge of a large garden behind the east side of Bridge Street. The site of this park was occupied by Albion Street, Steel Street and Volunteer Street.[192] The area west of Lower Bridge Street appears to have been more developed in medieval times. Cupping Street, Castle Street, Bunce Street and Castle Esplanade (*Nun's Lane*) were all built upon by the thirteenth century. Yet here it is to be observed that the Castle and Gloverstone were never part of the city nor even of the Hundred of the city. Chester Castle was,

---

[188] Assembly Book, AB/3, f. 27, City Record Office.

[189] *Venella que ducit de Wolfeyette usque ad Clavertonlone* 1387–8 Portmote Rolls, MR/58; *a lane leading out of Pepper Street touards Clayton Lane* 1760 Corp., C/Ch/2A/28.

[190] Sheaf 3, 43, No. 8980: Lavaux took it to be a continuation of Newgate Street whereas it is a continuation of *Claverton Lane.*

[191] Corp., C/Ch/2A/33, and James Hunter's map of Chester, 1789.

[192] Sheaf 3, 43, No. 8980.

and is, a parish of Broxton Hundred; Gloverstone was a township of St Mary on the Hill parish, and part of Broxton Hundred; and St Mary's church although standing geographically within the medieval city, was nonetheless the mother church of a parish which lies in Broxton Hundred.

It would seem that the medieval walls include territory originally not inside the city: they appear to have been deliberately thrown out to the river to west and south so as to expand the city at the expense of those jurisdictions and manors whose territorial disposition antedates the new line of wall. The date of the expansion is now up for debate. It looks as if the new boundary of the city reached to the river, between *Claverton Lane* (Duke Street) and St John's, by Domesday Book. Was this boundary marked by rampart or wall?

The city walls are not specifically recorded until the thirteenth century.[193] The gates of the city begin to appear regularly in record at about the same time, e.g. Bridgegate in 1288,[194] Newgate in 1258,[195] Shipgate in 1270,[196] Watergate c. 1270.[197] Earlier than this we find only the unidentified *Clippe Gate*, recorded only as *porta Clippe* 1121–9 (1285),[198] probably derived from an Old Norse by–name *Klyppr*;[199] Eastgate in 1153,[200] Northgate in 1096.[201] These evidences do not prove what date the southward extended walls were built. But some light may be thrown upon this by the name of one of the gates in the southward–extended wall, i.e. of a gate in that part of the medieval wall which stands outside the Roman circuit, and a gate, furthermore, in that very stretch of wall which runs between *Claverton Lane* and St John's. The important name here is that of Newgate.

---

[193] *murus Cestrie* is mentioned 1217–32, Miscellaneous deeds in Chester Record Office, in the context dealing with land 'sub muro ad exitum de *Clauertunelane*', i.e. land against the wall at the end of Duke Street; c. 1225 CAS 10, 18; and c. 1240 Br. Mus. Add. Ch. 49984.

[194] *le Briggegate* Court 154, 166.

[195] *porta de Wlfild* c. 1258 Vernon MSS., Box 3, C1, No. 13.

[196] *le Schipjete* 1270–3 Sheaf 3, 33, No. 7459.

[197] *porta aque* 1268–71 Br. Mus. Add. Ch. 40001.

[198] Chester I, 49.

[199] v. E.H. Lind, *Norsk–Isländska Personbinamn fran medeltiden,* Uppsala, 1920–21, 205. s.n.

[200] *porta orientalis* 1153–81 (14) Chester I, 50.

[201] *porta de North* 1096–1101 (1280) Chester I, 3.

Newgate appears as *porta de Wlfild* c. 1258[202] and the name *Wolfeld Gate, Woolfield Gate,* was regular until the fourteenth century and continued in use until the seventeenth. In the fourteenth century a contracted form of *Wolfeldyate* came in, i.e. *Wolfeyette,*[203] and this form, *Wolf Gate,* is quite regular in the fifteenth and sixteenth centuries. In 1553 the old gate was rebuilt and called *Newegatt,*[204] and this name, *Newgate,* persists although the gate was occasionally called *the Pepper Gate*[205] and *St John's Gate*[206] because it was at the end of Pepper Street and led to St John's.

The etymology of this gate–name has to be derived from the form *Wolfeldeyate* 1294,[207] *porta de Wlfild* c. 1258,[208] *Wolfuldegate* 1304.[209] This looks like 'wool–field' or 'wolf–field'. But there is evidence that *Wolfelde–* is a rationalisation of a form of name which had become unintelligible by the thirteenth century, i.e. the origiñ and meaning of the name were by then forgotten. An older form appears as *porta Wlfadi* late–13.[210] *Wlfadi* here is the genitive–singular of a latinised personal– name *Wlfadus.* The name 'Wlfadus's gate' would seem be a monkish dedication to the prince and martyr *Wulf(h)ad,* St Werburgh's brother, son of Wulfhere king of Mercia (657–74), whose edifying legend is told in Dugdale's *Monasticon Anglicanum,* 1673, II, 119–126.[†] This dedication is, itself, an attempt to make sense of an unintelligible name. The initial *W–* in *Wlfadus,* represented doubled *u,* i.e. *uu* (< long *u*) with dipthongisation and stress shifting; and the persistent *–l–* in the second syllable of the other forms, indicate that *Wlfadus* and *Wolfeld* are representations of an original form *Ulfaldi.* The name of the gate is 'Ulfaldi's gate', from the Old Norse nickname *Ulfaldi*[211] 'the hump– back', from Old Norse *úlfaldi* 'a camel'.[†] This nickname appears again

---

[202] Vernon MSS., Box 3, C1, 13.

[203] 1387–8 Portmote Rolls, MR/58.

[204] Morris, 237.

[205] 1656 Morris, 237.

[206] 1656 Ormerod, I, 134.

[207] Vernon MSS., Box 3, C1, No. 14.

[208] Note 202 *supra.*

[209] Chamb (R. Stewart–Brown, *The Accounts of Chamberlains and Other Officers of the County of Chester,* Record Society of Lancashire and Cheshire 59, 1910), 73.

[210] Chester II, 599.

[211] *v.* E.H. Lind, op. cit. 390, s.v.; cf. R. Cleasby & G. Vigfusson, *An Icelandic–English Dictionary,* Oxford, 1874, s.v. *úlfaldi.*

at Claughton near Birkenhead in the lost place–name *Vlfeldesgreue* 1340,[212] 'Ulfaldi's grove' (from Old English **græfe**, 'a wood, a grove' as in numerous place–names ending in *–greave, –grave*). A suggestion in this direction was made in 1939 by a contributor to *The Cheshire Sheaf*[213] signing himself 'V. L.', who said that the gate might have been named after a man called *Wolfeld*. Wolfeld is a quite credible anglicisation of the Old–Norse nickname in this place–name.

The derivation of the old name of Newgate as 'Ulfaldi's gate' would be significant. Like the unidentified *Clippe Gate* it contains a Scandinavian nickname, and must have been named after a Scandinavian. What is more, the name–forms are not originally anglicised, these men are named in Norse, not in Anglo–Norse. At Newgate it is significant that the personal–name form is Old Norse *úlfaldi* not the equivalent Old English *olfend* 'a camel' (later 'an elephant'); and that the meaning of *Ulfaldi* was so completely lost by the thirteenth century that the form was rationalised to *Wolfeld,* rather than translated into English *Olfend.* The name 'Ulfaldi's gate' was given to Newgate when Norse speakers with Scandinavian names were about the town, at a time when such a name as *Ulfaldi* was intelligible, and before the Scandinavian language was so lost to use as to produce the English rationalisations shown by the thirteenth–century spellings of this name.

Now, it is not hard to find Scandinavians in Chester. Domesday Book tells us that a man with the Danish name *Gunnwor* held half of *Redcliff* in 1066. Coins struck at the Chester mint in the tenth and eleventh century bear moneyers' names which are of Norse–Irish origin. In Bridge Street is St Olave's church.[214] The dedication is to St Olaf the King (of Norway; killed 1030). The earliest recorded dedications to St Olaf elsewhere in England[215] are at York 1055, Exeter 1063, Southwark a. 1085, Chichester late 11, Grimsby 1100–35, and London c. 1100. The Chester church, not mentioned in DB (1066 or 1086), was already in existence in 1119, the date of the *confirmation* of a grant of this church to St Werburgh's abbey: the grant being confirmed in 1119 was made by

[212] Palatinate of Chester, Forest Proceedings, in Public Record Office, Chester 33/3/m.1. But the final el. may be OE **grēne**, 'a green'.

[213] 3, 34, No. 7556.

[214] *ecclesia Sancti Olafi* 1119 (1150) Chester I, 41, n16.

[215] *v.* Bruce Dickins, 'The Cult of St Olaf in the British Isles', *Saga Book* XII, 53–80.

Robert Pincerna ('the Butler') in the time of Richard earl of Chester (1102–1120). This church of St Olaf in Chester was presumably built sometime between 1086 and 1119. It was parochial. The medieval parish was entirely within the city (the area approximately bounded by Duke Street, Park Street, Albion Street and Bridge Street) and looks as if it were an enclave taken out of St Michael's parish which adjoins it to north and south. This may be taken as evidence of the prior existence of St Michael's parish.

It is interesting to note that in a grant of land adjoining this church in 1230–34[216] the tenants named are Hugo and Nicholas *Ulf* and a witness is John son of *Ulfkell*.[217] These surnames are the Old Norse personal–names *Ulfr* and *Ulfkell*. We see here the persisting traces of a Scandinavian community: Scandinavian personal–names and surnames persisting, modified by English forms, among the landowners and tenants of the St Olaf parish. It might easily be supposed that this church had been founded especially to serve the needs of a Scandinavian community in Chester;[218] and being extra and superfluous to the ordinary parochial needs of the city, it fell upon hard times when the Scandinavian community was so absorbed into the general population that it lost its distinctive identity. Perhaps this decline of a distinctive Scandinavian community was already measurable early in the twelfth century: the endowment of St Olaf's may have been handed over to St Werburgh's by Robert Pincerna before 1119 because the place could no longer be easily supported. Certainly this church's history is a tale of poverty, neglect and calamity. In 1393 its poverty caused it to be united with St Mary on the Hill. In 1414 and 1459 Papal dispensations make allowance for its poor endowment. In 1722 there was no minister, the minister of St Michael's had been taking care of it for the past twenty years, and the church was unfit for services other than baptism and burial. In 1841 the church was closed and its parish was merged into St Michael's.

This tale of woe is an ironic commentary. St Olave's is the most powerful historical monument of the medieval city. It commemorates the

---

[216] Hemingway II, 126.

[217] This John son of *Ulfkell* may be that John *Ulkel* who was a sheriff of the city 1245–6 and 1256–7.

[218] The Irish connexions of such a community in the tenth century would probably be reflected by the dedication of St Bridget's church.

importance of this tired old city when she was in the vigour of her second magnificence.[219] St Olave's is a proof that Chester was a place with a position in that wide Scandinavian common–market of the Northern world in the eleventh and twelfth centuries. Its presence and its antiquity put Chester upon a par with York and London just as clearly as does the presence and antiquity of the fortress of the Twentieth Legion.

St Olave's church may serve as the focus of a speculation which gives significance to the old name of Newgate. We may see in St Olave's an evidence for a distinctively Scandinavian community in Chester in the eleventh century: a community with a Norse (and Irish) bias rather than a Danish one, as would be expected from the Irish Sea geography of the city, and from the influence of the Wirral Norsemen about the district.[220] This community had lost its distinct identity and social viability by the thirteenth century. Even by the twelfth the management of its church is being put into the hands of St Werburgh's. The vestiges of the Norse community in the thirteenth century are seen in the personal–nomenclature of some landholding citizens, but their names are hybridized; they are already Anglo–Scandinavian by name, and if we are to judge by the townsmen's inability to comprehend the meaning of the name 'Ulfaldi's gate' in the thirteenth century, it looks as though the *Ulfs* and *Ulfkells* of that age had all but forgotten their Scandinavian ancestral tongue. The form of the name *Wolfeld–gate* (Newgate) indicates that a gate in the post–Roman — the medieval — line of wall was given its name in an age when nicknames in the Norse linguistic form were used in Chester, and when a man with such a name figured sufficiently in local affairs to have a town–gate called after him. Either this gate was already there when this Norse speech and its users arrived, or it was built in their day. The name *Wolfeld–gate* would appear to belong to an era which ended in the twelfth century. It is likely to belong to that period when the Scandinavian influence would be strongest in the town, the tenth and eleventh centuries.

---

[219] Chester was a great city at three ages: once in Roman times, again in the Anglo–Saxon and Norman times from the tenth to the twelfth centuries, and finally under Edward I and III. The agony of the Civil War siege, the last spasm of importance, happened almost by accident.

[220] See my 'The Background of Brunanburh', *Saga Book* XIV, 303–316 [= *supra*, Appendix I: A].

Such speculation as this is a legitimate extension from the place–name evidence: but it cannot be proved by these rules of art. From the inferences of the name–forms, there would be no objection to the projection of a wall with Newgate in it, from the Roman wall to the river, before Domesday Book when this line was the boundary between the city and *Redcliff,* at a time when the city was under strong Norse influence: such a line of wall as might well have been drawn at the time of the refortification of Chester by Æþelflæd Alfred's daughter in 907.

THE ROWS

The exercise in speculation just now performed might be repeated with regard to another peculiarity of the city, the Rows. The names of the rows are more intricate than, and just as interesting as, the names of the streets of the city. Bridge Street Row East was the site of *le Coruyserrowe* 1356,[221] *Corvisor's Row* 1651,[222] 'the shoemakers' row'[223] and *Mercers Row* 1656,[224] *le Mercerrowe* 1503,[225] 'the mercers' row'.[226] Bridge Street Row West does not seem to have had any distinctive name in medieval times (unless it be the location of *le Sadelererowe, Sadelerisrowe* 1342,[227] *Sadelesrowe* 1304,[228] 'the saddlers' row'[229]). At the north end of this row, on the corner of Bridge Street and Watergate Street, stood the *Seldes* — 'the stalls'; *le Seldez* c. 1540,[230] *undecim selde vocat' selde sutorum in*

---

[221] Corp., C/Ch/2/1.

[222] Sheaf 3, 26, No. 5898.

[223] From Middle English **corviser** 'a shoe–maker'. One Richard *le Corueiser* of Chester is named c. 1258 (Vernon MSS., Box 3, C1, No. 13). *Corvisor's Row* was said in 1356 (Corp., C/Ch/2/1) to be in Bridge Street, but in 1651 (Sheaf 3, 26, No. 5898) it was said to be in Eastgate Street: it was therefore probably on the corner.

[224] Ormerod, I, 135.

[225] Sheriffs Books, Chester Record Office; cf. Morris, 294.

[226] From Middle English **mercer** 'a cloth–seller'. One Robert *le Mercer* was sheriff of Chester 1248–52, he is called *le Prudmercer* in 1250, 'the proud mercer'!

[227] Br. Mus. Add. Ch. 50152–4.

[228] Chamb 74.

[229] From Middle English **sadelere** 'a saddler'. Add. Ch. 50152 seems to place it in Bridge Street near White Friars street, and the Crownmote Rolls for 1392–3 (QC/R10) show saddlers in business in Bridge Street.

[230] Sheaf 3, 11, p. 1.

Bruggestrete 1278[231] 'eleven stalls called the shoemakers' shops'. In 1425[232] there is a conveyance of 'two cellars with their appurtenances built under a certain shop called *Stonesseldes*, lying in Bridge Street, Chester, i.e. upon the corner of Watergate Street'. *Stonesseldes* means 'shops or stalls made of stone or built of stone'. By contrast with these stone–built jobs, we find, just round the same corner in Watergate Street but adjoining Bridge Street, *le Staven Sildes, le Stavyn Seldes* 1508,[233] two cellars and vacant ground on the south side of Watergate Street near the west side of Bridge Street; 'stalls built of, or furnished with, staves or poles'.

Watergate Street Row South appears as *le Fleshrewe* Edward III,[234] *Flessherowe* 1356,[235] *le Fles(s)heuer Rowe* 1420,[236] and so on until *The Flesher's Row* 1578,[237] 'the butcher's row'.[238] Watergate Street Row North does not appear to have a distinctive name in medieval times. Northgate Street Row West was the site of *Iremonger Rowe* 1550,[239] *le Irnemongerrowe* 1330,[240] 'ironmongers' row'.[241] This row housed *Shoemakers Row* 1860,[242] *the Shoemakers Row* 1704,[243] which adjoined St Peter's churchyard. Eastgate Street Row South was *le Cornmarketrowe* 1343.[244]

It is the row on the north side of Eastgate Street and the east side of Northgate Street which is most heavily recorded. It was called *Pepper*

[231] Ancient Deeds in Public Record Office, No. B.3474, cf. Ormerod, II, 169, Sheaf 3, 34, No. 7513.
[232] Vernon MSS., Box 3, C11, No. 21.
[233] Corp., C/Ch/2.7. Morris, 251, reads *Stabyn Seldys* but I have not seen this form.
[234] Morris, 294.
[235] Chester Plea Rolls (Reports of Deputy Keeper of the Public Records 28, 58).
[236] Morris, 251, lit. *Flesh–, Flesshener Rowe*.
[237] Morris, 294.
[238] From Middle English **flesh–hewere** 'one who hews flesh; a butcher'.
[239] Ministers Accounts, Public Record Office, S.C.6/Edw. VI/65.
[240] Vernon MSS., Box 3, C1, 22.
[241] From Middle English **iren–mongere** 'an ironmonger'. Raynold *le Yrenmonger* owned land in Northgate Street in 1285 (CAS 10, 45). He may even have given name to the Row.
[242] White.
[243] Assembly Books, AB/3, f. 124v.
[244] Vernon MSS., Box 3, C1, No. 32.

Alley Row in 1894,[245] *Pepper Alley* in 1831,[246] from the name of the alleyway towards St Werburgh's churchyard, probably an instance of the modern use of 'pepper' for a rowdy person, a hooligan. The row has had many names given it. It was the site of *The Butter Shops* from 1280 to 1591;[247] it was *Baxter Row* or *Baker's Row* from 1293 to 1502;[248] here also was *le Cokesrowe* 'the cook's row' from 1330 to 1449.[249] In 1330 the Pepper Alley Row belonged to Reginald *de Thlene* of Leen Lane. Another name at the row alludes specifically to its rows–passage, perhaps not unconnected with its 'Pepper–Alley' reputation, and invites comparison with Northgate Street Row East which was called *Broken Shin Row* in 1817[250] and 1831,[251] and is still an uneven walk. This name for Pepper Alley Row is *The Dark(e) Row* 1591[252] to 1650.[253] The earlier form of this name was *le Dirke Loftez* 1488,[254] *le Darke Loftes* 1541.[255] Pepper Alley Row was also known as *The New Buildings* 1635[256] and 1688[257] because it was completely rebuilt in 1592.[258]

As can be seen from the selection of notes presented here, the Rows teem with names left upon them by the doings of Chester's inhabitants. One may speculate whether these rows have a connection with an older

[245] Morris, 295.

[246] Hemingway, I, 386; cf. note 161 *supra*.

[247] *le Botershoppes* 1280 (n.d.) Sheaf 3, 36, No. 7959, *le Butterscoppes* 1293 Chester Indictment Rolls, Public Record Office, Chester 25/1/m.3.

[248] *le Bakersrawe* 1293 Chester Indictment Rolls. Chester 25/1/m.3, *le Baxterrowe* 1330 Portmote Rolls, MR/30, *Baxter Row* 1502 Sheaf 3, 26, No. 5845. In 1330 (Vernon MSS., Box 3, C1, No. 22) this row was between Eastgate Street and St Werburgh's churchyard and was probably associated with St Giles's bakehouse, belonging to Boughton Spital, first mentioned in 1313 as 'a house with a furnace and a plot of land at *le Wodefen* which house is called St Giles's bakehouse' (CAS 2, 166–168; Morris, 157) when it was leased to Roger le Kylwe, baker.

[249] 1330 Vernon MSS., Box 3, C1, No. 22; 1449 Vernon MSS., Box 3, C2, 37.

[250] J.H. Hanshall, *History of the County Palatine of Chester,* 289.

[251] Hemingway, I, 386, cf. Sheaf 3, 43, No. 8958.

[252] Morris, 294.

[253] Parliamentary Surveys, Public Record Office, Cheshire 13 A, B.

[254] Corp., C/Ch/10. An eighteenth–century quotation in Sheaf 3, 19, No. 4552, seems incorrect to date this 1448.

[255] Corp., C/Ch 13.

[256] Sheaf 1, 1, p. 276.

[257] Assembly Book, AB/3/f. 16v.

[258] Sheaf 1, 1, p. 276.

age of the city than that of their emergence into record. The word *row* (Old English **rāw**) in these names means 'a row of buildings, a row of houses'. A distinctive feature of the rows or ranges of buildings along the principal streets of Chester is the first–floor gallery passageway. The rows fronting the main streets from the Cross have public footways along them, inside their first–floor fronts, lined with shops and chambers, and above the street–level frontage which is level with their cellarage. The rows–passages in front at the centre of the town are at the same level as the ground at the back of the buildings. It is this distinctive gallery feature which is now called, by transference or metonymy, a *Row*. The proper term for these passages, referring to them specifically rather than to the range of buildings they traverse, is now obsolete. It is found in *communis via vocata Lofts* 'the public thoroughfare called *Lofts*' 1492 (17),[259] referring to the Eastgate Street Rows, and in the name 'Dark Lofts' given to Pepper Alley Row.[260] This is the word *loft* from Old Norse **lopt**.

The origin and purpose of the style of building found in the Rows, a range with a public thoroughfare along it inside the first–floor front, is not known, although much considered.[261] The most familiar analogy might be the galleried yard of a medieval inn. But the use of the word *lofts* for the rows–passages suggests that the origin of this peculiar facility may have been in a row of lofthouses (Old Norse **lopt–hús**), each with a sub–structure at ground level on the street frontage, with a stall on the ground in front of it, and a 'cellarage' inside the sub–structure; and with a dwelling in the loft, perhaps with a shop in its front part, reached by a flight of steps from the street. For the convenience of trade and passengers, such lofts would have been connected by board–walks along the outside of the building at loft–level, probably standing over the stall–structures. Such an arrangement would have tended to become permanent, and architecturally integral, when bigger superstructures were needed and developed in the cramped space available along the streets, so that the board–walks, originally external

---

[259] Sheaf 3, 30, No. 4917; Br. Mus. Harleian MS. 7568, f. 158.

[260] *v. supra.*

[261] *v.* CAS 6, 57–9; 8, 48–66; Morris, 288–294; Ormerod, I, 386–9; there is a good specimen diagram in *Medieval Archaeology* 6–7, 1962–3, 230, fig. 74.

and over the front–stall, would be under the overhang of the next higher storey, whose supporting pillars would now form the outer wall of the loft–passage and the ground–floor frontage stall. The occurrence of loft–houses in Chester would have been a possibility in the tenth and eleventh centuries, in an age of marked Scandinavian influence.

The last stages in the evolution of the Rows, the incorporation of the loft–level passage–ways and the street–level stalls into the advanced frontages of the rows of houses, leaves its echo in the terminology of later contexts such as 'a waste part of the Roe or ground before a messuage on the west side of Bridge Street' in 1643;[262] or 'a shop on the north side of Watergate Streete . . . together with the row and stall before the shop' in 1670;[263] or 'part of the row enclosed by him into a chamber in the row before his house in Bridge Street, being eight feet, and also eight feet in the street by him lately enclosed and taken into his cellar or shop under his said house' in 1675;[264] or 'a passage called the Rowe on the west–side of Bridge Street' in 1692;[265] or 'a house in Foregate Street on the north side of the row or passage there' in 1699;[266] or 'a row or parcel of ground ten yards long by two and a half in breadth before a certain piece of ground lately purchased by . . . whereupon a messuage or dwelling house formerly stood, in the Foregate Street, with liberty to enclose and build upon the same so as to range even in front with the messuage now or late in the holding of . . .' in 1703;[267] or 'a shop in or adjoining the row on the east side of Bridge Street . . . and all that shop lying under the said shop' in 1706;[268] or 'a shop or stall or row at a house called the Harp and Crown in Bridge Street' in 1707.[269]

[262] Corp., C/Ch/2. 27.
[263] Corp., C/Ch 647.
[264] Corp., C/Ch/2/33.
[265] Corp., C/Ch/2/38.
[266] Corp., C/Ch/4/69.
[267] Corp., C/Ch/4/70.
[268] Corp., C/Ch/2/46.
[269] Corp., C/Ch/2/49.

HANDBRIDGE AND HERONBRIDGE

To round out this series of exercises in archaeological extrapolation from place–name etymologies, the place–names Handbridge and Heronbridge offer examples of more simple difficulty, where the form and meaning of a place–name are on the one hand obscure and on the other hand misleading.

Handbridge is a curious name. The place is called *Bruge* 1086,[270] and the simple name 'Bridge', meaning 'place at a bridge', representing Old English *brycge* dative singular (i.e. locative) of **brycg** 'a bridge', persists in occasional use down to 1527.[271] The modern form begins to emerge in *Honebrugge* c. 1150 (1400),[272] early 13,[273] and down to 1450,[274] *Hondbrigg* 1285,[275] *Hondbrugge* 1386[276] and down to *Hondbridge* 1656,[277] *Hondebrigg* 1361[278] and down to 1516,[279] *Honbrugge* 1334[280] and down to *Honbrigge* 1616,[281] *Hande–* 1511 (1571),[282] *Han–* 1541[283] *et seq., Hand–* 1544[284] *et seq.* Many other variant forms of the prefix occur, e.g. *Hune–* 1289, *Howne–* 1315, *Hun–* 1327, 1471, *Horne–* 1350, *Honder–* 1369, *Hony–* 1369 (1551), *Honse–* 1391, *Hound–* 1482, *Hunde–* 1488, 1506; and all the forms of the prefix can be accounted for

[270] Domesday Book, 3 times, ff. 266, 266b.

[271] *manerium de Brygge* 1527 Chester Recognizance Rolls, Reports of the Deputy Keeper of Public Records 39, 232, cf. *manerium de Bryge* 1528 (17) Cholmondeley MSS., Cheshire Record Office, H/79.

[272] Calendar of Patent Rolls, cf. CAS 13, 93.

[273] 1209–29 Br. Mus. Add. Ch. 43969.

[274] Br. Mus. Add. Ch. 43518.

[275] Vernon MSS., Box 3, C1, No. 27.

[276] Br. Mus. Add. Ch. 50201.

[277] Ormerod, I, 134.

[278] *Black Prince's Register,* III, 409.

[279] Chester Exchequer Appearance Rolls, Public Record Office, Chester 5/1/8 Hen. VIII.

[280] Chester Recognizance Rolls, Public Record Office, (Deputy Keeper's Reports 36, 522).

[281] Sheaf 1, 1, 255.

[282] Chester Recognizance Rolls, Public Record Office, (Deputy Keeper's Reports 39, 108).

[283] W. Dugdale, *Monasticon Anglicanum* (1817–30), IV, 316.

[284] Br. Mus. Add. Ch. 50248.

as effects of that rounding and over–rounding of *a* to *o* to *ow* in the north–west–midland dialect of Middle English, and the insertion of an epenthetic *d* between *n* and *b* which has been reinforced by a popular identification of Middle English hon–, hun– with forms of Old English **hand, hond,** 'a hand' and Old English **hund** 'a hound, a dog'.

For the place–name Handbridge, E. Ekwall[285] supposed the Old English personal–name *Hana* (from Old English **hana** 'a cock'). This would serve the formal transmission well enough, for Old English *Hanan–brycg* would lead to Middle English *Hane–, Honebrugge* in this dialect. But Handbridge is not so named until the twelfth century, and it is recorded as *Bruge* in 1086: we are dealing with a Middle English modification of the place–name. Again, Ekwall proposes Old English **hana** 'a cock', in the place–name Handforth (near Stockport)[286] and etymologizes it 'cock's, or Hana's ford'. He takes Handforth and Handbridge, and Handford in Staffordshire, together as being all 'cock–ford, cock–bridge' or 'Hana's ford, Hana's bridge'.[287] However, for Hanford in Dorset he admits[288] the Old English word **hān** 'a rock' (cf. Modern English *hone* 'a grind–stone, a hone').

It looks as though we ought to reckon *Han(d)ford, –forth,* as a type of place–name, i.e. a commonplace description which would recur with the recurrent juxtaposition of a ford and a rock (**hān, hone**). Hanford and Handforth would denote a ford marked by a rock or stone, either because they lie on a river at a rocky place, or because their course was marked by a stone, in the way that, say, a Stapleford would be marked by a **stapol** (Old English 'a pillar'). The word **hān** is not unheard–of in English place–names. For example, it is a major affix in the place–name Sutton at Hone, Kent. On this argument, Handbridge would mean 'the

---

[285] *The Concise Oxford Dictionary of English Place–Names,* 4th ed., s.v.

[286] Handforth appears as *Haneford* 1153–81 (1285) (Calendar of Charter Rolls), *Honeford* late 12 (*Facsimiles of Early Cheshire Charters*, No. 14), *Hondford* 1238 (17) (Chester Recognizance Rolls, Deputy Keeper's Reports 36, 382), 1371 (Bromley–Davenport MSS, John Rylands Library, Box 6/14), *Handforde* 1536 (J. Leland, *Itinerary*, ed. L. Toulmin Smith, V, 26).

[287] See E. Ekwall *The Concise Oxford Dictionary of English Place–Names,* 4th ed., s.nn.

[288] Op. cit., s.n.; setting aside the etymology offered by A. Fägersten, *The Place–Names of Dorset*, Uppsala, 1933, 9, Old English *hēan–forde*, 'at the high (i.e. deep) ford'.

place called Bridge which is at a *hone,* a rock, and is thus called *Rock Bridge'*. There is a prominent outcrop of rock at Handbridge, and the place could well be called *'Rock' Bridge.* A deed of 1736[289] describes *Paradise Croft* in Handbridge as belonging to five houses 'standing on the Rock in Handbridge', Paradise being a row of cottages between Percy Road and the main street of Handbridge, off Bottoms Lane. Alternatively, the *hone* at Handbridge may have been artificial, i.e. a standing–stone of some kind at some significant point in the hamlet. The solution of the formal problem in this place–name creates the possibility of an archaeological problem.

The place–name Heronbridge has been *made* to look difficult. Popular etymology has given it a significance it does not deserve. Heronbridge appears as *pons ferreus* 1354 (1379),[290] translated as *the Iron Bridge* in fifteenth–sixteenth–century documents,[291] and also appearing as *le Irenbrigge* 1506,[292] *the Irne Brige* 1540,[293] *the Yorne Brige* 1547,[294] *the Yern Bridge* c. 1574,[295] *Heron Bridge* 1831.[296] All these forms testify to a popular tradition that there was at this place a bridge of iron, as if the place–name contained Old English **iren**, Middle English **yrne**, **irne**, **iren**, 'iron'. This association with *iron*, which begins with the *pons ferreus* form in the 1354 charter of the city, has been improved upon and accounted for in various ways. In 1574[297] the name *Yern Bridge* was explained as because the Romans built a wooden bridge here with 'a grate of Iern', a portcullis, in the middle. It was discussed by R.S.B. (R. Stewart Brown) in *The Cheshire Sheaf,* 3rd Series, 31, No. 7035 and by W.F.I. (W. Fergusson Irvine) in op. cit., No. 7044. R.S.B. supposed Heronbridge a Roman ford and discussed the possibility of ironwork here. W.F.I. observed traces of iron slag close to the place where the road from Chester to Eccleston crossed a watercourse which runs into

---

[289] Sheaf 3, 31, No. 6779.
[290] Calendar of Charter Rolls, 1379, p. 259.
[291] Sheaf 1, 1, 189; Morris, 210–218, 537.
[292] Ministers Accounts, Public Record Office, S.C.6/Hen. VIII/1520.
[293] Morris, 210–218.
[294] Minister Accounts, Public Record Office, S.C.6/Edw. VI/61.
[295] Sheaf 3, 22, No. 5232.
[296] Bryant's Map of Cheshire.
[297] Sheaf 3, 22, No. 5232.

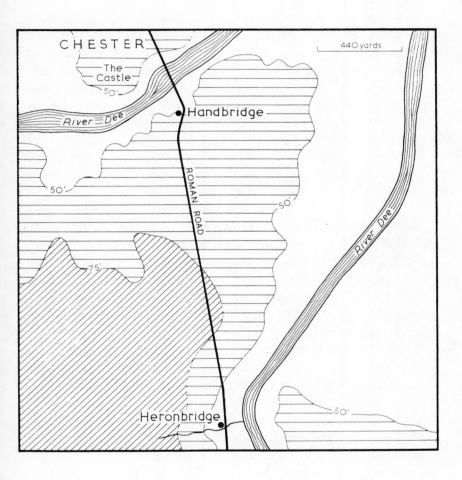

Figure C 3: The Site of Heronbridge.

R. Dee, the crossing being at the house called Heronbridge. The place is on a Roman road, and it is possible that there was a ford here in Roman times. But the bridge here need not be so ancient as that, and the association with *iron* is accidental.

The accident by which Heronbridge is associated with iron, is phonetic and etymological. The same sort of accident is seen in the Latin form *oculus crucis* 1394, 1403,[298] for Roodee. There the Latin text translates the English place–name Roodee in its Middle English form *Rood–eye*, 'the island of the Rood; Rood–island'.[299] But the latiniser has taken Middle English *eye* to be from Old English *ēage* (Latin *oculus*) 'an eye', instead of from Old English *ēg* (Latin *insula*) 'an island; a water–meadow'. So he gives us *Rood–eye* as *oculus crucis* instead of *insula crucis*. The *pons ferreus* form for Heronbridge would appear to be such a latinisation of a place–name *hyrne–brycg* 'bridge at the nook or corner'. The place–name element Old English **hyrne** appears, in numerous instances throughout Cheshire, to have been pronounced *yrne* or *hyrne* [(h)irn] in the Middle English dialect of the county. This would sound and look and develop like Middle English *yrne* the Cheshire form for Old English **iren** 'iron'. The words **hyrne** 'a nook, a corner, a secluded place' and **yrne** 'iron', both develop an alternative disyllabic form *hyren, hyryn* or *yren*. Thus we find the element **hyrne**, most frequently noted in minor place–names by the very nature of its meaning, in the field–names *Deyhiren* (lost, in Hurdsfield), Stubborn Oryon (Kinderton), Irons (Great Warford and Edge), Irons Lane (Barrow), Tom Irons (Stretton), Iron Field (Dodcott cum Wilkesley), Iron Dish (Frodsham Lordship and Helsby), Big and Little Irons (Tattenhall), *Hyron Yate* (lost, in Eccleston), Little Highon (Dunham on the Hill). There was even a lane–name in Chester *a certain way called le Hyryn* in 1510,[300] which contains this element **hyrne**. The place–name Heronbridge means 'bridge at a **hyrne**; bridge at a secluded corner'. Heronbridge would indeed be at a **hyrne**, see Fig. C 3. The situation is over a hill from Heronbridge, down in a hollow. The bridge from which the place is named would have carried the Chester–Eccleston Roman road over the

[298] Morris, 261, 302.
[299] From Old English **rōd** 'a cross, a rood', and **ēg** 'an island, a water–meadow'.
[300] Sheriff's Books, Chester Record Office.

watercourse running from a recess in the high bank overlooking the Dee meadows towards the pronounced bend in the river at this point. So far as the place–name is concerned we can forget about *iron*. Perhaps this will simplify the archaeological problems which the place–name's misconstruction has created: the supposed iron bridge here is a product of the latinity of an indifferent toponymist long ago.

The place–names of the city and its environs have not all been presented here: there is much more to see and say. But it is sufficient at this time to throw light upon the problems solved and created by a name–study. Perhaps even the failure to solve a problem by name–study methods can be seen to be a provocation of discussion and review. This would serve scholarship and possibly also clarify our vision of the history of Chester.[301]

Additional Notes [A.R.R.]

For fuller discussion of all Chester names mentioned, see **5:1** 1–84.

p. 337, *Wulf(h)ad*. For St Wulfhad, see A.R. Rumble, '*Ad Lapidem* in Bede and a Mercian Martyrdom', in *Names, Places and People: an Onomastic Miscellany in Memory of John McNeal Dodgson*, ed. A.R. Rumble and A.D. Mills (Stamford, 1997), 307–19.

p. 337, *Ulfaldi*. However, the ON by-name was rejected (in favour of OE *Wulfhild*, fem., or ON *Ulfhildr*, fem.) at **5:1** xliv (**4** 319) and 26.

[301] I am grateful to Mrs. B. Garbutt who typed this text, and to Mr. K. Wass who drew the maps, my colleagues at University College London. The preparation of the maps was assisted by a grant from The Chambers Research Fund, University College London. I owe a great deal, for assistance during several years' researches, to the Archivists of the City and of the County.

D. ALLITERATIVE PLACE–NAMES

[Reprinted from 'Two coals to Newcastle', in *Otium et Negotium: Studies in Onomatology and Library Science presented to Olof von Feilitzen*, ed. F. Sandgren, Acta Bibliothecæ Regiæ Stockholmensis 16 (Stockholm 1973), 46–8.]

Place–name scholars in Germany have discerned groups of place–names which alliterate and which are thought to mark the settlements of related kinship–groups.[1] In some such groups, the relating factor consists of the personal names which appear as first elements in the place–names. These personal names conform to a common Germanic pattern in showing the tradition of personal–name themes and of alliteration of personal names within the family group.[2] Anglo–Saxon personal names also follow such family models. For example, the famous Anglo–Saxon family, Æþelwulf king of Wessex 839–55 and his sons Æþelbeald, Æþelbeorht, Æþelræd and Ælfræd, bears a set of personal names which alliterate in Æ–, with common themes *Æþel–* and *–ræd*. It might, therefore, be expected that English place–names will occur in geographical groups with such kinship characteristics as first–element personal names with alliteration and common themes.

Such a group of alliterating place–names occurs in the Nantwich Hundred of Cheshire[3] in the country round about the town of Nantwich. The group[4] consists of the place–names

Wisterson (lost, Ch **3** 42, SJ/6752; *Wistetestune* 1086 DB, *Wichtrichestona* 1096–1101, *Wictredest'* 1194)

Woolstanwood (Ch **3** 44, SJ/6756; *Wolfstanwod* 1283)

Wistaston (Ch **3** 45, SJ/6853; *Wistanestune* 1086 DB)

---

[1] A. Bach, *Deutsche Namenkunde*, II. *Die deutschen Ortsnamen,* Part I (Heidelberg, 1953), §§ 342–44.

[2] A. Bach, *Deutsche Namenkunde*, I. *Die deutschen Personennamen*, Part 2 (Heidelberg, 1953), §§ 325–27.

[3] *The Place–Names of Cheshire*, Part **3**, EPNS 46 (1971), 1–159.

[4] Listed here in order of appearance in *Cheshire*, Part **3**, by page–number, with Ordnance Survey Grid Reference and early spellings.

Walgherton (Ch **3** 73, SJ/6948; *Walcretune* 1086 DB, *Walhreton* c. 1275)

Willaston (Ch **3** 78, SJ/674525; *Wilavestune* 1086 DB)

Wybunbury (Ch **3** 80, SJ/700500; *Wimeberie* 1086 DB, *Wybbunberi* 1199–1216)

Wilkesley (Ch **3** 93, SJ/628410; *Wiuelesde* 1086 DB (*–de* for *–cle*))

Wirswall (Ch **3** 112, SJ/5444; *Wireswelle* 1086 DB)

Wrenbury (Ch **3** 119, SJ/5947; *Wareneberie* 1086 DB, *Wrennebury* 1230)

Worleston (Ch **3** 151, SJ/6656; *Werblestune* 1086 DB (*–rbl–* for *–rvl–*), *Werflest'* 1175).

These ten place–names are the names of parishes and townships, that is to say, of the main settlements in their district. The townships of Wisterson, Woolstanwood, Wistaston, Walgherton, Willaston and Wybunbury are contiguous. These six place–names contain, as first element, OE personal names alliterating upon *W– — Wihtrēd* occasionally confused with *Wihtrīc* (Wisterson), *Wulfstān* (Woolstanwood), *Wīgstān* (Wistaston), *Walhhere* (Walgherton), *Wīglāf* (Willaston), *Wīgbeorn* (Wybunbury) — and so also do Wilkesley (OE *Wifel*) and Wirswall (OE *Wīghere*) which are a little farther off. Within this set of personal names in *W–* there occur sub–sets characterised by personal name themes, i.e. *Wīg–* (*Wīgstān, Wīglāf, Wīgbeorn, Wīghere*), *–stān* (*Wulfstān, Wīgstān*) and *–here* (*Walhhere, Wīghere*). It would be possible to augment these sets by bringing in minor place–names like those of the lost places *Waterdeslake*[5] (containing OE *Hwætrēd,* lying in Nantwich township, the adjacent township to Wisterson (OE *Wihtrēd*)) and *Wlfrischishalc*[6] in Church Minshull township; containing OE *Wulfrīc* which would link with the *Wulfstān* of Woolstanwood and perhaps with the occasionally substituted *Wihtrīc* of Wisterson).

These sets of personal names with alliteration in *W–* and with shared themes, *Wīg–, –stān, Wulf–, –here,* could represent the names of a kindred, and the group of place–names (adjacent township– and parish–names) in which they occur might represent settlements in the territory of a clan whose leading men had names which alliterated in *W–*.

---

[5] *Cheshire,* **3**, 41.
[6] *Cheshire,* **3**, 159.

E. THE WELSH ELEMENT IN THE FIELD–NAMES OF CHESHIRE

[Reprinted from BNF NF Beiheft 23 (1985), 154–64]

The ancient county of Cheshire, the province named after Chester, occupied that region of the North–West Midlands of England which adjoins the medieval frontier between England and Wales. The territory was taken from the Britons, ancestors of the Welsh, in the period 613–689 A.D. during which the Anglian Kingdom of Mercia emerged, especially under King Penda (626–654 A.D.), to assume, between 633 and 642 A.D., the resistance against the expansion, between 613 and 657 A.D., of the Anglian Kingdom of Northumbria; a resistance which had hitherto been conducted by the North Welsh Kingdom of Gwynnedd.

A number of the major place–names in Cheshire are relics and memorials of that epoch, and they have been analysed and interpreted in my article, 'The English Arrival in Cheshire', *Transactions of the Historic Society of Lancashire and Cheshire* 119 (1967), 1–37, especially, 23–32 [see above, Appendix I: B, especially, pp. 288–298] and: *The Place–Names of Cheshire, passim.* Some of them measure a deterioration in the social esteem with which the English colonists regarded the indigenous Celtic population. The place–names *Combermere*, Ch **3**, 93,[1] and *Comberbach* Ch **2**, 111, allude to the Britons by Old English **Cumbre**, 'the Britons', the loan–word from Primitive Welsh[2] **Cömmri* (Welsh *Cymry*), i.e. the polite word properly used by the sixth– and seventh–century Britons themselves (and still used by presentday Welshmen as the name of their nation) adopted by the Anglo–Saxons with reference to a respectable people. But the place–names *Walton* Ch **2**, 157, 158, and *Wallasey* Ch **4**, 323, allude to the

---

[1] Such references throughout, are to J.McN. Dodgson, *The Place–Names of Cheshire*, by Part and page, as follows: *The Place–Names of Cheshire*, Part **1**; Part **2**; Part **3**; Part **4**; Part **5:1**.

[2] The terms Primitive Welsh, Old Welsh, Middle Welsh, Modern Welsh, are specified in K. Jackson, *Language and History in Early Britain*, 5–6.

Britons by OE *Walas,* plural of Old English **walh** 'foreigner, slave', a less respectful term used for a subjected people. Such a set of place–names relates to the epoch in which the Angles met and subjected the Britons in Cheshire.

The place–names *Tarvin* Ch **3**, 281, and *Macefen* Ch **4**, 37 and xii, appear to refer to a Welsh frontier established before the withdrawal of Welsh political control from the territory: the Mercian King Æthelræd I established the English minster of St John the Baptist at Chester in 689 A.D., by which date the Welsh frontier must have been upon the River Dee. In 613 A.D., the Northumbrian King Æthelfrith fought a battle at Chester which was still, at that date, in British territory. The two place–names *Tarvin* and *Macefen* are linguistically of Welsh origin, not English. *Tarvin* represents Welsh *Terfyn* 'place at the boundary'. *Macefen* represents Welsh **Maes–y–ffin* 'open land at the boundary'. They indicate a boundary belonging to a Welsh–speaking community; a boundary and a community which both persisted long enough in the presence of the English newcomers for these to adopt the Welsh place–names which marked that boundary. *Tarvin* may have been, originally, the name of the River Gowy near which the place lies. This river has always been the northern part of the eastern boundary of the Hundred of Broxton, one of the immemorial subdivisions of the county of Cheshire; *Macefen* lies near the south–eastern boundary of the Hundred.

To the east of the line between *Tarvin* and *Macefen,* that is, the eastern boundary of Broxton Hundred along the River Gowy, there are some twenty–five place–names with a Celtic element, widely scattered about the county territory. West of this line, eighteen such names occur in the much smaller area which lies between the medieval Welsh frontier along the River Dee and the 'lost frontier' along the east boundary of Broxton Hundred. Of the eighteen, there are four in the remote extremity of the Wirral peninsula, five are near the ancient city of Chester and the lands which project into the Welsh territory west of the River Dee, and nine are in the southern part of the region, in the districts which belonged to the medieval feudal Barony of Malpas (see Fig. E 1).

The major place–names, then, indicate a persistent Welsh presence in this corner of the English territory. However, one needs to bear in mind, that the major names may reflect the survival of the nomenclature of a long–passed epoch; they may belong to the seventh–century stratum, their

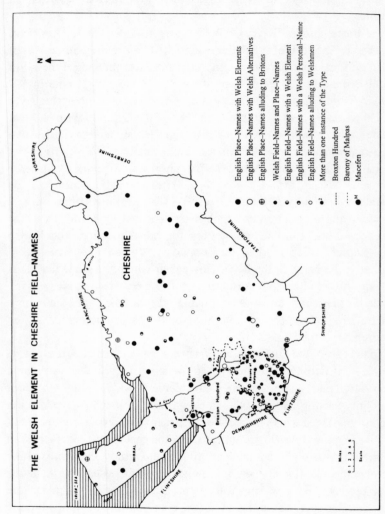

Figure E 1: The Welsh Element in Cheshire Field–Names.

Celtic element may be Primitive Welsh rather than Old Welsh or Middle
Welsh or Modern Welsh.[3]

Now, the analysis of the major place–names can be supplemented by
an examination of the field–names in Cheshire. There emerges a number
of medieval and modern field–names which have a Welsh element or
personal–name or structure, or which allude to Welshmen.

I. FIELD–NAMES IN THE WELSH LANGUAGE

In Cuddington township, Ch **4**, 28:

1. *Argoedd* 1838[4] 'near the wood', Welsh **ar** 'opposite', **coed** 'a
wood'.

In Cholmondley township, Ch **4**, 21:

2. *The Brynn* 1787, *Brynn* 1670, 'the hill', Welsh **brynn**. The Welsh
element **brynn** found in 2, 3, and 4, is also seen in the names *Bryn,
Bryn Farm* and *Brynn Bank* Ch **3**, 198, 203, in a district recorded as
le Brynne 1391, *the Brynne* 1779, *Brynnyl* 1467. The definite article,
and the composition with late Middle English **hyll**, 'hill' in 1467,
indicate that here was a hill named 'the Brynn', as if the Welsh *brynn*
'hill' had been a loan–word in English. Compare 33.

In Ridley township, Ch **3**, 313:

3. *Brin, Bryn* 1840, *Brins* 1677, *Brinn, Bryn Field* 1796; probably
these were two fields formed from a piece of land named 'Bryn'.
Compare 2.

In Odd Rode township, Ch **2**, 306:

4. *Brinne* 1705, Welsh **brynn** 'hill'.

In Oldcastle township, Ch **4**, 44:

5. *Big Vron* 1838, 'the big field named *Vron'*. The initial [v] shows
that this field has been originally named in Welsh *y vronn* 'the
hillside'; Welsh **bronn** with definite article. Compare 49.

---

[3] See note 2.
[4] Name–forms and dates are cited from my *The Place–Names of Cheshire*, in
which the documentary sources are specified.

6. *Henfaes, Henfas* 1838, 'old land', i.e. formerly used, now disused, ground; from Welsh **hen** 'old', **maes** 'open land'. The word order, adjective–noun, indicates a general sense, 'old land', i.e. this is not *maes–hen* 'the old field'.

7. *Little Cae Maur* 1838. Probably this field was enclosed out of a bigger one, which thus became divided into unequal parts, this being the smaller one. If the original field had been named *Cae Maur* we should then have had *Great Cae Maur* and *Little Cae Maur* as names of the parts. Only the latter one has survived. The field–name *Cae Maur* 'big enclosure' is Welsh, from **cae** 'enclosure' and **mawr** 'great'.

In Carden township, Ch 4, 53:

8. *le Bulgh* 1312; the Old French definite article with a Middle English spelling for Welsh **bwlch** 'a gap, a pass'.

In Shocklach Oviatt township, Ch 4, 66:

9. *Dale Vaughan* 1839, *Dole Vechan* 1528, *Dole Vaughan* 1778, *The Doll Voughan* 1637; Welsh **dôl** 'meadow', **bychan** (feminine *bechan*) 'little'; the English definite article in 1637 suggests that the name *Doll Voughan* was, or had been, understood as an appellative not just as a name.

10. *Caytanguistil* 1396; 'Tangwystl's field', Welsh **cae** 'enclosure' with the Welsh feminine personal–name *Tangwystl*. A lady of the same uncommon personal–name, inaccurately recorded as *Tanglust,* appears as a twelfth–century ancestress in the pedigrees of the noble families Egerton of Egerton and Cholmondeley of Cholmondeley,[5] feudal lords in this part of England since medieval times.

11. *Cae Coed, Car Coed* 1839, *Kay Koyd* 1637, 'enclosure at a wood' Welsh **cae**, **coed**; the 1839 spellings indicate a faulty English pronunciation of **cae**.

12. *Cae Ddu, Cae Ddu Mawr* 1839, 'the (great) black field', Welsh **cae** 'enclosure', **du** 'black', **mawr** 'great'; the lenition represented by the spelling *ddu* is incorrect after the masculine substantive *cae*, it would be correct after a feminine substantive. The document of record, the schedule of field–names in an Award of The Tithe Redemption Commission, was probably written by an Englishman who used, or heard, a mispronunciation.

---

[5] G. Ormerod, *The History of the County Palatine and City of Chester*, ed. T. Helsby, II, 628, 637.

13. *Cae Ithel* 1839, and 14. *Cae Robin* 1839; Welsh **cae** with the Welsh personal–name *Ithel* and the English personal–name *Robin.* Both are in Welsh word–order. Compare 29, 31.

15. *Gwern y ddavid* 1839 'marsh which belongs to a certain David'; Welsh **gwern**; the same land is described as *Dauiesacr' de Ridlegh' in Weisfordesmor'* 1331, in a classic Middle English formula for 'Davy de Ridlegh's acre in *Weisfordesmor*'. The same land is called *Croftdeuet* 1331 (from Middle English **croft**, 'a plot of land') and *Weyryloth Dauid* 1552 (from Welsh **gweirglodd** 'meadow'; compare 23), in both of which the word–order is non–English. The unexpected form *–deuet* for the masculine personal–name, Middle English *David* or Welsh *Dafydd*, indicates a confusion with the element **defaid** seen in No. 30.

16. *Gwern Wen* 1839, 'the white marsh', from Welsh **gwern** 'marsh', and **gwen** 'white'.

17. *Maes Lidiat* 1839 'field at a swing–gate', from Welsh **maes** 'open land' and **llidiat**, a loan–word from Middle English **(h)lidiate**, Old English **hlid–geat**.

In Chorlton township, Ch **4**, 27:

18. *Teir Main* 1838, 'narrow piece of ground', from Welsh **tir** 'land', and **main**, adjective, 'narrow, cramped'.

19. *Ten Main* 1838, 'small farm', from Welsh **ty'n** for **tyddyn** 'small–holding, homestead', and **main** 'narrow, cramped'.

20. *Higher Crunn, Lower Crunn* 1838, probably two fields formed out of one piece of ground called **Crunn* 'the round one', from Welsh **crwn** adjective, 'round'. Compare 26.

In Broxton township, Ch **4**, 12:

21. *Nant Chathul, boscus de Chathul* 1333. This records a modification (by Welsh **nant** 'wood') of an English place–name *Chathul*, 'hill at the woodland', a hybrid from Old English **hyll** and Primitive Welsh ***cēd** (< British ***cēto–**) the antecedent of Welsh **coed**. The Welsh construction *Nant Chathul* 'the wood of *Chathul*' is exactly equivalent to the Latin one; the Middle English equivalent would have been **Chathulwode*. The occurrence of this Welsh form throws interesting light on the linguistic history. *Chathul* is a formation in which Old English **hyll** has been combined with Primitive Welsh ***cēd**, (not yet developed to Welsh **coed** but perceived as Old English **cæt, *cēt*) and thus the name belongs to the earliest interface between the English and Welsh languages in this part of England. And this early hybrid place–name has subsequently

been incorporated into a Middle Welsh place–name. The archaic element *cēd is also found in the major place–name *Cheadle* Ch **1**, 246, *Cedde* (?rectius *Cedele*) 1086, *Chedle* 1153–1180, in which Old English **lēah** 'open woodland, lightly–wooded country' is affixed to a place–name *C(h)ed* (Primitive Welsh *cēd 'woodland').

In Bradley township, Ch **4**, 11:

22. *Bourth* 1838, is a problem. Perhaps it represents a Welsh form *y *berth* 'the hedge', from the Welsh feminine substantive **perth**, but the vowel looks as if the name were derived from *y *borth* 'the harbour, the port', from the Welsh feminine substantive **porth**. The feminine gender would explain the initial *b*, but the sense would be improbable. Perhaps the origin of the field–name *Bourth* was Welsh *y *porth* 'the gate–way', from the Welsh masculine substantive **porth**. An English writer or speaker has made a mistake in spelling or pronunciation.

In Clutton township, Ch **4**, 72:

23. *Wargloss* 1840, an English representation of Welsh **gweirglodd** 'a meadow'; the final *–ss* represents either an English plural or genitive–singular inflexional *s*, or the substitution of sibilant [s] for the dental spirant [θ] represented in the Welsh *dd* spelling in **gweirglodd** (Compare 15).

In Weston township, Ch **3**, 75:

24. *Cae Hyn* 1845, either 'the older enclosure' or 'enclosure at the ash trees', from Welsh **cae** 'enclosure', with either **hŷn**, comparative of the adjective **hen** 'old', or **ynn**, plural of **onnen** 'an ash tree'.

In Caldecott township, Ch **4**, 62:

25. *le Cammek* 1321, 'the crooked field', Welsh **cameg** 'a bent thing, a bend'.
26. *Cruin* 1839, *Kay Crune* 1598, 'the round, circular, enclosure', from Welsh **cae** 'enclosure' and the adjective **crwn** 'round'. The 1839 form must be interpreted as a substantive use of the adjective, meaning 'the round one'. Compare 20.

In Egerton township, Ch **4**, 33:

27. *The Kennant, Kennant Field, Kennant Meadow* 1838, an English adoption of a place–name from Welsh **ceunant** 'stream in a wooded hollow'.

In Churton–by–Farndon township, Ch **4**, 73:

28. *Quotkey Yollen* 1494, 'Iolyn's hedged–in field', from Welsh **coetgae** 'a quickset hedge, land enclosed by a hedge', and the Welsh masculine personal–name *Iolyn*.

In Horton township, Ch **4**, 55:

29. *Cae William* 1838, 'William's field', from Welsh **cae** and the English personal–name *William;* the word–order is Welsh. Compare 31, 13, 14.

30. *Werny David* 1838, represents either Welsh **gwerni Dafydd* 'David's marshes', like 15, or **gwern y defaid* 'marsh of the sheep', from Welsh **defaid**, plural of **dafad** 'a sheep'.

In Church Shocklach township, Ch **4**, 63:

31. *Cae Kendrick* 1839 *TA*, 'Cynwrig's field', from Welsh **cae** and the Welsh masculine personal–name *Cynwrig* (anglicized *Kendrick*, as in the modern English surname). The word–order is Welsh.

In Tushingham–cum–Grindley township, Ch **4**, 46:

32. *Talretheragh* 1348, 'Rhydderch's end', from Welsh **tâl** 'the end or top of something (a hill)' and the Welsh masculine personal– name *Rhydderch.*

II. FIELD–NAMES WITH A WELSH ELEMENT

In Wardle township, Ch **3**, 322:

33. *Brinshill* 1840, a hybrid place–name, 'the hill of *Brin*', a composition with English **hill** upon the genitive inflexion of a place–name from Welsh **brynn** 'hill'. Compare *Brynnyl* 1467, a similar composition noted under 2.

In Burwardsley township, Ch **4**, 93:

34. *Caycroft* 1476, a reduplicating composition of English **croft** 'a small enclosure' and Welsh **cae** 'croft at (the field named) *Cay* (< **cae**)'. Compare 37.

In Shocklach Oviatt township, Ch **4**, 66:

35. *Wern Hill* 1839, 'hill at–, of– or called *Wern*'; a hybrid place–name from English **hill** suffixed to a place–name *Wern*, from Welsh **gwern** 'marsh'.

36. *Westford Moor* 1839, *Weysfordesmor* 1316, 'the marsh at Weysford', from Old English **mōr** and a place–name *Weysford.* The Welsh equivalent is inaccurately written *Qwern Waysford* 1379, instead of *Gwern–*; the unvoiced initial, [kw] for [gw], may be the result of an English mispronunciation.

37. *Sokelachismor* 13th century, 'the marsh belonging to Shocklach', a composition of Old English, Middle English **mōr** 'marsh' upon the genitive singular inflexion of the place–name *Shocklach.* The place–name is recorded with the English formula down to *Shokelage mor'* 1445, but the Welsh formula appears in *Guernshoklege* 1362, *Gwerneshockelage* 1562. Here, Welsh **gwern** 'marsh' is equivalent to Middle English **mōr(e)**.

In Malpas township, Ch **4**, 38:

38. *Key Field* 1841, *Kayefeld* 1524. Another instance of a hybrid field–name in which the English element is affixed to a Welsh one, which is thus translated, compare 34. This field–name means 'field at –, field called –, *Kaye*' (Welsh **cae** 'enclosure').

39. *Coids Croft* 1777, a composition of English **croft** 'small enclosure' upon the genitive singular inflexion of a place–name *Coid* (from Welsh **coed** 'a wood').

40. *Pentre Field* 1841, 'field at –, field called –, *Pentre'. Pentre* is a place–name from Welsh **pentref** 'manor house, chief house in a settlement'. Compare 45, 46. The Welsh element appears also in an alternative Welsh name for Woolfall Farm in Audlem township, Ch **3**, 86, *Pentry Cloud* 1831, 1842, from Welsh **pentref** and **clawdd** 'a dyke, a ditch, a hedged bank'. This name, meaning 'mansion with a moat about it', is not recorded before, nor since, the nineteenth century and appears to have been a house–name used by the farmers in residence about 1820–1830; presumably they were Welsh speakers.

In Church Shocklach, Ch **4**, 63:

41. *Key Field* 1839, 'field named Key', analogous with 38; in this instance and 38, it is difficult to ascertain whether the Welsh word **cae** was understood as a Welsh word or as an English loan–word; compare 42.

In Handley township, Ch **4**, 90:

42. *Handley Keys* 1838, a group of fields, 'the *Keys* at, or belonging to, (the village of) *Handley*'. The name indicates that, at some time previous to this date, the Welsh element **cae** had been adopted as a loan–word in English whence it entered into the local nomenclature.

In Oldcastle township, Ch **4**, 44:

> 43. *Great Wern* 1838, 'the big division of the ground called *Wern*';
> Welsh **gwern**, as the name of a tract of marsh, modified by the
> English adjective.

In Chidlow township, Ch **4**, 20:

> 44. *Red Gough* 1841 is tautologous. The name alludes to the colour
> of the soil here, formed from red sandstone; and it means 'the red
> field named *Gough*'. The form *Gough* [gʌf] is not to be derived from
> the English surname *Gough* (from Welsh **gof**, 'smith') here, and it
> looks as though it represents a Middle English modification of Welsh
> **coch** [koχ] with characteristic phonetic substitutions [k/g], [χ/f].
> Welsh **coch** adjective means 'red', and the field–name *Gough*
> represents a substantive use of the adjective, meaning 'the red one'.

In Broxton township, Ch **4**, 12:

> 45. *Nant Meadow* 1839, 'meadow at –, meadow called –, *Nant*'
> (Welsh **nant** 'a wood').

In Clutton township, Ch **4**, 72:

> 46. *Pentry Field* 1846, compare 40.

In Carden township, Ch **4**, 53:

> 47. *Pentre Field* 1840 (perhaps associated with *le Pentref* early 14th
> century, compare 40, 46.

In Tarvin township, Ch **3**, 281:

> 48. *Press Hill* 1838, 'hill at –, hill called –, *Press*', a hybrid with
> English **hill** affixed to a place–name from Welsh **pres** 'brushwood,
> scrubland'.

In Middlewich township, Ch **2**, 240:

> 49. *Rosemedow* 1373, 'meadow at –, meadow called –, *Rose*', from
> Middle English **medow** suffixed to a place–name *Ros(e)* from Old
> Welsh **ros** (modern Welsh **rhos**), 'moorland'.

In Onston township, Ch **3**, 200:

> 50. *Bronnegge* 1354, 'the hill edge at –, or called –, *Bronn*'; Middle
> English **egge** (Old English **ecg**) suffixed to a place–name *Bronn*
> (Welsh **bronn** 'hillside'; as in 5). Compare 33.

III. FIELD–NAMES WHICH ALLUDE TO WELSHMEN

There is, among the field–names of Cheshire, another category, which refers to Welshmen; these are much less interesting indicators of a Welsh presence. Examples 1–50 require a linguistic presence, and are, more or less, Welsh names. In contrast, a set of English field–names, mostly modern, containing the terms 'Welsh' and 'Welshman', allude to an ethnic or social presence which is not always reflected in the language of local nomenclature.

> 51. *Welsh–, Welch Bank, Croft, Meadow* etc. in nineteenth–century sources, in the townships of Leftwich Ch **2**, 207, Sandbach Ch **2**, 273, Smallwood Ch **2**, 318, Church Shocklach Ch **4**, 66, Hoole Ch **4**, 131, Storeton Ch **4**, 256. However, the example in Church Shocklach, *Welch Meadow* 1839, probably means 'meadow on the Welsh side of the River Dee'.
>
> 52. *Welch–, Welshman's Acre, Croft, Field* etc. in nineteenth– century sources in the townships of Daresbury Ch **2**, 149, Wharton Ch **2**, 215, High Legh Ch **2**, 50, Byley Ch **2**, 234, Partington Ch **2**, 28, Burwardsley Ch **4**, 95, Dodleston Ch **4**, 158, Norbury Ch **3**, 111.

Earlier references are:

> 53. *le Walsemanesland* 1278, in Woodbank township, Ch **4**, 208, was held by Adam *le Waleys* (Adam 'the Welsh') in 1284; (from Old English, Middle English **land**).
>
> 54. *Walshemansiche* 1386 and *Walsmanheth* 1423, in Runcorn township Ch **2**, 176, from Middle English **siche**, 'a watercourse', and **heth** 'a heath'.
>
> 55. *The Welchmans lytle croft* 1581, in Daresbury township Ch **2**, 148, could mean either 'the little croft of the Welshman' or 'the Welshman's part of *Little Croft*'.
>
> 56. *Wellchmans Croft* 1700 in Bickley township, Ch **4**, 6.

The place–names *Welsh Lane,* Over township Ch **3**, 175, Welsh Row, Nantwich Ch **3**, 34, are associated with Welsh salt–traders and pack–horse men, travelling along the salt–ways from Cheshire to Wales. But *Welsh Row* in Nether Alderley Ch **1**, 98 cannot be clearly explained in that way. And, for most instances, the historical and personal circumstances which produced these 'Welshman' field–names cannot be traced.

This type of field–name may be the memorial of a Welsh landowner or tenant in the township at the time of record, or it may commemorate a long–standing local tradition of such an association having existed many years earlier. A more immediate evidence of the Welsh presence is that type of field–name which is based on a Welsh personal–name, presumably that of an owner or tenant of the land in question.

IV. FIELD–NAMES WITH A WELSH PERSONAL–NAME

Cae Kendrick 31, *Gwern y ddavid* 15, *Werny David* 30, *Talretheragh* 32, *Quotkey Yollen* 28, and *Caytanguistil* 10, are instances of a Welsh field–name containing a Welsh personal–name; however, there is a number of instances of a Middle English field–name containing a Welsh personal–name. In some, the Welsh personal–name has an English genitive singular inflexion in *–es,* evidence of the personal–name's being recognized and adopted by the English.

In Wigland township, Ch **4**, 50:
57. *Kenanescroft* 1317, from Old English **croft** with the Welsh personal–name *Cynan.*

In Great Mollington township, Ch **4**, 177:
58. *Edeuenetisgrave* 1286, from Old English **græfe** 'a grove' with the Welsh personal–name *Ednyfed,* see Ch **4**, 179 and xiv.
59. *Gruggeworth* 1292, from Old English **worth** 'a curtilage, private ground' and the Welsh surname *Gryg,* see Ch **4**, 179 and xiv.

In Tilston township, Ch **4**, 58:
60. *Ennyons Croft* 1552, from Old English **croft** and the Welsh personal–name *Eynon, Enniawn, Ennion.*

In Malpas township, Ch **4**, 38:
61. *Cams–, Gams Hillock* 1841, from Modern English **hillock** and the Welsh surname *Gam.* There is a place–name *Gam's Wood,* first record 1831, in Edge township, Ch **4**, 32.

In Foulk Stapleford township, Ch **4**, 105:
62. *Wrennowes Meadows* 1572, *campus de Wronowe* mid–thirteenth

century, named after one *Wronou* de Stapleford, lord here c. 1300 A.D., whose personal–name was Welsh *Grono,* a short form of *Goronwy.* Compare 63.

In Burton–in–Wirral township, Ch **4**, 211:

63. *Granowes Fielde* 1592, from the Welsh personal–name *Gronw,* a contracted form of Goronwy. Compare 62.

In Lower Whitley township, Ch **2**, 134:

64. *Griffiths Field* 1845, *Gryffythesfelde* 1561; from the Welsh personal–name *Gruffud* (> modern English *Griffith*).

In Tushingham–cum–Grindley township, Ch **4**, 46:

65. *Wlethereslond* 1354, from Middle English **land** with the Welsh personal–name *Gwledyr.*
66. *Madocuswalle* 1334, 'Madoc's spring', from Middle English **walle** (< Old English Mercian **wælla**) with the English genitive inflexion of the Welsh personal–name *Madog).*
67. *Ithelliscroft* 1295, from Middle English **croft** with the Welsh personal–name *Ithel.*

In Little Sutton township, Ch **4**, 195:

68. *Howelstylth* 1432, from Old English **tilð** 'arable land, ploughed land' and the Welsh personal–name *Houel.* Compare 69.

In Great Sutton township, Ch **4**, 193:

69. *Howell's Field* 1843, *Howellesfeld* 1398, *Howelsfeld* 1432, from Old English **feld** and the Welsh personal–name *Houel.*

In Cuddington township, Ch **4**, 28:

70. *Croft Iyagow* 1308, 'Iago's croft': a curious field name: the word–order is Welsh, as if this were a Welsh field–name using the English element **croft**. The personal–name is Welsh *Iago.*
71. *Blethums Croft* 1838, from the Welsh personal–name *Bleddyn.* Compare 72.

In Malpas township, Ch **4**, 38:

72. *Blethens Croft* 1582, from the Welsh personal–name *Bleddyn,* compare 71.

In Great Meols township, Ch **4**, 296:

73. *Iagowesmedwe* late–13th century, from the Welsh personal– name *Iago* and Middle English **medwe** 'a meadow'.

In Church Minshull township, Ch **3**, 154:

74. *Yevanscrofte* 1523, from Middle English **croft** with the Welsh personal–name *Ievan*.

In Churton–by–Farndon township, Ch **4**, 70:

75. *Madokesfeld* 14, from Middle English **feld** with the Welsh personal–name *Madog*.

In Tarporley township, Ch **3**, 294:

76. *Maleres rudyng* 1339; Middle English **ryding** (Old English **ryding** 'cleared land') and the Welsh personal–name *Meilyr*. Compare 77.

In Edleston township, Ch **3**, 140:

77. *Maylers Ryddynge* 1417, from Middle English **ryding** and the Welsh personal–name *Meilyr*. Compare 76.

In Cholmondeley township, Ch **4**, 21:

78. *Meyleresleghe* 1323, *Meylerestele* 1362, from Old English **stīgel** 'a stile' and Old English **lēah** 'a woodland glade', with the Welsh personal–name *Meilyr*; these names are associated with *Hugo filius Meylor* of Cholmondley, 1331 A.D.

In Handley township, Ch **4**, 90:

79. *Morgan's Mow* 1838, from Old English **muga**, Middle English **mowe** 'a mound, a haystack'; perhaps named after *Morgan de Mulneton* who was lord here in the thirteenth–century. *Morgan* is a Welsh personal–name.

In Faddiley township, Ch **3**, 142:

80. *Ouwanis Ruding* 1271, from Old English **ryding** and the Old Welsh personal–name *Ouein,* Welsh *Owen*.

In High Legh township, Ch **2**, 45:

81. *Owencrofte* 15th century, from Middle English **croft** and the Welsh personal–name *Owen*.

In Bradley township, Ch **4**, 11:

   82. *Urian Rydding* 1537, from Middle English **rydding** (Old English
   ryding) with the Welsh personal–name *Urien*.

The field–names reviewed in this paper, some of them in the Welsh
language, others in the English language which contain either a Welsh
element in their vocabulary or structure, or a reference to Welshmen, are
a body of evidence for a continuous presence of Welsh, and Welsh–
speaking, inhabitants in Cheshire throughout the medieval and modern
periods, despite the fact that the border between Cheshire and Wales was
a military frontier for long periods between the eleventh and fourteenth
centuries.

These field–names are evidence of a Welsh cultural and linguistic
presence; they do not tell us anything about the number of Welshmen
present at any one time, nor about the proportion of Welshmen to
Englishmen in the population at any one time. We are probably not
seeing, in these field–names, the manifestation of a large Welsh
population in Cheshire; the geographical distribution of the field–names
(see Fig. E 1) is not sufficiently widespread for that. It is a remarkable
feature of that distribution, that it shows a heavy concentration of
instances in the same extreme south–western part of the county which
contains the largest proportion of the Celtic–influenced major place–
names of west Cheshire, that part of Cheshire in the south end of Broxton
Hundred which lay in the territory of the feudal barony of Malpas.[6]

The distribution map, nevertheless, does not portray the fact that, in
most townships where Welsh or Welsh–influenced field–names occur,
such names are heavily outnumbered in our records by English field–
names. There are few townships which have so many Welsh names as,
say, Shocklach Oviatt, beside R. Dee at the south–west edge of the
county. It is not possible to suppose, from these field–names, that there
was in medieval or modern times a predominantly Welsh, Welsh
speaking, population even in this district. But we have to recognize that
these field–names testify to a population tolerant of its Welsh–speaking
component, and prepared to adopt their alternative Welsh forms of

---

[6] G. Ormerod, *The History of the County Palatine and City of Chester*, ed. T.
Helsby, II, 592.

field–names. Thus, it would appear that this Welsh population was socially influential although it was not a majority, and this observation prompts comparison with the status and influence of the landed gentry in medieval England.

We have noted, when considering *Caytanguistil,* an important Welsh element in the pedigrees of the Norman and English medieval feudal lords of the district. The township of Bradley–near–Malpas, Ch **4**, 11, which was occasionally called *Welsh Bradley* in the seventeenth century in order to distinguish it from the two other Cheshire places named Bradley (Ch **3**, 228 and **2**, 97), does not contain numerous Welsh field–names (see 22); but the lord of this manor in 1260 A.D. was one *Madoc de Bradeley,* whose Welsh personal–name is an indication of a Welsh relationship in his pedigree and connexions. The lady *Tangwistl* who was ancestress of the Egerton and Cholmondeley families, barons of Malpas, and the lady *Gwenllian,* the thirteenth–century ancestress of the medieval lords of Tushingham[7] bore Welsh personal–names; two of Tangwistl's Cholmondeley descendents in the fourteenth century bore the name *Kendrick* (i.e. Welsh *Cynwrig*; compare 31); between 1288 and 1347, the lordship of Cuddington was held by *Iorwerth ap Madoc ap Eignon de Cudynton,*[8] whose personal–name and patronymics are unmistakably Welsh; in 1363 there came of age one *Wenthlian* daughter and heiress of *Wylym ap Johann* who lived at Cuddington;[9] in 1313 *Hova filius Gronow* was lord of Chidlow.[10]

These few instances taken at random from the local history, indicate a strong and persistent tendency among the feudal lords in the barony of Malpas and its subordinate domains, to take Welsh personal–names, and to use Welsh patronymics in *ap* 'son of'. It seems fair and permissible to suppose that all these phenomena, the Welsh personal– names and the Welsh field–names, are manifestations of a recurrent and persistent Welsh element and influence in the pedigree and culture of the feudal lords of the district, a result of dynastic marriages between the English and Welsh landowning families across the national frontier, and the consequent movement of some Welsh speaking retainers into these domains in

[7] Op. cit., II, 658.
[8] Op. cit., II, 645.
[9] Op. cit., II, 645.
[10] Op cit., II, 660.

England, and of some English–speaking retainers into the adjacent Welsh counties of Flint and Denbigh. The reciprocal effect cannot yet be studied, because no survey of the field–names in these counties has been published and it will be some years before current research is applicable.[†]

Additional Note [A.R.R.]

pp. 354–370. For Flintshire names, see now Hywel Wyn Owen, *The Place–Names of East Flintshire* (Cardiff, 1994).

APPENDIX II
THE ENVIRONMENTAL BACKGROUND

By Denise Kenyon

INTRODUCTION[1]

Cheshire is typically regarded as a county of green pastures, the rolling grass plains which feed the dairy herds which in turn produce a cheese famous since at least Camden's day.[2] In fact Cheshire is a county of considerable diversity and environmental extremes. These extremes are most marked when contrasting the eastern parts, especially the north–eastern sector, with the western third of the county. The peat–covered grits and shales of the Carboniferous deposits which form the Pennine slopes can be contrasted with the blown sand deposits of Meols and Hoylake on Wirral. In the centre of the county the Mid Cheshire Ridge, marking the junction between Keuper and Bunter Sandstones, is covered by brown soils and podzols. The landscape there contrasts strongly with that of the plains on either side with their sticky gleyed clays overlying glacial till. On the plains themselves a distance of only a few metres on the ground may separate well drained, fertile brown earths covering small outcrops of sandstone or gravel ridges from the more ubiquitous, poorly drained, heavy clay soils.

RELIEF

Cheshire is loosely bounded by major geographical features: the Dee valley and the sea to the west; the Mersey valley in the north; the Pennines along the eastern margin. Only in the south is the border less

---

[1] A more extensive discussion of the environmental background to settlement in Cheshire can be found in D. Kenyon, 'Archaeology, Place–Names and Settlement in Lancashire and Cheshire c.400–1066', unpublished Ph.D. thesis, University of Manchester, 1984, chapter 5.

[2] J. Beck, *Tudor Cheshire*, Chester 1969, 41.

clearly defined, merging almost imperceptibly with the northern parts of Shropshire and Staffordshire, though the narrow, steep–sided valley of the Wych Brook offers some definition in the south–western corner of the county. Much of Cheshire is low undulating plain, rarely rising above 50m. The plain is split up into a western and a central division by the Mid Cheshire Ridge, the chain of hills and west–facing escarpments which frequently attain elevations of 150 to 200m, running from Halton in the north down through Frodsham and Helsby, past Beeston and Bickerton, and on towards Malpas in the south.[3] In the east rise the Pennines reaching altitudes of over 500m at Whetstone Edge. In the west the Wirral peninsula, formed by the lower reaches and estuaries of the Dee and Mersey, juts out towards the Irish Sea. The peninsula's generally undulating relief is occasionally broken by pronounced hills especially on the western side where Thurstaston Hill (90m) and Poll Hill (104m) can be found.

The main rivers in Cheshire, the Bollin, Dane, Dee, Gowy, Mersey, Tame, Weaver, and Wheelock, all drain westwards into the Irish Sea Basin.

SOLID GEOLOGY[4]

The geological formations of this part of the North–West of England primarily comprise rocks of the Triassic Age with a few older Carboniferous deposits along the Pennines. Apart from a small outcrop of later Jurassic rock in south Cheshire, there is no evidence for rock formation in the county after Triassic times.

[3] There is a chain of hill–forts along the ridge: Helsby, Bradley and Woodhouses; Eddisbury, Oakmere and Kelsborrow; Maiden Castle (Bickerton); a newly discovered site extending back into the Bronze Age at Beeston; and a possible hillfort at Halton. See W.J. Varley, *Cheshire before the Romans*, Chester 1964; J. Forde–Johnston, 'The Iron Age Hillforts of Lancashire and Cheshire', LCAS 72 (1962), 9–46; for Beeston see MedArch 25 (1981), 200.

[4] The principal sources are as follows: maps published for the Institute of Geological Sciences (Drift and Solid), Old Series, 1" Series, 1:50,000 Series; W.B. Evans, A.W. Wilson, B.J. Taylor and D. Price, *The Geology of the Country around Macclesfield, Congleton, Crewe and Middlewich*, Memoirs of the Geological Society, 1968; W. Edwards and F.M. Trotter, *British Regional Geology: The Pennines*, 3rd ed., HMSO, London 1954; B.A. Hains and A. Horton, *British Regional Geology: Central England*, 3rd.ed., HMSO, London repr.1975.

The Carboniferous rocks of the Pennines in east Cheshire occur widely in the Macclesfield Forest area as successive Millstone Grit series, including the various shales, sandstones and grits. The succeeding coal measures are found sporadically to the north–east of Macclesfield itself, in the Hurdsfield–Kerridge–Pott Shrigley area, and further north around Marple and Romiley. The Bunter rocks, which form the lower part of the Trias, are common in western Cheshire and Wirral. There, outcrops, especially of Pebble Beds and Conglomerates, as at Barrow, Dunham–on–the–Hill, Eastham and Eccleston, jut through the glacial till. The islands of well drained land thus formed amid the heavier clays of the plain constitute prime early settlement sites. In the west of the county the Bunter rocks are not overlain by rocks of the later Keuper series though they are covered by superficial deposits of glacial material (drift). In the eastern half of Cheshire, however, rocks of the Keuper series are found. Their eastern limit is marked by the Pennines; their western edge is defined by the Mid Cheshire Ridge. These Keuper beds consist of Keuper sandstones overlain by Keuper Marl, a thick and widespread deposit which is especially common in the Weaver Basin. Isolated outcrops of Keuper are rare. Some of the Keuper Marl is very rich in minerals,[5] for example the large amounts of rock salt in the Weaver Basin, and, on a smaller scale, the copper ores at Alderley Edge and along the Bickerton–Peckforton Fault.

Most of these solid rocks are covered by superficial deposits of glacial and post–glacial age, in thicknesses ranging from a few centimetres to over 100m.

DRIFT GEOLOGY

During the succeeding Quaternary period a great variety of deposits were laid down. They are generally termed 'Drift' deposits to distinguish them from the earlier 'Solid' rocks upon which they rest. The several advances and retreats of the ice–sheets left behind a mass of drift material comprising till (Boulder Clay) and various glacial sands and gravels. The

---

[5] The term 'marl' can be rather misleading in a Cheshire context. The word is traditionally used to denote a highly calcareous clay used as a fertilizer since at least medieval times, hence the number of marl pits dotting the landscape today. See W.B. Mercer, *County Agricultural Surveys*, 4, *Cheshire*, London 1963, 6.

composition of the glacial till varies, partly with the source of the
ice–sheets and glaciers by which it was transported and partly as a result
of periglacial processes. Consequently some is very stiff and clayey in
texture, some is sandy, some stoneless, some stoney.

The most extensive deposit is the reddish brown, slightly calcareous,
clay which is thought to derive from the Irish Sea area (Northern Drift).
It is medium to fine textured with various amounts of stones and is the
predominant drift form in west–central Cheshire where it covers the
plains and the lower slopes of Macclesfield Forest. Fluvial–glacial sands
and gravels, which are believed to represent periods of glacial retreat
during which water released by melting ice–sheets deposited sand over
the preceding till, is the second most frequently encountered drift material
in Cheshire. Deposits are scattered across the whole of the plains and
occur widely in Delamere Forest, to the south–east of Crewe and
Nantwich, and in a broad eastern belt from the Staffordshire border
northwards, through Macclesfield, up to Manchester. The later glacial
sands merge into river terrace sands which occur at various levels along
the main rivers. Shirdley Hill Sand, an important deposit around the
Mersey, is a wind–blown deposit composed almost entirely of pure silica.
It was used in glass manufacturing at the Roman industrial site at
Wilderspool.[6] More recent deposits include not only these blown sands
but also alluvium and peat which were mostly laid down after the ice had
finally retreated. Alluvium is a silty clay with occasional layers of gravel.
Its low–lying position along rivers and coasts makes it particularly liable
to flooding.

Peat is found at both of the altitudinal limits in Cheshire. Hill or
climatic peat (Blanket peat) covers most of the Pennine plateaux. It is a
fairly uniform deposit consisting principally of decomposed cotton grass
(Eriophorum) and bog moss (Sphagnum). According to the local
topography, peat growth began at any time between around 5000 B.C.
and 3000 B.C.[7] There has been widespread erosion and loss through peat
cutting. In the lowlands, peat deposits (basin peat) occur scattered in
hollows across the plains and in Delamere Forest. Peat is also found in
hollows or flashes resulting from salt subsidence as at Smallwood near
Sandbach and Wybunbury Moss in south Cheshire. Lowland peat

---

[6] T. May, *Warrington's Roman Remains*, Warrington 1904, 37ff.

[7] J.H. Tallis, 'Pre–Peat Vegetation of the Pennines', *New Phytologist* 63 (1964),
363–73, esp. 371.

deposits comprise reed swamp, fen and fen carr peat formed in shallow water conditions. Raised mosses like Alsager Moss are formed from basin peat deposits when there is excessive rainfall. The major lowland mosses and marshes have now been drained and reclaimed for agricultural purposes though Wybunbury Moss has been conserved as a nature reserve.

SOILS[8]

There are five main soil groups in Cheshire: brown soils, podzols, stagnogleys (surface–water gleys), ground water gleys, and peat soils. Each has its own sub–groups defined according to their clay, loam, humus and sand content, and their tendency to waterlogging. As a comparison between the soil and drift maps shows, there is a remarkably close correlation between soils and drift types in Cheshire.

Brown soils are naturally the most fertile and adequately drained soils in Cheshire. They include brown earths (*sensu strictu*), brown sands and gleyed brown earths. In Cheshire they are recorded as the Wick, Bromsgrove, Bridgnorth, and Newport series (map units 18–22). These soils are found mostly on well–drained sites, often on small hills or slopes, overlying sands, gravels, outcrops of sandstone and river terrace deposits. They occur in the Wirral peninsula, along the fringes of Delamere Forest, and along the Mid Cheshire Ridge. They can also be found in the south–east corner of the county along the Dane valley and in the Macclesfield Forest area. On the plains they occur as both large and small isolated patches varying in size from barely 1km across to several kilometres wide. Examples of these 'islands' of good soil are Farndon and Eccleston in the Dee valley and Acton in the Weaver valley.

Podzols, poor sandy soils with marked leaching of nutrients, develop where deciduous forest has been replaced by conifers and heathers on thin soils overlying sand and gravel spreads. A good example is the large

---

[8] The principal sources are as follows: R.R. Furness, *Soils of Cheshire*, Soil Survey Bulletin, 6, Harpenden 1978; R.R. Furness, *Soils in Cheshire*, I, *SJ 45E/55W*, Soil Survey Record, 5, Harpenden 1975; R.R. Furness and S.J. King, *Soils in Cheshire*, II, *SJ 37*, Soil Survey Record, 17, Harpenden 1973; S.J. King, *Soils in Cheshire*, III, *SJ 65*, Soil Survey Record, 43, Harpenden 1977.

expanse of the Delamere series in the central Delamere Forest area (map unit 23). On the Cheshire plains the Reaseheath series (map unit 23) is another example.

Surface–water gleys are normally wet for significant periods during the course of a year and usually have a gleyed horizon within about 40cm of their surfaces. Artificial drainage is required as the downward movement of water is slow. Surface–water gleys with a distinct topsoil form stagnogley soils (*sensu strictu*), the most widespread soil type in the whole of the county. These soils overlie the thick glacial till of the plains of west and central Cheshire. The whole group includes soils of the Rufford, Clifton and Salop series (map units 25–9).

Ground–water gley soils tend to be saturated from below by regional groundwater or by water held by a deeper impermeable layer. There are several subgroups in the county where they occur chiefly as the Blackwood series (map units 31–4). These soils are found mostly along the river flood plains and at river estuaries like the Dee, Gowy and Weaver where they cover alluvial deposits.

Raw peat soils and earthy peat soils occur sporadically across Cheshire, being located in enclosed hollows, raised mosses and, more commonly, along the Pennines where they have been mapped as the Wilcocks and Winter Hill series (map units 30, 35–7).

Most of the land in Cheshire today has a broad land–capability classification of between class 2 and class 4 according to Bibby and Mackney's system.[9] Brown soils tend to fall into class 3 and occasionally class 1. The more prevalent gley soils tend to fall into classes 3 and 4. Peat soils vary from class 1 (when reclaimed) to class 6 (unreclaimed). Many of the soils of Cheshire today are therefore capable of supporting arable crops, given a moderate level of investment in terms of drainage, fertilizers and other current agricultural practices. Land–use potential in earlier times, without the benefit of modern agricultural technology, would have been far more restricted. The fact that much of Cheshire has now been turned over to grass reflects the increased importance of dairying and stock–rearing in the county since at least Tudor times.

[9] J.S. Bibby and D. Mackney, *Land Use Capability Classification*, Soil Survey Technical Monograph, 1, 1969.

CLIMATE[10]

Altitudes varying from below 15m in the west of the county to above 500m in the east contribute to the local variations in the climatic regime across Cheshire. The climate is typically slightly cool and slightly moist becoming appreciably cooler and damper as one approaches and scales the Pennine heights. In Wirral, west Cheshire and across the central plains, average annual rainfall is less than 30cm, just over half that found on the higher Pennine slopes where over 50cm is frequently reported. The temperature range is less extreme than the moisture range: average annual differences usually lie between 1°C and 2°C. The environmental extremes between the east and the west of the county would have been more critical in earlier times,[11] but even now relief, soil and climatic factors combine to produce a difference of nearly seven weeks in the length of the growing season for grass[12] between the west of the county (256 days) and the easternmost margins of Cheshire (209 days).

---

[10] The principal sources are as follows: V.C. Bendelow and R. Hartnup, *Climatic Classification of England and Wales*, Soil Survey Technical Monograph, 15, Harpenden 1980; L.P. Smith, *The Agricultural Climate of England and Wales*, Ministry of Agriculture, Fisheries and Food Technical Bulletin, 35, 1976; P.R. Crowe, 'Climate', in *Manchester and its Region, A Survey prepared for the British Association for the Advancement of Science*, ed. C.E. Carter, Manchester 1962, 17–46.

[11] For climatic change see H.H. Lamb, *Climate, Present, Past and Future*, 2, London 1977, and *Climate, History and the Modern World*, London 1982. For the effect and importance of climatic change in marginal areas see C.G. Johnson and L.P. Smith, *The Biological Significance of Climatic Changes in Britain*, London 1965; G. Manley, 'The Effective Rate of Altitudinal Change in Temperate Altlantic Climates', *Geographical Review* 35 (1945), 408–47; M.L. Parry, *Climatic Change, Agriculture and Settlement*, Fishbourne 1978; C.D. Smith and M.L. Parry, *Consequences of Climatic Change*, Nottingham 1981; *Climatic Resources and Economic Activity*, ed. J.A. Taylor, Newton Abbott 1974. For the debate on the historical significance of climatic change, see *Climate and History*, ed. T.M.L. Wigley, M.J. Ingram and G. Farmer, Cambridge 1981.

[12] That is, the number of days when the temperature rises above 5.6°C.

ENVIRONMENT AND SETTLEMENT

It has become fashionable to minimize the importance of geographical determinism as a factor influencing settlement location,[13] but one cannot deny the paramountcy of geographical factors both in the short term — and perhaps more importantly — in the long term development of settlement in Cheshire. The county lies at the junction of Fox's Highland and Lowland Zones.[14] Fox contrasted the archaeology of the northern and western uplands of Britain with those of the southern and eastern lowlands, attributing the differences in population levels, settlement types and material wealth to the very different geographical natures of the two zones. This division of the country into two geographically–determined archaeological zones is perhaps an outmoded concept today: the situation is, of course, far more complex and fragmented. Yet even in the twentieth century there are still very strong divisions between North and West Britain on the one hand, and the East and South of the country as a whole. These divisions to a large extent perpetuate the differences in population levels, settlement densities and levels of material wealth documented by a series of fiscal records from Domesday Book onwards.[15]

The origins of these socio–economic divisions have been clouded by the mists of time but one must not ignore the fundamental geographical reasons which underlie differences which have subsequently been distorted by historical and human agencies.

Environmental factors are particularly important in areas which are marginal in terms of agriculture and/or permanent settlement since they are extremely sensitive to the slightest environmental fluctuation.[16] Cheshire is marginal in two ways. Firstly, it is, as a county, marginal for arable farming. Secondly, it contains land at the upper and lower

[13] See T. Rowley, *Villages in the Landscape*, London 1978, 16ff, 25 ff; C.C. Taylor, *Village and Farmstead*, London 1983, 12ff.

[14] Sir Cyril Fox, *The Personality of Britain*, 1st ed., Cardiff 1932.

[15] H.C. Darby, *A New Historical Geography of England*, Cambridge 1973.

[16] J.A. Taylor, ed. cit. in n.11; C.G. Johnson and L.P. Smith, op.cit. in n.11. For the effect in Scotland, see M.L. Parry, op. cit. in n.11; for North Wales see N. Johnson, 'The Location of Rural Settlement in Pre–Medieval Caernarvonshire', BBCS 29 (1980–2), 381–418.

altitudinal thresholds for permanent settlement. In marginal areas even a small change in environmental factors can make the difference between a successful harvest and a harvest failure, between land viable for permanent settlement and land unsuited to settlement. Along the Pennines, for example, a long–term drop of only 0.5°C in average annual temperature can lower the upper altitudinal threshold for cultivation by about 70m.[17] A small rise in sea level, before the construction of elaborate flood defences in modern times, would have inundated large areas of land at the estuaries of the Dee, Gowy and Weaver.[18] Areas not at the altitudinal thresholds could also be affected, since agricultural productivity — the quality and quantity of both grain harvests and grass yields — would be detrimentally affected by poor weather conditions.[19] As a corollary, a rise in average annual temperature of 0.5°C can raise the upper threshold for cultivation by about 70m and similarly have a beneficial effect on yields.

Indirect evidence for climatic change in Cheshire before the keeping of modern records can be derived from studying the sequence of bands of unhumified sphagnum which mark recurrence surfaces in peat deposits.[20] Such layers were laid down during unusually wet conditions and may be associated with periods of climatic deterioration. Recurrence surfaces have been noted in peat deposits from mosses at Congleton, Lindow, Oakmere and Wybunbury in Cheshire, and from the surrounding mosses along the Mersey valley and in the south

---

[17] For a discussion of the altitudinal lapse rate, see G. Manley, op. cit. in n.11, and S.J. Harrison, 'Problems in the Measurement and Evaluation of the Climatic Resources in Upland Britain', in J.A. Taylor, ed. cit. in n.11, 47–63.

[18] Prior to large scale drainage using Irish labour and Italian and German prisoners of war there was an estimated 3000 acres of land subject to flooding on Frodsham Marshes alone, see W.A.C. Carr and W.B. Mercer, 'Reclamation of the Frodsham Marshes', *Journal of the Royal Agricultural Society of England* 108 (1947), 112–26.

[19] Studies on corn yields in Iowa have shown that yield increases almost linearly as the soil temperature 4" below the surface rises from 60°C to 81.3°C; above this temperature the yield decreases, see Chang Jeu–Hu, *Climate and Agriculture: an Ecological Survey*, Chicago 1968, 96; in Iceland a decline in summer temperature of 1°C reduces hay yield by 15–17%, M.L. Parry (citing Bryson), op. cit. in n.11, 73.

[20] *The Environment in British Prehistory*, ed. I.G. Simmons and M.J. Tooley, London 1981, 212–16, 251–61.

Pennines.[21] Changes in relative sea level have been discerned by studying the regressive/transgressive overlaps shown in deposits along the Morecambe Bay coastline, from North Wales to the Lake District, and in particular from the type site at Lytham on the west Lancashire coast.[22] The data from deposits in the North–West of England closely correlates with climatic and sea level data from elsewhere in the British Isles and north–west Europe.[23]

On the strength of this evidence it can be demonstrated that Cheshire experienced a period of climatic deterioration, the weather becoming noticeably cooler and wetter, after Romano–British times. Because of the lack of direct corroborative dating material, and because of the vagaries

[21] H.J.B. Birks, 'Pollen Analytical Investigations at Holcroft Moss, Lancashire, and Lindow Moss, Cheshire', *Journal of Ecology* 53 (1965), 299–314 and 'Late Glacial Deposits at Bagmere, Cheshire, and Chat Moss, Lancashire', *New Phytologist* 64 (1965), 270– 85; J.W. Franks, 'Abbots Moss, near Oakmere', unpublished pollen diagram, Dept. of Botany, University of Manchester; B. H. Green and M. C. Pearson, 'The Ecology of Wybunbury Moss, Cheshire, II: Post Glacial History and Formation of the Cheshire Mere and Mire Landscape', *Journal of Ecology* 65 (1977), 793–814; M.D.V. Raybould, 'Congleton Moss: The Development of a Peat Bog and the History of its Vegetation within its Surrounding Area', unpublished dissertation, Dept. of Botany, University of Manchester; J.H. Tallis, 'Studies on Southern Pennine Peats, I–III', *Journal of Ecology* 52 (1964), 323–53; J.H. Tallis and H.J.B. Birks, 'The Past and Present Distribution of Scheuchzeria Palustris L. in Europe', *Journal of Ecology* 53 (1965), 287–98; J.H. Tallis and V.R. Switsur, 'Studies on Southern Peats, VI: A Radiocarbon–Dated Diagram from Featherbed Moss, Derbyshire', *Journal of Ecology* 61 (1973), 743–51.

[22] The principal sources are as follows: M.J. Tooley, *Sea–level Changes in North West England during the Flandrian Stage*, Oxford 1978, and 'Sea–level Changes in Northern England', *Journal of the Geological Association* 93 (1982), 43–51; *Archaeology and Coastal Change*, ed. F.H. Thompson, London 1980; C. Kidson and M.J. Tooley, 'The Quaternary History of the Irish Sea', *Geological Journal*, Special Issue, 7, Liverpool 1977.

[23] For the early period a range of other 'proxy data' is used as well as recurrence surfaces. This data includes rates of tree–ring growth, ice layers (varves) at the polar ice–caps, past distributions of certain temperature–sensitive species of flora and fauna.

For the correlation with the North–West, see H.H. Lamb, op. cit. in n.11; B.Aaby, 'Cyclic Variations in Climate over the past 5500 years Reflected in Raised Bogs', *Nature* 263 (1976), 281–4; I.A. Morrison, 'Comparative Stratigraphy and Radio–carbon Chronology of Holocene Marine Changes on the Western Seaboard of Europe', *Geoarchaeology, Earth Science and the Past*, ed. D.A. Davidson and M.L. Shackley, London 1976, 159–63.

of radio–carbon dating for the historic period,[24] the chronology of the change is necessarily imprecise, but it can be said with certainty that the poorer weather was being felt by the fifth century, and was probably at its worst during the sixth century. There followed a gradual recovery which can be traced in the proxy data from c. 850 A.D., and which increased in pace in the immediate post–Conquest period. It culminated in what is sometimes called 'The Little Climatic Optimum' of the twelfth and thirteenth centuries in England. Average annual temperatures seem to have been approximately 1°C higher than in the post–Roman period.[25] This was succeeded by another period of climatic deterioration of varying severity during the later Middle Ages, reflected by series of bad harvests and crop failures from the second decade of the fourteenth century onwards. This period of poor climate was at its nadir in the seventeenth century which witnessed Frost Fairs on the Thames and has been dubbed 'The Little Ice Age'. Thereafter climatic records show that our climate has fluctuated considerably, though the general trend seems to have been upwards.[26]

Major changes in sea level have occurred during the last two millenia. Levels were high in late Roman times, falling to their lowest point around 630 A.D. Levels than rose to another peak around 1000, since when they have fallen to their current level. Coastal flooding may also occur as a result of raised ground–water levels during periods of extreme climatic wetness, as in the sixth century, and as a result of storm surges. The latter can be particularly severe along the Morecambe Bay coastline which experiences the second highest tidal range in Britain.[27] At the north end of the bay ranges as high as 11.5m have been recorded between MHWST and MLWST; the distance is less at the southern end of the bay. Britton

[24] This is because of oscillations in the decay curve of the carbon atom, see S. Fleming, *Dating in Archaeology: A Guide to Scientific Techniques*, London 1976, 56ff., and reports in *Radiocarbon* (Supplement of the *American Journal of Science*), esp. J. Klein et al., 'Calibration of Radiocarbon Dates', *Radiocarbon* 24 (1982), 103–50.

[25] H.H. Lamb estimates a change of between 0.7°C; M.L. Parry suggests the rise was lower, around 0.5°C.

[26] For an indication of modern climatic fluctuations see J. Gribbin, 'Hot News on Global Warming', *New Scientist* 1448 (21st March 1985), 4.

[27] The highest range is experienced along the Bristol Channel from Ilfracombe to Swansea.

has listed four occasions when inundations occurred: one of the fifth
century affecting the coast from the Severn to the Dee; a mid–seventh
century inundation of Lancashire and Cheshire; an inundation of the Dee
in 885; and an inundation affecting Stanlow and the Dee as far as Chester
in 1279.[28] Further flooding also occurred in the mid–fourteenth century
when 30 carucates of land were reputedly lost to the sea.[29]

The combined effects of sea level changes, storm surges and so on
caused severe coastal erosion along stretches of the north–west littoral in
earlier times. In Cheshire the changes are most conspicuous in the altered
shape of the tip of the Wirral peninsula around Meols and Hoylake.[30] The
important Roman, Anglo–Saxon and medieval beach– head trading marts
located on this part of the peninsula have been lost to the sea and are only
known through the numerous finds of ancient artifacts found along the
foreshore and recorded in the nineteenth century.[31] Coastal change in
Cheshire is not a solely negative process, however, and several thousand
hectares have been added as a result of the progressive silting up of the
major river estuaries and large–scale drainage and reclamation of
low–lying mosses. The former Roman harbour on the Dee at Chester is
now the Rood Eye racecourse, whilst the reclaimed marshes at Frodsham
have been used for agricultural purposes, including sheep grazing, since
the time of the earliest recorded attempts at drainage and reclamation in
the fourteenth century.[32]

In view of the obvious influence of environmental factors it is not
surprising to find that in Cheshire early settlements are concentrated in
certain well defined areas.[33] Land between 15m and 61m, especially in
the milder, drier west and central parts of the county was favoured. Land
below 8m and above 152m was avoided. The better–drained brown soil
groups overlying river terrace deposits, small and medium sized

[28] C.E. Britton, *A Meteorological Chronology to A.D. 1450*, HMSO, London
1937.

[29] W. Hewitt, *The Wirral Peninsula*, London 1922, 45.

[30] Ibid. 11ff.; G.D.B. Jones, 'Archaeology and Coastal Change in the North
West', in F.H. Thomson, ed. cit. in n.22, 87–102.

[31] Principally published in A. Hume, *Ancient Meols*, London 1863; see D.
Kenyon, op. cit. in n.1, chapters 1 and 2 for a modern review of the material and its
significance.

[32] W. Hewitt, op. cit. in n.29, 49 ff.; W.A.C. Carr and W.B. Mercer, op. cit. in
n.18.

[33] D. Kenyon, op. cit. in n.1, 394–6.

sandstone outcrops, and gravel ridges along the larger river valleys were preferred over both the thick gleyed clay soils covering the till and the thin acidic podzols of the central Delamere area and parts of east Cheshire. Peat and alluvial soils were avoided.

Settlements whose place–names contain elements indicative of formation in the earlier Anglo–Saxon period up to c. 650–750, such as **hām** and certain topographical elements, and which are frequently ancient parish[34] or estate centres, typically occur in such favoured locations. Examples include Eastham, Frodsham and Weaverham, Farndon, Bowdon and Malpas (*Depenbech*). In fact the Cheshire **hām**s, and to a lesser extent the **–inghām**s, lie in some of the best locations in the county.[35] It is more difficult to generalize in the case of topographically named settlements since they are a less well defined group.[36]

As demand for land rose, permanent settlements spread further on to the heavier clay soils. These soils are more difficult to cultivate since they are prone to gleying and are slower to warm up for the spring sowing. The practice of raising the ground into pronounced ridges ('ridge and furrow') was therefore practised not only in medieval times in Cheshire[37] but well into the nineteenth century when Cheshire farmers were exhorted to raise the land into butts 5.5yds wide for easier drainage.[38] The increase

[34] That is, recorded as a parish church centre by *Taxatio Ecclesiastica Angliae et Walliae c.1291*, Record Commission, London 1802, 248–9.

[35] An assessment of site suitability in terms of soils, drift, relief and climatic regime, and expressed as a numerical value out of 20, showed that the **hām**s, with the exception of Frodsham (17), could be rated at 18 or 19 out of 20. Apart from Altrincham (18), the **–inghām**s were assessed at only 17 out of 20, see D. Kenyon, op. cit. in n.1, 568 ff.

[36] Farndon, Bowdon and Malpas (*Depenbech*) were rated at 19, 18 and 18 respectively. Elements such as **ford** occur as both early and late settlement names. **Ford** is in fact one of the commonest of all the topographical elements in use during the Anglo–Saxon period, see M. Gelling, *Place–Names in the Landscape*, London 1984, 67ff.

It should also be recognized that Anglo–Saxon estate centres may have been located for the best exploitation of the whole estate rather than for their immediate access to good quality land *per se*.

[37] D. Kenyon, 'Aerial photography and the Open Fields: Open Field Agriculture in Medieval Cheshire', in *The Changing Past*, ed. N.J. Higham, Manchester 1979, 59–65.

[38] W. Palin, 'The Farming of Cheshire', *Journal of the Royal Agricultural Society of England* 5 (1845), 57–111; J. Caird, *English Agriculture in 1850–1*, 2nd ed., London 1968, 25.

in population levels of the later Anglo–Saxon period, both as a result of natural growth and as a result of incoming Scandinavian settlers, provided the impetus for this expansion of settlement which was in turn facilitated by the ameliorating climate after c. 850.

Growth assumed the form of an internal colonization movement as improved agricultural productivity increased the carrying capacity of the land and thereby enabled a higher settlement density. The increased density manifested itself in the fragmentation of large estate units[39] as individual thegns acquired rights over land (*bōcland*). The development is marked by the appearance of a new class of place–names, those of the personal–name + **tūn** type.[40] In Cheshire such names are frequently found as the names of settlements like Alvaston, Cholmondeston, Tetton and Warburton whose locations are, in geographical terms, poorer than the locations enjoyed by **hām**–named settlements.[41] Furthermore, place–names consisting of personal–name + **tūn** are rarely found as the names of ancient parishes.[42]

It can also be argued that settlements like Caldecot, Stoke and Keckwick, which bear names in **cot, stoc, wīc**, appeared at this time: that they were secondary settlements whose foundation belonged to the late Anglo–Saxon period of internal colonization and estate fragmentation.[43]

---

[39] *ex inf.* Dr N.J. Higham.

[40] M. Gelling, *Signposts to the Past*, London 1978, 177 ff.

[41] These places had the following locational values out of 20: Alvaston 15, Cholmondeston 14, Tetton 15, Warburton 13, see D. Kenyon, op. cit. in n.1, 655 ff.

[42] Dodleston is the only instance in Cheshire.

[43] M. Gelling, op. cit. in n.40, 183; D. Kenyon, op. cit. in n.1, 701 ff, and chapter 6, 415 ff. This is essentially an expansionist view of later Anglo–Saxon England. According to this interpretation there was a gradual recovery of population and settlement levels after the recession of the sixth century. This is fully corroborated in the case of Cheshire by the archaeological and vegetational evidence. Pollen diagrams from the North–West, for example, show a pronounced period of woodland regeneration and abandonment of agricultural land following the major Iron Age / Romano–British clearance phase and preceding the later Anglo–Saxon clearances. This view can be contrasted with that of Sawyer. According to Sawyer the rural resources of much of England were already fully exploited by the seventh and eighth centuries: elements like **cot, stoc, wīc**, were used to denote the lesser components of old multiple estates: their independence as settlements, not their original foundation, belongs to the later Anglo–Saxon period, see *Medieval Settlement*, ed. P.H. Sawyer, London 1976, 1–7, and idem, *From Roman Britain to Norman England*, London 1978, 132–67.

The internal movement was complemented by an external colonization movement directed at the altitudinal margins, in particular the foothills and valleys of the Pennines. Worth near Poynton and Hollingworth form part of a group of late upland places called **worð** distributed across the Pennines of north–east Cheshire and south–east Lancashire.[44] Names like Godley and Matley, also in the north–east Cheshire uplands, embody OE personal–names, and may be the counterpart of the names in personal– name + **tūn**.[45] Scandinavian and Scandinavianized place–names along the Wirral coast and Mersey estuary are an indicator of the attack on the lower altitudinal margins. Names such as Meols and Tranmere which are derived from ON **melr** 'a sandbank' bear eloquent witness to the nature of the land on which the Scandinavians were permitted to settle freely in west Cheshire.[46]

According to some arguments, these internal and external colonization movements overreached themselves by causing settlements to spread on to poorer soils which were incapable of sustaining long–term settlement and cultivation. In other parts of England the large numbers of deserted medieval villages are often cited as proof of this phenomenon.[47] This is certainly a valid argument in places like Dartmoor where high altitude settlements were speedily abandoned after the end of the medieval period, and a study of some of the West Midlands examples has emphasized the role played by environmental factors in their abandonment.[48] The situation in Cheshire with regard to the reasons for settlement desertion in and after the medieval period is more difficult to ascertain. There is as yet no comprehensive listing of deserted sites. The situation is aggravated

[44] D. Kenyon, op. cit. in n.1, 701–4 and Fig. 8.10 (p. 1344).

[45] Ibid. 690 ff.

[46] Ibid. 716 ff. The difference is even more marked in Lancashire, ibid. 721 ff. and Figs. 8.16, 8.17, 8.20 (pp. 1351 ff).

[47] M.W. Beresford and J.G. Hurst, *Deserted Medieval Villages*, London 1971, 21 ff.

[48] C.D. Lineham, 'Deserted Sites and Rabbit Warrens in Dartmoor', MedArch 10 (1966), 113–44; C. Dyer, 'Deserted Medieval Villages in the West Midlands', *Economic History Review*, 2nd series, 35 (1982), 19–34; G. Beresford, 'Climatic Change and its Effect upon the Settlement and Desertion of Medieval Villages in Britain', in C.D. Smith and M.L. Parry ed. cit. in n.11, 30–9.

by the dispersed nature of so many of the settlements in Cheshire[49] and by the lack of national population and fiscal data for the medieval period.[50] The afforestation policies of the Norman earls were directly responsible for the loss of *Aldredelie* and *Done* in the Delamere area[51] whilst the disappearance of hamlets at Eaton near Chester and at Tatton in north Cheshire can be attributed to the emparkation activities of the Grosvenors and Egertons in Georgian times.[52] One may legitimately doubt whether strong flourishing communities on good quality land would have suffered such fates. However, because of the tentative nature of the current list of deserted sites in the county, it is too early to discern any correlation between place–names and desertions.

---

[49] D. Sylvester, 'Rural Settlement in Cheshire', LCHS 101 (1949), 1–37, and *The Rural Landscape of the Welsh Borderlands*, London 1969; D. Kenyon, 'Rural Settlement Patterns in Medieval Cheshire', unpublished M.A. Thesis, Dept. of Archaeology, University of Manchester, 1974.

[50] Cheshire, as a County Palatine, was exempt from national taxation and so there is no equivalent of the Hundred Rolls or Poll Tax.

[51] Both were 'waste and in the earl's forest' by 1086, see B.M.C. Husain, *Cheshire under the Norman Earls*, Chester 1973, 54 ff.

[52] D. Sylvester, 'The Manor and the Cheshire Landscape', LCAS 70 (1960), 1–15. For the Grosvenors at Eaton see D. Kenyon, op. cit. in n.49, 60–1, 73, and map 20; for the Egertons at Tatton, see N.J. Higham, 'Medieval Tatton: the Reconstruction of a Landscape', *Cheshire History* 9 (1982), 31–42, and interim excavation reports in *Cheshire Archaeological Bulletin*.

By F.I. Dunn

The following abbreviations are used:

EDT	The invaluable series of maps and apportionments (*TA*, *TAMap*) made for most parishes in accordance with the Tithe Act, 1836, 6 & 7 William IV c.71 s49. *EDT* refers to copies of maps in the Chester Diocesan Record Office and is followed by a number indicating the parish or township in question.
EDV 7/1	Replies by the clergy of the Diocese to articles of enquiry sent out in 1778 by Bishop Porteous preparatory to Visitation. The original returns are held in the Chester Diocesan Record Office. Later 'articles' are also useful to consult, e.g. *EDV* 7/2 (1789), *EDV* 7/3 (1804), *EDV* 7/4 (1811), *EDV* 7/6 (1821).
Leycester	'A Survey of All the Churches & Chappels in Cheshire. Carefully Collected in Every Hundred by it Selfe, togather with the Townes belonginge to every Parish, and the Mise thereof; By me Peter Leycester Anno Domini 1671': Cheshire Record Office, Tabley MS DLT/B/27 ff. 37–73. A condensed version was printed by Sir Peter Leycester in his *Historical Antiquities . . . concerning Cheshire* (1673), 192 ff and reprinted Orm[2] I 399 ff.
NotCestr	*Notitia Cestriensis or Historical Notices of the Diocese of Chester* by Francis Gastrell, Bishop of Chester (1714–25). Original MS versions are held in the Chester Diocesan Record Office. MS EDA 3/3 was edited by F.R. Raines for the Chetham Society Vol. VIII, 1845, to which page numbers refer.
1740 Map	*A Map of the Diocese of Chester divided into Deaneries* by T[homas] H[utchinson] (c. 1740). This printed map aims to differentiate parish churches, parochial chapels, chapels of

ease etc., though no parish or township boundaries are
shown. The dating is approximate and is deduced from the
map's dedication to Samuel [Peploe] Bishop of Chester
(1726–52). A later (apparently early 19th cent.) printed table
is generally found in company with the map.

[1] The north–westerly tip of Ince around 'Holme House' was in Stoke
parish (*EDT* 374/2).

[2] Stanlow was a Cistercian monastery founded 1178 which removed to
Whalley, La in 1296 after an inundation by the sea. It was probably
part of Great Stanney before this and remained extra–parochial after
the dissolution of the cell maintained here by Whalley Abbey (see Ch
4 185). *Leycester* gives a classic description: 'Stanlow–house formerly
an Abbey is now in no Parish, nor hath it any Constable: but is a
Priviledged place'.

[3] The parish of Stoke contained the townships of Stoke, part of Whitby
(see *EDT* 426/2) and the part of Ince that lay in Eddisbury Hundred
(see note 1, *supra*). Stanlow and Great Stanney, though extra–
parochial, seem later to have been included in Stoke parish, though
anciently Eastham may have been the mother church. Great Stanney
was extra–parochial as a result of being granted to Stanlow Abbey
1178 (see Ch **4** 182). Stoke was probably originally part of the parish
of Chester St. Oswald which still had burial rights there in the late
13th cent. (Orm^2 II 389).

[4] Earnshaw, a detached part of Rudheath Lordship in Sandbach parish.

[5] Detached portions of Baddiley in Acton.

[6] Detached portions of Newhall and Dodcott cum Wilkesley in Acton.

[7] Detached portions of Whitegate parish.

[8] A detached portion of Cheadle Moseley.

[9] A detached portion of Marston.

[10] Stublach, in Middlewich parish.

[11] The extra–parochial status of Rudheath Lordship, despite parts being
placed with various parishes for various purposes, is explained Ch **2**
198.

[12] A detached portion of Bradley.

[13] The township of Newhall was partly in Audlem parish and partly in
Wrenbury chapelry, with small detached parts in Acton parish proper
(see note 6 *supra*).

14 No Town, a curious detached portion of Rudheath in Twemlow township (Ch **2** 230–1).

15 Hilbre Island and Little Eye form the township of Hilbre, a detached part of the parish of Chester St. Oswald. It may have been part of the parish of West Kirby before a cell of the abbey of St. Werburgh was founded there (Orm² II 501).

16 Part of the south–west corner of Claughton cum Grange adjoining the Oxton boundary was in Woodchurch parish (*EDT* 47/2).

17 Blacon cum Crabwall, though reckoned as one township, is distinctly divided in that Crabwall lies in the parish of Chester St. Oswald, having been given to the abbey of St. Werburgh, while Blacon is in the parish of Chester Holy Trinity (Orm² II 575–7).

18 A small southerly portion of Coole Pilate was in the parish of Audlem.

19 The apparent complication of the parishes of Whitegate and Over is explained by the presence of the Abbey of Vale Royal. The church of the tenants of the abbey was made parochial at the dissolution of the abbey by statute 33 Henry VIII cap. 32, the parish being known as Whitegate or New Church (Orm² II 145 and Ch **3** 164).

20 Iddinshall was a detached part of the parish of Chester St. Oswald (Orm² II 305).

21 Bosden is the detached part of the township of Handforth cum Bosden in Cheadle parish (Orm² II 645).

22 The ancient parish of Cheadle comprises primarily the townships of Cheadle Bulkeley and Cheadle Moseley, so intermixed that it is impossible to depict on any small scale map. The townships may be distinguished by reference to the respective tithe maps (*EDT* 90/2 and *EDT* 91/2). For an explanation of this complicated state of affairs see Orm² III 621 ff.

23 Bache, Great Boughton, Newton by Chester, Croughton, Wervin and a small part of Upton (*EDT* 407/2) all lay in the parish of Chester St. Oswald.

24 Claverton, Marlston cum Lache, Moston and the greater part of Upton all lay in the parish of Chester St. Mary.

25 Portions of Weaverham township comprising Hefferston Grange, Weaverham Wood and parts of Sandiway were in Whitegate parish (see note 19 *supra* and Ch **3** 206–7).

26 A few fields of Norley lay in Crowton in Weaverham parish and, similarly, a few fields of Crowton lay in Norley (*EDT* 302/2).

27   Dutton lay in the parishes of Great Budworth and Runcorn (*EDT* 146/1 and 2). Poolsey, al. Poosey, a detached chapelry (lost, but mentioned in *EDV* 7/1, 1778) of Runcorn parish, apparently lay near the Dutton/Bartington boundary in the township of Dutton (Ch 2 113). Poolsey chapel was built c. 1236 (*Leycester*). Its decline was attributed to 'ye Neighbourhood resorting to the Domestic Chapel of Dutton' (NotCestr).

28   Stockton Heath is a hamlet in the township of Appleton, Great Budworth parish (*EDT* 17/1) [*contra* Ch 2 145].

29   Mutlow, the possible meeting place for the Domesday Hundred of *Hamestan*, in Marton township, was in the parish of Gawsworth (Ch 1 81).

30   Middleton Grange was an extra–parochial township and was not officially included in Aston by Sutton until 1843 (Ch 2 161).

31   It has been conjectured that the ancient chapelry of Poynton included Woodford as well as Worth (Orm^2 III 684), but *EDV* 7/1/99, 1778 states categorically, 'Woodford is not in the Chapelry'.

32   Birkenhead was an extra–parochial liberty created out of Claughton township to contain the demesne of Birkenhead Priory.

33   About thirty fields at the north–east corner of Baguley lay in Northenden parish (*EDT* 34/2).

34   Leese is a township of Goostrey chapelry detached by Church Hulme chapelry.

35   Sir Peter Leycester, in the mid 17th century, wrote of 'an ancient free chapel at Warburton now usually taken for the parish church' (Orm^2 I 566). It is shown as chapel of ease to Lymm (1740 Map).

36   Grafton was an extra–parochial liberty, which, though often regarded as a township of Tilston, did not officially become so until 1841 (Ch 4 61).

37   The township of Ashton on Mersey lay partly in Bowden parish and partly in Ashton upon Mersey parish. The parts are completely intermixed and may be identified by reference to the respective tithe maps (*EDT* 22/1 and *EDT* 23/1).

38   Little St. John, Chester, al. St. John of Jerusalem's Hospital, was stated in 1778 to consist of the Bluecoat Hospital, six almshouses and the Northgate Gaol (*EDV* 7/1/3).

39   Four fields at the north–eastern tip of the township of Backford were in Stoke parish (*EDT* 31/2).

40   Sixteen fields at the southern tip of Hoole township lay in the parish of Chester St. John (*EDT* 305/2).

MAP 2   391

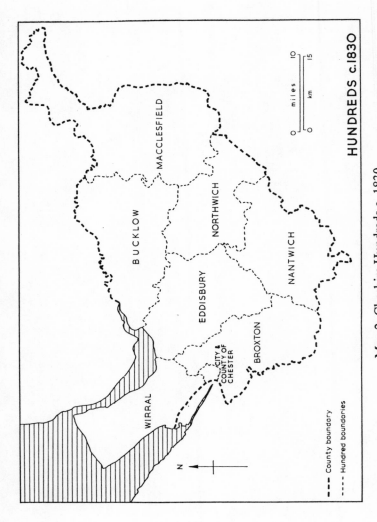

Map 2: Cheshire Hundreds c. 1830.

Reproduced from the *Victoria History of Cheshire*, volume ii, p. 30, by permission of the General Editor.